D1201763

HOOVER
THE FISHING PRESIDENT

Kennebago Lake, Maine, May 29, 1939.

COURTESY QUEENS BOROUGH PUBLIC LIBRARY, LONG ISLAND DIVISION, NEW YORK HERALD TRIBUNE COLLECTION

HOOVER

THE FISHING PRESIDENT

Portrait of the Private Man
and His Life Outdoors

Hal Elliott Wert

STACKPOLE
BOOKS

Copyright © 2005 by Hal Elliott Wert

Published by
STACKPOLE BOOKS
5067 Ritter Road
Mechanicsburg, PA 17055
www.stackpolebooks.com

All rights reserved, including the right to reproduce this book
or portions thereof in any form or by any means, electronic
or mechanical, including photocopying, recording, or by any
information storage and retrieval system, without permission
in writing from the publisher. All inquiries should be addressed
to Stackpole Books, 5067 Ritter Road, Mechanicsburg,
Pennsylvania 17055.

Printed in U.S.A.

First edition

10 9 8 7 6 5 4 3 2 1

Library of Congress Cataloging-in-Publication Data

Wert, Hal Elliott.
    Hoover the fishing president / Hal Elliott Wert.— 1st ed.
       p. cm.
    ISBN 0-8117-0099-2 (hardcover)
    1. Hoover, Herbert, 1874–1964. 2. Fishing. 3. Presidents—
United States—Biography. I. Title.

    E802.W47 2005
    973.91'6'092—dc22

                                                    2004011467

To Andrew, Allison, and Sarah Wert

semper pesco
(fish always)

Man's life is but vain, for 'tis subject to pain,
    And sorrow, and short as a bubble;
'Tis a hodge-podge of business, and money, and care,
    And care, and money, and trouble.

But we'll take no care when the weather proves fair;
    Nor will we vex now though it rain;
We'll banish all sorrow, and sing till to-morrow,
    And angle, and angle again.

                 —IZAAK WALTON (1653)

Contents

	Foreword	xi
	Acknowledgments	xv
	Prologue	xix
1.	A Boyhood in Iowa	1
2.	A New World in the Great American West	23
3.	From Stanford to the Stars	48
4.	A Relentless Pursuit of Money	70
5.	The Great Humanitarian	88
6.	The Restorative Blessings of Nature	100
7.	The Fisherman President	181
8.	Fishing for Fun and to Wash Your Soul	219
9.	It's the Old Horse for the Long Race	288
	Notes	350
	Index	381

Foreword

It is a great pleasure for me to offer a few thoughts about one of my personal heroes and his passion for fishing. As I turned the pages of this outstanding new biography, I could not help but think that Herbert Hoover was never more at peace than he was standing in an Oregon stream in search of rainbow trout or trolling off the coast of Florida for fighting fish. Public service was his vocation, but fishing was his respite from a hectic world.

In fact, the sport was something of a spiritual experience for him. "He found God in a trout stream as well as a church pew," Richard Norton Smith once wrote about our thirty-first president. Hoover was fond of saying that fishing was a lesson in democracy—"for all men were equal before fishes." And let us not forget that before he was elected president of the United States, Hoover presided over the Izaak Walton League. His inaugural address to the League is worth quoting at length:

> Man and boy, the American is a fisherman. That compre-
> hensive list of human rights, the Declaration of Indepen-

dence, is firm that all men (and boys) are endowed with certain inalienable rights, including life, liberty, and the pursuit of happiness, which obviously includes the pursuit of fish. . . . The great majority of us (except public officials) really work no more than eight hours a day except during the stress of planting or harvesting or elections. If we sleep eight hours we have eight hours in which to ruminate and make merry or stir the cauldron of evil.

This civilization is not going to depend upon what we do when we work so much as what we do in our time. . . . We go to chain theaters and movies; we watch somebody else knock a ball over the fence or kick it over the goal post. I do that and I believe in it. I do, however, insist that no other organized joy has values comparable to the outdoor experience. . . . The joyous rush of the brook, the contemplation of the eternal flow of the stream, the stretch of forest and mountain all reduce our egotism, soothe our troubles, and shame our wickedness.

Izaak Walton did not spend his life answering a bell. He never got the jumps from traffic signals or the price of wheat. The blessings of fishing include . . . discipline in the equality of men, meekness and inspiration before the works of nature, charity and patience toward tacklemakers and the fish, a mockery of profits and concerts, a quieting of hate and a hushing to ambition, a rejoicing and gladness that you do not have to do a blanked thing until next week.

Hoover's love of fishing never left him. A year before his death in 1964, the former president published *Fishing for Fun and to Wash Your Soul,* certainly the most personal and whimsical of his many books. Under headings such as "Where Ponce de Leon Lost the Fountain of Youth" and "Fishing Presidents and Candidates," the old man distilled the experiences of a lifetime, registering a wry protest against "civilization, cement pavements, office buildings, and radios," not to mention such deadening realities of modern life as "telephone bells, church bells, office boys, columnists, pieces of paper and the household chores." No one ever went to jail while fishing, said Hoover—"unless they forgot to buy a license."

Forgive me if I also quote Hoover's eloquent testimonial to my native state: "Oregon," wrote Hoover, "lives in my mind for its gleaming wheat fields, its abundant fruit, its luxuriant forest vegetation, and the fish in the mountain streams. To step into its forests with their tangles of berry bushes, their ferns, their masses of wild flowers, stirs up odors peculiar to Oregon. Within these woods are never ending journeys of discovery, and the hunts for grouse and expeditions for trout." I could not have said it better myself!

He was never more poetic about fishing than in the wistful postscript entitled "Home Again," in which Hoover declared, "There are two things I can say for sure. Two months after you return from a fishing expedition you will begin again to think of the snowcap or the distant mountain peak, the glint of sunshine on the water, the excitement of the dark blue seas, and the glories of the forest. And then you buy more tackle and more clothes for next year. There is no cure for these infections. And that big fish never shrinks."

Although I am not much of a fisherman myself, I did learn about fishing and many other things from the man himself. As a graduate student at Stanford University, I studied Hoover's leadership in establishing federal labor policy, and Mr. Hoover graciously agreed to discuss my thesis with me in his office at Stanford. Although I still remember the excitement of entering that room more than fifty years ago, I can't remember much of what was said. Perhaps the most important result of the meeting was that he granted me permission to use his papers and showed faith that this young graduate student would produce a useful study.

I stayed in touch with Mr. Hoover by mail after I left Stanford, but the high point of my contact with him came in the summer of 1959 during my first term as governor of Oregon. Mr. Hoover invited me to be his guest at the Bohemian Grove encampment that July. It was an extraordinary opportunity to talk with him about politics and public service and all manner of subjects including fishing.

Mr. Hoover and I wrote and spoke to each other several times over the years, and I value those contacts immensely. Indeed, I still have among my book collection several Hoover volumes, including a personally inscribed copy of *Fishing for Fun.* Forty years after his death, Mr. Hoover's message in that book has lost neither its appeal nor its charm. Life consists of more than making a living, he insisted. "It is the break of the waves in the sun, the contemplation of the eternal flow of the stream, the stretch of forest and mountain in their manifestation of the Maker—it is all these that soothe our troubles, shame our wickedness, and inspire us to esteem our fellow men—especially other fishermen."

Hal Elliott Wert has expanded on Hoover's slim volume and documented the contours of Hoover's passion for fishing. Hoover comes alive in Wert's lively prose, as he struggles with enormous challenges of feeding the world and reorganizing the federal government. Wert shows that, in spite of his considerable responsibilities, Hoover always set aside a few days each year to cast his line into a bubbling brook or sail off in search of the one that got away. Hal Wert reveals a side of Hoover that is not available in other biographies.

So I commend this volume to all who enjoy reading or fishing or both. It is a book that will inform and entertain you regardless of your political philosophy. I suggest that you take the book along on your next fishing trip. You can read a few chapters as you wait for the big one to snatch your line and take you on your next great adventure. Happy reading and happy fishing!

Sen. Mark O. Hatfield
May 2004

Acknowledgments

Hoover the Fishing President would not have been possible if it had not been for a large number of people who gave both their time and talents to help make the book possible. Former senator Hatfield, when asked to write the foreword, immediately said yes and consented to a telephone interview concerning his trips to the Bohemian Grove. To him I say, thank you. Leslie Hoover Lauble welcomed me to her home in Oregon and allowed me to plow through family picture albums and examine a wonderful collection of her great-grandfather's fishing equipment. Tim Walch, Director of the Herbert Hoover Library in West Branch, Iowa, read the manuscript and encouraged me to finish the book. George Nash, eminent Hoover biographer, read the manuscript, saved me from a number of mistakes, and offered encouragement when I was floundering. Theodore A. Wilson, Professor of History at the University of Kansas, read all of the manuscript and offered suggestions for improvement, as did Kendrick A. Clements of the University of South Carolina. Robert W. Demeritt of Barstow School, a friend of thirty years, was kind enough to ensure that I made no mistakes with the Chinese romanization system in the chapter in which the Hoovers faced the Boxers. Robert and his wife, Mary Anne, read the manuscript and offered cogent advice. Harvey Hix, Vice President for Academic Affairs at the Cleveland Institute of Art, read the first draft, a duty beyond the demands of friendship, and made many useful suggestions.

Lee Nash, Professor of History at George Fox University, invited me to participate in the university's ongoing Hoover Seminar. Lee and his charming wife, Grace, were enthusiasts of both Hoover and fishing from the start, and Lee has done numerous favors, including finding several of the guides who "fished Hoover" on the McKenzie River. George Fox University Archivist Dick Votaw and his assistant Anita Cirulis worked to restore several of the photographs from their treasure trove of early Hoover material. Dwight Miller, retired Senior Archivist at the Hoover Library, read the first half of the manuscript and has been a constant source of information and a good friend.

Always helpful were the Herbert Hoover Library staff in West Branch, Iowa: Dale Mayer, Cindy Worrell, J. Patrick Wildenberg, Matt Schaefer, and Spencer Howard. A special thanks to archivist Lynn Smith and Audio-Visual Specialist Jim Detlefsen, who were forced to deal with me weekly. Most of the photographs in the book were scanned by Jim. Elaine Danielson, Carol Leadenham, and Heather Wagner at the Hoover Institution at Stanford University were invaluable in helping find obscure material on fishing. Thanks also to Kathleen Collins, President of Kansas City Art Institute; Gary Sutton, Dean of the Faculty; Phyllis Moore, Director of the School of Liberal Arts; and the Board of the Kansas City Art Institute for a number of Faculty Development Grants and the sabbatical that made finishing the book possible. The library staff of the Kansas City Art Institute, M. J. Poehler, Leesa Duby, and Sally Closson went the extra mile to find material I needed.

Ed Stelfox of the Lane County Oregon Historical Museum produced the best unpublished photo of Herbert and Lou Henry Hoover, one taken by C. L. Stevenson of the Hoovers fishing together on the McKenzie River. Thanks also go to the following Oregonians, all of whom contributed much new material and unpublished photographs to the Hoover fishing story: Curt Lantz, Manager of the Deschutes Historical Society in Bend; Julia Moore of the Woodville Museum, Rogue River; Nancy Noble,

Polk County Oregon Historical Society; the Oregon State Historical Society; Bill Miller and Carol Harbison-Samuelson of the Southern Oregon Historical Society; Jan Collins of the Josephine County Historical Society, Grants Pass; Joanne Ward, Librarian at the Columbia Gorge Discovery Center, The Dalles; Nancy Sieberts, Museum Aide, Klamath County Museum, Klamath Falls; and Vivienne Wright, former owner of Holiday Farm near Blue River, who was kind enough to consent to a telephone interview and send along photographs of Hoover on the McKenzie.

Dee Anna Grimsrud, Reference Archivist, Wisconsin State Historical Society, helped track down Hoover and Coolidge photographs, as did Kathy Laakso of the Douglas County Historical Society in Superior. Ted Conant of Conant Studios, Marinette, Wisconsin, graciously granted permission for me to use photos taken by his great-uncle during Hoover's fishing trip to Pembine in 1938. Thanks also to all of the following people and organizations, who helped locate material for the book: Barbara Davis and Leila Wiles (Librarian) of the Izaak Walton League of America; Betty Mitchell of the Lake Tahoe Historical Society; W. D. Barry of the Maine Historical Society; Scott Saga, Curator of Collections, Thomas T. Taber Museum of the Lycoming County Historical Society, Williamsport, Pennsylvania; Kathryn Hodson, Special Collections Reader Services Liaison, University of Iowa Libraries; Dawn Hugh of the South Florida Historical Association; Tom Hambright at the Key West Public Library for help on Long Key; Jerry Wilkinson, President of the Upper Keys Historical Society and author of the Internet History of the Keys; John Hyslop, Queens Borough Public Library, Long Island Division, for help with the New York *Herald Tribune* photo collection; Kris Hager of Quorn, Iowa who found a photograph of Grandma Minthorn's house and the LaMar Polo Team; Judy Bowman and Margaret Henreich of the Plymouth County, Iowa, Historical Association; Ruth Bartels of the State Historical Society of Iowa-Des Moines and the State Historical Society of Iowa-Iowa City; Catherine Hanson-Tracy, Reference Librarian, and Janet Clemmensen, Library Technical Assistant, at the California State Library in Sacramento; Kenneth R. Clark and his Internet History of Shasta Springs, California; Marilyn Cox, Director of the Historical Society Museum, Montrose, Colorado; Paula Ruth, Head Librarian, Weiser, Idaho, Public Library; Michael Maher, Librarian, and Dr.

Lee P. Brumbaugh, Curator of Photographs, Nevada Historical Society, Reno, Nevada; Leslie Childers, Museum Curator, Lincoln County Historical Museum, Pioche, Nevada; Cindy L. Brown, Reference Archivist, Wyoming State Archives, Cheyenne, Wyoming; Jim H. Bradshaw of the Lafayette *Daily Advertiser,* Lafayette, Louisiana; and Janet Hooker, Archivist, Arkansas History Commission.

To my agent, Fritz Hanson, whom I caused great anxiety, and my editor at Stackpole, Judith Schnell, for patience above and beyond the call—thank you. My family and friends were fated to hear more about Hoover and fishing than they ever wanted to know; on mention of the subject, friends fled through the front door and my children scattered. But even with all of the marvelous assistance I have received, any mistakes are mine alone.

Prologue

While researching Hoover and his programs to feed Europe during both World Wars, I persistently ran into material on Hoover as a fisherman. It was quickly evident that Hoover had led an adventurous life in the outdoors and that fishing was a key to better understanding a very private man. It was also clear that very little had been written about the Hoovers' association with the world outdoors. Hoover wrote dozens of articles on fishing, and his wife, Lou Henry, wrote about camping and hiking for the Girl Scouts. Biographers and historians touched on the highlights of their adventures only in a secondary way, as a means of adding color, rather than as something central to their analysis. Partly, this was taking the easier road, for discovering details of their outdoor life proved a laborious task. Hoover considered his fishing time private and therefore rarely revealed any details as to where, how often, or with what he fished.

The oral history collections at the Hoover Library were invaluable in ferreting out details, as was the newspaper clipping file. Much of the best information, however, came from state historical societies, county museums, and local newspapers. The national media might not have paid much attention to a fishing trip taken by the secretary of commerce or a former president, but local papers did. In Oregon, where Hoover was a hero before his presidency and remains popular, local and state coverage was extensive. In several areas where Hoover fished, I was able to find accounts written by his fishing guides or their families or friends.

Hoover, who pulled fish from the Wapsinonoc in West Branch, Iowa, as a boy, developed into a preeminent fishermen, one of the best known in the country, just a few notches below Zane Grey and Ernest Hemingway. Hoover mastered nearly every kind of freshwater and saltwater fishing. After 1946, when President Harry Truman returned Hoover to government service, Americans came to know the man more fully and to learn more about his fishing trips to Florida and Oregon. Hoover, who had given up politics by the end of World War II, became in the 1950s an elder statesman who dispensed a wide array of advice and commentary on the nation's problems and on the benefits of fishing— a latter-day Izaak Walton. But Hoover's presidency remained clouded by the Depression, and his earlier accomplishments moved to the back of the American psyche.

To the present generation, the Hoovers are people relegated to history books, along with Calvin Coolidge, William Howard Taft, and William Henry Harrison. But the mention of Hoover can still evoke memories among those who survived the Great Depression. Often people remember jingles such as this one:

> Worldwide Depression, Everywhere
> Herb Hoover is to blame.
> Disaster in the Earth and Air,
> Herb Hoover is to blame.
>
> I find my eyes are getting dim,
> Herb Hoover is to blame.
> My bank account is very slim,
> Herb Hoover is to blame;

> My oldest boy is running booze,
> And little Jennie smokes and chews,
> I'm nearly dying of the Blues,
> Herb Hoover is to blame.

Others recall invective little rhymes that stuck in your brain and ran round and round:

> Mellon drove the engine
> Hoover rang the bell
> Wall Street blew the whistle
> And the country went to hell.

And then there are those powerful Depression icons that persist in the popular imagination: Hoovervilles, Hoover hogs, Hoover flags, Hoover blankets, Hoover carts, and Hoover Pullmans.

Walk into any bookstore, particularly one of the large chain stores, make your way to the presidential biography section, and run your finger along the shelf. A lot of books have been written about the forty-three presidents, but the list of those who have maintained the interest of the American public is short. An occasional breakthrough, such as the brilliant biography of John Adams by David McCullough, is there, and maybe a biography of Washington or Jefferson, but probably not both. Most likely, a Jackson biography, a Lincoln biography, and three or four books about Teddy Roosevelt grace the shelves. There are usually one or two books on Wilson, a half shelf on Franklin and Eleanor Roosevelt, one or two on Truman and Eisenhower, and two full shelves on the Kennedys, who remain a virtual publishing industry. After JFK, two or three titles appear on each of the more recent presidents, except for the raft of books on Reagan and Clinton. Significantly, there are no books on Herbert Hoover. You are lucky to find a Hoover title in a used bookstore, though the large Internet book services have more choices. If you want to know something about Herbert and Lou Henry Hoover, you have to make a special effort. Hoover remains in the minds of the public and most historians as a failed American president, a cold man, indifferent to his nation's suffering during the Great Depression.

The popular views of the three Republican presidents between Wilson and Roosevelt are that Warren Harding was a corrupt man who prevailed over a scandal-ridden administration,
Coolidge was a do-nothing president with a sharp tongue, and
Hoover was a president who made a very bad situation worse. To
the younger generation, all three names mean nothing.

Then why a book about Hoover? Historians in the last fifteen
years have been much kinder to our thirty-first president, and
several economic historians have credited Hoover's analysis of
the Depression, linking it to the international financial crisis
emerging from World War I, as correct, though his efforts to deal
with the economic crisis, while sometimes extraordinary, were
too little too late. Regardless of Hoover's failings or the enduring
fame of the Roosevelts and the Kennedys, Herbert and Lou
Hoover deserve more attention. Their lives were much more
interesting than is generally supposed. In fact, they were often
genuinely exciting. Hoover's life spanned nearly a century, and
he was a thinker and doer who shaped the way we live. It is hard
to imagine a couple who worked harder or accomplished more
than the Hoovers. Just as important, their lives posed a solution
to the problem of modernity, the transformation of an agrarian
society into a modern industrial giant. The Hoovers, like so many
Americans of that period and even now, to use an old expression,
had a pair of pants on each leg. One leg was firmly planted in
rural Iowa, with its attendant values, and the other leg was
squarely in the new upwardly mobile, urban professional class.
Hoover's idea was to combine the best of the old with the new, to
minimize the assured loss associated with major changes he was
helping bring about, to try not to be the agent of our own society's destruction.

The Hoovers' solution, the voluntary cooperative restruc-
turing of American society, largely failed, but for a time their
approach represented the hopes of millions. Hoover's ideas were
pleasing and promised to bridge the widening gap between past
and present. Bert and Lou were the new man and woman of
bourgeois America, and they carried the new professional class's
standard, its hopes and dreams. To Hoover, his election to the
presidency represented a mandate to implement his solutions
posed by the problem of a rapidly transforming society. It was a

"New Day." A more radical solution to the same set of problems, which also failed, was the road traveled by John Reed and Louise Bryant. For Hoover, fishing became symbolic of his effort to transcend the earthquakelike separation of historical epochs. Fishing and the beauty of nature pulled forward those simpler times, recalling the garden in which we once had lived and had so radically transformed.

Hoover likely will remain somewhere around thirtieth on polls rating the presidents. Because of his accomplishments in his postpresidential years, he, like Jimmy Carter, won a place in the hearts of Americans. Nevertheless, he will continue to be viewed as a president who, although he was a decent, upstanding, caring human being, committed to government service, was a failure while in office—a man who failed the challenges of his time, a man who failed to master events and therefore was mastered by them. Hoover was a victim of the values he held and of his own experiences. But a closer examination of Hoover's life reveals a private, shy man largely unknown to the American public. Ironically, that is exactly what Herbert Hoover intended.

Stoicism, his Quaker upbringing, and a deep commitment to privacy made Hoover difficult to know. Except for an infrequent glimpse behind the wall of seclusion, whatever unhappiness or disappointments the Hoovers might have suffered in their marriage, or whatever difficulties or disappointments they had in their family, remain essentially hidden. The Hoovers' success in warding off the world is a constant source of frustration to the historian. The downside of public persons who insist on private lives is that a lack of personal letters and diaries turn historians to other figures, people who are more accessible and can be more easily reconstructed.

Through a range of sources, I have been able to clarify many details concerning the Hoovers' life outdoors, and I have discovered the details of many fishing trips that were previously unknown. On the other hand, I have often run into dead ends, destinations regarding which no information was available. In other situations, I have not had a specific document as evidence but have had to rely upon deduction and inference. Through all of this, my goal has been to tell more fully the little-known but exciting story of the Hoovers' lives and to demonstrate how important the outdoors was to their understanding. I hope that I have managed to put flesh on their bones, as well as fish on Herbert Hoover's hooks.

HAL ELLIOTT WERT
Kansas City Art Institute
February 2004

1

A Boyhood in Iowa

Herbert Hoover's initiation into the deep mysteries of the piscatorial art began when he was eight years old, on the creeks and rivers that punctuated the fertile prairie surrounding West Branch, Iowa, a tiny village in the eastern part of the state. His equipment was a marvel of simplicity: a willow pole, butcher-string line, and hooks that sold for a penny apiece. Hoover liked to say that hooks sold ten for a dime, but the dime was hard to get.[1] Bait consisted of minnows, worms, grubs, mayflies, cicadas, katydids, grasshoppers, and a potpourri of other insects. Night crawlers and angleworms were favorites. Young Iowa fishermen spent a good deal of time preparing wooden cheese boxes, tin canisters, buckets, and various containers in order to house the bait they persistently hunted. Picking up huge, slimy, wiggling night crawlers on dewy nights or turning over spades full of black prairie earth in pursuit of slippery angleworms or fat, white-bodied, orange-nosed grubs was almost as enjoyable as fishing. The angleworms were amazingly agile and often quickly disappeared into the tunnels of their own making. Dexterity was

West Branch, Iowa, 1880s. COURTESY HERBERT HOOVER LIBRARY, WEST BRANCH, IOWA

needed to catch them. Fish worms quickly grasped between the index finger and thumb could be pulled from their chambers. Occasionally, when pulled on hard, the worm stretched out taut—like a rubber band—and then, surprisingly, easily broke in two. The grubs, however, when exposed by the shovel, curled up in tight semicircles and rolled slowly about in protest against the invasion of their dark, dank realm. Boys easily caught huge grasshoppers, thick in the tall, red-stemmed prairie grass, and squeezed their thoraxes to make them "spit tobacco," a process that forced a blackish brown liquid to bubble from between their mandibles.

Flying grasshoppers with wings of red or yellow, trimmed with black, were extremely difficult to catch by hand—perhaps the greatest challenge. The protruding bulbous eyes and sensitive antennae of these armored leaf-eating machines saw and heard all. Even when approached with stealth, the wily insects nearly always detected their pursuer, springing into the air with a loud, shrill staccato chatter, and flew no more than ten or fifteen yards, landing with a thump. On sweateringly hot summer days, small barefoot boys chased these six-legged Pied Pipers down dusty serpentine roads. After an assortment of bait was at last assembled, it was time to fish. Dreaming of success, the fishermen headed for the creek to try their luck.

To ready the fishing line, a cork bobber was attached in order to set the depth of the hook. Several inches above the hook, a lead sinker or a small rock ensured that the bait stayed submerged. Then the bait was securely attached so that it hid the hook but still looked natural or wiggled enough in the water to entice a fish. To bring him luck, the hopeful fisherman spat on the bait. Hoover explained that fishermen were a superstitious lot and maintained that "all American small boys spit on the bait."[2]

Now came the most challenging part: The line had to be thrown or cast to midstream without losing the bait or without catching the trees or hooking the tall ragweed or button weed that often lined the creek banks. Sometimes this took several attempts, and each boy developed his own technique—a subject that produced numerous arguments about who had the best solution. Occasionally a fish would tug the bobber in the first few minutes, but more often it was Lady Luck and patience that yielded a catch from Wapsinonoc Creek.

Once the fish took the bait, the boys learned to set the hook and pull in the fish. To land the catch, it was necessary to extend the line and pole as far away from the body as possible while running the trailing line through the other hand. When the pole and line were fully extended, the boy grasped the line and repeated the process until the fish was snug against his hand. Setting the pole on the ground, he ran the other hand slowly over the fish to smooth down the fins and avoid getting spiked—a painful experience that almost always drew blood and produced purple streaking around the wound. Removing the hook was also a tricky procedure. Even small fish would expand their bodies with air, wiggle, and attempt to escape. A misstep and the fish was lost. With the fish securely in hand, a stringer was run through the fish's mouth and out the gill. The last step was to slip the fish back into the water and tie the rope to a stick stuck into the ground at the edge of the creek.

Digging through a cheese box for a worm or reaching into a grass-filled jar in search of a grasshopper, the boy again baited his hook, cast his line, and sat down in anticipation of hooking an even bigger fish. Come late afternoon, stringers of mud cats, sunfish, pumpkinseeds, chubs, and redhorse were carried home to appreciative mothers, grateful for a change in diet, but exasperated by the wet and muddy condition of their charges. Hoover, reflecting upon his fishing experiences as a boy in Iowa, remarked that he had "lived in the time when a fish used to bite instead of strike and we knew it bit when the cork bobbed. And moreover we ate the fish."[3] For Hoover, these rich childhood experiences instilled in him a love of fishing and a love of the outdoors. Throughout much of his long and productive life, he repeatedly returned to nature for recreation, solitude, escape, and renewal. Later in his life, when alone in a fast-rushing trout stream, he felt closer to the creator of all things.

Hoover, who would become thirty-first president of the United States, was born on August 10 or 11, 1874, in West Branch, Iowa, to Jessie and Hulda Hoover. In the commotion attending the baby's arrival, nobody noticed whether it was just before or after midnight. The following morning, his father, quite pleased at having a second son, bragged to a neighbor, "Well, we have another General Grant at our house."[4] Named Herbert at the suggestion of his aunt Ann, he was soon dubbed Bertie by family and friends. Bertie was preceded by a brother, Theodore, nicknamed Tad, born in 1871, and followed by a younger sister, Mary, called May, born in 1876.

Bertie, as a child, along with many other family members, suffered the croup, a viral infection of the upper and lower breathing tract. One snow-covered winter day, when he was roughly two and a half years old, he coughed, choked, turned purple, and keeled over, seemingly dead.[5] After placing him on pillows on a high table, his mother, father, aunts, and cousins worked furiously to save his life. In their frantic attempts at reviving him, his aunts vigorously rubbed his body with goose grease. When he did not respond, they swathed his body in an onion poultice. Both failed. One of Bertie's cousins was hurriedly sent to find his uncle, Dr. Henry John Minthorn, who was out on daily house calls. Told that his nephew was near death, Henry John drove his spirited horses at a gallop to reach the stricken boy. As he reined in the sweat-covered team, Grandmother Minthorn burst from the house and shouted, "Bertie is gone."[6] Henry John leaped from the buggy, ran to his house next door, retrieved two blankets, and ran back to the Hoovers'. There he

Birthplace of Herbert Hoover. COURTESY HERBERT HOOVER LIBRARY

found Bertie laid out on the kitchen table given up for dead, a dime on each eyelid, awaiting burial preparation. The young boy indeed seemed gone, but among those gathered, someone noticed a faint tremor of life. Dr. Minthorn acted quickly. Wrapping Bertie in blankets, he pulled out the boy's tongue, cleared the phlegm from his clogged throat, and slowly and gently revived his patient using mouth-to-mouth resuscitation.[7] As devout Quakers, the family attributed Bertie's miraculous comeback to God's direct intervention. Grandmother Minthorn solemnly proclaimed, "God has a great work for that boy to do; that is why he was brought back to life."[8]

Fully recovered, Bertie grew into a healthy, round-faced, slightly chubby young boy. He was inquisitive but naturally quiet, shy, and reserved. Like so many other youngsters of that time, he went on to survive a number of childhood diseases— mumps, measles, diphtheria, chickenpox, and recurring bouts of the croup. Sickness attacked the West Branch area often, and the inhabitants were additionally exposed to the dangers of typhoid fever and malaria. Four years later, in 1880 when Bertie was six, his father was not granted a similar reprieve. At age thirty-four, after developing a severe cold, Jesse Hoover, successful blacksmith and budding entrepreneur, died suddenly from "rheumatism of the heart"—rheumatic fever, another contagion that claimed many.[9] Bertie was too young for his father's death to have much of an immediate impact, and his father remained dimly remembered in the young boy's mind. His life, of course, now moved in a different direction. For his older brother, Tad, then ten, their father's death left "a void unfillable and unfilled forever."[10]

Hulda Hoover struggled with providing for and raising three children without the aid of a husband. For spiritual comfort, she turned to the church. Always a deeply committed Quaker, she took to the circuit, sometimes for two or three weeks at a time, and was in demand as a speaker and preacher—especially at the quarterly meeting of Friends in Muscatine, Iowa. Conservative Quakers objected to her singing hymns in church, but the Society of Friends was in transition, and the evangelical reform elements appealed to many believers.[11] Hulda knew where she stood: She was an activist evangelical who supported reform. While their mother traveled to meetings as far away as Kansas, the children were cared for by relatives or friends. Tad boarded with the Cook family, who lived down the street. To earn his keep, he performed whatever chores needed to be done. These often included gathering kindling or weeding the garden. Bert stayed with Uncle Allen Hoover, but he was too young to do much work and not much was expected. May stayed with Grandmother Minthorn, a woman to whom she was greatly attached.[12]

Attending Quaker services that lasted nearly all day Sunday was a trial for the children, but their mother's break with the conservative wing of the church made the day easier, for now there were a sermon and music. When younger, the two Hoover boys sat on the men's side of the meetinghouse, May was on the other side with the women, and all waited for hours for the Lord to move someone in the congregation to speak. Sometimes no one was touched by the inner light and not a word transpired. After several hours had passed, all went home.[13] Hoover recalled the long hours of silence in the unadorned, cold, gray meetinghouse with a special poignancy, a place where "a small boy was not even allowed to count his toes."[14] This disciplined waiting may have taught patience, restraint, and forbearance, but the Hoover boys and most of the Quaker children of West Branch bore these Sunday sessions with equanimity, for their reward came later that day when they escaped into the surrounding woods and fields. Not until Hoover became secretary of commerce did he begin to warm again to his Quaker religious heritage.

Growing up on the Iowa farming frontier necessitated a self-reliant life in the outdoors. Very few items in the Hoovers' lives were storebought—the land provided for nearly all the family's needs, and the young people of this small village worked alongside adults to gather and cut wood, dry herbs, gather walnuts and hickory nuts, tap maple sap for syrup, milk cows, slaughter animals, muck stalls, hoe corn, and prepare vegetables for canning. But even after adding the busy schoolday to church and the endless list of chores, there was still some time left for other pursuits. In the opening lines of *A Boyhood in Iowa*, Hoover nostalgically recalls his Tom Sawyer-like childhood: "I prefer to think of Iowa as I saw it through the eyes of a ten-year-old boy—and the eyes of all ten-year-old Iowa boys are or should be filled with the wonders of Iowa's streams and woods, of the mystery of growing crops. His days should be filled with adventure and great undertakings, with participation in good and comforting things."[15] In Hoover's Garden of Eden, the rhythmic change of seasons provided the children of West Branch an opportunity for swimming in summer, sledding in winter, and hunting, fishing, and exploring nearly all year round. Bertie, Tad, and May, along with the other children of the town, participated in Iowa's offerings with relish.

Bertie, now usually called Bert, early on demonstrated a flair for fishing by hooking the big ones. He once hauled in a twelve-inch sucker from Wapsinonoc Creek—"a record," his brother Tad maintained, "a famous fish in those days and not surpassed in his time."[16] When the boys had caught enough fish or were overcome with hunger, they gathered wood, built a small fire, and then gutted, scaled, and slow-roasted their small fish on green willow sticks. Later in life, Hoover, having eaten at some of the best restaurants in the world, adamantly maintained that no dish, not even one prepared at the Ritz or in the kitchen of Maxim's, could match the succulent flavor of a "punkin seed" on a stick.[17] After this "gourmet repast," the boys usually plunged into their favorite swimming hole near the Burlington, Cedar Rapids, and Northern Railroad trestle bridge. Though the swimming hole was shallow and only some thirty feet across, it provided opportunities to zip down the slippery mud bank like greased lightning

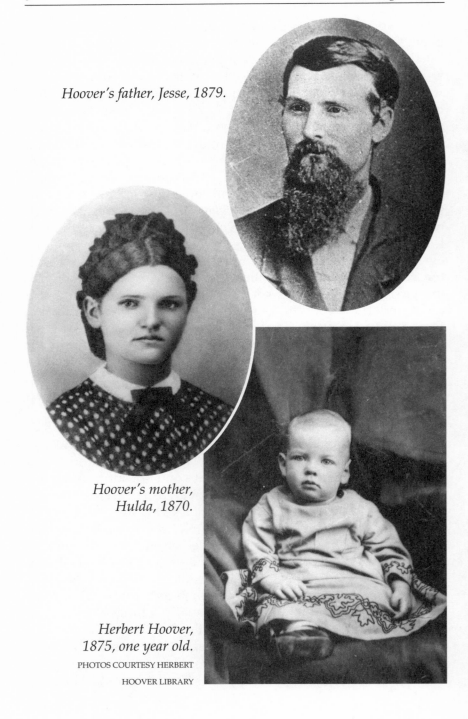

Hoover's father, Jesse, 1879.

*Hoover's mother,
Hulda, 1870.*

*Herbert Hoover,
1875, one year old.*

PHOTOS COURTESY HERBERT

HOOVER LIBRARY

and splash into the water. If not in the mood to swim, the boys built dams and skipped stones. The winner was the boy whose stone skipped the most times and went the farthest. Dam building was hard work, and many of the boys soon tired or turned to other pursuits. Not Bert, who spent hours constructing dams and diverting water, his fascination for this activity seemingly endless. Happy, worn out, and with evening approaching, the small band of mud-covered boys trudged home through the spreading dusk to a sure scolding and a hot meal.

Another of Bert's and Tad's favorite pastimes was to walk along the railroad grade in search of agates and fossils, as the Burlington line had used for ballast glacial gravel that had been dumped in a line across Iowa during the ice age. Occasionally Bert or one of his friends would find a geode, a piece of coral, or a crinoid stem, considered exceptional treasures.[18] To see the magnificent marbling and wonderful colors of the agates, the boys would work their finds on a grinder, but lacking more sophisticated polishing equipment, it was necessary to lick the stones to be able to show them off. Bert and Tad excitedly cracked open geodes with a hammer to reveal the marvelous crystalline interior. It was not surprising that years later, upon entering Stanford University, both boys were drawn to geology and mining.

The whole Hoover clan enjoyed picnicking, camping, and fishing. All agreed that one of the best spots in the area was on the banks of the Cedar River some ten miles east of West Branch. Jesse Hoover, before his untimely death, especially enjoyed summer trips to the Cedar and was particularly fond of the picnic lunches lovingly prepared by his wife, Hulda. Participation in these festive forays began when neighbors and relatives were persuaded that an outing was in order. Earnest preparation began days before the event. Extensive discussions determined where to picnic, where to camp, what would be eaten, and what to take along. Then the women baked breads, biscuits, pies, and cakes midweek, and as departure time neared, a flurry of activity commenced. Fresh corn, field corn if its milk had just come in, was picked and left in the husk to be roasted in hot coals. Green beans and ham hocks simmered on the cookstoves, as did a cornucopia of other vegetables—potatoes, beets, and peas. Chickens were caught, killed, plucked, and roasted. Hams retrieved from the smokehouse were scrubbed and sliced. Girls aided their mothers in gathering blankets, pillows, jackets, and extra clothing throughout the house and then were sent scurrying down steep, damp cellar stairs, soon to emerge laden with jars of pickles, chow-chow, salted cherries, honey, jam, and sweet tomato preserves. Picnic baskets were carefully packed and set near the door or on the back porch for loading. The men and boys prepared the buggies and wagons, rounded up and filled the lanterns, gathered all the necessary tools, and readied the fishing gear. The night before, the boys, lanterns held high overhead, searched for night crawlers and packed the slick bait in wooden cheese boxes filled with moist black earth. Anticipation swelled, as early Saturday morning, wagons and buggies loaded, dogs yipping, the whole kit and caboodle headed for the Cedar River.

For several hours, the small caravan traversed a rutted road through grasses intermingled with wildflowers. Here and there, a patch of long-stemmed or blue-stemmed prairie grass survived amid imported rivals. Sunflowers, black-eyed susans, Quaker ladies (bluets), blazing-stars, Queen Anne's lace, and thistles blossomed in profusion. In the narrow open spots between the trail and prairie, the wild rose led a perilous existence. Beyond the prairie, the road wound its way down into the green hardwood forest that filled the valley of the Cedar. The women spread out picnic cloths in an open meadow, while the men watered the horses and turned them out to graze. Seated on the ground, the entire party feasted on the contents of the picnic baskets, then lounged under the tall oaks, elms, and walnuts, escaping the midsummer heat in the cool of the shade. Nearly all activity ceased.

On this particular outing, Bertie, no more than three or four, took this opportunity to wander off to explore on his own. A short time later, he came hightailing out of the woods, tears streaming down his face and holding the top of his head. He had stumbled into a nest of blue and green hornets, two of which had stung him on the head. As the stingers embedded in his tender scalp swelled, Bertie began to howl. Raised from their lethargy, the picnickers looked on as Jesse Hoover applied a poultice of soft yellow clay to the injury. Tad recalled, "I remember as if it were yesterday a tear-stained, fuzzy-headed little boy sleeping peacefully after a period of great emotion, with a large pyramid of mud drying in his hair."[19] Refreshed, and with Bertie recovered, the

A Hoover family reunion, ca. 1878. Bertie is at the top, second to the left of the boy in the tree. COURTESY HERBERT HOOVER LIBRARY

Quaker families packed up and pushed on to their campsite on the banks of the Cedar. Uncle Benajah and the boys' favorite cousin, George, had arrived the day before and put in an afternoon of fishing. Their efforts were rewarded with a good catch of speckled river catfish (channel catfish)—enough to feed all for supper. This large, meaty catfish was a West Branch favorite and a special treat.

Bertie and Tad, 1879. COURTESY HERBERT HOOVER LIBRARY

Sometime in the first two years after Jesse Hoover died, probably when Bert was around seven or eight, their mother, in need
of a respite and eager to be on the Quaker circuit again, sent the
children to stay with relatives. One of their uncles, Maj. Laban
Miles, who was the U.S. Indian agent to the Osage nation in

Pawhuska, Oklahoma, volunteered to take Bert. This interlude in Indian Territory proved one of the greatest adventures in his early life. Laban's wife, Agnes, came to West Branch, where she visited relatives while she waited for her husband to arrive from Washington, D.C. Then they took Bert back to Oklahoma with them, first by train to Arkansas City, Kansas, and then by buggy to the capital of the Osage nation at Pawhuska.[20] The trip took several days, during which the three travelers jostled along the rutted prairie road amid a profusion of wildflowers and grasses. The vast prairie stretched in all directions as far as the eye could see, broken only by an occasional hill or a few scattered trees.

The Miles family and their small guest from Iowa numbered among the few whites in the small reservation settlement. For the next few months, Bert and his three cousins attended the Indian school, including Sunday school; observed an elaborate Osage wedding; and spent many hours exploring the surrounding hills and streams. Classes were conducted in English, and most of the Indian children were eager to demonstrate their newly acquired language skills. A visiting missionary once asked the children of the Sunday school if they knew the week's Bible lesson. Several blurted out excitedly, "Ananias set fire to his wife." The preacher, at first dismayed by this strange response, soon realized the children's innocent mistake. The Bible lesson was "Ananias and

Bertie at Osage Indian wedding ceremony, Pawhuska, Oklahoma, 1882. Hoover is at the far left. COURTESY HERBERT HOOVER LIBRARY

Sapphira, his wife."[21] While in Oklahoma among the Osage, Bert added to his fishing knowledge by learning to use a bent pin as a hook and then cook his catch on the lid of a discarded tin can. Other acquired Indian skills included snaring rabbits and ground squirrels and making bows and arrows from the Osage orange tree.[22] Upon his return home, Bert had many adventures to relate and many new things to teach his friends. His confidence outdoors continued to grow.

All three Hoover children returned from their stays with various relatives and were reunited once again with their mother in West Branch. In the rhythmic change of seasons, the onset of fall meant the beginning of school, bringing in the harvest, and rigorous preparation for the coming long, hard winter. It also meant trips to Aunt and Uncle Merlin Marshall's farm, halfway to Iowa City, to gather walnuts and hickory nuts underneath a canopy of red, orange, and yellow foliage. Here Bert and Tad played in their uncle's collection of discarded farm machinery, but massive pumpkin wars were the real fun. Uncle Merlin grew a huge number of pumpkins to feed his dairy herd. As the pumpkins ripened, they were brought by wagon into the farmyard and stacked pyramid-style. These orange piles were often twenty feet high and fifty feet long. The boys could do whatever they wanted with the pumpkins, as long as they ended up in the cattle troughs as feed. In his memoirs, Tad Hoover described the melee: "We made 'Jack-o-lanterns' of every sort our fancy could conceive, and arranged them by companies and battalions and brigades. Then we attacked them, foot and horse, with a corn-cutter, a weapon like a machete or a Circassian sword, and annihilated the whole array. There was no limit to the slaughter save from physical exhaustion with the rather hard chopping."[23]

As winter set in, the children of the village looked forward to an array of new activities, which included sledding, skating, and hunting. The Hoovers lived at the bottom of Cook's Hill, the steepest and longest sled run in town. On cold, dark winter evenings, nearly all of the boys and many of the girls trudged up the long hill, sleds in tow, and gathered in small groups, chattering and laughing, waiting for their turn. Some lay down in the snow and waved their arms back and forth to make angels. With little artificial lighting in the village, the stars gleamed against an ink black winter sky. Children pulled their heads back and looked up in wonder at the bright stars, slowly turning in a circle to search for familiar constellations. To the north, Draco, Hercules, and Cygnus were easily spotted. Then came a giant Pegasus, followed by Capricornus, Sagittarius, and Virgo. To the south, Orion hugged the horizon. Just before the children completed the turn, heads now pushed back so far that their mouths hung open, the Big Dipper appeared almost straight overhead, radiant in the cold, crisp night.

The boys picked up their sleds with both hands, held them close to their chests, ran as fast as possible on the packed snow, and hit the slope of the hill hard. Many years later, on a return visit to West Branch, Hoover recalled the thrill: "To satisfy our human cravings for speed, we slid down at terrific pace with our tummies tight to home-made sleds."[24] Brother Tad also vividly remembered the glories of sledding as he raced down Cook's Hill, "with heels high in the air and toes to be put down to port or starboard as the needs of navigation demanded."[25] Both boys had homemade sleds, Tad's constructed by the wagonmaker, and Bert's by his father in his blacksmith shop. Neither sled was particularly fast, although Tad's, painted a bright red and green, was more attractive and faster. Both boys soon traded their homemade sleds for secondhand factory-built coasters.

Girls were expected to approach the art of sledding differently. They sat on their sleds and steered with their feet, the proper way for young ladies. Pushed from behind by a friend or a beau, the girls started down the slick, well-worn icy track at breakneck speed. Sitting on the sled made navigation more difficult. The girls compensated by hunkering down as far as possible and shifting their weight on the curves, but spills occurred frequently.

As the evening progressed and the temperature dropped, most of the wet, frozen children headed for home. Now came the penalty paid by all young sledders. Regardless of their pleas, attentive parents removed the children's stiff, frozen shoes or boots and ice-crusted socks and pants, and plunged their blue-tinged toes and feet into buckets of ice water—a well-known remedy for frostbite. The parents of West Branch accepted the prevailing theory that ice water warmed feet more rapidly than warm or hot.[26] Their torture over, the shivering children slipped between cold sheets on quilt-covered beds.

Ice skating was popular but of short duration. When the ice froze thick on the Wapsinonoc, the skating was wonderful, but as the snow piled up, the little creek was buried under a thick, heavy blanket until spring. Snowbanks, however, could be used in a practical application. As Christmas neared, the Hoover children and their numerous cousins got together to make tree decorations and candies and cookies of various kinds. They strung popcorn, bittersweet, and dried berries to wrap around the tree and painted and tied dried pinecones with ribbons. Popcorn rolled in sorghum molasses provided sweet treats. But the favorite, and the most difficult to make, was maple sugar eggs. After poking a small hole in each end of the egg, the child leaned over a bowl, held the delicate oval between the forefinger and thumb of both hands, placed his or her puckered lips to the end of the egg, and blew gently and steadily. The trick was to blow hard enough to force the content of the egg out the other hole without breaking the shell. Cousin Harriette Miles fondly remembered, "Bert and I were clumsy and broke so many eggs."[27] This difficult step was only half the process. Melted maple sugar was carefully and slowly poured into the blown-out eggshell, which was then taken outside and buried in a snowbank to harden. The results were delicious.

Winter brought hunting and trapping as well, although the Hoover boys set wooden cracker-box traps held up by sticks (figure-four traps) in open areas along the edge of woods all year long. Their cousin George subscribed to *Youth's Companion,* a publication strictly forbidden by Tad and Bert's parents, and occasionally loaned copies to Tad. This taboo magazine featured adventure stories and activities for boys. Cousin George, slightly older, was an additional source of envy and hero worship because he was allowed a gun. Tad, with borrowed magazine deftly hidden, went out behind the blacksmith shop, out of sight of his father and mother, and clandestinely devoured each illicit issue.[28] One issue told how to fasten live trapped rabbits to one's belt. One trapper held the rabbit while the other stretched out its legs and used a knife to punch two holes through the muscle tissue just behind the knee joint. Then a string was pushed through the incisions and the rabbit attached to the hunter's belt.[29]

Early the next morning, a cold, snowy day, the young trappers reached underneath one of their wooden cracker boxes to discover that they had a catch. It was decided that Bert would hold the rabbit and Tad would punch the holes. Bert expressed reservations, but being the younger, he went along with the plan. When Tad began to push the knife through the rabbit's leg, it reacted to the pain by squirming free from Bert's grasp. Leaping to the ground, the rabbit bounded off across the snow-covered field. Long after both boys were grown, Hoover maintained that his brother never forgave him for allowing the rabbit to escape, and that just when it seemed the incident was forgotten, the old accusation would surface again. This episode had a lasting effect on Hoover, who never became a hunter. When he recalled this story from his youth, he confessed: "I never see rabbit tracks across snowy fields that I do not have a painful recollection of it all."[30]

The following summer, 1882, Hulda and the children traveled to the newly built town of Quorn in western Iowa, not many miles from the Missouri River and Dakota Territory, where they spent more than a month with their uncles Merlin Marshall (of pumpkin patch fame) and Samuel Hammer. Plymouth County and the lands to the north and west, across the river, were just opening up to farming. Uncle Merlin and numerous citizens of West Branch, along with a cavalcade of humanity, were unable to resist the lure of cheap land and new opportunities. The whole area had a speculative boomtown atmosphere. Among the strangest sights on the prairie were the English aristocratic land developments in and around Quorn, with sixteen- and seventeen-room "manor houses," a prairie social club with billiard tables, a cricket field, a lawn tennis court, and a horse-racing track. Additional British amenities included polo matches and a weekly Sunday fox hunt. If no red fox could be found, a coyote seemed a spiffy substitute.[31]

Equally strange was the sight of a hotel pulled across the prairie by twenty wagons and fifty or so horses and mules. The railroad bypassed the little town of Quorn. Rather than be left behind, stranded on the prairie, the citizens demonstrated amazing initiative and decided to move the entire town to Kingsley, less than a mile away and site of the railhead. The decision made, a scramble ensued as homeowners and businesses jockeyed for the best locations in Kingsley. Houses were jacked up and then lowered onto four wagons, one at each corner, pulled by teams of four to six mules. The stores, the bank, the saloon, the town hall, and finally the hotel were all moved in this manner in two days. Less than a month later, what had been Quorn became wheat.[32]

Tragedy, however, had struck northwest Iowa the preceding winter. A severe outbreak of diphtheria claimed the lives of hundreds of settlers, among them all three of the Hoover children's small cousins. Tad and Bert, without companions, were left to find their own entertainment. A favorite pastime included fishing for chub on the west fork of the Little Sioux River on the edge of town near the Heacock Mill. If the boys tired of fishing, hunting for prairie chicken nests was a pleasurable way to fill out a day. Success was nearly assured, as thousands of birds nested in the tall, thick, unplowed prairie grasses, a "sea of grass" that stretched far beyond the Missouri River. In between forays into the open fields, Bert began to put together a collection of crooked sticks—crooked in unusual, almost impossible ways. Tad noted that his brother's collection of weird sticks was quite intriguing and revealed Bert's budding interest in science, later to be fulfilled at Stanford.[33]

At summer's end, it was time to go home. On the way, the Hoovers visited other Iowa relatives, and the boys used every stop as an opportunity to fish. Each summer, the fatherless family visited and stayed with relatives or the children were sent off individually. Thus family ties were maintained and strengthened, especially on the paternal side; some of the burdens of being a single parent were lessened; Hulda gained time for herself and for her preaching; and a good deal of money was saved, since others provided room and board.

In the summer of 1883, Bert was sent back to northwest Iowa, this time to stay with his uncle Miles Pennington Minthorn, who homesteaded in Sioux County just to the north of Uncle Merlin Marshall in Plymouth County. Uncle Miles, it seemed, had also succumbed to the magnetic attraction of cheap land. That summer, Bert lived in a sod house and spent many a day proudly perched atop the lead mount of a team of plow horses that broke the virgin prairie soil.[34] That same summer, back in West Branch, Tad and Bert picked strawberries for two and a half cents a quart for a neighbor, Thompson Walker. This hard work produced the first money either boy had earned, about $7 each.[35] Some of their money went for clothes, but the brothers delighted in having lunch together at Crew's grocery store. Tad remembered that "the bill of fare was limited to dried herrings, cheese, crackers and apples, with a drink of water from the bucket by the door."[36] The price for being "men about town" was three to five cents a meal.

In the winter of 1884, the Hulda Hoover family's unconventional but innovative lifestyle came to a sudden and tragic end. Around February 1, Hulda contracted a fever while out conducting a meeting and preaching in the little town of Springdale, just east of West Branch, and returned home with a bad cold. No buggy or rail transportation was available, and as she had frequently done in the past, she had walked the three miles. All of the usual folk medicines were tried, all failed, and her condition steadily worsened. As the days turned into weeks, she languished, and it became clear that her chances for recovery were not good. The fever she suffered was typhoid, and her cold turned to pneumonia. At age thirty-six, two years older than her husband before her, Hulda Hoover died of this double affliction on Sunday morning, February 24, 1884. A few days later, the three children watched as their mother's coffin was lowered into the snow-covered frozen earth. Bert and his brother and sister were given another lesson, as Hoover later phrased it, from the "Montessori school in stark reality."[37] Brother Tad best captured the tragic circumstances: "A lad of that age" [he was twelve] feels . . . a helplessness and despair and a sort of dumb animal terror. What will become of him and these two others in the same boat. The Lady of the golden sunshine . . . had gone away, and there were left only three small children, adrift on the wreck of their little world."[38]

A few days later, the three grieving and disoriented orphans were sent to Grandmother Minthorn in Kingsley, Iowa. The Hoover-Minthorn clan assembled and discussed who would take the children. On her deathbed, Hulda had stated her wishes, but now it was necessary to gain the consent of those she had recommended and to see to the details of the arrangements. This was not the first time the Hoovers had faced such a momentous decision. The children's great-grandmother Rebecca Yount Hoover lived outside of West Branch in a portion of the farmhouse of their great-uncle Benajah Hoover. There she raised two orphaned second cousins, Emma and Annie Miles.[39] Death was an all too frequent visitor on the nineteenth-century midwestern farming frontier.

Bert's schoolteacher, Mollie Brown, argued vehemently to be allowed to adopt the young boy, but she was unmarried, and it was decided that Bert would be better off raised in a family to whom he was related. Laban Miles in Oklahoma also spoke for Bert, but again the family decided that growing up in Indian Territory might restrict the boy's future opportunities.[40] The impracticality of all three children being taken in by one family necessitated their separation. Bert joined the family of Allen and Millie Hoover, who farmed about a mile north of West Branch. May, who already spent much time with Grandmother Minthorn, remained in her care in Kingsley. Tad temporarily stayed with Uncle Merlin Marshall, also of Kingsley. His mother had wished that he be raised by his uncle Davis Hoover, her late husband's brother, who lived some three miles outside Hubbard, Iowa, in Hardin County, and this was agreed to. A few weeks later, one of the children's great-uncles, the Rev. John Yount Hoover, retrieved Tad and Bert in Kingsley, dropping Tad off in Hubbard and bringing Bert back to West Branch. The three children now lived with three different families in three different parts of the state. Tad wrote a poem that captured the uncertainty of their situation:

Orphans

We were orphans three
   Bert and I and little Marie
Bert was eight, a chuck of a boy,
   Brimful of tricks that boys enjoy.
Marie was six and all the day
   She would sing in her bright, cute way
A brown-haired, sweet little girl,
   With none in life to say her nay.[41]

Though the loss of their parents and their separation from each other were extremely difficult, a heavy burden borne for years, Tad, Bert, and May were fortunate that they were members of a large, loving, middle-class, extended Quaker family—a frontier clan that all helped and supported each other.

The Hoover children may have been orphaned, but they were not abandoned, nor were they destitute. Upon their father's death, their mother had inherited cash and property worth $1,850.31, not an insignificant amount of money for that time.[42] Extremely frugal, Hulda Hoover pinched every penny by buying as little as possible and making things last. She took in sewing and rented out the north room of their house. Even though she traveled extensively in the service of the church, by the time of her death, she had increased the family's net worth to $2,500.[43] She felt that education was imperative—she wanted her children to go to college—and education cost money. All of the relatives desired that the children's money be spent properly and carefully accounted for. To ensure that this happened, the family asked the Probate Court of Cedar County, Iowa, to appoint Lawrie Tatum of Springdale as executor of their inheritance. Tatum, a Quaker minister, lawyer, author, former Indian agent, and friend of the family, was a man who could be absolutely trusted to wisely guard and administer money. The estate was divided equally three ways, and it was agreed that small amounts would be paid out to those relatives who kept the children. As the meeting concluded, Tatum pulled Bert aside and advised him to be kind, brave, prudent, and a help to his aunt and uncle. He pressed a small black book into Bert's hand and instructed him to write down money he received and all of his expenditures. "God bless you, my boy," he said as he turned and strode through the door.[44]

For the next eighteen months, Bert lived in West Branch with his aunt and uncle and their son, Walter, who was about his age. Aunt Millie was an excellent cook, and her Sunday dinners were locally renowned. As an adult, Hoover proclaimed that her cooking was superior to that of the finest chefs of Europe. His aunt's and uncle's kindness, along with the good food, endeared them to him for the rest of his life. Here, in this supportive environment, Bert coped with the death of his parents and readjusted to the rhythm of farm life, putting in the row crops and seeing them through to harvest. Sometimes at night he missed his mother terribly, crying himself to sleep.[45] He and his cousin Walter walked the two miles to school in West Branch. At school, Bert found a surrogate mother in Mollie Brown, who took a special interest in his development and provided a strong shoulder for him to lean on. Bert continued to fish and hunt with Walter. They also played marbles and mumblety-peg and, along with other town boys, engaged in another favorite pastime—dirt-clod fighting.[46]

Another of Bert's uncles, Henry John Minthorn, a missionary and the doctor who had saved his young life, was the head of the newly founded Friends Pacific Academy in Newberg, Oregon. The Minthorns had recently suffered a tragedy of their own when their only son, Benjamin Bruce, died at age seven on September 22, 1884. Henry John wrote to Allen Hoover back in West Branch and suggested that Bert come and live with him in the Chehalem Valley, attend the academy, and become a stand-in for the child they had lost.[47] Thinking of the boy's future and his mother's wish for his education, Aunt Millie and Uncle Allen reluctantly agreed to Henry's proposal. Tatum, his legal guardian, concurred with the dictum uttered by Horace Greeley, "Go West, young man, and grow up with the country," and concluded that Oregon held brighter prospects for the boy than did West Branch. He therefore authorized the expenditure of $33.33 from Bert's trust, the exact price of the ticket.[48]

To keep Bert from having to travel alone on such a long trip, Uncle Allen inquired about and discovered a family named Hammel who were emigrating to Oregon. They agreed to allow Bert to join them and promised to see him safely to Portland. Aunt Millie readied the young boy for his strenuous journey. Clothes were repaired, a bedroll put together, and a basket found to house his food and supplies. Ample amounts of fried chicken, ham, meat pies, fruit, and bread were stored in the basket along with two bottles of hive syrup—medicine for croup. Tucked in his coat pocket was the small accounting book given him by Lawrie Tatum, in which he had carefully recorded all of his expenditures since picking strawberries—his first income.[49] Eleven-year-old Bert boarded the train laden with food and was able to feed the Hammels for most of the long trip. In addition to his ample larder, telescope bag, bedroll, and treasured collection of sticks, Bert had two dimes in his pocket.[50]

2

A New World in the Great American West

Like so many Iowans before him, Bert set out on the Oregon Trail.
Not by covered wagon, but by train, a train specially equipped to
serve emigrants to the Pacific Northwest. The trip lasted seven
days. Travelers in second class brought along their own food and
bedding and slept in railroad cars lined with wooden seats that
transformed into beds. At the end of the car was a coal-burning
cookstove. The stove was kept going by the brakeman, and anyone in the car could cook food if he or she so desired. A large
enameled pot of hot coffee was always available. The train
stopped for half an hour at regular intervals to allow the first-
class passengers to eat prepared meals in Harvey restaurants.
Many from second class rushed from the train to wash up (water
on board was a scarce commodity) or to purchase food to be
cooked on the stove. Often people cooked in groups, shared food,
got to know one another, and created a party atmosphere, talking, singing, playing cards—activities that helped pass the endless hours of travel across half a continent. A black porter was
assigned to each car and was fed by the passengers, and each

night he helped fold down and make the beds and each morning reversed the process.[51] Bert reported the scenery along the route in a letter to his favorite teacher, Mollie Brown, and confided that he was disappointed in the Rocky Mountains, which to him seemed nothing more than "piles of dirt." Devil's Slide and Castle Rock stood out in Bert's mind from other famous sights. In the soft, diminished daylight hours of late fall, he described the scenery through which the train passed as "an independent film in my memory."[52]

In November 1885, Uncle Henry John met Bert when he arrived at the train station in Portland, Oregon. While the trip was a great adventure for a young boy, he must have been filled with uncertainty concerning his new adoptive parents and his new home. On the twenty-five-mile wagon ride from Portland to Newberg, he had a taste of how different his new environment really was. It would be a few weeks before he would undertake his first explorations and realize more fully that he had been thrust into an unspoiled natural world far different from the pastoral one he had left behind in Iowa. For a young boy enamored of the outdoors, one who loved to fish and found pleasure in solitude, Oregon was close to Eden.

The landscape possessed a cathedral-like scale. Fir trees with trunks four feet or more across were routinely felled and burned to make way for rich farmland—an arduous and time-consuming undertaking. To the west of the Willamette Valley, in the coastal mountain range, huge sitka pine trees with trunks twenty feet or more in width grew in dense virgin forests that descended quickly to a rugged, steep, rock-strewn coastline that was incessantly pounded by a cold, turbulent ocean. To the east, out past Mount Hood, stretched more forest that abruptly gave way to a high desert plateau, and to the north, just above Portland, was the Columbia. In this mighty river swam salmon fifty times bigger than Iowa bullheads and "punkin seed" perch. Others, too, who had traveled to Oregon and the Pacific Northwest were captivated with its natural beauty. The journalist George Bailey, who at twelve, after the death of his father, was sent to spend summers a little farther north on islands in Puget Sound, described succinctly the outlook of German immigrants who lived in solitude in the great forest: "They were in paradise and they knew it.

*Newberg, Oregon, in 1888-89. Herbert Hoover lived in the house on
the far right.* COURTESY GEORGE FOX UNIVERSITY, NEWBERG, OREGON

Scions of a nation of forest worshippers, they were quietly devo-
tional in their cathedral."[53]

The Newberg in which Hoover arrived was a small frontier
town of one hundred or so residents, and only a few hundred
people lived in the surrounding valley. Dr. Minthorn drove the
wagon past the partially completed Friends Pacific Academy,
Bert's new school, and on to a two-story white frame house that
the Minthorns had completed four years earlier, in 1881. Bert's
aunt Laura and her two daughters, Tennessee, age eleven, and
Gertrude, three, were in the backyard stirring a large wash boiler
suspended over an open fire. The female family members were
making pear butter and asked the new arrival if he wished to
help by stirring the simmering tub of pears. Bert had never seen
or tasted a pear, and Aunt Laura encouraged him to eat all he
wanted as he stirred.[54] He downed spoonful after spoonful of the
delicious warm concoction. Hours later, this "Oregon wonder"
produced stomach cramps, and for several days Bert scampered
between house and outhouse. It was a long time before he ate
another pear.[55]

That evening, Bert unpacked. He was given his own room on the second floor, and after a fitful night's sleep, he awoke to his new surroundings. One of his first acts was to walk across the parlor in front of the assembled family and place the remaining bottles of hive syrup on the mantle above the fireplace. He explained that he did not think he would need the croup medicine in the future. Placing the bottles on the mantle may also have symbolized his open determination to make a fresh start. Indeed, he did not need the medicine again, as his chronic respiratory infections vanished, relegated to the past, safely stored as only a memory.[56]

To Bert's consternation, the Minthorns of Oregon were quite a different family from his own, and different as well from Aunt Millie and Uncle Allen, with whom he had spent the last eighteen months in Iowa. Uncle Henry John was a disciplinarian, a strict but quirky Quaker, who believed in consistent hard work. "Idle hands were the work of the devil," and the whole Minthorn family worked like the devil to ensure that there were no idle hands. Being a Quaker was a serious, high-minded business. The taciturn, stern, reserved, and sometimes forbidding Henry John enjoyed serious intellectual discourse on serious subjects. He delighted in terse conversations on his favorite topics, health, medical practices, and religion—things of an educational nature. Dr. Minthorn had a plethora of experience that was unusual for a Quaker. As a boy, he had driven wagons that transported runaway slaves on the Underground Railroad to freedom in Canada, and later, to the extreme displeasure of his pacifist family, he joined the 44th Iowa Infantry Regiment of the Union army and fought in the battle of Shiloh during the Civil War. This deeply religious man boldly recommended, "Turn your other cheek once, but if he smites it, then punch him."[57]

Educated at the University of Iowa and the Philadelphia College of Medicine, Minthorn secured an appointment as a government doctor and assisted in the return from exile of Chief Joseph and the Nez Perce. This exciting humanitarian assignment was followed in 1879 by an appointment as agent and physician to the Ponca tribe in Indian Territory. Still restless, in 1882 this wandering Quaker then went to head the Chemawa Indian School in Forest Grove, Oregon, and from there on to another Indian school in Oklahoma. In 1885, the Quaker community of Newberg sought a superintendent for the newly established Friends Pacific Academy. The elders selected Dr. Minthorn, and in September, the half-completed academy opened its doors.[58] Bert Hoover arrived in November, and his education began at once. He was enrolled in the grammar section of the academy and took six courses, all taught by his aunt. School started promptly at nine in the morning with prayer and a twenty-minute session on morality and character building. At four o'clock in the afternoon, school finally ended. Sunday provided no respite from unending routine—first Sunday school, then on to church, and then afternoon Bible study. The final meeting of the day was a Quaker children's temperance group called the Band of Hope.[59]

Dr. Minthorn was the only physician in Newberg, and as such, he often made house calls far out into the surrounding country. In the winter in the wet rain forest of the Pacific Northwest, this meant muddy, treacherous roads, floods, fog, and penetrating cold. The solution to this perpetual sea of mud was to build what were called "corduroy roads." A roadbed a few feet high was constructed and the surface covered with four- to six-inch fir logs embedded in the roadway at right angles. To cut building costs the logs were rarely split and laid in flat side up, so travel was rough and loud.[60] Sometimes the doctor took Bert along with him for company and as an assistant or the buggy driver. As the two of them jostled along on washboard roads, Henry John occasionally held forth for hours, espousing the philosophy he had nurtured over a lifetime and reduced to neat aphorisms, skills he had honed as a minister and a missionary. "The worst thing a man can do," he exclaimed, was "to do nothing." On leading a God-fearing, moral, and happy existence, he held that three things were necessary: "a right relation to God and understanding of his will; good health; and something worth doing and doing well."[61] To make himself heard above the clamor from the roadway, he was forced to speak in a loud voice, sometimes almost a yell. In this boisterous "mobile Montessori classroom," Hoover learned much.

Other than philosophy, Dr. Minthorn's other favorite topic was advances in medical science, a subject on which he kept abreast. More rarely, he commented on literature or history. To Bert's advantage, he did not take an overly conservative view to reading books other than the Bible, and the academy encouraged

Friends Pacific Academy, 1880s. Hoover is in the front row, third boy from the left. COURTESY GEORGE FOX UNIVERSITY, NEWBERG, OREGON

students to read in a library of carefully selected titles. Henry John read widely and the Minthorn home contained books on history and geography, as well as biography and fiction, although it was several years before Bert developed an interest in these subjects.[62] Bert's mother, Hulda, had opposed fiction and history as too worldly. In fact, she had forbidden anything beyond the Bible other than stories of people saved from "demon rum."

Uncle Allen and Aunt Millie had been right when they argued that the Oregon Minthorns were the best educated and most sophisticated members of the family, and that Bert's education would be enhanced by being in their care. Dr. Minthorn's pronouncements, however, were not always on the highest level. Every so often after a house call, as the buggy bounced along toward Newberg, he emphatically complained, sometimes exploded, about how people failed to take care of themselves—especially "white trash." He alleged that people's sicknesses were far too often their own fault and that people "like that" almost always lacked the money to pay. In spite of these outbursts, this country physician refused to take payment for his services from poor non-Quakers, noting that Quakers were always able to pay their bills.[63] What he despised most was that ignorance seemed so widespread and needlessly ruined so many lives. From the doctor's perspective, education and Christianity were the twin solutions to the world's problems.

Work consumed another big block of Bert's time. The day started early, and seven days a week, before and after school and church, there were chores to do. His tasks included watering and feeding the family's two horses. He was also responsible for bringing in the cow from the pasture and seeing to it that she was milked. Chopping wood and making sure Aunt Laura had a sufficient fuel supply rounded out his regular duties. On Saturdays, Bert often spent much of the day burning felled cedar trees on some acreage his uncle wished cleared. The technique was to

Hoover's uncle Henry John Minthorn, 1883–84.

COURTESY HERBERT HOOVER LIBRARY

drill two holes into the end of a felled log or into a stump at angles that met about a foot into the wood. This process was repeated as many times as was necessary along the length of the log or the width of the stump. Burning charcoal was then stuffed into the top bored hole. Blowing into the lower hole started an internal fire, and with luck, large sections of the log would burn. At first "it was sport," Bert recalled, but it soon turned into drudgery in the face of the great number of remaining trees. "The view of these battalions of tall trees in the moonlight haunted me as an advancing and unconquerable army."[64] Yet one by one the trees were felled and burned, the army conquered.

Hoover complained in letters to his cousin Harriet Miles in Oklahoma about the strictures of his Quaker environment and the incessant hard work foisted upon him, "unhappy experiences" and "unhappy days."[65] The tone of voice in which Aunt Laura chided him when her supply of wood dwindled galled him: "It is time thee gets in the wood." He chafed under the stern discipline of his uncle. Henry John arrived home late one night to discover that Bert had failed to fill the water tank in the paddock and that the horses had nothing to drink. A sleepy boy was roused from his bed and sent out to fill the tank to overflowing. While Minthorn made his point, Bert harbored resentment. Even though he objected to being told what to do, he ended up doing what was asked of him. He demonstrated his displeasure with an attitude of stubborn, passive defiance.

Henry John prized his two horses, liked taking care of them, and enjoyed driving his buggy as fast as possible. Bert, to the contrary, heartily disliked horses, resented taking care of his uncle's "pride and joy," and suspected that all horses and mules possessed difficult dispositions. Once, coming back from a camping trip in the mountains, Bert's uncle asked him to drive the wagon pulled by two mules. On the way down a steep hill, the empty wagon jackknifed and threw off the bed. The mules panicked, pulled the front wheels from under the careening wagon, and sent Bert flying into the air. Bert, uninjured, sat amidst the wreckage as the two mules raced down the mountain, front wheels in tow.[66] In future years, when necessary, Hoover made use of horses, mules, and donkeys, but his negative opinion of the equine species remained fixed. As it was often necessary to deliver medicine to places outside Newberg, Dr. Minthorn would ask Bert to run the errand and suggest that he take a horse or the horse and buggy. Bert invariably refused, but against his better judgment, he was occasionally persuaded. He once took a horse at the doctor's insistence, leaving mounted but returning hours later on foot, the horse following along behind. Such stubborn clashes characterized the relationship between Bert and his uncle. From Bert's point of view, far too much of his time was taken up with chores, school, and religious training. His uncle, while well meaning, was too intrusive, too inflexible.

On those few occasions when Bert did rebel or break the rules, the repercussions were not severe so much as exasperating. Once, to avoid the long, boring Sundays in church, he and his cousin Agnes Hammer, a girl he always called "Tack," persuaded eight of their younger cousins to skip church in favor of a fishing expedition. Agnes's older sister, who was in charge of the children, agreed to sleep late the next morning in exchange for a bag of candy. The band of recalcitrant children slipped out of the house around five the following morning and were gone all day. The adults were upset that the children had disobeyed but also feared for their safety. The rebellious fishermen somehow avoided a catastrophe when they flipped the boat and all ten floundered in the shallow water of the small lake. That evening, they arrived back home covered with mud, no fish in hand, and in great fear of the punishment that surely awaited them. Nothing was said, and the sinners were sent to bed without supper. A worried Bert could not sleep and snuck into Tackie's room to ask what she supposed would happen to them. Tackie crept downstairs and asked Aunt Laura, the most approachable of the older Quaker women. Aunt Laura reported that a family council had been held, and it was decided to meet in the morning. The following day, a special gathering was held in the church to determine the children's fate.[67] The congregation prayed for their guidance and redemption. The horrors of hell that awaited sinners who failed to obey were graphically portrayed to them, and they were repeatedly exhorted to mend their ways or face eternal damnation. The long ordeal finally ended. Hoover angrily confided to a cousin that he did not believe in a wrathful creator; "my God is a good, kind God."[68]

One Fourth of July in Newberg, when he was thirteen or fourteen years old, Bert and his friends attempted to contribute to

the patriotic fervor of the day by making their own fireworks—
a large cherry bomb. They filled a drain tile with gunpowder,
sealed both ends with clay, and inserted a fuse. The boys lit the
fuse, which was far too short, and scampered away, but they were
caught in a hail of shrapnel from the explosion of their ingenious
device. Recalling this event, Hoover remembered that "Dr. Minthorn was busy for hours picking pieces of tile out of the skin of
small boys. He engaged in no reprimands."[69]

In the Minthorn home, Bert missed the warmth and love that
had been openly shown him by his parents. Given his character
and his sense of loss over the death of his mother and father, his
new environment was difficult. As he grew into a man, however,
his resentment toward Henry John subsided and eventually grew
into a respect for his intellect, principles, and commitment. Tad
described the doctor as a "romantic figure," one of "great energy
and personal magnetism." Admiration for his guardian increased
when Bert discovered that no money had been taken from his
trust to pay for his support. His $533.99, safely invested in Iowa
by Lawrie Tatum at 8 percent interest, had grown to $822.67 dur-
ing the years he lived with the Minthorns. Later in life, looking
back from a position of success, Hoover correctly judged that
"adolescent impressions are not of historical importance."[70]

Even in a disciplined household like the Minthorns, all was
not work, church, and school. Bert had time for baseball, a game
he enjoyed playing and watching throughout his life, as well as
jigsaw puzzles, swimming, camping, exploring the surrounding
fields and forest, and dam building. The Minthorn family took
vacations several times a year, camping and fishing in the mountains that surrounded Newberg or having a campout at the beach
that included fishing, digging clams, and harvesting oysters.
Another of Bert's aunts, Harriet Minthorn, lived on a ranch in
southern Oregon just a few miles from the Rogue River. It was
here on family visits that Bert first fished the wild, untamed
Rogue. These excursions ranged from several days to several
weeks.[71] On these family outings, or on trips with the neighborhood boys or by himself, the thing Bert liked best, the thing that
produced real pleasure, was bait fishing for trout, salmon, and
anything else he could catch in the teeming rivers and creeks
around Newberg. To the west of town, running down from the
mountains, flowed Chehalem Creek, dammed at the Ramsey Mill

Fred and Hattie Minthorn home, Rogue River, Oregon, the place where Hoover stayed when he first fished the Rogue.
WOODVILLE MUSEUM, ROGUE RIVER, OREGON

about a mile upstream from its confluence with the Willamette. In the spring, here and in the two small streams to the east, Hess Creek and Spring Brook Creek, as well as in all of the tributaries of the Willamette, the native Oregon cutthroat trout made their annual run. Hess Creek wandered through the grounds of the Friends Pacific Academy and provided Bert with fishing close at hand. All of the creeks around Newberg contained several varieties of Dolly Varden trout, a trout named for a female character in the Dickens novel *Barnaby Rudge*. This eminent Victorian writer described his character, Dolly Varden, as "the very impersonation of good-humor and blooming beauty." Some New World Izaak Walton, perhaps in good humor, named this handsome fish Dolly Varden.[72]

As in West Branch, the boys of Newberg frequented a favorite swimming hole on Chehalem Creek just above the dam.[73] The millpond provided more familiar fishing opportunities for suckers, bullheads, and small panfish. In winter, the fast current and murky waters of the Willamette spoiled fishing, but the rest of the year, fish were in abundance, although different species swam in front of Newberg in the different seasons. The cycle included trout and salmon smolts (young fish on their way to the sea), bass, yellow perch, crappie, Columbia River chub (squaw-fish or pikeminnow), and on the best of days, the lucky fisher-man might land a salmon or steelhead. If he chose, Bert, in the Willamette, could go after an Iowa Hoover family favorite, the bottom-feeding channel cat, a fish he knew how to catch. For a boy burdened with school and chores, one with a chip on his shoulder, the easily accessible rivers and streams in and around Newberg were his refuge.

At age thirteen, many boys looked forward to summers filled with play and adventure, but Bert Hoover, after graduating from the grammar school department of the academy in 1887, spent much of his thirteenth summer weeding onions for his uncle Ben Cook in Sherwood, Oregon. Weeding onions was a difficult job. The fields were often wet, and the weeders wore knee pads to protect against moisture. Sometimes for as long as twelve or thir-teen hours a day, Bert and his cousin Alva Cook crawled up and down the long rows of onions cleaning out weeds. Remuneration consisted of fifty cents a day and room and board. He slept on a straw mattress in the loft of a rustic pine wood cabin.[74] Entrance to the loft was gained by scaling a ladder propped outside against the side of the building. The onion job over, a tired Bert returned to Newberg and finished out the summer working in the local brickyard. His tenacity had paid off, as he had earned $30.[75]

As much as Hoover loved to fish and camp, from an early age he put work, in this case earning some money of his own, ahead of pleasure. While Henry John gave Bert and his own two children a $5 a month allowance, Bert took great pride in having a degree of financial independence.[76] Like his mother, he guarded his money and his new nest egg tenaciously. Money, hard earned from long hours in the onion fields, would not be casually spent, and his allowance only increased the size of his cache. A sense of responsibility and frugality had been bequeathed to him by his Quaker family. This new financial liberty empowered Bert, increased his sense of self-worth, and gave him greater control over his own life. Freed from having to ask for things he desired, Bert occasionally allowed himself to buy things he wanted. In the ongoing battle with his stern uncle, a struggle to make a place for himself, hard work, and financial independence were critical components. The lessons that Bert carried from childhood were that love and respect were earned. Throughout his long life, Hoover was driven always by the need to be useful.

In September 1887, Tad arrived from Iowa. The two brothers had been separated for more than two years and were delighted to be reunited. Tad, infatuated with Mark Twain's *Life on the Mississippi*, had decided to work as a boatman on the Willamette or the Columbia, but Uncle Henry John and Aunt Laura dissuaded him, making a case for the necessity of a good education. Dr. Minthorn pontificated, "Go to school, first, last and all the time."[77] Following this wise advice, Tad enrolled in the Pacific Friends Academy. The main building of the school had just been completed, and the two brothers slept in a room on the first floor. Bert ate with the Minthorns and worked after school and on Saturdays for Isaac Miles, another cousin, while Tad was fed by a nearby family and cut wood for $2 a cord on Saturday. The beauty of Oregon, however, was tempered by the enormous number of fleas that attached themselves to man and beast. Tad was tormented all winter long. To keep from scratching, he tied his hands together at night. His open sores healed, but he was still bitten repeatedly. Finally the problem was partially solved by scrubbing the floor with kerosene. Bert also suffered that winter with painful earaches. None of Dr. Minthorn's remedies brought relief to either boy.[78]

At fourteen, in 1888, Bert graduated from the Friends Pacific Academy and moved with his aunt and uncle to Salem. All of the furniture, the buggy, the wagon, the household goods, and the Minthorns made the trip by river steamer. Bert and Tad drove the livestock overland and arrived several days later. Tad helped the family settle in and then returned to the academy, where he boarded with another uncle and continued his education. Dr. Minthorn, tiring of Newberg and the academy, had undertaken a new venture—the Oregon Land Company. The Willamette Valley was undergoing a transformation from wheat growing to prunes, pears, apples, berries, and hops—specialty agriculture. The newly formed land company bought large tracts, broke them up into smaller parcels, set out fruit trees, and sold these "ready-made farms" to newer arrivals. The improved land held by the company to the southeast of Salem around Silver Falls City was some of the best in the state, and parcels sold for considerable sums. On

Tad, Bert, and May, Salem, Oregon, 1888. COURTESY HERBERT HOOVER LIBRARY

some properties, the company even constructed the houses and outbuildings; they were pioneer speculators and developers.[79]

Minthorn and his Quaker partners advertised the agricultural glories of Oregon in more than a thousand newspapers in the Midwest and East. In bold letters, the broadsides and newspaper ads proclaimed, "NO HYDROPHOBIA, NO TARANTULAS, NO CEN-TIPEDES," but failed to mention the legions of fleas.[80] Those in search of a promised land, mostly Quakers from America's heartland, flocked into the valley. The Minthorn's new house was not finished when the family arrived in midsummer, and all lived in the barn until the house was completed. A few months later, Bert was thrilled when his sister, May, and Grandmother Minthorn made the long trek from Kingsley, Iowa, to Salem. The three orphaned children now lived within thirty miles of one another and were frequently together. Their grandmother unfortunately had been forced to move to Oregon because of the failed investments of her son-in-law—the holdings in Kingsley and West Branch, Iowa, so carefully acquired were now gone. Henry John came to the rescue and built a small house for her and May next to the one he had just completed.[81]

The thriving Oregon Land Company hired Bert as the office manager at $20 a month. He threw himself into the job, mastered it quickly, and made himself indispensable. With his incredible capacity for work, he was in the office early in the morning and left late in the evening. One of his specialties was overseeing the company's extensive advertising. He also arranged all business meetings, was in charge of filing, and learned accounting from another employee, "a sad and dour Scotsman."[82] Bert's enthusiasm for accounting did not last, and he concluded that "it was a cheerless calling." But when anyone in the office needed a document, Bert knew where it was. When anyone needed information on a past business deal or the stage of negotiations on a present deal, Bert knew the details. His salary soon rose to $35 a month, a hefty figure for a fifteen-year-old boy.[83] Brother Tad, who had again rebelled and been out on his own, returned to Newberg and worked for a short time as a printer's assistant at the local newspaper for $1 a week plus room and board.

Bert lived with the Minthorns and was accountable to Aunt Laura, though he spent evenings studying mathematics at Uncle

State Insurance Company. Hoover is on the far right in knickers. The Oregon Land Company was the next business to the right.

COURTESY MARION COUNTY HISTORICAL SOCIETY, SALEM, OREGON

Ben Cook's newly opened Friends Polytechnic College. Between his salary and his inheritance, he was easily able to pay the $60 tuition fee. Busy from morning to night, he often slept in the back room of the Oregon Land Company office and ate in nearby restaurants. Strong's was a favorite place where he could eat his fill.[84] In his business dealings and for recreation, Bert needed to get around Salem quickly. After considerable deliberation, he justified the purchase of a second-hand high-wheel—a velocipede. The high-wheel, an extremely popular machine, but one from which Bert fell frequently, was challenged by the new "safety bicycle." The high-wheel and the new rear-wheel sprocket-driven safety bike were the latest thing and had taken America by storm. The safety bike was made to order for Bert; it was much smaller, faster, more maneuverable, had cushion tires, and did not eat hay. Almost two months' salary was sacrificed for a new Victor bicycle. Although Hoover was frugal, if he really needed or wanted something, he would spend the money—especially if the purchase had a utilitarian aspect. The new bicycle increased his mobility, which in turn increased business.[85] He was now able to deliver medicine for the doctor and avoid the horse and buggy. Of even greater importance, it was lots of fun.

One of Bert's friends, Burt Brown Barker, recalled tying their bikes to the back of horse-drawn streetcars and being towed around town. The Salem Street Car Company was also a part of the Oregon Land Company improvements owned by Uncle Henry John and partners. Inadvertently, the construction techniques of the streetcar company made bike riding great fun. The space between the tracks was filled in with fir planks and provided the boys of Salem with a marvelous roadway often traversed at breakneck speed. Tad frequently joined Bert in racing about town.[86] Sometimes when the car company was short of drivers, despite his disdain for horses, Bert filled in, particularly during the Oregon State Fair, held for five days each August. On the way to the fairgrounds, the streetcar passed by some of the lots and houses offered by the Oregon Land Company. The ambitious young Hoover never passed up an opportunity to make money.

Bert's commitment to his "wheel," however, was total. His Uncle Henry John claimed that once, starting out on a camping trip to the mountains, Bert "got out his wheel," intending to ride along with the wagon and buggy even though it was a twenty-five-mile trip uphill. Several members of the family encouraged him to put the bicycle in the wagon and ride along, but he replied that he would beat them to the campsite and be there waiting for them. When the Minthorn party entered the campsite hours later, there sat the tenacious Bert, wet, but smugly enjoying his victory over horse-drawn conveyances. He had accomplished this feat by descending into a thousand-foot canyon, carrying his wheel upstream three or four miles, climbing back out of the canyon, and then riding as fast as possible to the agreed upon rendezvous.[87]

Regardless of Bert's fishing, camping, and business success, he remained socially awkward and keenly aware of his orphan status and general shortcomings. In both West Branch and Newberg, he had received support and comfort from two teachers in their late twenties, women who may have served as stand-in mothers for a lonely, shy young boy. Mollie Brown had shown Bert genuine affection in Iowa, and after his mother's death, she had pushed hard to adopt him. In Newberg, Bert had become quite attached to his Sunday school teacher, Evangeline "Vannie" Martin, whose Sunday afternoon class was a respite from the harsher environment in which he usually found himself.[88] In Salem, it was not long before Bert established a close relationship with Miss Jenny Gray, the third and most important of the women teachers who rallied to his support. She was a tall, attractive, distinguished-looking woman in her early thirties.[89]

Miss Gray, as Hoover always called her, took a general interest in the working boys of Salem and one day walked into the land office reception room. He was alone, working the desk, and Miss Gray took the opportunity to ask him about his schooling. Bert replied that he was in night school and fully intended to complete his education. He volunteered that he also spent time fishing and camping. She continued to question him and asked what he read. Unsatisfied with the short list he reported—the Bible, the encyclopedia, prohibitionist novels, and a few other disparate titles—Miss Gray asked that he accompany her to the small Salem lending library. There she pulled from the shelf a copy of *Ivanhoe* and handed it to Bert, saying, "I think you'll find this interesting." Bert loved *Ivanhoe*. A whole new world of literature was opened to him. "Suddenly," Bert reported, "I began to see books as living things and was ready for more of them." Next, Miss Gray recommended *David Copperfield*. Years later, when in his eighties, in a tribute to his benefactor, Hoover reminisced, "I can still remember the harshness of Murdstone, the unceasing optimism of Micawber and the wickedness of Uriah Heep. I have met them alive many times in after years."[90] Bert went on to Thackeray and Irving, and then began to read biographies—Washington, Lincoln, and Grant. Under Miss Gray's tutelage, he commenced a lifetime of reading. He judged that textbooks were necessary but thanked Miss Gray for showing him that it was literature "which stimulated the imagination and a better understanding of life."[91]

Miss Gray, however, did far more than hand Bert a few books to read. She invited him and his friend Burt Brown Barker to her house for dinner and to social functions that she had arranged with other young people. Jenny Gray's father was quite wealthy, and the house was big and beautiful, yet she disparaged material things and argued that character was far more important than money. At table, both boys became acquainted with a new array

Jenny Gray and family, ca. 1890s. Miss Gray is seated on the steps, top right. COURTESY MARION COUNTY HISTORICAL SOCIETY, SALEM, OREGON

of foods and learned manners, how to converse, and how to dine, not just eat. They were exposed to a wider, more sophisticated world. At Miss Gray's, the boys put powdered (not granulated) sugar on their strawberries.[92] In Salem, though they remained working boys, their status was greatly enhanced. They were no longer "greenhorns," but they were still quite rough.

After Hoover left Salem, Miss Gray married, at the insistence of her mother and against her wishes. She had two children but finally divorced the husband she did not love, and against whom Burt Brown Barker had warned her, a man he called a "rounder and a rotter." Some years later, on the way home from a shopping trip in downtown Salem, she stepped off the trolley car in front of her house and tragically was run over by a meat truck. Ironically, the truck was driven by a very young teenage boy, who did not think to apply the brakes. Barker, knowing how upset Hoover would be over Miss Gray's death, withheld the news for many years.[93]

In Salem, Bert achieved a high degree of independence, and on weekends he returned to his favorite pastimes—fishing and camping expeditions in Oregon's verdant wilderness. One memorable fishing experience occurred when Bert and his friend Burt Barker visited Bert's uncle Samuel Hammer, another Iowan who had succumbed to the temptation of cheap land. He lived on the high prairie around Crooked Finger on the Crooked River, a beautiful, sparsely settled area in the central part of the state. Shortly after arriving, Bert and Burt set off on a daylong foray with a rifle and fishing gear. That evening, they returned empty-handed and with a jammed rifle. Moved by their disappointment, Uncle Samuel agreed to take them out again the following morning and help them sharpen their fishing skills, if the boys agreed to help with the hay later in the day. By noon, Samuel had caught about thirty trout. When he called the boys for lunch, Bert refused to come until he had landed a fish. Uncle Samuel went down to the river to watch as Bert struggled with a large, feisty trout. Still a bait fisherman, Bert yanked too hard when the large fish struck the line and pulled the bobber under. In his exuberance, he ended up throwing three trout over his head into the weeds far back on the bank. He searched diligently but could not find the fish. Samuel showed Bert how to set the hook after the fish ran with the bait and how to work his catch in close to shore. By midafternoon, Uncle Samuel reported that the threesome had caught one hundred trout, the daily limit. The successful fishermen climbed out of the steep canyon that lined the Crooked River and spent the rest of the day baling hay on the open, semi-arid prairie.[94]

Shortly after this summer fishing trip, the Hammers moved again, this time to Scott's Mills, a homestead just above the orchard development of Uncle Henry John, some twenty-five miles east of Salem in the foothills of the Cascade Mountains. Other Hoover cousins, Isaac, Prudence, and Abigail Miles, had also moved from Iowa to Scott's Mills. As children, the Hoover boys had played dolls with the two girls at their cousin Harriette Miles's home in West Branch.

Uncle Samuel invited his nephews to visit, promising good fishing and the possibility that they might see a bear, so the boys jumped on their bicycles and pedaled out to Scott's Mills. They spent several days exploring and fishing Butte Creek, only to be disappointed because the trout would not bite. While exploring, the boys accidentally interrupted a large bear eating salal (juniper berries) and red huckleberries. Tad described the startled bear: "He crashed through the matted growth of the big burn [a huge area devastated by a forest fire] like a locomotive gone wild."[95] Tad Hoover loved to fish, and he also loved the forests and rivers of Oregon as much as did Bert, later recalling: "Those early Sunday mornings in Oregon, with the dawn just breaking over the Cascade Mountains, the delicate perfume of orchids in the fir woods borne in the clear morning air, the twitter of waking birds, and leap of a ten inch Dolly Varden trout in some splashing brook in the everlasting hills—it was an hour when young gods were abroad and the world was young and mighty fine."[96]

Back in Salem, Bert's business success continued as he thought of more ways to make money. Buyers responding to the national ads of the Oregon Land Company arrived at the railroad station, found a hotel, and the next day wandered into the office. Burt devised a system whereby he met potential buyers at the train station and drove them to rooms he had rented in private homes. This service not only impressed the clients, but it also kept them out of the hands of rival land development companies. Profits from the room rentals were Bert's to keep.[97] Always busy, this industrious and ambitious young man still found time on the weekends for fishing and camping. His passion was redoubled by an encounter while fishing the North Santium River, a fine fishing stream that empties into the Willamette north of Albany and was just south of Henry John's "orchard community" in Scott's Mills. Rainbow and cutthroat trout, steelhead, and a spring run of chinook graced the waters of the Santium.

Bert and three other boys were fishing from the riverbank with worms when an older fisherman give each one three artificial wet flies and encouraged the boys to abandon bait fishing. For Bert, his new flies, "a coachman, a gray hackle and a professor," proved both a revelation and an incentive.[98] Fifty-five years later, in his *Memoirs*, Hoover called the gift "powerfully productive in the mountain streams."[99] Bert used the flies over and over, never dreaming that they would wear out. In fact, they proved to be so effective that even after "the feathers had all worn off, the trout still rose to the flies."[100] The worm, the butcher-string line, and the willow-stick pole were now put aside for a bamboo pole with the fly tied directly to the end of the line. Hoover, arguing for simplicity and efficiency, claimed that the action and the "potency" of the bamboo pole and fly exceeded that of new "cosmetically" treated flies that were attached to gut leaders and costly manufactured rods. His conversion to fly fishing was a significant rite of passage, one of Hoover's first steps up the socioeconomic ladder he was so anxious to climb, but a step he was surely unaware of at the time.

Fish no longer nibbled at the bait and tugged under the bobber; instead, sixteen- to twenty-four-inch trout would strike the fly with force—especially the steelhead. Bert had entered a new world of fishing, considered the highest form by most of its aficionados, one in which he began to learn how to cast, how to drop the fly accurately and delicately in front of the fish, how to use the fly to imitate various insects, how to play the fish, land it, and carefully remove the hook. He loved the world of fly fishing, with its rich, specialized vocabulary and endless number of accoutrements. Given his reticent character and the satisfaction he obtained from being by himself for hours at a time, fly fishing was a perfect fit. Hoover's love of the outdoors may have been reinforced by the loss of his parents and his difficulties with the Minthorns, providing him an attachment that seemed more reliable than most human interactions, but it seems more likely that the sport simply provided him a respite from a busy life. When Bert went fishing, he typically went with a small group of close friends, often men from the land office who were older than he was, but he also often fished with his brother, Tad. While in the stream, he usually moved away from his companions to spend hours by himself, fishing and enjoying the beauty of nature. He liked grilled fish, camp life, and the companionship and conversation of evenings spent around a campfire. Of all the many styles of fishing that Hoover would come to master, he preferred to fly-fish, wading his favorite trout streams until he was too old to maintain his balance in the cold, rushing water.

In the business world of Salem, fishing was a topic often discussed. Debates raged over which of Oregon's many rivers was the best. Nearly everyone had a favorite that he ardently defended. The rule "in important things truthfulness, in personal matters latitude" was strictly adhered to. Eager for more fishing, Bert ranged farther from Salem as he explored and fished the Rogue River in southwest Oregon, staying on the ranch of Aunt Harriet Minthorn, who lived nearby. He had visited the Rogue with his uncle's family when he was younger and a bait fisherman. The Rogue in the 1880s was a rushing river famous for steelhead and salmon in an isolated wilderness of pristine beauty. Fly-fishing the Rogue was a new, exciting experience. Bert was becoming a sportfisherman.

Closer to home, Bert delighted in fishing the McKenzie River, an eighty-nine-mile tributary that runs into the Willamette just north of Springfield. The river was named for Donald McKenzie (1783–1851), who was a partner with John Jacob Astor in the Pacific Fur Company and led an overland expedition to Astoria in 1811–12 in the quest for plentiful furs that preceded the rush for cheap land. McKenzie, a Scot, was a muscular giant who weighed more than three hundred pounds. After arriving in Astoria, he spent the next two years in the employ of the North West Company, exploring the Willamette and McKenzie River valleys. Extremely energetic, his men called him "Perpetual Motion" McKenzie.[101] To this day, the river remains one of the best trout-fishing rivers in Oregon, famous for its redside rainbows. The river drops quickly into its valley through steep, forested canyons punctuated by large boulders and whitewater riffles. There are only a few places where the surefooted angler may gain entry and attempt to wade these fast waters. *Fishing in*

Oregon claims that the McKenzie is "one of those rivers that weaves its magic around anglers," and that magic touched Bert Hoover, who fished the McKenzie often.[102]

For the fly fisherman on the McKenzie, a boat is a necessity. Many different types of skiffs and dories were then used, especially long, narrow, low-sided contraptions made of cedar or fir planks. When Bert first fished the river, the boats were board-and-batten constructed, sealed with tar and very heavy. They lacked maneuverability and were generally used to ferry passages across the river, steer logs downstream, and serve as rescue vessels.[103] These ungainly craft were ill suited to fly fishing. Over time, local craftsmen responded to the demands of the McKenzie by designing a unique boat. Experiments in design were under way when Bert floated the river, but the famous McKenzie river boat, the boat that could "float on the dew," came later.[104] Regardless of the type of boat, standing, feet braced against gunwales, drifting cross-stream, was an exciting, effective way to fly-fish. From Blue River, eventually a Hoover favorite, to the confluence with the Willamette, the river widened out and the trout fishing was excellent. In 1890, there was no shortage of fish, and Bert caught redsides, rainbows, cutthroat, steelhead, chinooks, and whitefish. The McKenzie was a fisherman's paradise. After each fishing trip, Bert returned to the hectic pace of his life in Salem refreshed and reinvigorated. He had established a pattern that he would follow most of his life.

Tad, who had returned to school in Newberg, was constantly at odds with his Quaker relatives; finally he rebelled and went to work as a printer's assistant. Once again, Henry John stepped in, offering to pay half of Tad's expenses if he would enroll as a student at William Penn College in Oskaloosa, Iowa. Tad jumped at the opportunity to be in school and out of Newberg.[105] With Tad in college, Bert began to question what was in his own future. A visitor at the land company office had trumpeted a career in engineering, especially in mining. Uncle Henry John offered Bert the same deal he had offered Tad—he would pay half of all expenses if Bert attended college. He suggested Earlham College in Indiana, where he had supposedly arranged a partial scholarship.[106] But Earlham had no engineering program, and Bert had heard much concerning a new university about to open in Palo Alto, California. Stanford University, in the beautiful San Clara Valley, had the added attraction of being tuition free. Entrance examinations were to be administered in Portland.

Bert signed up, and with his usual zeal, he studied hard. But his education had been spotty, and he failed the entrance examinations. Joseph Swain, who had administered the test and was a mathematics professor at Stanford and a Quaker, was impressed with Hoover's concentration and determination. In his mind, Bert Hoover was the kind of student who would do well in college if given the opportunity to succeed. After an interview in his hotel room, he admitted Hoover on the condition that he come to Stanford for tutoring and preparatory study before the fall term began. On his way out of Portland, Swain stopped in Salem and assured Henry John that Bert would do fine at Stanford and that the family need not fear a secular education.[107] This gesture by the Quaker professor was probably precautionary, a response to Bert's fears, as Dr. Minthorn himself had attended secular colleges and sent two of his daughters to the University of Iowa and one to Columbia College. Determined that he would overcome his deficiencies, Bert quickly grasped the opportunity offered him by Swain and buried himself in geometry texts for the rest of the summer.

In late August 1891, having just turned seventeen, Bert and a friend from Salem, Fred Williams, whose father was a banker, boarded the train for the new university springing up on the eight-thousand-acre ranch of Sen. Leland Stanford. Hoover would not again live in Oregon, but he later returned many times to fish the rivers and streams to which he had become attached. He wrote in his *Memoirs:* "Oregon lives in my mind for its gleaming wheat fields, its abundant fruit, its luxuriant forest vegetation, and the fish in the mountain streams. To step into its forests with their tangles of berry bushes, their ferns, their masses of wildflowers stirs up odors peculiar to Oregon. Within these woods are never-ending journeys of discovery, and the hunts for grouse and expeditions for trout."[108] As the train made its way south through a seemingly endless wilderness, Hoover surely reflected on the vicissitudes of his boyhood along the farming frontiers of Iowa and Oregon, and pondered what lay before him in the golden hills south of San Francisco.

3

From Stanford to the Stars

Herbert Hoover and his friend Fred Williams got off the train in Menlo Park, California, on the morning of August 30, 1891. The two drowsy boys clambered aboard the horse-drawn bus that took them past the "university," a whirlwind of construction, a maze of incomplete buildings amidst vineyards and stubble wheat fields. The bus crossed a wooden bridge and the driver pointed out a lone stately cedar, exclaiming that the ranch was named for the tree, Palo Alto, Spanish for tall tree.[109] The vehicle turned and proceeded down a long, tree-lined avenue to Adelante Villa, the boardinghouse where the two soon-to-be students stayed and where they would be tutored in geometry and English. Bert, to pay for his room, board, and tutoring, was assigned to take care of a horse once again and drive the two miles to Menlo Park for groceries, supplies, and the mail.

English, including spelling, was his poorest subject and the test he was most likely to fail.[110] In the time remaining, he studied hard to pass the seven examinations. By the end of the month, Bert had passed all but English. Nevertheless, he was admitted to

Stanford's pioneer class of 1891 with the stipulation that he pass the English exam sometime before he graduated.[111] Bert was elated with his achievement. He and Fred moved into Encina Hall, the first two students in the uncompleted dormitory, and cautiously commenced their university life. Of the 559 students who poured onto campus, Bert Hoover was the youngest.

Bert declared his major mechanical engineering and took a curriculum laden with mathematics and mechanical drawing, but at the beginning of the second semester, he switched to geology and began a course of study under the new chairman of the department, Dr. John Caspar Branner. By mid-semester, Bert had obtained a second job, as Branner's office assistant, a job he held on to, along with working for a San Jose laundry on campus, until his graduation in 1895. His three years' experience running the office of the Oregon Land Company paid off. At Stanford, Bert clung to his workaholic ways in ardent pursuit of his goals.

Later in the semester, Dr. Branner, impressed with his new office assistant, offered Hoover summer employment as a surveyor in the mountains of Arkansas. Hoover jumped at the opportunity, for a salary of $40 a month meant that his dwindling inheritance would last longer and that his sophomore year was assured. With school out, Bert rode by train to Arkansas, where his task was to map the rock outcroppings along the northern face of the Ozark Mountains. He occasionally rode a horse or mule, but most of the time he walked and worked alone. The Ozarks were extremely isolated, with rough terrain and few roads. His Oregon experience, with the extended camping trips, the long hikes through deep canyons, and the long bicycle treks, served him well—he was tan, trim, and physically fit. The mountain streams of Arkansas held marvelous trout, but he had no time for fishing and barely finished his survey assignment by the end of summer. Bert arrived late back at Stanford, where he assisted Dr. Branner in the office and enrolled in a heavy load of science classes.

Hoover's financial situation remained difficult, as he had spent almost half of his trust fund during his freshman year. To save money, he moved out of the expensive dormitory and into the Roomer Boarding House, living and sharing expenses with several friends. By economizing, with his contract with the San Jose laundry and his monthly salary as office assistant, he made it through his sophomore year of school. In running the laundry, he met a tall freshman from Iowa who also was working his own way, Ray Lyman Wilbur, a man who became a lifetime friend, an avid fishing companion, president of Stanford University, and eventually Hoover's secretary of the interior. When school ended in June, Bert went to work in the Geology Department, helping construct a huge topographical model of Arkansas that was shipped to the Chicago World's Fair for display in the Arkansas Pavilion. Later that summer, the relief map won a prize for being one of the top displays.

In mid-July and August, Dr. Lindgren arranged for Bert to go to work for the U.S. Geological Survey on a team mapping the High Sierras and the desert in Nevada. Lindgren headed the team, and Hoover was his "cub assistant."[112] The team worked the snow line on horseback. They camped out and were supported by a number of teamsters and a competent camp cook. Once again forced to spend a great deal of time on horseback, Hoover commented:

> In those long mountain rides over trails and through the bush, I arrived finally at the conclusion that a horse was one of the original mistakes of creation. I felt he was too high off the ground for convenience and safety on mountain trails. He would have been better if he had been given a dozen legs so that he had the smooth and sure pace of a centipede. Furthermore he should have had scales as protection against flies, and a larger water-tank like a camel. All these gadgets were known to creation prior to the geological period when the horse was evolved. Why were they not used?[113]

Among the Lindgren survey party was a foreign visitor who had never seen a rattlesnake and expressed keen interest in seeing one. Bert was ambling along the trail on horseback when he heard the all-too-familiar rattle along the edge of the trail, and his horse shied wildly. He dismounted, picked up a large, heavy stick, and hit the snake hard on the head. Then he wrapped up the diamondback in his bandanna and attached his trophy to the front of his saddle. As horse and rider plodded along toward the campsite in the warm afternoon sun, both were nearly asleep. In this dreamlike state, he imagined the response his gift would elicit from the amazed foreign guest. Suddenly his imaginings were shattered by a loud rattle. The snake had revived and shaken its tail vigorously. When the horse heard this fearsome noise just behind its ear, it panicked. Bolting off at a gallop, the frightened horse plunged into the bush despite all efforts by Bert to regain control. Some five miles later, the distraught animal threw its rider. Disheveled but unhurt, Hoover began the long walk back, which gave him plenty of time to construct a plausible story. The lesson that Hoover learned from this experience was not that it was dangerous to hit rattlesnakes on the head with sticks and attach them to one's horse in a flimsy bandanna. To the contrary, he concluded that the episode "added to my prejudices against horses in general."[114]

In the fall of 1893, Bert moved back to Encina Hall and enrolled for nineteen credit hours. His Iowa trust fund, so diligently administered by Lawrie Tatum, had dwindled to $110.26. As the end of the second semester approached, Hoover prepared for another rugged summer outdoors. Dr. Branner had again secured for him an appointment with the U.S. Geological Survey. He and several friends decided on a long camping trip to Yosemite. To finance the trip, the boys persuaded the San Francisco *Examiner* and other city businesses to pay them to repaint advertising signs along the route and to put up new ones wherever possible. Having raised several hundred dollars, the boys bought a wagon and two mules and set off on the 227 miles to Yosemite, the beautiful and mysterious valley to the east.[115]

The five Stanford boys and two boys from rival Berkeley joined the team of advertising men, who spent the next ten days, in Hoover's words, "putting up eyesores, advertising coffee, tea, and newspapers."[116] Upon arriving in the valley, the hungry boys, after days of dirt, dust, and canned beans, decided to splurge and eat in one of the better tourist hotels. For seventy-five cents apiece, they stuffed themselves. The campers elected one of the beautiful open meadows not far from El Capitan and sent up their tents.

Yosemite, a natural paradise, was a geologist's dream, a place of spectacular rock formations. From the floor of the valley, the outcroppings quickly ascend to more than thirteen thousand feet. Swift rivers such as the Merced cascade down the mountain and plunge over the precipices to the valley below. Yosemite Falls, the highest in North America, is 2,425 feet high. Several groves of giant sequoias grace the lowland meadows. These trees reach a height of two hundred feet or more and are among the oldest living things on the planet. Mariposa Grove, which contains almost two hundred of the huge trees, is where the largest, a tree named Grizzly, still stands. Grizzly is well over two hundred feet in height, weighs a thousand tons, and is twenty-seven hundred years old. An early explorer, among the first whites who entered the valley in 1849, wrote of Yosemite, "As I looked at the grandeur of the scene, a particular exalted sensation seemed to fill my whole being, and I found my eyes in tears with emotion."[117] John Muir, conservationist, founder of the Sierra Club, and the man most responsible for preserving Yosemite, wrote in *My First Summer in the Sierra* that "these sacred mountain temples are the holiest ground that the heart of man has consecrated."[118]

Within a hundred yards of the boys' campsite was that of Professor Joseph Le Conte, a famous geologist who was conducting a summer workshop for university students. At night, after having spent the day in exploration, the seven boys were welcomed in Le Conte's camp, where he gave evening fireside talks on the geology of the valley. Hoover reported that he and his six companions "listened spellbound" to the explanations of how the valley came to be.[119] The spell of this intellectually exciting sojourn was broken, however, when a telegram arrived at the camp informing Bert that his job with the U.S. Geological Survey had come through. Plans to fish the rivers and lakes for trout evaporated. The boys pooled their remaining money to pay Bert's stage fare to the Stockton river boats, some eighty miles away, but they were short the necessary cash. Bert packed up enough food to see him through and hiked the eighty miles to the boats. It took him three hard days to cover the distance, but he arrived on time at the Lindgren camp in the High Sierras on July 1, 1894.

Already behind schedule, the small survey party, consisting of Lindgren, Hoover, and a cook, was further delayed by a nationwide rail strike, which kept them in Placerville until the third week of July, when the strike finally wound down. Then, splendidly equipped with two specially built wagons and extra horses, they at last struck out for their mountain rendezvous. It was questionable whether Lindgren and Hoover could finish mapping the glacier sheets in the Pyramid Peak area to the southwest of Lake Tahoe before winter storms closed the passes.[120] For the next three months, Bert camped under the stars, slept on the ground, and did what he loved best. In a letter to Dr. Branner back at Stanford, he declared the region "the roughest country that God or man ever saw."[121] But the hardships were compensated for by good food—ham, Boston baked beans, and buckwheat cakes. Mapping the High Sierras was not like Hoover's summer in Arkansas, when he subsisted on sowbelly and cornbread and slept in a cramped, uncomfortable bed in a crowded cabin. In an effort to complete the mapping, Lindgren and Hoover clung to the snow line of the mountains, worked seven days a week, and took maximum advantage of the shortening days. Occasionally, if the survey party reached camp earlier, Hoover took the opportunity to fish for trout. Finally, on October 17, the two surveyors and their cook were "driven clear out of the mountains by a [snow] fall of seven feet."[122] Bert returned to Stanford five weeks after the fall term had commenced.

Shortly after his return in October 1894, Hoover noticed a new girl in the geology lab. He asked another young lab assistant who the new girl was and was told her name was Lou Henry. Even more surprisingly, she was not just taking a course in geology, she was a major. Hoover wrote to his friend Nell Hill and in a single short paragraph revealed his burgeoning interest: "We have a young lady taking geology as a specialty now a very nice young lady too."[123]

Lou Henry was tall, attractive, and athletic. Bert was at once attracted to "her whimsical mind, her blue eyes, and a broad grinnish smile that came from an Irish ancestor."[124] When first introduced by Dr. Branner and asked to comment on some lab samples, the tongue-tied Hoover put his hands in his pockets and fumbled with coins while he attempted to formulate an answer. He was not impressive, a tall, thin boy with a mop of hair, a shy young man who walked around campus and the geology building with his eyes focused upon the ground. Nonetheless, Bert overcame his shyness enough to scramble to be the one to assist Lou in the lab. He was even more enthusiastic about departmental field trips into the areas near Stanford. The usual practice was to arrange special outings for the female students interested in geology, based upon the assumption that they were less physically inclined and needed assistance. Lou was used to long, tough hikes in rugged terrain. She showed up for the regularly scheduled field trip dressed in a sweater, a short skirt, and proper walking shoes, with a small red bow under the collar of her blouse that accentuated her femininity. On the way up into the hills, the cavalcade of geologists ran into the university fence line. Lou amazed her male counterparts by vaulting the fence.[125] Her straightforward, plainspoken manner, her intellectual curiosity, and her physical prowess soon won her acceptance in the Geology Department. These qualities, coupled with her naturalness, supple figure, broad smile, sparkling blue eyes, and thick dark hair, won for her as well the heart of Bert Hoover. Lou was once asked who would marry a woman geologist. She firmly replied, "I want a man who loves the mountains, the rocks, and the ocean like my father does."[126] In Bert Hoover, she had met her match. She was an unusual woman with unusual interests. He was smitten.

As Bert and Lou became better acquainted, they soon discovered that Lou had been born in Waterloo, Iowa, only seventy miles from West Branch, the same year as Bert, 1874, but six months earlier. Both native Iowans, they shared a certain affinity. Lou's father, Charles, was a banker by trade, but his avocation was as a naturalist. A progressive Republican, he maintained that a woman could do anything a man could do. He taught Lou to hunt, fish, hike, camp, ride, and shoot—she was an excellent shot. On her maternal grandmother's farm, near Shell Rock, Iowa, she and her father took long walks through the woods and fields. On each of these expeditions, her father identified the flora and fauna and taught Lou their names.[127] Together they assembled collections of rocks and minerals; pressed, dried wildflowers, grasses, and leaves; bird's eggs; butterflies and other insects; and small mammals and reptiles. Lou kept lists and descriptions of all she had seen. Her habit of keeping lists and making extensive notes stayed with her throughout her life. Sometimes after a day of strenuous hiking, father and daughter pitched a tent and cooked over an open campfire whatever they had hooked, shot, or trapped. As the embers died down and the darkness increased, they lay back and studied the stars. Constellations observed were duly noted the following morning.

*Lou Henry, age ten,
Waterloo, Iowa, 1884.*
COURTESY HERBERT HOOVER
LIBRARY

Picking blackberries was another favorite activity, as was gathering hickory nuts in the fall. In the winter, Lou learned how to set snares for rabbits. She was a very good ice skater, enjoyed horseback riding, and in her teens finally learned to ride sidesaddle. In the 1890s, roller skating became the rage across the United States, and Lou joined the craze. When she was ten, she won the grand prize, a pink umbrella, for navigating an obstacle course on roller skates in the fastest time.[128] Like Bert, she was introduced to fishing early on. She and her father fished the Cedar River in a flat-bottom boat using butcher-string line and penny-apiece fish-hooks. On the Cedar, coincidentally one of the Hoover family's favorite places to fish and camp, Lou caught speckled river cat-fish and bullheads. Even as a very young girl, she was able to land the fish and knew how to unhook them without getting stung.

Lou's mother was thought to suffer from tuberculosis, and her doctor had recommended a drier, milder climate. The Henrys tried Texas but returned to Iowa. Then in 1887, they ventured to Kansas. The Henrys spent only a few months in Clearwater, a small town roughly twenty miles southwest of Wichita. Though the stay in Kansas was short, the prairie, covered with sunflow-ers, greatly influenced Lou, who loved to sit in the prairie grass and sketch the flowers.[129] In the fall of 1887, the family headed west to California, where they lived in several places. In the latter part of 1890, the Henrys permanently settled in the old mission town of Monterey. Wherever they lived in California, Lou and her father explored the surrounding countryside, hunting, camp-ing, and fishing. At sixteen, while living in Whittier, she recorded in her diary on February 2, 1890: "Sherman Wiggins came for Papa to go after coyotes, but I went instead. We were gone from four o'clock until dark, but didn't even see a coyote, altho' we came nearly getting an immense badger."[130] A week later, Lou and her classmates and close friends Frank and Jessie Naylor rode horses up the side of Barney Rock. They followed the ridge-line between two canyons to the highest point. In exploring the ridgetop, Lou remarked that the riders took "the longest, steepest places where there was the least foothold for the horses, utterly spurning roads and trails."[131] She concluded the day's adventure by writing, "It was by far the roughest climb I ever had, and we just had a big time."[132] Outdoor adventures also figured promi-nently in papers that Lou wrote in her English classes. An essay saved by her father was titled "A Foretaste of Camp-life."[133] Lou's thoughts were never far from the great outdoors.

After graduating from the Bailey School in Whittier, Califor-nia, Lou attended the Los Angeles and San Jose Normal Schools, where she studied to become a teacher. She graduated in 1893. Her years in teachers' college were punctuated with many fish-ing, hunting, and camping forays in the wilds of California. When she transferred to San Jose Normal School, she was near

Bailey School camping trip to the Puente Hills, summer 1889. Lou Henry is third from right. COURTESY HERBERT HOOVER LIBRARY

enough to Monterey that she and her father could resume their outdoor forays. After graduation, Lou returned home and worked as a teller in her father's bank. The following year, she taught third grade in Monterey. Her epiphany occurred one evening when she attended a lecture on geology given by Dr. Branner titled "The Bones of the Earth." At the conclusion of this inspirational talk, she knew that her calling was to study geology at the new university in Palo Alto.[134]

In the spring of 1895, after a semester of limited courtship, Hoover's relationship with Lou transcended the scientific, manifesting itself in a whirlwind of social activity. The young couple attended the sophomore ball, junior hop, charity ball, and senior ball as well as a myriad of other social functions. A favorite was to attend concerts in the old chapel.[135] Hoover, proud of himself in this unaccustomed role, declared that he had become "quite a social swell. Enjoyed myself better than ever in my life."[136] Lou helped her shy, introverted escort improve his social skills, but their spring fling taught both that they preferred a more moderate, more private lifestyle.

Stanford students came from all over the country, but by far the largest number were from California. Many had spent a good

Lou Henry fishing with her father, 1880s. COURTESY HERBERT HOOVER LIBRARY

deal of time as they grew up in the outdoors, hiking, camping, hunting, fishing, and exploring. This guaranteed that outdoor clubs were among the new campus organizations and social clubs. Groups of students rented horses, mules, buggies, and wagons and took trips into the High Sierras, to the beach, or into the hills that rose around Stanford. Bert and Lou participated in these outings as often as possible and enjoyed the field trips required by the Geology Department. In the spring of 1895, when the tall grass around Stanford was green, Bert and Lou explored the exposed limestone strata in the hills surrounding the Santa Clara Valley. The fields were filled with blooming orange California poppies and a riot of lupine, with its distinctive pea-shaped flowers in purple, pink, blue, white, and yellow. Meadowlarks nested by the thousands and filled the air with their song. Near the base of the outcroppings were lavender, lilac, and white-flowered wild clematis vines, a favorite spot for breeding tow-hees.[137] The young couple thoroughly enjoyed each other, shared their interest in geology, and preferred to be outdoors. In the last few weeks before graduation, Bert and Lou spent as much time together as possible, for once school ended Bert would again disappear into the High Sierras in the employ of the U.S. Geological Survey.

A whirlwind semester of social events, courtship, and study had been wonderful, but at this late date, Bert still had not passed his English requirement. Not quite sure how to solve this problem, he was rescued by the intervention of Professor Smith. Recognizing that Bert was on the verge of failing to graduate, Smith called him into his office and suggested that he rewrite and carefully proof a paper he had previously turned in. Smith argued that the paper clearly demonstrated Hoover's ability to express complex ideas in written English. Bert agreed and rewrote the paper. Smith then corrected the paper a second time, and Bert again made all the necessary changes. Then Smith took the paper to Professor Anderson and argued that Anderson should clearly be able to see that Hoover was competent in English and deserved to graduate. Anderson concurred, and Bert graduated with the pioneer class of 1895.[138]

At Lou's invitation, Bert traveled to her home in Monterey, where he spent a week as a guest of her family.[139] Although most of the letters between the young couple have since been destroyed, Bert and Lou were plainly in love and planned to marry. It is not clear whether they discussed marriage and their future, but by the end of the week, that understanding was implicit. Nonverbal communication, with each being able to intuit correctly the other's intentions, characterized their long and lasting relationship. The two of them could happily spend entire evenings together and not exchange a word. On other occasions, either or both would hold forth profusely on subjects dear to their hearts. Neither enjoyed chitchat, especially not Bert.

Of immediate concern, Lou had three years left at Stanford, and Bert needed a job. Hoover's goal was to earn enough money that he and Lou could marry and he could see his brother and sister through Stanford. His summer work with the U.S. Geological Survey might become a full appointment. At week's end, Hoover said good-bye to Lou and her family, leaving for the Sierras outfitted in high-topped boots and a brown duck suit.[140]

Throughout the summer and into the early fall of 1895, Dr. Lindgren and his hardworking assistant diligently mapped the area of the High Sierras around Lake Tahoe, Mono Lake, and the deserts of western Nevada. As luck would have it, Hoover again ended up with a difficult horse, one he described as "diabolically wicked." The bronco had the unusual name of Napoleon von Sandow, so christened because he could "unthrone any monarch" in the survey team who was foolish enough to mount him. Mounting Napoleon and staying atop, however, was possible only after having the unenviable experience of trying to saddle him. When the potential rider attempted to tighten the girth by securing the cinch strap, Napoleon expanded his chest prodigiously. Hoover and Lindgren laughed at the horse's antics, which reminded them of the immensely popular strong man and weight lifter at the 1893 Chicago World's Fair, Eugene Sandow, who greatly expanded his enormous chest when he flexed. Adding the "von," a Prussian pomposity, further embellished the horse's title.[141]

The task of the summer surveyors was to complete the study, begun the previous summer, on the geology of gold. Long, hard hours of work along the snow line of the jagged peaks were again the norm. Evenings, if one could stay awake, were spent in shop talk and occasional reading by the light of the fire. After weeks of camping in the wild, the survey crew would come down out of the mountains and use the opportunity to stay in hotels, usually the better resort hotels on Lake Tahoe. Hot baths, clean sheets, a choice of good food, and rest and relaxation were welcome respites. These breaks also provided opportunities to read and to write letters, something Bert was not good about doing. But Jenny Gray would have been proud of Bert's continued commitment to literature.

The previous summer in Yosemite, Hoover had walked in the footsteps of John Muir. Now, on the eastern slopes of the Sierras, he crossed the paths of two of America's more famous literati: Mark Twain and Bret Harte. In the mountains around the campfire and in the lounges of various hotels, Hoover probably read

Lou Henry, 1891. COURTESY HERBERT HOOVER LIBRARY

Twain's *Roughing It.* Reading Twain's descriptions of Lake Tahoe while he worked the same region must have been exciting. At the very least, he was impressed enough to appropriate one of Twain's rambunctious metaphors and add a twist of his own when writing to his sister, May, on August 4, 1895. Describing Tallac, a resort complex with magnificent vistas nestled on the shores of Lake Tahoe, Hoover wrote, "The best I can say for it is that its surrounding atmosphere would energize an Egyptian mummy and give him an appetite like a Florida Alligator."[142] In *Roughing It,* Twain had written, "Three months of camp life on Lake Tahoe would restore an Egyptian mummy to his pristine vigor, and give him an appetite like an alligator."[143] Revealing his egalitarian streak, Hoover further commented that Baldwin's Tallac House restaurant had about as much chance of satisfying a Florida alligator's appetite "as a spring chicken would an elephant."[144] He wondered how a hungry geologist fresh from the mountains could possibly put meat on his bones eating "pattie-foi-gras."[145]

Hoover's geology class, ca. 1893. Hoover is second from left.
COURTESY HERBERT HOOVER LIBRARY

In a letter to Nell Hill written in July, Hoover recounted a Mark Twain-like night spent in a small mining town. Sarcastically, he wrote, "Had a ball in town last night."[146] In one of the dance hall saloons that he entered, the whiskey, or forty rod mountain red-eye, as the local distillation was called, flowed freely, and as the evening progressed, the dancers became more animated.[147] Quarrels over dance partners and other whiskey-inspired arguments ended with two men shot, a sure sign among the denizens of the mining camps that the evening was a success. In the saloon, no one's spirits were dampened by the turn of events. The dancers, oblivious to the pools of blood here and there on the floor, continued their madcap frolic. Hoover described this macabre scene: "The floor became slippery, then sticky and finally brown again. I did not dance. I am timid about arguments on a six shooter basis. As morning approached the whiskey became worse in quality and more wicked in result until all were in the gutter from loss of trolly connection or injury of machinery."[148]

Hoover's boundless enthusiasm for the Sierras temporarily brought out the writer in him. His newsy letters, usually about his financial difficulties and his accomplishments at Stanford,

Kappa Kappa Gamma sorority. Lou Henry is fourth from left.
COURTESY HERBERT HOOVER LIBRARY

now waxed eloquently on the breathtaking beauty of the mountain peaks in the vicinity of Lake Tahoe—perhaps further inspired by Twain's eloquent descriptions. Hoover rarely elaborated on the beauty of nature in any but a prosaic manner, but now, for the first time, he expressed his deep romantic feelings toward nature that had been developing in him since he was a boy. He rarely spoke of or wrote about nature's beauty or other sensitive topics, such as his love for Lou. For Hoover, feelings were private. Deeply held feelings were expressed through action and attitude, not words. In his letters from multiple campsites in California and Nevada in the summers of 1894 and 1895, as well as in his *Memoirs,* Hoover is always the protagonist in a heroic, larger-than-life American adventure story, the geologist-engineer, whose major theme is man against nature, progressive, pragmatic, and pregnant with possibility. The young Stanford graduate embodied the heady optimism of the late nineteenth century and saw himself in the vanguard of a technological and managerial revolution that would bring good things to man.

During respites on Lake Tahoe and on forays into the mountains, Hoover and his survey team rarely fished, lacking time and physically exhausted. Mark Twain had fished there and reported

Lou Henry camping, 1895. She is second from left.
COURTESY HERBERT HOOVER LIBRARY

that try though he would, he caught but one fish a week on the crystal clear, mirrorlike lake. "We could see trout by the thousand winging about in the emptiness under us, or sleeping in shoals on the bottom, but they would not bite—they could see the line too plainly, perhaps. We frequently selected the trout we wanted, and rested the bait patiently and persistently on the end of his nose at a depth of eighty feet, but he would only shake it off with an annoyed manner, and shift his position."[149] Perhaps it was Mark Twain's peevishness that turned off the trout, for he seems the only one denied the lake's lavish bounty. Tallac House was famous for its guests' catches of silversides and boasted of spectacular trout fishing in its advertising literature. The silversides catches numbered in the hundreds per day, and fishermen averaged fifteen to twenty trout per hour, weighing approximately two pounds each.[150] Why Mark Twain failed to entice the trout to rise remains a mystery, as does how Hoover managed to resist this limitless opportunity. Though Hoover may have fished from the steamer *Tallac* or from the shores of the lake, there is no historical record that he did.

After a week of indulgence in civilization, Dr. Lindgren, Hoover, the two teamsters, the cook, and the small pack train of seven horses and four mules wound their way south through the Nevada desert. On their right rose the sheer rock walls of the Sierras, and on their left the vast emptiness of the desert stretched endlessly. Hoover described the torturous trek: "If the Good Lord made a few Trial Hades before the completion of the final resort he must have had his Experiment Stations N[orth] of Mono Lake."[151] A few days later, the exhausted survey crew reached its destination, the alkaline American Dead Sea of which Mark Twain wrote:

> It is one of the strangest freaks of nature to be found in any land, but it is hardly ever mentioned in print and very seldom visited, because it lies away off the usual routes of travel and besides it is so difficult to get at that only men content to endure the roughest life will consent to take upon themselves the discomforts of such a trip. Mono Lake lies in a lifeless, treeless, hideous desert, eight thousand feet above the level of the sea, and is guarded by mountains two thousand feet higher, whose summits are always clothed in clouds. This solemn, silent, sailless sea—the lonely tenant of the loneliest spot on earth—is little graced with the picturesque.[152]

Somewhere along the godforsaken route, the cook became ill, and the two teamsters took him to a doctor in the nearest town. During the four-day interlude, Hoover became the camp cook. Hoover maintained that his cooking was just fine; Lindgren commented circumspectly that "a College education is invaluable to a cook."[153]

Between Lake Tahoe and Mono Lake, Hoover and Lindgren spent the rest of the summer and early fall completing their survey. Shortly after leaving Reno for California in September, one of the teamsters quit and headed back for civilization. As Hoover's luck would have it, he was asked to drive the buckboard pulled by four government mules "over the worst road ever made."[154] That night, the survey crew camped at Donner Lake. Hoover commented that the lake was the site "where the Donner party gave up the ghost." He was referring to a wagon train that in 1846 had pursued a rumored shortcut across Utah, Nevada, and the Sierras. Numerous delays slowed the wagon train's progress, and the attempted October mountain crossing ended in tragedy. Snowbound in the high mountains and low on supplies, most of the trapped pioneers resorted to cannibalism in order to survive. Hoover more fully understood the Donner party's fight against the cold, for though it was but early September, nearly an inch of ice formed that night on the surface of the lake. After a long, cold night on the ground, he complained that he "had neuralgia in one jaw and a general bad humor that kept those four mules pretty well on the jump."[155]

Now south and west of Lake Tahoe, Lindgren and Hoover decided that the following morning they would attempt a Donner-like shortcut—a descent through the American River Canyon with horses, mules, and buckboard. The mountaineers in

Fishing on the dock at the Tallac Hotel, Lake Tahoe, California.
COURTESY LAKE TAHOE HISTORICAL SOCIETY, SOUTH LAKE TAHOE, CALIFORNIA

The Tallac Hotel. COURTESY LAKE TAHOE HISTORICAL SOCIETY, SOUTH LAKE TAHOE, CALIFORNIA

the area warned the survey crew that the proposed descent was impossible. Displaying the arrogant bravado and self-confidence for which he would become famous, Hoover responded, "But they are not geologists."[156] Lindgren and Hoover undertook the treacherous descent as planned and were successful. The little party worked its way through the narrow canyon for several days and arrived back in civilization at Placerville.

As the long summer of mountain surveying came to an end in mid-October, Hoover faced the task of finding full-time employment. A future with the U.S. Geological Survey was a chancy year-to-year prospect dependent upon the whims of congressional appropriations. With nothing definite on the horizon and his cash savings dwindling, the young Stanford graduate headed for the mines of Nevada City and Grass Valley.[157]

Degree in hand, Hoover went from mine to mine applying for an office job but was repeatedly turned down. He was willing, he said, "to get a start anywhere near the bottom of any mine staff."[158] The Cornish miners who had been promoted up from the bottom of the work ladder and now ran the mines were suspicious of "them college educated fellas."[159] Hoover's $40 was gone, and the hotel keeper where he roomed, a Mr. Rector, extended him credit. He finally found work in the lower levels of the Reward Mine, pushing an ore cart on a ten-hour night shift. The pay was $2 a day, and the crew worked seven days a week. Hoover did not become depressed and wrote in his *Memoirs* that he did not consider himself "a down-trodden wage-slave."[160] This attitude was bolstered by the fact that he likely was one of the few miners who possessed a college degree and considered the job temporary. After just a few weeks of this grueling labor, the ore deposits of the Reward proved less rewarding, and Hoover was laid off. Desperate for a job, he showed up early at the employment office every day, only to be turned away. "I then learned what the bottom levels of real human despair are paved with."[161] This sojourn at the bottom was short-lived; a job turned up at the Mayflower Mine as a mucker.

By Christmas, Hoover had saved $100, but he realized that he had no future in the mines of California or Nevada. If he and Lou were to marry, he had to secure something more substantial. Dr. Lindgren had once introduced him to Louis Janin, a very successful San Francisco mining engineer. Hoover had tried the bottom, he reasoned, so why not go to the top? Later, reflecting on this period in his life, he commented that "his education had prepared him for something better in life than competing with a mule."[162] In February 1896, Hoover left the goldfields of California to be reunited with Tad and May in Oakland.

Grandmother Minthorn had died in the fall of 1895, and May moved from Oregon to live with Tad, who for financial reasons had dropped out of William Penn College in Oskaloosa, Iowa, and was working as a linotype operator for the Oakland *Tribune.* Cousin Harriet Miles also moved in and helped run the household while she attended the University of California.[163] When Bert arrived, it was the first time the siblings had lived under the same roof since the death of their mother in 1884.

In his search for a job, again demonstrating the chutzpah that would secure him his fortune, Hoover used Lindgren's name to obtain an appointment with Janin. Over lunch, Janin explained that he regretted that there were no positions open in his firm. As an aside, he commented that the only job open was that of office boy. Hoover jumped at the chance, telling himself that "something might turn up if I kept near the throne."[164] Once again this ambitious young man started at the bottom. With his usual acumen, Hoover soon made himself indispensable and quickly was given important assignments by Janin. His salary rose to $7 a day plus expenses, and he was sent to many locations throughout the West to evaluate mines, as well as to Florida to help construct a levee at Lake Okeechobee. A short time later, his salary was again increased. He was now making $2,000 a year.

The reunion of the brothers and sister would not last long, however. The happy interlude was interrupted in fall 1896 by opportunity. Louis Janin received a telegram in October from the London international mining investment firm of Bewick and Moreing. This British concern asked Janin to recommend an experienced gold-mining engineer approximately "thirty-five years of age with seventy-five years of experience" to engage in exploration and assist in developing mines in Australia.[165] American mining technology and management techniques were recognized as superior to those employed by European companies, and American engineers were in great demand.[166] Janin, not surprisingly, turned to his competent twenty-two-year-old assistant— Hoover had been right that it paid to stay near the throne. He worried that Bewick and Moreing would reject him because of his age and lack of experience, but Janin reassured him that things would work out fine. Despite his anxieties, Hoover was keenly aware that the opportunity before him was the solution to his family's problems. The salary of $6,000 would allow him to marry Lou Henry, pay for his brother's education at Stanford and his cousin Harriet's education at the University of California, and provide for his sister, who would return to Oregon.

Hoover left no stone unturned in his effort to build an impressive résumé. He compensated for his lowly status by putting together a large packet of letters of recommendation, many of them written by people of stature in the mining field. To appear to be in his mid-thirties, he grew a mustache. In March 1897, the awaited job offer arrived. Employment secured, Hoover bought a life insurance policy, arranged for a portion of his salary to be distributed to his "wards," purchased a top hat and frock coat, and sailed for London.[167]

4

A Relentless Pursuit
of Money

Hoover determined to make good but could hardly know that the road he had set upon would lead him far beyond the arid wastelands of western Australia, a place he described as "three yards inside civilization," a place where it was cheaper to bathe in beer than in water.[168] On exploratory expeditions around Kalgoolie, Hoover suffered the swarms of blackflies and blowing red dust, and lived on tinned sardines and cocoa. From the mining hellholes of the great Australian outback, he moved on to become a globe-trotting inspecting engineer (exploration and mine examination), assayer, metallurgist, business reorganizer, systems and efficiency expert, and speculator. His beginning with Bewick and Moreing in Australia would lead him to China, London, Russia, Burma, and a dozen other countries. Camping and fishing would take a backseat as during the next twenty-two years he worked at breakneck speed, often eighteen or more hours a day. As a result, he amassed a fortune in a short period of time. From 1897 to 1914, he labored as a "mine doctor" as he was fond of describing his business activity, but in 1914, by chance, he entered public service. From 1914 until 1919, he became a great food czar in charge of feeding millions of starving human beings.

The Sons of Gwalia Mine assayed by Hoover in western Australia produced substantial profits, bringing Hoover to the attention of senior management, who decided that he was the right man to go to China to work with the imperial government to develop mining sites in the north. Opportunity knocked again at Hoover's door. His only stipulation was that he be allowed to return to the United States before departing for Tianjin (then Tientsin). Management concurred. Hoover, unsure of himself, cabled Lou Henry with an indirect offer of marriage. The telegram read "Going to China via San Francisco. Will you go with me?"[169] She responded yes.

On February 10, 1899, Herbert Hoover and Lou Henry, in matching brown suits, were married at her parents' home in Monterey. The civil ceremony was conducted by Father Raymond Mestres, Catholic priest and friend of Lou's. It was a service that suited the couple's modern eclectic views. Although her parents were Episcopalians, Lou declared herself a Quaker, and she was not asked to obey, only to love and honor. The newlyweds also had no time for a typical honeymoon, but the monthlong boat journey to China aboard the *Coptic* provided a wonderful opportunity for a leisurely renewed acquaintance between a couple who had not seen each other for nearly two years.[170] Stops in Honolulu at the Royal Hawaiian Hotel and tours of Yokohama, Tokyo, and Kyoto added spice to the adventure.

China, in the aftermath of a disastrous war with Japan in 1894–95, was torn apart by warring factions, sporadic civil wars, and the ravenous appetite of the competing Western powers bent on colonizing, annexing, or leasing as much of the Celestial Empire as possible. It was a fascinating and dangerous place to be at the end of the nineteenth century. It was also a place where foreigners lived opulent lifestyles in secluded international compounds. The Hoovers, twenty-five years old, commanded a salary of around $20,000 a year and soon lived in a mansion in Tianjin's foreign settlement, attended by nine servants; Bert once boasted fifteen.

While Bert scoured northern China for gold, Lou furnished their rental house, hired a Chinese teacher, and worked hard at learning to speak Chinese, an activity considered odd by many of the other women in the foreign community. In the three years the Hoovers stayed in China, Hoo Loo's (Lou's Chinese name) Mandarin progressed rapidly. Hu-hua (Hoover's Chinese name) managed to learn around a hundred words. Forever after, when a social situation demanded subtle communication, sotto voce, Bert and Lou relied on Chinese. The couple loved Chinese culture, and Lou began to collect blue and white porcelains from the Song (Sung), Ming, and Qing (Ch'ing) dynasties. In time, she put together a distinctive collection of great value. Aristocratic life in the British-dominated foreign settlement revolved around social gatherings and horses. Bert seemed fated to be intimately involved with the animal he disliked until the advent of the automobile. Lou participated with more enthusiasm than did Bert in the steady flow of social events, but that was partially due to his long treks into the provinces. Both preferred each other's company, but they did what was expected of them to maintain their position.

Bert put together a large collection of books on Chinese mining techniques and had them translated into English. It was from one of these ancient histories that Hoover first learned of a fantastic silver mine in the north of Burma, a mine that would eventually add greatly to his fortune.[171] Lou devoted a great deal of time to writing sketches of Chinese personalities and places. She went so far as to contact a literary agent in New York and solicit his opinion on publication. In her completed manuscript, which was never published, she views the Chinese from a romantic, turn-of-century, reductive point of view—as quaint, exotic, inscrutable, and unfathomable.[172] Both Hoovers' love for China was a love for the Chinese past, for accomplishments achieved long before. Contemporary China was a place in long decline, with little know-how and little initiative. Individual Chinese could be exceptional, but the Chinese as a "race" were considered indolent.[173]

Though they viewed foreigners through a eugenic lens, the Hoovers were progressives and were far more receptive to the ways of other cultures than were most of those with whom they associated. Both Hoovers were also very nationalistic, a nationalism that bordered on jingoism. In their letters and statements, it was clear that they felt that American technology, American initiative, and American democracy had pushed the United States to the forefront of the Western civilized world. For Hoover, the differences between the United States and Australia or England were frustrating enough, but China was in a world by itself. In Australia, Hoover's British Empire peers claimed that his initials H. C. stood for "Hail Columbia."[174] Though he was usually shy and reserved, American know-how and cultural superiority were topics to which he quickly warmed.

Bert and Lou were in China a little over a month when they learned that May had married a plumber she met in San Francisco, a man named Cornelius Van Ness Leavitt. Chagrined, both brothers disapproved of the match, repelled by Leavitt's working class status and lack of ambition. While Bert's and Tad's wives and families became close, May's marriage created a permanent barrier among the Hoovers.

Often Lou accompanied Bert into the interior of China. These journeys were like luxurious camping trips. Ponies, donkeys, carts, baggage carriers, grooms, and cooks made their way through the high desert plateau in search of precious metals. The Hoovers thoroughly enjoyed these outings together, with evenings around the fire and late-night reading in their tents— life in the great outdoors.[175] In the 1920s, Hoover claimed that he had fished the rushing rivers of northern China on these outings, but there is no mention of fishing in his correspondence. By late spring of 1900, however, these sojourns were becoming more dangerous. There had always been bandit gangs, robbers, and the possibility of other disasters, both man-made and natural, but more recently, a group of anti-Western religious fanatics, the Heavenly Fists (dubbed Boxers by the Western press), attempted to ethnically cleanse China of long-nosed foreign devils.

Hoover took the danger seriously, and by May 1, he had recalled all of his company's geological survey teams from the north of China.[176] Raids on isolated Western outposts increased and in early June 1900, the Boxers attacked the foreign concession in Beijing (then Peking) hunting down, killing, and torturing all those who consorted with foreigners. A contingent of eighteen hundred Russian soldiers on their way to relieve the siege of the foreign settlement in Beijing was attacked while in Tianjin. The Russian commander, realizing that so small a force would be unlikely to reach the capital city, stayed to protect the weakly defended foreign community composed of four hundred men, three hundred women and children, and roughly eleven hundred soldiers and sailors of various nationalities—American, Austrian, British, German, French, Italian, Japanese, and Russian. For the next several days, the besieged settlement held out against repeated attacks by five thousand Chinese soldiers and howling, shouting, long-haired hordes of Boxers, some twenty-five thousand strong. The Hoovers, always enamored of adventure, got all they wanted in the next few weeks.

Working around the clock, Bert fought fires, repaired holes torn in the fortifications by shell fire, served as a messenger, stood night watch, scrounged supplies for the hospital, and ensured that the thousand or so Chinese who remained in the settlement had adequate food and water. To reach all points in the compound quickly, Bert returned to a form of transportation he trusted—the bicycle. Lou, who refused shelter with the other women and children, strapped a .38 Mauser pistol to her belt, stood night watch, and served as a nurses' aide in the hospital.

As the siege progressed, casualties mounted while supplies dwindled. Thousands of shells arced into the settlement daily, as did thousands of rifle rounds. Lou had two close calls. While riding her bicycle near the perimeter wall for protection, a rifle bullet ricocheted, puncturing her front tire. Exhausted and nearly dazed from days of long service in the hospital, Lou attempted to relax by playing solitaire in the parlor of the Hoover home, when an artillery shell burst through a rear second-story window and exploded in the hall, blowing out the front door and destroying the entryway. The newel post exploded and the floor was covered with shell fragments. Frederick Palmer, a famous *Collier's* war correspondent, walked into the living room, still filled with plaster dust, where Lou continued her card game. Looking up and smiling, she commented, "I don't seem to be getting this."[177]

After a harrowing summer under fire, the Hoovers survived the Boxers' siege of Tianjin. Lou especially reveled in the battle and wrote to a friend that she had missed "the most interesting siege of the age," though in truth the Hoovers were both lucky to be alive.[178] In later years, the Boxer Rebellion and their China experiences were subjects that the reserved Hoovers were always eager to talk about.

Bert returned to their home to face the damages. Artillery shells had chewed up the yard, garden, and stable. The house

Lou Henry, Boxer Rebellion site, Tianjin, China, 1900. The cannon was used to defend Tianjin. COURTESY HERBERT HOOVER LIBRARY

had taken five direct hits. Much of their furniture was damaged, most of their clothing was ruined, the silver had disappeared, and all six of their horses were dead or missing. The Hoovers sold almost everything that remained intact, packed their personal belongings, and sailed for London aboard the German trunk steamer *Weimar*.[179] In London, Hoover reported on conditions in China and argued that if Bewick and Moreing acted quickly, there was money to made in the Kaiping coalfields in northern China—the trick would be to beat the Germans and the Russians. The Chinese were predisposed to cooperate with the British rather than the other two more difficult powers, who would not likely share mine management.

In China, Bert successfully organized a new coal-mining company, but he left after nine months because of extreme difficulties with European managers appointed by Belgian investors. At sea on the way to England in September 1901, the Hoovers were again about to enter a new phase of their life. Like Australia, China had been profitable, and Bert had moved up the ladder of success. The Kaiping coal-mining venture and other Chinese investments had added $250,000 to his mounting fortune. The Hoovers arrived in London rich and well known in international mining circles. It has often been said that "chance favors the prepared," and as chance would have it, one of the four senior partners in Bewick and Moreing wished to retire. Hoover became the new senior partner, with a 20 percent interest in the firm, an opportunity to acquire even more money, but he was a senior partner of a different stripe.[180] Rather than stay in London and deal with the financial end of the firm, Hoover became a kind of roving field agent, a front-line troubleshooter who focused on reorganizing existing investments in order to increase profits and who sought out and evaluated new mining properties. From 1902 until 1908, he was always on the move, working extremely long hours in far-flung regions of the world.

The Hoovers attempted to establish base camps in London and California, and whenever possible Lou traveled with her workaholic husband. On August 4, 1903, Lou gave birth to a son, Herbert Charles Hoover. Both parents were delighted, and young Herbert almost immediately began to travel with the family. When he was five weeks of age, Lou placed him in a basket, and she and Bert boarded a steamer for Australia. Bert took along an automobile.[181] He had bought his first the year before in France, a Panhard, recognizing at once that like the bicycle, this mode of transportation might free him forever from horses, mules, donkeys, and camels. While these new automobiles were not always mechanically reliable, Hoover soon loved to drive.[182]

By 1904, extensive travel, business difficulties, family pressures, and long hours began to take their toll on Hoover. Night after night, he wore out the carpet with his incessant pacing, a habit probably developed while a student at Stanford. Back and forth, back and forth he trudged, his hands behind his back, deeply engrossed in thought. He was unable to sleep more than three or four hours a night, his memory was slipping, and he had difficulty concentrating.[183] His penchant for pacing the floor while mulling over problems or worrying was exacerbated by mounting legal problems. His doctor ordered a long, two-month cruise to South Africa as a cure and insisted that Lou and the baby would be a distraction. Reluctantly Bert agreed to the remedy and asked a friend, J. H. Curle, an economics journalist, to

Bert, Lou, and Fluffy, the White House, Waltham on the Thames, London, England, 1902. COURTESY HERBERT HOOVER LIBRARY

accompany him. Lou, too, concurred with the doctor's recommendation. She and young Herbert spent the summer outside London in the country.

On the voyage to South Africa, Hoover spent most of the time in bed, but when he reached Johannesburg, refreshed and relaxed, he used his "vacation" to survey several mines and fish in the highland streams. Fishing, as it had for him as a boy in Iowa and Oregon, provided a safe haven from a hostile world. Fishing calmed his frayed nerves, washed his soul, and restored his spirits. He was back in London by fall to deal with a lawsuit and trial brought against Bewick and Moreing by Chinese mining interests over ownership of the mines. As the trial carried over into the new year, Bert and Lou began to think of California—home, friends, and a real vacation.[184]

In March 1905, the court rejected the Chinese claims. Hoover was exonerated. In late April, Lou and baby Herbert left for the United States, and Bert followed shortly thereafter in May. The first stop in California was at Lou's parents' home in Monterey. Everyone was interested to hear about the Boxer Rebellion and the young couple's close calls, but no overseas adventure could compete with the presence of a grandchild. Herbert was the center of attention throughout the weeklong stay. From Monterey, Bert and Lou made the short trip to Palo Alto to stay with Tad and his wife, Mildred, who were also on vacation.[185] In June 1899, Tad had married Mildred Brooke, a woman he had known since they were children in West Branch. In 1901, he graduated from Stanford with a degree in geology and went to work as a mining engineer in Bodie, California. He suggested that they return to their home in Bodie and then go camping in the High Sierras. Both couples instantly agreed, eager to be again in the wilderness of their beloved California. A real adventure seemed in order. After much discussion, they decided to attempt to cross the Sierras on horseback and work their way down into Yosemite Valley from the backside. If all went well, it would take two days to cross the snowfields. All agreed to this exciting but difficult trek.

Tad rounded up the necessary horses and equipment, and the expedition set out from Bodie to Mono Lake. On the steep descent into the basin that surrounded the lake, they enjoyed the incredible wide open views spread before them. In the background, to the west, rose a magnificent wall of snow-capped Sierra peaks, most over twelve thousand feet in height.[186] After lunch in Lee Vining on the shores of the lake, the Hoovers sought out a guide familiar with the mountain trails. A long, steep afternoon ride, a climb of several thousand feet in elevation, ended when the trail reached the campsite of the California state road commissioner near Lee Vining Canyon. The commissioner, Nate Ellery, had been a friend of Bert's since their student days at Stanford. Ellery was the engineer in charge of building a highway through the Sierras. In the summer of 1905, the work crews were slowly pushing the road through the extremely rugged terrain of Tioga Pass. That night, Tad, who had volunteered to be camp cook, prepared his first meal. After dinner, he was relieved of duty for the remainder of the outing. In his *Memoranda*, he commented with typical Hoover humor, "I cannot understand why, as I am a first-class camp cook, probably the best there ever was."[187]

Early the following morning, in the chilly mist, the Hoovers began the climb, soon reaching the snow line. The hard-packed crust that coated the top of the deep snow held the weight of the horses, at least most of the time. By midmorning, the climbers had covered roughly ten miles, an excellent beginning, but then the trail steepened dramatically. Skinners and drivers who had previously scaled the mountain sunk poles into the ground just beyond steep inclines or rock shelves. At these points, the lead ropes of heavily laden pack animals were hitched to the poles to prevent them from tumbling backward down the trail or off the side of the mountain when they lunged forward to make the climb. Once the front feet of the horse or mule was securely on the next level, it used its strong back legs to step up. Often human assistance was necessary to push or pull. This arduous process was repeated until the trail leveled out or the summit had been reached.

When the Hoovers' small pack train started up the steep grade, the guide led each of the horses over the snow-covered rock shelves without securing their lead ropes to the poles. When the last packhorse in the line, a heavily loaded bay mare, stepped up, the weight of her load shifted, and she pitched over backward off the mountain. Tad, who brought up the rear, witnessed the calamity:

> I counted slowly the number of times she revolved, one, two, three, four, five, six, seven, eight, nine, and landed "crash" in a willow thicket, about two hundred feet below. When the dust and shower of ladies' lingerie, tinned meat, biscuits, knives, forks, plates, and toilet articles had settled down, Bert and I climbed down the rocks and took up a collection. The mare was trembling with fright in the willows, but beyond about two dozen small cuts, which bled considerably, she was not injured.[188]

Nearly three hours were consumed in picking up as much camping paraphernalia as possible. Food was most important, as the two engineers had calculated the party's needs precisely, with no reserves. The loss of time extended the snowfield crossing by at least a day, though with careful rationing, supplies would hold out. After the mare was carefully repacked, the Hoovers and their guide pushed on. For a while the party moved along steadily, but the heat from the noonday sun began to melt the icy crust. Suddenly the lead horse broke through the surface, plunging into snow up to its withers. Bert, Tad, and the guide unpacked the struggling animal and worked to pull her free. It was agonizingly difficult. By pulling on the lead rope, they coaxed the frightened creature to put her front legs on the ice crust, but when the horse attempted to pull herself out, the crust broke, and she sank once more into the deep snow. The horse at last secured a solid footing and was pulled free and repacked.

The party moved forward cautiously, angling down across the snowcap in an effort to find firmer ground. It was not to be. Now one horse after the other broke through the thin crust, floundering in the deep snow. The Hoovers worked feverishly: unpack, unsaddle, pull, push, cajole, curse, drag, saddle, and repack. They refused to give up. Their faces reddened from exertion, and their clothes were soaked with sweat. Each person wore blue sun goggles made of a gelatinous material to protect against snow blindness. Heat and perspiration slowly melted the flimsy goggles. Streams of indigo sweat ran across their cheeks, down their necks, and soaked their collars. It was difficult to see as the melted jelly stung their eyes. When the goggles finally disintegrated into a gooey mess, the struggling mountaineers squinted against the intense glare that reflected from the snow. Stubbornly they pushed on, resolved to cross the snowfield. Hard work in a hot sun at over ten thousand feet brought on bone-tired fatigue, but no member of the party succumbed to altitude sickness. For eight hours, the battle to cross the snowfield went on, but only ten hard-fought miles had been won.

As dusk and the cold night air descended on the mountaintop, Lou discovered a frozen track made by an avalanche. It was only eight inches wide and was just below the snow, but it was wide enough to provide footing for the horses and promised a way out. The track ran up the side of the mountain at a forty-five-degree angle for about a hundred yards. The party tied all of the lead ropes together, and taking one end of the homemade line, Bert scrambled up the narrow, icy pathway. A rock at the crest of the ridge served as a hitch, and the horses were brought up one at a time. The whole disheveled party slid down the other side into a natural amphitheatre.[189] In the growing darkness, the outline of buildings were barely visible. Fortune smiled on the climbers, for they had stumbled into the abandoned Tioga Mine.

Most of the buildings had collapsed long before, but the stable and the assay office were in fairly good shape. The discredited guide and the horses were bedded down in the stables, and the Hoovers claimed the office, which had last been used to store charcoal. The party discovered an old stove in a far corner and put it back together. They melted tubs of snow and cleaned the room. Several hours later, the two couples had hot water, a hot meal, a heated room, and drinking water for the horses.

Before dawn the next morning, Bert and Tad hiked to the top of Tioga Pass to find a solid trail over the top of the Sierras. Looking to the west, the brothers estimated that they still had thirty difficult miles to go. The three hours lost when the horse toppled off the mountain proved decisive. It would take two to three more days to work their way through the icefields and over the peaks. The horses had not eaten anything since passing the tree line and were worn out by difficulties encountered the day before. They could not go two or three more days without food. Food for human consumption was also in short supply and would be insufficient if once again the ice crust failed to support the weight of the horses. Good judgment prevailed; the campers could go no further. Bert and Tad returned to the assay office and explained to Lou and Mildred that it was too risky to proceed. Though disappointed, all settled for a good breakfast.

Still early in the morning, the little pack train worked its way back across the snowfield without mishap—the ice crust held. The previous day's exciting events gave way to a routine leisurely ride back to Bodie. Tad, who generally shared his brother's feeling toward the equine species, had been riding a sorrel mare named Polly, a horse he described as having "pronounced criminal instincts. Her whole ambition in life seemed to be to throw me off, or to rear up and fall backward and crush the life out of me."[190] She did possess one virtue, which was "a very easy pace . . . when she did want to behave herself."[191] Mildred, on the other hand, had been riding a large, black Morgan, a gentle creature, but one that possessed a hard gait. Now Tad and Mildred traded horses. Under Mildred's gentle urgings, the mean-spirited Polly underwent a conversion experience; she became cooperative and easy to handle for the remainder of the trip.

Near midmorning, the riders entered Nate Ellery's camp. Invited to an early lunch, and still recovering from the hard physical exertion in the deep snow, the weary adventurers consumed a huge amount of food. To the consternation of the black cook, dozens of hot biscuits, ham, sausage patties, and quarts of hot coffee disappeared down their gullets. Later that day along the trail, the Hoovers met a Piute Indian who wished to trade goods. After some haggling over the price, Tad bought a wildcat skin. On the north rim of Mono Lake, Lou, encouraged by her brother-in-law, dismounted and disappeared over the top of some sand dunes in search of Indian arrowheads. She was rewarded with an excellent find—a large specimen with all points intact. In June, an array of wildflowers were in bloom on the high desert plateau. Lou and Mildred carefully identified and recorded each species. Just outside Bodie, the list had grown to 125 varieties. Lou, ever the scientist, later cross-referenced her list from this outing against her lifetime list. The Hoovers returned happily tired from this latest adventure, one that fortuitously did not end in disaster. Tad best summed up the trip from the young couple's perspective: "So ended the famous attempt of the Hoover family to break into the back door of Yosemite."[192]

Back in Bodie, Bert had an opportunity to do something he had not done since he left South Africa—fish. He and Tad fly-fished the cold, spring-fed waters of Bodie Creek. They were successful, and fresh trout was served that evening for dinner.

In late June, their wonderful California vacation over, Bert, Lou, and baby Herbert left for New Zealand and Australia. For almost five months, Bert inspected the mines of Bewick and Moreing. Lou traveled to Tasmania and on several occasions went with Bert to Westralia. She began to collect rock samples for Dr. Branner and ship them back to Stanford.[193] In November, business concluded, the Hoovers left once more for England. At a stop in Cairo, Lou stayed on to see Egypt and collect Red Sea rock samples. Two weeks later, she sailed for London and joined Bert. Back in England, Bert decided, after extensive investigation, that zinc might prove more profitable than gold and threw himself into this new endeavor enthusiastically. The following year, Bert and Lou were elated when Tad and Mildred and their two young daughters, Mindy and Hulda, moved to London. Tad had secured employment with a subsidiary company of Bewick and Moreing. Bert maintained that he had not interceded on Tad's behalf; nepotism was on his list of taboos.[194]

Soon the two couples found houses close to one another and began to spend much time together. Both brothers maintained intense travel schedules and were often away from London for extended periods of time. But when in England, their leisure activities included motoring in the English countryside. Bert began to develop a passion for English history and missed no chance to visit historic sites. On his long ocean voyages, he read history voraciously and planned out what he wanted to see on his return home. One such trip was a two-week tour of Scotland by automobile with Ray Lyman Wilbur, another old friend from Stanford.[195] Sunday drives often included a picnic, on the ground, under trees, West Branch style. The food, too, was usually Iowa fare that recalled the Hoover clan's trips to the Cedar River when Bert and Tad were young. After lunch, nearly all would take off their shoes and socks, wade into the stream, and join the two brothers in building dams and trapping minnows—another activity that carried over from their youth. While these outings included family traditions from their Iowa boyhood, they were picnics on a much grander scale. Both families, including their dogs, packed into a large, chauffeur-driven, open touring car. They brought along the maid, who set out the food while the Hoovers gathered nuts, picked wildflowers, and played along or in the stream.[196] No picnicking West Branch Quakers relaxing under leafy hardwood trees had ever been served tea at four o'clock in the afternoon by domestic servants.

Always loath to participate in upper-crust English society, with its rigid class values, the Hoovers built a social circle largely around Americans, many of them engineers or Californians. The previous year, another American couple, Edgar and Abigail Rickard, had moved from San Francisco to London. Edgar and his brother published the leading journal on mining in America. Hoover convinced Edgar that the center of international mining was London, and that there was a real need of an independent publication that focused on the business aspects of mining as well as on the technical. Rickard's new *Mining Magazine* became very successful, and Edgar and Abigail became lifelong friends of the Hoovers.[197] Rickard later served for many years as Hoover's business manager and advisor. Despite their dislike of certain aspects of British society, the Hoovers and the Rickards partici-pated with relish in the cultural offerings of turn-of-century England. The two couples also started a joint savings program that they called the Seeing Cairo Fund.[198] Hoover fondly reported that "at one time its assets rose to $5,000 or $6,000. In any event, out of it we saw all the 'sights,' including cathedrals, museums, galleries and restaurants of most of Europe—England, Germany, France, Russia and Italy and every way station—with all the abandon of tourists."[199]

The first fifteen years of the new century were an age of heady optimism, of unparalleled achievement, and the future looked bright. The British empire was at the height of its power, no major international war had afflicted Europe since Napoleon was defeated at Waterloo in 1815, the economies of the modern countries were booming, and science and technology promised to solve most social problems. The horsemen of the apocalypse seemed banished. Hoover held that England before the outbreak of the First World War "was the most comfortable place to live in the whole world. That is, if one had the means to take part in its upper life. The servants were the best trained and the most loyal of any nationality. The machinery for joy and for keeping busy doing nothing was the most perfect in the world."[200]

A second son, Allan Henry Hoover, was born into this comfortable English setting on July 17, 1907. Like his older brother, he was to become a world traveler at a tender age. The family, along with Lou's sister Jean and Hoover's journalist friend J. H. Curle, left for Myanmar (then Burma) in late August with their two children in tow, two-month-old Allan in a basket, to evaluate a reportedly fabulous silver and lead mine in the far north of the country near the Chinese border, an area today known as the golden triangle. The journey was arduous, but Hoover remarked that "traveling with babies is easier than with most grown-ups."[201]

From Rangoon, the Hoovers traveled upcountry to Mandalay by train. There they were met by the American mine manager C. D. Clark, whom Hoover had earlier sent out to Myanmar to undertake a preliminary evaluation. Lou, Jean, Herbert, and Allan stayed in Mandalay while Hoover and his mine evaluation team continued north by rail to Hsipaw. From Hsipaw, it was possible to proceed the fifty-one miles to Bawdwin only by horse on jungle trails. When the three surveyors arrived at the remote site, the slag heaps and tailings suggested that at one time the mine had been extremely lucrative. Obviously a huge number of miners had once worked the area. All signs pointed to the possibility of a profitable mine operation.

But misfortune befell the Hoovers in the jungles of Myanmar. Both Bert and Lou were bitten by malaria-carrying mosquitoes and contracted the disease. Bert's case of tropical fever was the worst. Suffering a high fever and chills, he slipped into a delirium. Delusional and incoherent for weeks, Hoover babbled poetic verse.[202] Those around him feared he had lost his reason. As the malaria burned itself out, so did Bert's efforts at becoming the Bard of Burma. He soon regained his faculties and returned to normal. Fortunately, the children did not become ill, and in later years, neither Bert nor Lou succumbed to recurring outbreaks. The long journey and the bouts of malaria, however, were worth it. Over the next ten years, the Bawdwin mine guaranteed Hoover's fortune.

For a long while, Hoover had been unhappy in his relationship with Bewick and Moreing. Financial scandals, lawsuits, and constant travel had taken their toll. Then, too, the Hoovers missed the United States, especially California, and both wanted their sons to be educated in America. "Hail Columbia" did not wish to see his children brought up in the British tradition. Hoover had begun the process of extricating himself from Bewick and Moreing before the trip to the great mine at Bawdwin, but on the boat home from Myanmar, he resolved to cut the final ties and become an independent entrepreneur.

Back in England, the Hoovers decided to look for a new residence. After a thorough search, they settled for an eight-room house in the Campden Hill neighborhood of Kensington, which they christened the Red House because of its big red front door. A huge mulberry tree graced the center of a large back garden that was surrounded by a wall. It was a perfect play area for Herbert, Allan, and their Irish terrier, Rags.[203] From 1908 until the outbreak of World War I, hundreds of guests came to dinner at the Hoovers'. Even if the host was in a reticent mood and said next to nothing, the rest of the company enjoyed sparkling conversation, often led by Lou, and wine from the Hoovers' well-stocked cellar, reportedly one of the best in London.[204] Many Californians, particularly Stanford alumni and students, thought of the Red House as a home away from home, an extraterritorial slice of

America in the middle of London.[205] Sunday dinner, unlike the other evenings, was nearly always reserved for family and friends. For Lou, the burden of running this complex household was reduced by employing a maid, a cook, a butler, and a personal assistant. Bert and Tad shared a chauffeur. Weather permitting, breakfast was regularly served on the patio from spring to fall.

Ever since working in Australia, Hoover had been interested in old mining techniques. He began to buy a book here and there, but as his collection increased, so did his ardor. While in China, he searched diligently for ancient mining texts. Word went out through the antiquarian dealers of China that a foreigner was buying anything in Chinese on mining. Hoover thus acquired a large number of books, and Lou's tutor aided him in deciding which ones to have translated into English. By the time the Hoovers left the Celestial Empire, they had put together an impressive collection.

In London, Hoover purchased mining treatises in many languages. One of their outstanding finds was a copy of Georgius Agricola's *De Re Metallica*. Bert and Lou, as geologists, were fascinated with this volume, a compendium on mining in the fifteenth century, based on actual fieldwork and copiously illustrated with nearly three hundred detailed woodcuts. George Bauer (Georgius Agricola was his Latinized name) lived between 1494 and 1555. A physician, he wrote many books on various scientific subjects, but for twenty years he labored on his crowning achievement, *De Re Metallica*. After publication, it quickly became the "how-to-book" as mining expanded out from Saxony and into Bohemia and Moravia. German mining towns such as Kutna Hory flourished on Czech lands.

Lou, who had studied Latin at Stanford, attempted to read the manuscript, but it proved extraordinarily difficult, as Bauer had created his own new Latin vocabulary to deal with technical mining terms that did not exist. With encouragement from Dr. Branner, the Hoovers decided in 1907 to undertake a translation. Enormous obstacles almost immediately emerged, and the would-be linguists decided instead to have an early German translation rendered into English. To facilitate the project, they hired several full-time translators over a number of years. Bert and Lou devoted most of their free time to the project, made all of the critical editorial decisions, and carefully reworked the translation four times. Bert wrote a lengthy scholarly introduction that put the book into historical perspective.

In 1913, after six years of labor, a beautifully bound illustrated English translation was published. Of the print run of three thousand, fifteen hundred copies were given away to research institutes, universities, libraries, and those with a professional interest in mining; five hundred were held back; and the remainder were offered for sale at $5 a volume. Printing costs were around $25 a copy, but the Hoovers hoped for the widest distribution possible.[206] They were rewarded for their efforts when awarded the gold medal for achievement by the Mining and Metallurgical Society of America. During these "scholarly years," Sunday or weekend outings in the countryside were greatly curtailed. At this point in his life, Hoover had no time for fishing, but he did assemble a large collection of English trout and salmon flies.

5

The Great Humanitarian

Until the outbreak of World War I, both Bert and Tad continued to work extremely hard and travel frequently. After leaving Bewick and Moreing, Hoover worked closely with other mining associates in a series of international projects, but he formed no company, maintaining his independence. To facilitate his vast international dealings, in 1908 he opened offices in London, San Francisco, New York, St. Petersburg, and Paris.[207] Lou accompanied Bert on his business trips whenever possible, but in the summer of 1908, the Hoovers rented a house on the Stanford campus, and when Bert returned to London in the fall, Lou stayed in California, where Herbert started school. From 1908 on, Lou spent the school year in California and vacations in London or on the road with Bert. Regardless of Hoover's efforts to spend more time in the United States and eventually return home, he was unable to arrange a visit from 1907 through 1909.

Hoover began to tire of mining and the relentless pursuit of money. By now he had amassed a fortune of several million dollars.[208] Nonetheless, he reasoned that there had to be more to life.

The desire to be of service or to enter public life was growing quite strong, though he understood that certain aspects of his personality—taciturn, authoritarian, and introverted nature—all but disqualified him from politics. One biographer wrote that he was as "emotive as a slide rule."[209] He put out feelers to the Taft administration in Washington and worked diligently to raise money for his alma mater, but nobody in Washington contacted him, and the thought of serving out his life as a Stanford trustee, a member of numerous corporate boards and prestigious social clubs, did not appeal to him. The restless and industrious Californian was not the kind of man who could spend the rest of his life "staying busy doing nothing."[210] Something deep inside him pushed him ever on to grander projects. Perhaps he was more like his uncle Henry John than he realized; he had become as restless as a Minthorn.

Just before the outbreak of World War I in August 1914, he thought he had found the solution. He was about to purchase a newspaper in California—the Sacramento *Union*. To friends, he confided that he might assemble a great chain of newspapers, something his fellow Californian William Randolph Hearst was doing with great success and to much controversy.[211]

The war, however, changed everything. Hoover was almost immediately drawn into the maelstrom. Thousands of American citizens were stranded in London, and thousands more were fleeing across the channel every day from the spreading conflict. A committee of prominent Americans in London organized to aid their fellow countrymen. It was not long before Hoover was asked to join the committee.[212] He leaped into this new project with considerable zeal. Several hundred thousand pounds were required and obtained, some of it Hoover's personal money. Lou dug out a hundred pounds the Hoovers kept at home in case of emergencies.[213] Those in need were interviewed, and the money was loaned on their signature alone, no collateral required. In addition to money, the Hoover Committee distributed food, clothing, and steamship tickets to America.[214] Some recipients felt that the accommodations they received were beneath their social status, but no first-class cabins were booked; many landed in steerage. Ambassador Walter Hines Page responded to the flood of "refugees" by requesting immediate aid from Washington. He was gratified to learn that the U.S. Congress acted quickly, voting $2.5 million to aid Americans in need. To avoid any problems involving currency exchange, the Wilson administration dispatched the $2.5 million in gold aboard the battleship USS *Tennessee*.[215] The American committee was to continue to provide aid until the gold arrived.

The tension caused by thousands of distraught travelers was occasionally relieved by comic situations. One near-hysterical woman refused to board any oceangoing vessel unless Hoover guaranteed in writing that she would not be torpedoed by German U-boats. Hoover thought for a moment, then grabbed a pen and paper and wrote the demanded guarantee. He later explained that if the woman arrived in New York safely, she would be well pleased, and that if she went down in the mid-Atlantic, the guarantee was likely rendered moot.[216] In addition to the difficult and the demanding, many strange people in strange occupations appeared before the Hoover Committee. Among the strangest were the remnants of a wild west show waylaid in Poland. Into the Savoy Hotel walked twelve American Indians and ten cowboys in full garb, and what a tale they had to tell. At war's outbreak, the army had confiscated the show's horses and ponies but left the elephant, lion, tiger, and orangutan. Unable to perform, and with banking suspended, the situation became more desperate each day. The showmen were unable to feed the animals or pay their hotel bill. Still, their leader, an Indian named White Feather from Pawhuska, Oklahoma, was determined to save the situation. As an interim solution, they killed the orangutan and fed it to the lion and tiger. Then they dressed in their most expensive costumes, abandoned all else in the middle of the night, and headed for England. On the road, in Hamburg, they picked up a twelve-year-old boy who had been on his way to Croatia to stay with his grandparents. The young man was delighted to be rescued by "real Americans," and fortuitously, he had enough money to feed the troupe until they reached London. His mother was informed by cable that he was safe and would be returning to America in the care of the wild west show. The cowboys and Indians, dressed in their colorful costumes, contributed much to the American Committee's efforts, lessening tensions by moving up and down the long lines and talking with those who anxiously awaited assistance.

Lou also walked the long lines of worried Americans and talked with hundreds. She soon noticed that many women and children were unaccompanied and in dire need. Immediately she called a meeting of the Society of American Women in London. The next day, Lou opened for business in the grand ballroom of the Savoy Hotel. Like the men's committee, the women's committee provided food, clothing, hotel accommodations, Atlantic passage, day-care facilities, sightseeing tours in and around London, loans, and cash. As more and more Americans poured into London, the Women's Committee met arriving trains and boats, gathering distraught and needy Americans.[217] During those hectic weeks, about fifty thousand U.S. citizens were aided in some way by the American Committee, thousands of them schoolteachers with very limited means. Of the $400,000 loaned out, less than $400 went unpaid.[218] "Hail Columbia" argued that such a high level of honesty, responsibility, and integrity was a testament to the American character.

For six weeks, the Hoovers worked at a frenetic pace. Both reveled in the role of service, and both found renewed purpose in their lives. Lou learned that her organizational skills were greater than she had known, and her confidence grew.[219] As the war settled down into a ghastly slaughter, Hoover kept his eye open for an opportunity to volunteer his considerable talents in a humanitarian cause. He did not have long to wait, because little Belgium, under a harsh German Army occupation, was quickly running out of food.

When the war began in August 1914, Belgium declared its neutrality, but it stood in the way of the impending German attack on France. The German high command asked the Belgian government for transit rights but was rebuffed by King Albert, whose response to the audacious request was that "Belgium was a country not a thoroughfare."[220] Huge German armies crashed across the border regardless of the king's pointed protestations, but the Belgian Army fought valiantly, slowing down the German drive. At the Marne, the French and Belgian Armies miraculously prevailed—the kaiser's armies were stopped. Both sides dug trenches and commenced a war of persistent attrition. Nearly all of Belgium was seriously damaged and under German control. The grain harvest was destroyed or abandoned and food in storage was confiscated by the German Army. Belgium had always imported large quantities of food but was now unable to do so because of a British blockade. Food quickly disappeared from stores in the major cities. Without outside assistance, the Belgian population faced hunger and perhaps mass starvation. This small, overrun country was a catastrophe waiting to happen.

Hoover, wrapping up the activities of the American Committee, was approached by a British group asking for assistance for the large number of Belgians who had found their way to refuge in Great Britain. Shortly thereafter, Hoover met Millard Shaler, an American mining engineer who represented a Belgian relief organization that was purchasing food supplies in England. Shaler described for Hoover the tragedy that was unfolding just across the English Channel. Convinced of Belgium's plight, Hoover opined that the solution was for a committee of prominent American citizens to work closely with the U.S. government to provide the needed supplies. U.S. Ambassador Walter Hines Page concurred and invited him to formulate a proposal; Hoover asked "for 24 hours to think it over."[221] That night, Hoover weighed his future. Although the war might make him richer, the Belgians offered a whole new challenge, a chance for continued service and perhaps a roundabout entry into public life. In the morning, he had breakfast with his good friend Will Irwin, a journalist, fellow Stanford graduate, and houseguest. Hoover stared intently into his breakfast plate for some minutes, then looked up and emphatically pronounced, "Let the fortune go to hell."[222] The decision made, he returned to the embassy on October 22 and within two days produced a plan and a committee. Hoover understood that he had come to love the challenge associated with large, difficult undertakings, projects that others would consider next to impossible. This business entrepreneur turned humanitarian committed himself to feed the Belgians.

The Commission for Relief in Belgium (CRB) developed into a huge international organization that fed an entire nation from 1914 to 1920. The CRB was a unique, thoroughly modern organization, and all later Hoover organizations would bear its stamp. Based on his past managerial experience, Hoover ensured that the lines of communication within the organization were clear. There was no doubt who was in charge. Hoover ran the show, but he allowed his lieutenants a great deal of latitude in accomplishing their assigned tasks. Just before American entry into the war in 1917, he turned over the lower-level operations to Holland and Spain, both neutral countries, but for more than two and a half years, he raised huge amounts of money, $25 million a month, from the French, British, and American governments as well as from international fund-raising campaigns. Saving the nine million Belgians from starvation took more than over $200 million, $24 million of which was spent on reconstruction at war's end.[223] Amazingly, administrative overhead was less than 1 percent.[224] But more interestingly, the CRB was a new-style quasi-private-public organization that filled the space between governments and corporations—a semiofficial hybrid NGO (nongovernmental organization). A member of the British Embassy staff accurately characterized the CRB as "a piratical state organized for benevolence."[225] Hoover's dramatic success in Belgium against heavy odds caused his reputation to balloon, and by 1917, many referred to him as the "Great Humanitarian" or "Hoover of Belgium." One of the finest tributes to his accomplishments came from Ambassador Page, who misjudged him but said that this "simple, modest, energetic little man, who began his career in California [would] end it in Heaven."[226]

As Hoover scuttled back and forth among London, Brussels, and Berlin, he picked up much valuable war information, all of which he reported to Col. Edward M. House, President Wilson's trusted aide, who was sequestered in a hotel room in New York City. House was impressed with the quality of information Hoover provided and with his suggestions on how to handle the belligerents.[227] Others, too, in Washington thought that there was a place in Wilson's government for Hoover, especially Justice Louis Brandeis and Federal Reserve Board member Adolph Miller. In April 1917, Hoover was asked to make a presentation to the Council of National Defense. Soon after, he was appointed war food administrator with cabinet rank, and the family moved to Washington, D.C. Although Hoover had hoped for a more prestigious position, he was well aware that entry into the administration was the most important thing.

Once in, Hoover, the consummate empire builder, knew what to do. His task was to ensure that the United States produced enough food to feed the American public, the rapidly expanding American Expeditionary Force, and those increasing numbers of

Hoover, war food administrator, ca. 1917. COURTESY HERBERT HOOVER LIBRARY

Europeans in need of relief. In an effort to ensure his success, President Wilson and the U.S. Congress bestowed upon Hoover czarlike powers. As he had in the past, Hoover attacked his new assignment with vigor. Once again he found himself working sixteen- to eighteen-hour days. The workload he faced as "food czar" was complicated, as he retained the chairmanship of the CRB.[228] Hoover created numerous agencies that helped accumulate huge amounts of food, but he relied heavily on voluntarism, firmly convinced that the American public would sacrifice individually for the greater good. To get across his message, "Food Will Win the War," Hoover conducted a huge publicity campaign that reached into every community in America. Millions of Americans jumped on the "save food" bandwagon and "Hooverized." Horace Albright, acting director of the newly created National Park Service in 1917–18, was reconnoitering the northwest corner of Yellowstone. He drove into Cooke City, Montana, an isolated mining town with few residents but a working hotel that housed a number of guests. Sugar was very difficult to obtain, but Albright reasoned that the hotel might have some. When he asked the elderly woman behind the desk, she quickly responded, "We're Hooverizing."[229] Obviously, the word was out.

To deal with the growing number of hungry people throughout Europe after the war, Hoover created the American Relief Administration (ARA), an organization that eventually fed millions. By pushing himself to his limits and innovatively using every means at his disposal, he was able to accomplish all that had been asked of him. The War Food Administration (WFA) and the ARA were roaring successes. His name had become a household word, and people in both political parties eyed him as a candidate as the 1920 presidential race heated up. Hoover had gotten his wish: He was at last on the "slippery road of public life."[230]

For years, Hoover had taken almost no time off, making do with an occasional Sunday stolen from a hectic work schedule. During all the seasons, but especially the hot Washington summers, the Hoovers, with old friends such as Hugh Gibson and the Rickards and new friends from the WFA such as Mr. and Mrs. John W. Hallowell, squeezed in as many Sunday picnics as possible. Children and dogs romped along streams while Hoover, interested children, and other adults, often some of the women as well as the men, built dams and engineered canals, complete with waterfalls and waterwheels. Model boats navigated the newly constructed waterways. Hugh Gibson wrote in his diary of one sharp November day: "We all got filthy dirty and fell in the water now and then and had a proportionately good time. The Chief looked like a tramp and I was worse if anything."[231] If the party arrived at their destination in midmorning, Hoover cooked breakfast. Gibson commented on one such outing in April 1920: "It isn't a picnic unless the Chief scrambles eggs over a hot fire in a short-handled frying pan, burning his hands and getting his eyes filled with smoke." He suggested to Hoover that he could avoid burning himself if he purchased a long-handled iron frying pan, "but that was turned down cold." Gibson remarked that he "made other suggestions but they got just as far."[232] Typically, later in the afternoon, meats were roasted over open fires while corn and potatoes cooked beneath the glowing hot coals. The picnic hamper included ham or chicken salad sandwiches, potato or tomato salad, hot coffee, hot beef bouillon, and, for Lou, lots of cold orange juice, her favorite beverage.[233] Early evenings around the campfire included songs and stories. Finally, cars loaded and dogs and children rounded up, the Hoover caravan, filled with happy but tired people, wound its way back to Washington.

Winter provided fewer opportunities, but Bert and Lou recalled with relish their long-ago cold, wintry days in Iowa and eagerly looked forward to cold snaps and a decent accumulation of snow. Washington, D.C., winters rarely met expectations, except the unusually cold winter of 1917–18, when, surprisingly, it was possible to build a snowman in the front yard.[234] More often, the Hoovers were forced by the mild Mid-Atlantic climate to gather family and friends for outings in the mountains. The adventurers motored west into the foothills of the Appalachians in search of good sledding hills and ponds with thick, smooth ice that would support the eager skaters. Roaring bonfires and hot cocoa sustained the enterprise. By the fire, Hoover held forth on the glories of sledding for Herbert and Allan and recalled how he and Tad had sped down Cook's Hill on store-bought coasters, runners made slick with beeswax. As winter's darkness settled in, the bone-chilled sledders packed into their cars, wrapped themselves in blankets, and snuggled in for the long drive back to

Washington. Fatigued by the cold, but hungry and thirsty, the Hoovers anticipated mugs of hot cocoa, hot coffee, and steaming bowls of beef stew or Virginia ham and beans prepared by their cook. As enjoyable as were these brief family outings, they were no substitute for a real vacation. Bert and Lou had attempted a getaway the previous year to North Carolina, but a freak snowstorm ruined their plans.

Then in June 1918, just before he again left for Europe to survey relief needs, a very tired Hoover accepted an unexpected invitation to spend a weekend fishing at the country home of Jay Cooke in Williamsport, Pennsylvania. Cooke, a prominent Pennsylvania Republican, owned the Ogontz Fishing Club, several miles of very good trout stream on Larry Creek. Ogontz, for whom the camp was named, was an Indian chief in Sandusky, Ohio, who had raised Cooke's grandfather. All the club members were family members, and the stream was fished only from April 15 to June 15, but for generations, the Cooke family had loaned out a rustic old sawmill that had been converted into a six-bedroom house to various family members during the short fishing season. Over the years the Cookes added an icehouse, a woodshed, a cave storage cellar, and a horse barn. In 1916, a room was added to the sawmill so that the men would have a place to play bridge and poker. The entire camp was "very primitive and marvelous," tucked away in an isolated second-growth forest and surrounded on three sides by mountains.[235] A visitor once commented in a letter that the "the four-mile trout stream tumbling over God-made and man-made dams, the clear quiet pools, the hemlocks and laurels, the carpets of tiny white violets, are wonderful."[236]

The Cookes entertained Hoover at their home in Philadelphia. After dinner, a small group of fishermen, including A. J. Heinz, the pickle king, took the night train to Williamsport. The weather was beautiful, clear and fair, and the fishing was good, the party catching as many as thirty trout a day. The small stream had yielded much larger catches in the decades right after the Civil War, but only if the fisherman used live bait. By 1918, upper-crust Americans thought it unsportsmanlike to use live bait, and even the use of wet flies was frowned upon—an English tradition, not an American. The challenge, the more difficult task, was to raise trout by use of a dry fly. It was even more prestigious if the dry fly had been designed and tied by the fisherman himself. The cooler waters of the upper stream produced feisty native rainbows, while the deep pools in the lower stretches hid the larger but more elusive brook trout. After two days of good fishing, good food, and evenings filled with conversation, Hoover holding forth on the trials and tribulations of Belgian relief, the overworked, ambitious humanitarian relaxed. He wrote in the Ogontz Lodge guest book that he had slept better than at any time during the past two years. On the train back to Washington, he likely recalled the wonderful fishing trips he had taken before he was consumed with making money, and perhaps fantasized as well about future escapes to isolated fishing lodges.

Back at the War Food Administration temporary headquarters in "Foggy Bottom," Hoover was once again buried in work. As the war raged in Europe, Hoover stockpiled American supplies, continued to provide aid for Belgium and northern France, and developed a plan to feed the starving Russians, former Allies now out of the war, their country mired in revolution. In September 1918, the Allied offensive drove the Germans back. Germany was near collapse, and it was clear that the war was coming to an end. Hoover realized that nearly all of the peoples of Europe who had been devastated by the fighting would desperately need food. From the Atlantic to Armenia, he said, two of the horsemen of the apocalypse, famine and pestilence, would ride across Europe. Only massive aid from the United States could prevent widespread starvation, political chaos, and the spread of bolshevism. Having no other options, the newly installed social democratic government of Germany reluctantly signed the proffered armistice on November 11, 1918. The extremely harsh terms of the agreement were to guarantee that the German high command could not restart the war. One of the more controversial provisions continued the Allied blockade that prevented Germany from importing food. After four years of vicious combat in which millions died, the huge German Army silently climbed from their trenches and marched back to their country, a hungry nation teetering on the brink of disaster.

President Wilson agreed with Hoover's assessment of European food needs and instructed the Great Humanitarian and a team of specialists to go to Europe on a fact-finding mission. On November 16, at a press conference held before boarding the steamship *Olympic,* Hoover predicted that he would be home before Christmas. It was not to be. Embroiled in feeding a starving Europe, and intimately involved in the political questions that swirled around the Paris Peace Conference, he would remain in Europe for the better part of the coming year. As usual, Hoover worked himself to the brink of exhaustion. Once again, he was successful, and the press worldwide furthered his reputation by noting his accomplishments through references to classical mythology and famous literature: his "colossal achievements," "Herculean endeavors," and "gargantuan undertakings."

Hoover rallied against the continuation of the Allied blockade after the Germans signed the armistice. He laid the blame for Germany's deepening troubles squarely at the feet of hardliners such as Winston Churchill. Hoover developed a dislike for Churchill that he never overcame. Bitterly disappointed in the Treaty of Versailles, he was convinced that the "Carthaginian Peace" would soon plunge Europe once again into war. Hoover argued with all those who would listen that food was the key element in building a lasting peace: "Food Will Win the World." Hungry people would seek radical solutions to alleviate their suffering, he said, and would quickly destroy the fragile new democracies created by the Big Four in Paris.

Unsuccessful at changing the course of the peace process, a worn-out and defeated Hoover prepared to return to his beloved California in the late summer of 1919. Just before leaving Paris, he was pulled aside by French premier Georges Clemenceau, a major contributor to the harsher provisions of the treaty, who fed Hoover's worst fears: "There will be another world war in your time and you will be needed back in Europe."[237] Hoover, however, maintained that he never wanted to see Europe again.[238] As he trudged up the gangway of the *Aquitania* to undertake yet another ocean crossing, he was in too deep a funk to recognize that his efforts had saved the lives of millions of human beings. John Maynard Keynes maintained that Hoover was the only man at Versailles whose reputation was enhanced.[239] The long days at sea did not restore his flagging spirit.

6

The Restorative
Blessings of Nature

The weary, disillusioned titan arrived home in California on September 13, 1919, and at once began to weigh his options. What would he do? What lay in his future? His brother, Tad, had sold all of their British holdings by 1915 and moved his family back to California, where he had opened an office in San Francisco.[240] The Hoover brothers' years as international businessmen working out of London were at an end. Late in the war, Bert had liquidated his last great mining asset, stock in the Bawdwin silver mine in Myanmar, for $2.5 million.[241] He was financially secure, though not fabulously rich; he had not built a fortune in mining as had the Guggenheims, and he was no mogul, no Newport robber baron. Newspaper ownership had attracted him in the past and did so again. The Sacramento *Bee* was for sale, and he made an offer. The Hoover telephone rang constantly, and Western Union delivery boys, enduring the September heat, pedaled hourly between the Palo Alto office and the Hoover home. Job offers, business deals, pleas to run for president, and requests for endorsements and for speaking engagements poured in. A legion of reporters constantly badgered him to discuss everything from the Treaty of Versailles to his thoughts on politics and the future of the country.[242]

Part of what made Hoover so popular with the public was his belief in the American future, built on the American past, in a time of uncertainty. Hoover provided a theory of continuity in a transitional age. For Americans, victory proved more difficult than war: In Paris, incessant squabbling over how to conclude the peace poisoned the process; in Washington, quibbling over the details of the treaty and the proposed League of Nations doomed ratification; rapid wartime economic growth turned to recession in the war's aftermath; race riots erupted in cities; labor union strikes turned violent; subversive red radicals set off bombs; and a flu epidemic killed 22 million people worldwide, 670,000 of them Americans.[243] In the winter of 1918–1919, after a second outbreak of the killer influenza, Lou, worried that her children might contact the disease, sent Herbert and Allan, along with the two Rickard girls, to stay in a house outside Washington in Chevy Chase.[244] The capital was hard hit and hundreds died, but Herbert came down with only a light case, and all the other Hoovers somehow avoided the disease. Added to the confusion pervading the country was Woodrow Wilson's tragic series of debilitating strokes. The nation seemed adrift—leaderless.[245] Hoover's appeal to reason, his commitment to American values, his deep belief in individualism, his progressive political point of view, and his seemingly pragmatic approach to solving problems spoke to many Americans. The Hoover message, a grab bag of attractive if not necessarily compatible ideas, particularly appealed to those in the upwardly mobile but insecure professional classes, a "new national class" that transcended particularism.[246]

Hoover, caught up in a torrent of publicity, wished for time with his family. Since the war's start in August 1914, he had been separated from Lou for long periods of time and had seen even less of his sons, Herbert, now fifteen, and Allan, twelve. Temporarily suspending the fishbowl pandemonium that swirled around him, he put his foot down, regally announcing that he would not answer telephone calls, read letters longer than one page, or give speeches.[247] It was high time, he said, to reacquaint himself with his children and bring his family back together.

As they had in the past, the Hoovers turned for renewal and

solitude to camping and fishing in the places they so loved—the High Sierras and Yosemite National Park. The family purchased a wide array of the best equipment money could buy. Then, with the car packed to overflowing, they struck out on a thirty-day outing in the wilderness, driving, camping, hiking, fishing, dam building, and recording all that they observed in nature.[248] Breakfast consisted of pan-fried bacon, eggs, and flapjacks. A light lunch of sandwiches and fruit held everyone over until dinner, when pan-fried fresh trout, macaroni with fresh-grated cheese and tomato sauce, and slow-baked potatoes filled the hungry campers' stomachs. If a salmon was caught, it was wrapped in green leaves, then in waxed paper and finally in layers of wet newspaper. Buried four inches under the fire, the salmon was baked for fifteen minutes per pound.[249]

Lou's daily explorations greatly expanded her list of flora and fauna, and Hoover was pleased to be able to instruct his sons in the art of fly fishing. His eager audience was also treated to a plethora of fishing stories that started in West Branch, then went on to the Williamette Valley in Oregon, and ended wherever they stood in the High Sierras—territory Hoover knew well from his summers with the U.S. Geological Survey. Herbert and Allan delighted in the attention shown them by their too-long-absent father. For the first time since the Hoover family's attempt to break in through the backdoor of Yosemite in 1905, Bert and Lou returned to their cathedral of nature.

A month in the outdoors with his family, though occasionally interrupted by Western Union or an enterprising reporter, restored Hoover's spirits. Fishing for trout and salmon in the fast rivers of California, coupled with the fishing weekend with the Cookes in Pennsylvania, reawakened in him a desire to fish. Lou, too, wished for time to fish and to ride horses, camp, and explore—particularly California. The Hoovers' return to the great outdoors in their quest for rest, relaxation, solitude, and spiritual renewal was successful, and the happy couple was amply rewarded. Lou sometimes accompanied her husband on various outings, and she also plunged into Girl Scout work and women's amateur athletics.[250] One of her favorite pastimes was to take weeklong horseback camping trips with friends. Bert now sporadically devoted to fishing the same intensity and commitment that he had previously reserved only for work. When not at streamside, Hoover talked frequently with close friends about fish, fishing, and the marvelous array of equipment associated with the piscatorial art—rods, reels, flies, and lures.

Hoover the engineer loved fine equipment, especially well-crafted rods, and he appreciated the art of fly tying. Some of the prized flies that ended up in his book of flies he had purchased years before, many in England, and there were the well-worn original three he had been given by the generous stranger on the North Santium.[251] The colors and variety of flies, the craftsmanship and ingenuity that went into making them, and the endless evolution of successful creations enchanted him as it enchants all fly fishermen.[252] But Hoover claimed that he was no purist and often threatened that if the trout would not rise to the flies, he would resort to bait. He now often speculated on coming fishing trips and on future forays into the wilderness for steelhead and trout. Each spring, the urge to get out into nature in pursuit of fish tugged at his soul, pulling him to streamside. As time went on, Hoover sought out pristine wilderness areas—the more remote, the better.

While the Hoovers camped and fished in the Sierras, work continued on Lou's dream house on the Stanford campus. For years this globe-trotting couple had coped with a life on the go and a home constantly filled with guests. For some time, Lou had wanted to build a spacious permanent home that would comfortably accommodate her growing family, domestic staff, and endless numbers of visitors. While war food administrator in Washington, Bert gave her the green light to build whatever pleased her and not worry about the costs.[253] Lou worked hard on a design and hired an architect, Louis C. Mullgardt. The plan to construct a twenty-room house atop San Juan Hill, at 623 Mirada Drive, for around $60,000, a large sum of money during World War I, was being drawn up while Bert was in the midst of a campaign asking the American people to reduce consumption for the war effort. Somehow the newspapers learned of the Hoovers' building plans and ran the story. The backlash was immediate and the secretary was embarrassed. Lou's dream house was put on hold until after the war. In one sense, Lou was relieved, as she did not like the ornate style Mullgardt proposed.[254] She dismissed the architect and bought a house on the Stanford campus as a temporary base camp in California.

When the war was over but Bert was still in Europe, Lou revived her plans for the house on San Juan Hill. Built in a Spanish flat-roofed style, a fifty-seven-room house with a fireplace in every main room, a beautifully landscaped yard, a swimming pool, and a tennis court, the sprawling complex took two years to complete and cost $137,000.[255] Obviously, Bert had been sincere when he told Lou that "the cost was secondary."[256] The house incorporated the latest technologies. The walls were constructed of reinforced concrete, the main rooms used indirect lighting and opened onto verandas, and the whole structure was fireproof.[257] Lou had included some special architectural features, with a hidden room at the top of a spiral staircase where she could be alone and look out on the front of the house to see what guests were arriving.[258] Bert's study was on the second story and contained two large plate-glass picture windows. The windows allowed a panoramic view across the northern horizon from east to west. On clear days, the view to the northwest included a barely visible Mount Tamalpais across the bay from San Francisco at the base of the Marin peninsula. The other window looked out over the water all the way to Alameda.[259] The study was big, a longish room that allowed Hoover to engage in his unbreakable habit of pacing back and forth as he mulled over solutions to problems.

Brother Tad, who won an appointment on the Stanford faculty in 1918, also purchased a large house on the Stanford campus. The following year, Tad, now called T. J. by family and friends, bought a piece of property along the coast, one that he had eyed for some time, a place called the Rancho del Oso.[260] T. J.'s house, while smaller than his brother's, had thirty rooms spread over three stories. Once again the Hoover brothers and their families were together as they had been in London in the early 1900s, but now the family reunion was more like the brief time the three children had been united in Berkeley in the 1890s because May, her husband, and son were frequent guests at the ranch. T. J., as he had in the past, continued his efforts to unite the family, tolerating May's alcoholic husband for the greater good.

Bert and T. J. regularly fished from beaches hidden in rocky coves.[261] At lunch, the two brothers built "Hoover-style" sandwiches, added condiments, and feasted on an assortment of midwestern side dishes, washed down with cold lemonade. After lunch, Bert particularly liked to sit and sort through colorful pebbles washed up by the breaking waves. For dinner, the catch became the entrée. Later they sat and smoked long-stemmed white clay pipes in front of an open fire. On other occasions, the two climbed the stairs to the comfortable roof garden atop the ranch house for a spectacular view of the Pacific Ocean, a perfect spot from which to watch the California sun slowly sink into the sea. But events soon intervened that rendered the reunion short-lived.

Although Hoover held no public office, he remained in the public eye. As the 1920 presidential race heated up, the Great Humanitarian was courted by both political parties, even though he had long ago registered as a Republican and had supported Teddy Roosevelt's bull moose charge in 1912. He chose not to actively run; disavowed Hoover Clubs, which were springing up like mushrooms around the country; and withdrew his name from presidential primaries when possible. In Michigan, where he could not withdraw, enthusiasts placed his name on both the Republican and Democratic ballots. He came in fourth on the Republican side, but surprisingly, he won the Democratic primary.[262] Only in California did he bow to pressure from those who had organized to advance his candidacy and wished to enter his name on the state primary ballot. This trial balloon assuaged his ardent supporters and provided an opportunity to test voter support for the Treaty of Versailles.[263] He did no campaigning in the California primary, and as he had predicted, he was soundly defeated. He commented that any Hoover "boom," like his son's "flivver," would take "a lot of people to start it, make a lot of noise," but all would have "to walk back home in the end."[264] As a consequence of his entry into California politics, he made an enemy of Sen. Hiram Johnson, a powerful isolationist who very much wanted the Republican presidential nomination and vehemently opposed the Treaty of Versailles and the League of Nations. Hoover, who just as vehemently opposed what Johnson stood for, intended to let the air out of his fellow Californian's presidential campaign. He did so with a faint-hearted effort and thereby incurred the permanent wrath of Johnson.

Summer 1920 found Hoover at the Bohemian Grove encampment for the first time. He had been nominated to this elite circle of mostly Californians and selected for membership in 1913, but his overseas relief work and time as war food administrator had prevented his attendance. The Bohemian Grove, shrouded in secrecy, was infamous because of its lodgelike hocus-pocus ritual—an exclusive Gridiron Club West. "Bohemian" referred to the fact that it provided an organized opportunity for rich, famous, and generally conservative men "to disregard conventional standards of behavior," and "Grove" to the camp's location just north of San Francisco on twenty-seven hundred sprawling acres covered with huge redwoods. For two weeks in July each year on the Russian River, the rich and the famous gathered to cavort in the woods, some say to drink and pee on the ferns. The club began in 1872 as a true haven for bohemians—artists, writers, and entertainers—though it soon took in businessmen and other members of the local elite to help pay the bills. An owl, which graces the club's letterhead and all official publications, became the logo because "a group of newspaper men gathered late in the evening in the club rooms after their papers had been put to bed. They called themselves the night owls."[265] Later, the owl was held up as the symbol of wisdom and silence, and members swore that anything said, heard, or seen at the Grove stayed at the Grove. The club motto, "Weaving Spiders Come Not Here," taken from *A Midsummer Night's Dream*, reminded members that business and politics were suspended while at the camp or in the club, but in reality, over the years, it became a den of weaving spiders.[266]

The first retreat into the bosom of nature, with a cluster of tents pitched on a hillside, took place in 1882 on a mere 160 acres.[267] The successful camp-out, the brainchild of Henry Edwards, a San Francisco businessman and club promoter, was commemorated by a plaque affixed to a beautiful redwood that read, "His hand first led us into the forest."[268] By 1900, the San Francisco business and social elite controlled the club and far outnumbered those from the arts. Unlike most of America's other watering holes for the wealthy, this club awarded artists, writers, musicians, and singers, who provided much of the camp's entertainment, associate membership, and they consequently paid reduced dues.[269] The club's commitment to the arts, though diminished and definitely not avant-garde, was not abandoned.

By the time Hoover first joined the revelers under the sprawling canopy of redwoods, the Grove had grown considerably, and the number of camps had increased dramatically. Though some were quite small, with half a dozen or so members, others had grown to be quite large, with several dozen or more. Associate members developed their own campsites and tended to divide up by occupation, writers in one camp and artists in another. From club offices in a six-story building in downtown San Francisco, the oversight committee maintained the constantly expanding camp.[270] In addition to the seventeen-day summer session, the club sponsored a spring program and a June picnic. The picnic was the only opportunity for members to bring wives to the Grove; women were forbidden at all other times. During the encampment, the wide selection of activities included fishing, trap and skeet shooting, walks on the nature trails, swimming, and canoeing. In addition to what the Grove provided the campers, campsites usually organized around business, professional, or institutional associations had special entertainment or special lunches or drinks that evolved over the years. Of note were the Poison Oaks, who sponsored a special Bull's Ball lunch; the Owl's Nest, who put on a breakfast fete of eggs Benedict and gin fizzes; the Jungle Camp, who specialized in fresh mint juleps; and the Halcyon Camp, who outdid themselves by building the world's largest martini maker, a three-foot glass contraption that dispensed the famous California cocktail—Hoover's favorite drink.[271] Card games of every variety were played: hearts, pinochle, bridge, and poker, often for very high stakes. Hoover described his time at the Grove as the "greatest men's party in the world."

And it was indeed. The opening gathering on Friday evening was a simple affair, as members continued to stream in at all hours from all over the country, some from foreign ports. A short welcoming ceremony at the campfire circle at six-thirty was followed by dinner in the Grove's outdoor mess hall underneath towering redwoods.[272] The long picnic-style tables made from redwood and fashioned in a semicircle were rustic but elegant. Some evenings, the tables were spread with tablecloths or festooned with large bouquets of flowers. All of the tables were adorned with shiny silver gas candelabra, whose flickering yellow flames produced an atmosphere of intimacy.[273] The men came to dinner here every night to eat the best food, talk, and enjoy each other's company. After the opening dinner, entertainment occurred at the campfire circle, but many returned to one of the numerous campsites scattered throughout the reservation to unpack, settle in, and see who had arrived.

The ensuing weeks offered Bohemians a wide array of entertainment, daily lectures, lakeside talks, Friday night entertainment, a ribald often risqué play called Low Jinks, and on the final Saturday night, High Jinks—the Grove extravaganza. The Grove play was usually quite well written and performed by a cast of at least one hundred, often in a Gilbert and Sullivan operatic style or like a Broadway musical or a Cecil B. DeMille dramatic epic. Will Rogers, a onetime guest before it was decided that he talked too long while at the Grove and too much after he left, gibingly likened the play he saw to the Oberammergau.[274] Many of the actors practiced for months to prepare for the performance, and production costs might run into the thousands of dollars. By the 1970s, the cost could be as high as $30,000 for a one-night production.[275]

Guests could come at any time during the encampment, but many tried not to miss the first Saturday evening, as it featured the Cremation of Care, an annual elaborate ceremonial presentation that supposedly freed Bohemians from their heavy responsibilities in order to frolic in the woods for the next two weeks. At the conclusion of the first Saturday night's dinner, the Cremation of Care would begin. Funereal music was heard out in the woods, and men carrying flaming torches and dressed in long red robes with pointed red hoods, solemnly led by a high priest, emerged from the darkness carrying a coffin that bore the body of Dull Care. Imps guarded the coffin, "devil-masked and garbed in crimson, horned and cloven-hoofed, brandishing torches."[276] The Bohemians, two abreast, arms folded, followed the procession to the lake, where they witnessed the coffin being loaded onto a small boat. Across the lake, in front of a forty-foot hollow concrete owl sculpture, a small flame burned in the Lamp of Fellowship. Now unfolded a thirty-minute drama in which a singing tree spirit, a hamadryad, invoked the beauty of nature, its restorative blessings, and the spirit of the Grove. To the tune of "The Barcarole," the song of Venetian gondoliers, Care's coffin slowly floated across the lake. Care was pushed upon a huge pyre by the pallbearers, but just before the torches set the blaze, a loud burst of thunder accompanied by a gust of wind halted the cremation. Laughing, mockingly, Care cried out that the Bohemians were fools if they thought he could be banished, and that once they left the Grove they would be back within the realm he rules. The high priest told Care that those assembled would be satisfied with the two-week respite, crying out, "Midsummer sets us free!" Far from subdued, Care bellowed, "I spit upon your fire." All the torches went out except for the flame in the Lamp of Fellowship. The priest, kneeling, begged for the intervention of the wise owl. The owl assured the priest that two weeks could be purchased, but only if Care was burned with a flame from the Lamp. Quickly the priest relit the torch in the small flame and hurled it onto the pyre. Care once again went up in flames as the orchestra and chorus grew louder. Bohemians began to celebrate, fireworks exploded in the background, and the band played a jazz rendition of "There'll Be a Hot Time in the Old Town Tonight." The encampment was officially open for another year and the spirits of the participant freed. The wise owl had once again granted a two-week indulgence, a temporary suspension of the rules.

Hoover may have recalled, as he stood among the celebrants under a shower of pyrotechnics, that "There'll Be a Hot Time in the Old Town Tonight" was the song played by the U.S. Marines as they entered the besieged city of Tianjin when he and Lou faced the Boxer threat in China. Whatever his thoughts might have been, for Hoover the ritualistic ceremony and the companionship found underneath the spectacular giant redwoods gave him much satisfaction, a feeling of being accepted and at home, both with nature and with other people. These strong feelings may well have been intensified by the traumas of his childhood. But in the protected environment of the Grove, he relaxed, let down his guard, and opened up as he rarely did elsewhere. He truly enjoyed himself and recommended to friends that husbands and wives occasionally take separate vacations. Hoover rarely, if ever, missed a summer session of "the greatest men's party in world."

Back in the whirlwind world of Washington politics, there was little time for Hoover to enjoy the afterglow. Sen. Warren G. Harding of Ohio won the Republican presidential nomination and went on to soundly defeat the Democratic ticket of James Cox, also from Ohio, and Franklin Roosevelt. As Hoover had foreseen, 1920 was a Republican year. But Hoover's incredible reputation, visibility, and growing political clout determined his future. He was offered and finally accepted an appointment as secretary of commerce in Harding's cabinet, but his appointment was not without controversy. A group of Republican senators, which included an outspoken Hiram Johnson, opposed his nomination. Sen. Frank Brandegee of Connecticut summed up the Republican old guard's assessment: "Hoover gives most of us gooseflesh."[277] Harding overcame strident opposition by brokering a deal in which Andrew Mellon, a fabulously wealthy investment banker and aluminum king from Pittsburgh, would become secretary of the treasury. Hoover used the impasse to increase his leverage, persuading Harding to allow him to restructure and expand the Department of Commerce. The president-elect had the last word: "Mellon and Hoover, or no Mellon."[278] Hoover was confirmed by the Senate on March 4, 1921. Plans to become a newspaper magnate evaporated for the second time, as the Hoovers headed back to Washington.

Lou bought a lovely twenty-two-room colonial house near Rock Creek Park at 2300 S Street. It sat on an acre lot that included oak trees from George Washington's era.[279] Like the house in California, this Georgian mansion sat on a hill, commanding a view of the District of Columbia. The rooms of the house contained beautiful artifacts that the Hoovers had purchased in dozens of foreign countries. Of special interest were the hundreds of pieces of Chinese blue porcelain ware—vases, platters, bowls, and large storage jars, many of which sat on Belgian lace doilies obtained during the food relief days.[280] The Hoovers, as usual, promptly established a domestic menagerie. From California came their old Irish terrier Rags, a dog they had acquired in England. A Belgian shepherd, which Hoover named King Tut, soon joined the family—a dog to which he and Lou would become greatly attached. After breakfast, in the backyard garden, Hoover fed Tut unwanted scrambled eggs with a fork.[281] Several cats also moved in, as did pet birds, turtles, and Allan's alligators, which for a short period of time wintered in an upstairs bathtub until they finally moved to the Washington Zoo.[282] To top it all off, two white ducks hung out on the front porch. The house at 2300 S Street, described by one relative as a very Hooverish home, was reminiscent of how the family had lived in London.[283]

Some of the neighbors did not cotton to the intrusive Hoovers. George Myers, the heir to the Bristol-Myers pharmaceutical fortune, who was described as a "terrific little fighting bantam," repeatedly complained about the pets, cats, children, and constant coming and going of guests.[284] Once, in the summer, when the Hoovers were out of town, Myers had two of his servants sneak into the backyard and chop down a magnolia tree he thought kept his grass from growing. Mark Sullivan, the famous journalist with whom Hoover had become good friends when he was war food administrator, and with whom he developed a deep intellectual relationship, lived several houses down the street. Hoover also became good friends with Harlan S. Stone, chief justice of the Supreme Court. Nearly every Sunday evening, they were guests at the Hoovers along with the Rickards. Bert and Lou did not give parties, nor did they often entertain formally, but the house was always full of guests, the best of the new professionals, movers and shakers, people full of new ideas—among them those committed to the economic ideas of Thornstein Veblen and thoughts on efficiency espoused by Frederick Winslow Taylor. It would not be an exaggeration to compare Hoover's openness to the scientific and professional community with that of John F. Kennedy's interest in the "best and brightest," but with one significance difference: Hoover had no interest in the glitter of Hollywood or in its stars. Lou, demonstrating her managerial skills as well as her patience, coped with a husband who sometimes invited three or four different groups of people to their home for the same dinner and forgot he had issued any invitations at all. Constantly busy, Hoover was often preoccupied, forgetful, and hot-tempered.

Kosta Boris, Hoover's valet, whom he had found in Europe in 1919, was dedicated to him, took care of the rambunctious dogs, and constantly amused Herbert and Allan. Tall, dark, and very handsome, he spoke English with a heavy Serbian accent.[285] The boys teasingly called him *"Factum factotum"* which might be loosely translated as "domestic maestro."[286] The Rickard girls and the Hoover boys were fond of listening to the latest music, jazz, on the player piano. Hoover would often cross the living room and glance disapprovingly, eyebrows raised, jowls more pronounced. Allan soon developed a ploy, quickly changing the piano roll and putting on "The Barcarole," one of Hoover's favorites, at his father's approach. Hoover would smile as he passed through the room.[287] Their home at 2300 S Street was a lively "Hooverish" household filled with the noise of children— nieces, nephews, and the offspring of friends, all of whom Lou treated as if they "were her own children."[288] T. J., who had come to dislike travel, rarely came East to visit, nor did May and her family make the long, expensive trip to Washington. To assure that his sister May could make ends meet, Hoover dutifully sent a check for $250 each month.

Hoover settled into Washington, plunged into his new assignment at Commerce, reorganized his neglected fiefdom, and returned to his workaholic ways. His predecessor, Oscar Straus, assured him that the job required no more than two hours a day. His major responsibility would be "putting the fish to bed at night and turning on the lights around the coast."[289] But to the contrary, a whirlwind of activity now besieged the once quiet department. In the eight years that Commerce was under Hoover, the department went from one of the smallest and least important to one of the largest and most influential. The quip in Washington was that "Hoover was Secretary of Commerce and undersecretary of everything else." This left little time for fishing, but despite the empire building, Hoover did manage two or three trips a year. In fact, his opportunities to fish were greatly increased, for the Bureau of Fisheries was within his domain. The temptation was the greater as the bureau also maintained several boats, the coastal survey vessel and lighthouse tender *Kilkenny* among them, which served at the pleasure of the secretary.

Secretary Hoover soon gave in to the temptation to board the *Kilkenny* and fish the Chesapeake. In October 1921, just a few days before his departure, he received an invitation to address the American Electric Railway Association convention in Atlantic City.[290] Hoover was concerned about the economic health and efficiency of the railroads, as the government had operated the lines during the war and they had only been returned to private ownership in 1920.[291] The Hoover solution: go fishing and write the speech on the boat. When the speech was completed, some- where in the middle of the Chesapeake Bay, an aide whisked the document off to Atlantic City, where it was delivered to the assembled railway men by Hoover's assistant, F. W. Feiker. The press jokingly noted, obviously seeing the secretary as a potential president, that Lincoln had jotted down the Gettysburg Address while riding on a train; Wilson typed up his own war message, alone in the wee hours of the morning; and Harding often set the type for his own speeches. Hoover was the first to write a speech in a boat while fishing.[292] But he was not the first to work on a speech while fishing. Daniel Webster was famous for holding forth while wading the stream. Webster's Mashpee Indian guide, John Attaquin, told Grover Cleveland that the senator talked to the fish "mighty strong and fine."[293]

For Hoover, fishing the Chesapeake Bay was a new experience, and his repertoire of fishing skills increased as he learned how to catch rock bass, hardheads (croakers), and perch. As he settled in at Commerce, he would miss few opportunities to get out on the water. Hoover took to the Chesapeake, with its thousands of miles of shoreline, hundreds of smaller bays, coves, and inlets, and honeycombed with islands, and fished there whenever possible. The beauty and diversity of the bay also enticed him to continue his explorations. But never quite free from his feelings of responsibility, whenever Hoover left Washington for a "working vacation," he was loaded down with papers and reports as well as rod and reel.

In June 1922, the Hoover family boarded the *Kilkenny*, sailed the Chesapeake, and viewed the historic plantations along the James River. The Chesapeake provided Hoover an unparalleled opportunity to be with his family, fish, still get in some work, and not be too far from Washington. For a week after Bert and Lou disembarked, their son Allan and a friend of his stayed on the boat. The two young boys had a marvelous time, fishing, sunning, and learning the workings of the boat, and enjoyed being on the water.[294]

Back in the capital, Hoover finished a book he had been working on for several years. It was a short book that set forth his views on how to reconcile the best of American tradition with the rapid changes brought about by modernization and the rise of a mass consumer society. He had begun to ruminate on how Americans differed from Europeans shortly after his arrival in Australia and in 1909 maintained that someday he wanted to write a book on business or social philosophy.[295] In 1922, he finally brought his ideas together in *American Individualism*, an attempt to quell the fears associated with a shifting economic and social paradigm.²⁹⁶ Hoover reassured his readers that America's strength and uniqueness lay in its commitment to individualism. He rejected all of the competing "isms" on the left, as he clearly understood the dangers of the totalitarian utopian worldview.²⁹⁷ He was horrified by the excesses of the Russian revolution.²⁹⁸ He also rejected the reactionary right, as well as those committed to Adam Smith's laissez-faire economics.²⁹⁹ Hoover took a middle-of-the-road progressive internationalist approach that essentially argued that we were free to build whatever kind of world we chose. A system that guaranteed individualism and cut out waste and inefficiency would increase productivity. The nation would flourish economically, and its spirit would be enriched as well as its pocketbook. The role of government was to ensure the right of equal opportunity, to act as an umpire.³⁰⁰ If citizens voluntarily cooperated with one another to ensure the general welfare, then affluence and leisure were within the nation's grasp. The idealism in Hoover's thinking was that the leading elements in any society would voluntarily reach a consensus and the general welfare would triumph over particular interest groups. As secretary of commerce, Hoover was hot to try out his ideas. When many of them did not work out, Hoover postulated that if he had more power—in other words, were he president—they would. *American Individualism* sold well and helped build Hoover's growing political constituency; it was another step on his trajectory to the pinnacle of political power. The response whetted his appetite.

The Bureau of Fisheries was a part of Hoover's growing empire at Commerce, and this made him responsible for the nation's fish. This new responsibility dovetailed neatly with his renewed commitment to fishing. More important, being in charge of both game and commercial fisheries brought out a side of Hoover not previously seen—that of conservationist. While a mining engineer, he had expressed no outrage at the devastation to the landscape and the pollution produced by operations under his management.³⁰¹ His growing concerns for the environment were likely tied to his renewed commitment to fishing. It was blatantly obvious that during the twenty years he had mostly been out of the country, serious declines had occurred in the fish population. The fishing party at Williamsport, Pennsylvania, in 1918 discussed the great number of trout that had once been caught in Larry Creek. During the monthlong camping trip the following year in the High Sierras, environmental degradation was observable. Hoover's boyhood recollection that the limit on the Crooked River in Oregon was one hundred a day contrasted markedly with his recent experience: "The time between bites [had] become longer and longer, and the fish have become wiser and wiser."[302]

As he had done in the past in mining, Hoover evaluated each of the bureaus in his charge and made personnel changes if they seemed warranted. At the Bureau of Fisheries, a longtime employee, Henry O'Malley, took over. In one of his first sessions with his new boss, he woefully described the deplorable condition of U.S. fisheries, a tale of overfishing and government neglect. Hoover responded to his new bureau chief's plea by ordering a scientific study in Alaska, as the territory was under federal control and he would not have to deal with state governments.[303] The report concluded that some salmon spawning streams had been destroyed, and halibut and cod were on the brink of extinction. Hoover offered up legislation, which was hotly opposed by the canners and commercial fishermen. As a compromise, the Commerce Department agreed to a one-year program of voluntary compliance, a method much favored by Hoover, but monitoring proved that as many as 25 percent of all fishermen violated the voluntary restrictions.[304]

Hoover quickly persuaded President Harding to issue an executive order. As justification, he warned that unless tough restrictions were implemented, the fish would soon be gone. He argued that vast fisheries along both coasts had been depleted. He may well have had in mind the disappearance in the 1890s of the huge schools of sardines off the California coast near Lou's hometown of Monterey. In 1924, Congress, after rancorous debate, passed the Alaska fisheries conservation bill.[305] To further safeguard the fishes of the northern Pacific, an international agreement was made with Canada. The restrictions seemed to work in the short run, and in a few years the fish and shellfish returned; halibut, cod, salmon, and crabs were again abundant in the market. By the late 1920s, however, the fish and seafood harvest began to steadily decline again.[306]

For Hoover, legislation or executive orders were always last resorts. "Statism," as he called it, was to be assiduously avoided. He continued to favor voluntarism and believed that when

shown a problem, the American citizen would respond in positive, cooperative ways to solve it. Natural resources had to be
managed and used efficiently. If this occurred, then resources
would be inexhaustible. The Hoover technique was to call a
national conference in Washington, D.C., and invite the leadership from the troubled area to attend. Some attendees objected
to the secretary's approach, pointing out that he controlled the
agenda and knew beforehand what solutions he wanted the conference to reach. Although these conferences appeared open and
looked as if solutions came from debate and compromise on the
floor, they did not. The critics were right. Hoover knew in
advance what he wanted, and the conferences were his way of
getting it. Unavoidably, with Hoover, the conferences and com-
mittees were the "shadow of the man."[307] It seemed to many that
the secretary's top-down administrative style demonstrated his
distrust of the very democratic process he so heralded.[308] That
Hoover had to be in control, in charge, was well established long
before he arrived in Washington. It would prove to be one of his
greatest weaknesses.

As the secretary analyzed the state of fishing throughout the
nation, he was handed a platform for his emerging views. In
1922, Williamson H. Dilg of Chicago, along with fifty-three other
men concerned about the decline in fish and the pollution of the
nation's waterways, organized the Izaak Walton League of America. Will Dilg was an uncompromising, combative firebrand for
conservation, "a charismatic evangelist."[309] Stumping Illinois,
then the Midwest, and eventually most of the nation, this tireless
crusader had enrolled one hundred thousand members by
1925.[310] To spread the word more effectively, he conceived the
idea of a magazine that featured prominent outdoor writers and
hard-hitting articles on environmental polluters and abusers. The
first issue of *Izaak Walton League Monthly: Defender of Americas
Out-of-Doors* in August 1922 included a clarion call to conservation featured on the front cover. The manifesto was written by
the popular writer Emerson Hough, whose novel *Covered Wagon*
was a best-seller. Hough attacked the federal and state bureaus,
other conservation organizations, the private hunting and fishing clubs, and sportsmen themselves—no one was spared. The
renowned fisherman, outdoorsman, and novelist Zane Grey was
in charge of a regular column on saltwater fishing. Dr. James A.

Henshall, author of the popular *Book of the Black Bass,* went after polluters and state legislatures that failed to rectify the painfully obvious decline in fish. In a nostalgic emotional appeal, Dilg published a two-page poem by Robert H. Davis titled "Rape of the River." Among these outdoor celebrities was Hoover, who, along with conservationist and newly elected govenor of Pennsylvania Gifford Pinchot, contributed short statements supporting Dilg's founding principles.[311]

Hoover's overview outlined his ideas on fish and fishing— the noble piscator, wholesome recreation, voluntary restrictions, prudent management, and a dramatic increase in fish nurseries and fish—many of the ideas that he had explored in *American Individualism.*[312] Hoover recognized—in fact, worked hard to strengthen—the burgeoning consumer society. This new society, which spread affluence more evenly, would create an increase in leisure time—time that could be spent badly or in a positive way. Hoover saw the outdoors as an ideal place for "constructive rejuvenating joy."[313] But Hoover and the Ikes, as members of the Izaak Walton League were soon called, recognized that constructive leisure outdoors would only increase pressures on the already threatened environment. Hoover became the honorary president of the league from 1926 to 1932.[314] The league, in agreement with Hoover's thinking, endorsed his views and supported his Alaska fishing proposals. The support was significant, for unlike its rival conservation organizations, Dilg's was a power to be reckoned with. Beyond their concern for the environment and desire for constructive leisure, Hoover and Dilg shared a deep love of nature and found spiritual renewal in the outdoors. As Hoover began to put down on paper his thoughts about the importance of fishing and nature, he was surely inspired by the words of Dilg: "My senses plead for the peace of forest glades, and my feet search for the feel of the trail. My eyes strain to view the flaming set of the sun and to watch the birds winging for home."[315]

Hoover's Alaska visit in 1923 was not just an ordinary inspection tour geared to solicit support for his fishing conservation policies. It would turn out to be his most bizarre and tragic fishing trip. President Harding, who was overworked and suffering from heart trouble, needed a vacation, but that was not the only purpose of the trip. Alaska was an administrative nightmare,

Williamson H. Dilg, right, founder of the Izaak Walton League of America. COURTESY IZAAK WALTON LEAGUE OF AMERICA NATIONAL ARCHIVES

with five cabinet officers and twenty-eight bureaus exercising authority over the region.[316] The president would conduct an inspection tour and then work out a reasoned reorganization plan, one in which Hoover hoped to play a leading role. A further incentive for Harding was his looming reelection campaign; he was less well known in the western states, and he wished to test out his ideas on the public. An extended presidential trip would generate a huge amount of press coverage. Harding would get to know the West Coast, and the West Coast would get to know him. He christened the trip a "voyage of discovery."[317] To Hoover's surprise, he was a last-minute addition to the presidential party, which included among its sixty-seven guests House Speaker Frederick Gillett of Massachusetts; a fellow Iowan, Secretary of Agriculture Henry Wallace, with whom Hoover often clashed; Secretary of Labor Hubert Work; Admirals Hugh Rodman and Joel Boone; Hoover's assistant, W. C. Mullendore; journalists Charlie Michelson of the New York *World* and Harold Phelps Stokes of the New York *Evening Post;* and a couple from Ohio who were friends of President and Mrs. Harding. The Hoovers caught up with the tour at Tacoma, Washington, on July 3.[318]

En route to Tacoma, the presidential train stopped in all the major cities from St. Louis west, and many of middling size to boot. It was a marathon, and usually this was the kind of campaigning Harding loved. He frankly said, "I like to go out into the country and 'bloviate.'"[319] Extemporaneous speaking was his forte. In each city, the president bloviated on a different subject, laying out the administration's positions and accomplishments. After the speeches, he shook hands with long lines of well-wishers and attended a large number of official functions. At various stops, a congressional delegation, the governor, and key politicians boarded the presidential train and rode at least partway across their states. At dozens of whistle stops, the president performed for the voters. Near Hutchinson, Kansas, the train stopped and Harding helped harvest wheat. Though dressed in white trousers and blue blazer, "he won the admiration of the crowd by taking his turn at the tractor."[320] Harding arrived in Tacoma exhausted, his blood pressure hovering around 180.[321]

Aboard the navy transport *Henderson*, Hoover found Harding upset and run down. The president invited him as a fourth at bridge, but little did he suspect the game would run from early morning until late into the night. Several days into the trip, Hoover maintained that Harding privately asked him what he would do if he suspected scandal in his administration. Hoover counseled the president to publicly come clean, but when he asked him pointed questions, Hoover reported that Harding

President Warren G. and Florence K. Harding, Metlakatla, Alaska,
July 8, 1923. COURTESY KEYSTONE MAST, UNIVERSITY OF CALIFORNIA–RIVERSIDE

remained silent.[322] Harding did reveal that he had discovered
that Jesse Smith in the Department of Justice had accepted loans
from oil concerns that did business with the government. He told
Hoover that he had confronted Smith and told him he would
be fired. Smith hurried home, burned his papers, and then shot
himself in the head.[323] Everyone knew that Smith had committed
suicide, but the reasons why were speculative. As the *Henderson*
cruised north through the narrow channels off the Alaska coast,
the president relaxed somewhat and seemed to be enjoying himself. Hoover wrongly assumed that Harding knew far more than
he had revealed. Harding may well have just been asking Hoover
if he knew anything. But from that point on, Harding's visible
stress, which was due to his failing heart, was interpreted by
Hoover as anxiety over scandal in his administration.[324] Naturally the secretary had serious concerns over what might have

befallen the administration, as he was a key player in it. Meanwhile, Harding spent hours viewing the spectacular scenery and continued to play round after round of bridge into the early hours of the morning.

Hoover often spent long days ashore, having scheduled hearings on his fishing restrictions program in several Alaskan cities. The president, the first American head of state to visit "Seward's Folly," went ashore, too, to participate in long welcoming ceremonies that surrounded each landing. Metlakatla was the first stop. The tiny fishing village, composed of a cannery, a wooden church, and a few wooden houses, greeted Harding's party with a Indian missionary band in white duck pants.[325] A crowd of about one hundred Indians surrounded the president. Some were dressed as working- or middle-class Americans, others were in native costume, and a few women were decked out in the latest flapper fashion. Metlakatla, however, was not just any ordinary Alaskan fishing village; it was an opportunity for a brief Hoover family reunion. Hoover's uncle Henry John Minthorn, who had died a few years earlier, had been a missionary in this village, a rolling stone to the end of his life. Aunt Laura, with whom Hoover had lived for six years, was a resident missionary who still worked among the Indians of Alaska's coast. Harold Phelps Stokes of the New York *Evening Post* described her as having "the light of the great cause . . . in those eyes, as one sees it so frequently in the eyes of devoted men and women working in the far mission fields of Hindustan or the Yangtse valley."[326] Hoover was genuinely glad to see her and insisted that she come aboard the *Henderson*. She agreed and rode with her nephew to the next stop—Ketchikan.[327]

For the next several weeks, the presidential party worked its way up the coastline visiting cities, attending receptions, surviving receiving lines, and holding hearings on fisheries issues. This whirlwind of activity, especially the train trip on the recently completed government line from Anchorage to Fairbanks, only increased the pressure on the president's heart—he tired easily, slept fitfully, and did not recover. The party continued to enjoy the wild Alaskan scenery, dined sumptuously on fresh seafood, and participated in the nightly sing-alongs. Lou Hoover even danced with Adm. Joel Boone, the president's physician.[328] Her husband did not like to dance, but he eagerly looked forward to an opportunity to fish. On July 18, the *Henderson* anchored at Seward. Hoover arranged for his meeting to end by eleven o'clock so that he could at last go fishing. He was joined by Mullendore and three others. Time was a factor, because nearly every afternoon, strong sea breezes churned up swells three to six feet in height. A launch was lowered, and the fishing party cruised up Resurrection Bay on a calm sea in search of a good fishing spot. The small launch was dwarfed by the wild Alaskan landscape, hemmed in by massive headlands that substituted for shore. Visible through breaks in the headlands were open alpine meadows surrounded by forests of spruce, hemlock, and alder, framed by towering snow-covered peaks, a landscape whose icy beauty harbored danger. A productive spot was found, and the men pulled sea bass and rock perch from the cold waters. Mullendore landed a large silver salmon, as did Alaska state senator E. E. Chamberlain. Hoover, having no luck with salmon flies, switched to trolling with spoons, but this too failed. He caught no fish.[329]

The next morning, the *Henderson* sailed for Valdez, where the party toured the Richardson Trail; viewed spectacular mountain scenery, waterfalls, and huge glaciers; and continued on to sightsee in Cordova. Secretary Wallace wrote home that the most interesting person he met on the whole trip was a woman in Valdez named Spitting Maud, "one of the notorious characters of the mining days."[330] On July 22, the ship reached Sitka, the old Russian capital. Crates of huge king crabs were brought aboard, a gift from the city to the president. As in Seward, only a half-day program was scheduled, and Hoover quickly arranged a fishing foray. Two small fishing boats were hired, and the fishermen traveled sixteen miles to a forest-covered emerald green island that the guides heralded as a good place to fish. Mullendore and Michelson did well trolling, catching thirteen salmon, two over twenty pounds, and one sea bass. The Hoover boat also was successful. Mullendore called the fishing expedition "a great afternoon of sport."[331]

Three days later, after sailing along the Alaska coast line, the *Henderson* passed through the Seymour Narrows and dropped anchor in the placid waters of Queen Charlotte Sound at the mouth of the Campbell River, one of the most famous salmon fishing rivers in Canada.[332] In the nineteenth century, the Campbell supported tens of thousands of beautiful green-backed tyee

Hoover, William C. Mullendore, and unidentified journalist, Resurrection Bay, Seward, Alaska, August 1923.

COURTESY KEYSTONE MAST, UNIVERSITY OF CALIFORNIA–RIVERSIDE

salmon, but the net boats, as they had done up and down the west coast of both North and South America, reduced the fish populations drastically.[333] The president decided not to fish, but Hoover, Lou, Secretary Wallace, Admiral Rodman, Edmund Starling, head of the Secret Service detail, and five others clambered into dinghies to fish the sound. The fishing guides rowed the prestigious guests back and forth across the mouth of the river. Several caught large cod, but Mullendore disparaged that cod gave no fight and were no fun to catch. He called them lazy "hogs of the sea."[334]

By three o'clock in the afternoon, most of the fishermen had had enough. The Hoovers had caught no fish, but their spirits were not dampened, so while the rest of the group went off to sightsee and drink Canadian beer (a rare legal opportunity as Prohibition was the law in the United States), Bert, Lou, and a few others returned to the river's mouth to fish. Hoover, trolling with a spoon, soon hooked into a large salmon, which he battled for more than an hour. When the fish was finally rolled into the boat, the secretary was pleased that it weighed fifty pounds. Admiral Rodman, chagrined by Hoover's good fortune, headed to shore to buy spoons, salmon flies, and other lures favored by the local fishermen, swearing that he would catch a fish bigger than Hoover's.[335] A few years earlier, in 1919, Zane Grey and his brother R. C. had fished the Campbell and caught forty- and fifty-pound salmon on locally crafted large silver spoons, that looked like, moved like, and were almost the size of a herring.[336] Five large salmon were landed, but the admiral suffered disappointment despite his special Campbell River spoons. With Alaska's long summer days, the Hoovers did not return to dock until nine-thirty that evening.[337] Tired and hungry, Hoover had the *Henderson*'s cooks prepare the day's catch for a late dinner.

Early the next morning, the *Henderson* weighed anchor and sailed for Vancouver, some ninety miles to the south. Hoover recalled that it was an "exceptionally hot day in July. There were great crowds, long parades, and many receptions. The President rode through the city bareheaded in the heat. He was called upon for five different speeches."[338] The next day in Seattle was even worse. Harding, while addressing sixty thousand people in the football stadium at the University of Washington, faltered, clutched the podium, and knocked his speech to the ground. Hoover picked up the pile of scattered papers and quickly rearranged them in the right order. The president continued without further incident.[339] That evening, the president returned to his private railroad car, sailed his straw hat across the sitting room, and said to Boone: "Doctor, I'll tell the world that one Warren Harding has had a most strenuous and fatiguing day and he is an exhausted man."[340] Harding's handlers at last realized that the president could not keep up the pace, yet no one suspected the seriousness of his condition. The stop in Portland was canceled, and the train proceeded on to San Francisco, but the trip would take another two days. Harding's other doctor, Charles Sawyer, and Secretary Work, who had been a practicing physician, were convinced that the president was experiencing an attack of ptomaine poisoning induced by eating Sitka crabs. He would be fine, they said, after he had rested. That night, the president was sick to his stomach and could not sleep. On the second night, Harding was even worse. Somewhere in northern California, in the middle of the night, Boone examined the president's heart and discovered that it was dilated.

In the morning, Hoover, Work, Sawyer, and Boone, as well as members of Harding's staff, decided he would go by ambulance to the Palace Hotel. Boone urged Hoover to contact Dr. Ray Lyman Wilbur, Hoover's old friend and now president of Stanford University, and arrange for Dr. Charles Cooper, a heart specialist, to see Harding immediately upon his arrival in San Francisco on Sunday July 29. Harding, now feeling better, refused the ambulance, dressed, and walked out into the railroad yard to a waiting limousine.[341] Tragically, the President would not leave the Palace Hotel alive. For a week Harding's condition seesawed. Agent Starling stopped by on Thursday afternoon to chat and complained to the president that he felt the fishing in Alaska was quite poor.[342] On the evening of August 2, while his wife, Florence, read to him, he suffered a major heart attack, recovered for a few minutes, and then died suddenly.[343] Hoover was one of the first to enter Harding's suite and soon left visibly shaken, tears streaming down his cheeks.

Those in the official party now bore the awesome responsibility of transporting the dead president back to Washington. The coffin was placed on risers so that it could be seen from outside the Pullman car. The train left San Francisco in the early evening of August 3, drawing large crowds of mourners in each town it passed through. In Omaha, throngs crowded the depot, and the high bluffs on the Iowa side of the Missouri River were thick with people. Chicago turned out as many as a million and half of its citizens. The police and the Secret Service walked in front of the funeral train, pushing back those who had broken through the security barricades and spilled onto the tracks. In Ohio, Harding's home state, some claimed that people lined the greater part of both sides of the tracks from the Indiana to the West Virginia border.[344] The public learned that Harding's favorite hymn was "My Redeemer Liveth." Hoover lamented: "Soon at every station and every crossroads the people sang as we passed. At the many places where we stopped a moment to give the people a chance of expression, bands and orchestras played it. My chief memory of that journey is of listening to this hymn over and over again, all day and long into the night."[345] The train reached Washington on August 7, a four-day trip. After an impressive parade through the streets of Washington, Harding's body was on view in the East Room of the White House. The following day, the coffin was moved to the rotunda of the Capitol, then he was ceremonially returned to his hometown of Marion, Ohio, where he was buried on August 9. The new president, Calvin Coolidge, and his entire cabinet were a few of the many who made the long trip from Washington to Marion.[346] Several days later, the exhausted government officials made their way back to the nation's capital. For Hoover, this bizarre five-week journey, his strangest fishing trip, finally came to an end.

Over the next year, Hoover continued to expand the Department of Commerce and deal with foreign trade, foreign loans, conservation, water resources, rural electrification, standardization, specification, better housing, better children, aviation, radio broadcasting, and a plethora of other projects. One of his biggest challenges was learning to work with his new boss. Coolidge was a radically different man than the more affable Harding. Harding had liked Hoover, admired his abilities, and gave him great latitude. Hoover, of course, took maximum advantage of this favorable situation.[347] Coolidge was more guarded, a politically savvy manipulator who was a master at outmaneuvering potential opposition. Many of those around him, behind his back, called him "the little fellow." Hoover immediately raised the new president's suspicions.[348] Coolidge suspected, rightly, that Hoover, whom he called "the wonder boy," wanted his job.[349] Then, too, Hoover caused problems by interfering in other departments' affairs and touching off bureaucratic feuds that would have to be resolved by the president. Last, and perhaps most important for the niggardly Coolidge, Hoover's long list of projects all cost money.[350] But Coolidge, forced to deal with the scandals still emerging from the Harding era, needed the immensely popular, competent, and untainted Hoover. The empire builder marched on under the careful watch of the chary president.

During the winter of 1924, Hoover branched out and undertook another new, but much more dramatic, kind of fishing. On his first working vacation in Florida, he went deep-sea fishing in the Florida Keys. How this came about remains unclear, though it likely was the result of a recommendation tendered to Hoover by Fred Walcott, a longtime associate and fellow angler, who had spent two weeks fishing in the Miami area a few years earlier.[351] But it may also have been the lure of the famous Long Key Fishing Camp. Newspaper stories and magazine articles on the glories of Florida abounded, many on the good fishing and the beauty and uniqueness of the Keys. The Long Key camp was nestled beneath a huge grove of elegant coconut palm trees that had been planted in the 1880s to produce rope for the navy.[352] In October 1908, the Key West *Citizen* reported, "Six buildings are being erected at Long Key for the use of tourists, and incidentally to allow the traveling public to stop over here and enjoy some of the best fishing in the world."[353] Business must have been good, because the following year, the camp included a seventy-five room, two-story hotel and fourteen cottages. In 1911, millions of Americans learned of Long Key when the famous writer Zane Grey came to fish, write, and winter. Grey, the reigning king of outdoor writers, passionately pursued the popular kingfish and managed to complete another novel, a best-seller, *The Light of the Western Stars*.[354] Grey eventually wrote nine books and published dozens of articles on the adventure and art of fishing. Many concentrated on the challenges of sportfishing, hooking the "big game" of the deep. His first fishing book, *Tales of Fishes*, written in 1919, was hailed by the *New York Times* as a classic to be treasured by the followers of Izaak Walton.[355] That information alone would have been enough to send Hoover, an enthusiastic reader of Grey's novels and fishing stories, scurrying to Florida.[356] In the High Sierras, Hoover had followed in the shadow of John Muir and Mark Twain. Now, in Florida, it was Zane Grey and Izaak Walton.

Year after year, Grey, like a migratory bird, returned to the isolated beauty of Long Key. In 1917, he and a group of other fishing enthusiasts founded the Long Key Fishing Club, declaring that they wished "to develop the best and finest traits of sport, to restrict the killing of fish, to educate the inexperienced angler by helping him, and to promote good fellowship."[357] Grey served as president from 1917 to 1920. The fishing club brought more notoriety to the Keys when a tournament was established that awarded gold, silver, and bronze buttons (medals) for catching large fish on specified tackle. The club was maniacal in its specificity. Florida deep-sea fishing opened on December 14 and ended on April 15. Club members who caught tarpon over 160 pounds received a gold button, silver for tarpon over 130 pounds, and bronze for those over 100 pounds. Awards were given as well to the person catching the largest bonefish on a six-thread line, and a special award was reserved for the woman using a twelve-thread line who landed the largest kingfish.

Stubborn and independent, when it came to fishing Grey was also an innovator. The sailfish, derogatorily named the boohoo, was not fished and was disliked because it would take bait meant for the more desirable kingfish. Grey's pursuit of the sailfish with light tackle opened up a whole new avenue of fishing. In the faddish 1920s, hooking a big sailfish was the ultimate achievement. Hundreds of would-be Zane Greys flooded to south Florida every winter in their quest for a trophy fish that would end up stuffed and hanging on their den or office wall. But at the Long Key Fishing Club, a fisherman deservedly won the top prize if he used nine-thread line to successfully subdue the season's longest sailfish. Only the most skilled or luckiest fishermen could successfully battle a large fighting sailfish on nine-thread line. Another challenge was to win a specially crafted rod offered by Grey's brother for the largest sailfish over sixty pounds caught on a six-ounce tip and twelve-thread line. Gold buttons were given for sailfish over sixty-five pounds, silver for over fifty-five pounds, and bronze for over forty pounds. The Long Key Club was a game fish sportsmen's paradise.

Headquartered at the Long Key Fishing Camp, Hoover immediately took to this tropical paradise and eagerly learned the art of catching sailfish, tarpon, marlin, barracuda, kingfish, bonita, amberjack, dolphin, wahoo, black sea bass, and eventually the cagey fighting bonefish. For the overworked secretary, hooking onto a large kingfish or huge tarpon that fought for hours was exhilarating—the height of sport. His goal was to hook a six- to ten-foot sailfish, but it was a pleasure he would be denied for many years. In the evening, sunburned and dead tired, the Hoover party ate grilled fish and reminisced about the day's catch. Hoover was always at his best in this intimate environment, surrounded by a small group of friends. He was sometimes the raconteur, holding forth on political subjects such as voluntary cooperation and standardization, or he might elaborate on mining in Australia, fighting the Boxers in China, or surveying the High Sierras. Given his travels, his repertoire of fascinating stories was nearly inexhaustible. Committed to getting the most out of his vacation, the secretary rose early, a lifetime habit, so that he might get in a full day of fishing. With a strong cup of coffee with cream and sugar in hand, he would greet later risers with "Isn't it a beautiful morning?" Hoover was elated with his Florida fishing experience, and he returned to deep-sea fish in the winter as often as possible. He later even managed a couple of west coast forays south into Mexican waters and on and around the islands off California.

Starting around 1923–24, Hoover's fishing trips and vacation time began to take on a pattern. In January or February, he traveled to Florida to deep-sea fish. In the spring, he took short trips on the Chesapeake or went trout fishing in the vicinity of Washington, D.C., but ranged as far as the Brule River in Wisconsin or Larry Creek in Pennsylvania. His regular pilgrimages to the Bohemian Grove afforded an opportunity, before or after, to fish the western lakes and rivers or do some deep-sea fishing in California, although this did not commence until 1926. In the early fall, it was back to the Chesapeake and then off to Florida, and then the cycle was repeated. Conferences sponsored by the many bureaus of the Commerce Department afforded additional opportunities.

In the summer of 1924, shortly after Calvin Coolidge won the Republican presidential nomination, Charles K. Field, Shirley Baker, and Hoover, members of the Stanford pioneer class of 1895, were invited to establish a separate camp at the Bohemian Grove. The Stanford men picked Kitchen Hill, a site across a gully named Pioneer's Gulch that was up a steep incline behind the Low Jinks stage.[358] So began Cave Man Camp, so called because of a large concrete caveman statue that had been abandoned on Kitchen Hill by previous frolickers after a play in 1910 titled "The Cave Man." Returning nearly every year, Hoover, Field, Baker, and their guests slept in tents perched atop the hill. In the winter of 1928–29, the Grove changed the rules and allowed permanent buildings.[359] A building boom hit Bohemia, and the Valhalla in the woods was reorganized, with the construction of an art gallery, a small hospital, a bar and grill, a clubhouse, a museum, a store, and miles of paved roads. Camps such as Stowaway and Mandalay built impressive complexes.[360] The men of Cave Man Camp began to build log cabins around a central screened-in dining hall and clubhouse, and to landscape the site. Eventually, nine cabins that accommodated thirty people straddled the ravine.[361]

As a founder of Cave Man Camp, Hoover was in the position to issue a number of invitations to America's power elite. To be invited to attend the Bohemian Grove summer encampment was tacit recognition in corporate and business circles that one had "arrived." Over the years, the Hoover guest list came to read like a who's who of rich, powerful Republicans. Hoover continued to revel in the activities of the annual encampment and was often chosen as a speaker for the final night's bonfire or lakeside inspirational talk. Hoover remained a loyal enthusiast of the Grove for the rest of his life, looking forward to each year's encampment. The Grove must be added to his growing list of escapist outdoor activities and to the rise in his fortunes. For Hoover, one of the greatest attractions was that as a member, he was protected from the public eye, guaranteed that anything said or heard was confidential, and assured the hale and hearty companionship he so arduously sought. Here was a place, among the tranquil beauty of the giant redwoods, where Hoover could relax and openly express opinions. "The Bohemian Grove is ultimately the American Dream come full circle: from cabin in the woods to cabin in the woods, in one generation."[362]

At the end of another summer's sojourn in sunny California, the Hoovers were back in the stifling heat of the capital. A respite in late August was a trip aboard the *Kilkenny* to fish and explore the lower Chesapeake Bay. The weather turned foul and forced a curtailment of the voyage, but the bass and hardnose fishing around Crisfield, Maryland, proved to be very good.[363] The Hoovers and their friends often fished the Chesapeake from the decks of the *Kilkenny*, though only a few of these outings are recorded. Mark Sullivan, Jr., recalled that in 1925, the Sullivans were guests of the Hoovers on a Department of Commerce vessel that used the canal system between the Chesapeake and Delaware

Bays, cruised the Intracoastal Waterway along the New Jersey coast, and then followed the Hudson River to West Point. The boat returned to New York, and everybody got off except Mark Jr., who now had the boat to himself all the way back to Baltimore—a marvelous adventure for a boy of seventeen.[364]

February 1925 found Hoover back in Long Key, Florida, in a renewed effort to hook a large sailfish. He was once more denied the prize—no sailfish. But compensation came on February 24 when trolling northeast of Key West onboard the *Kilkenny*. A fish forcefully struck Hoover's line, triggering a fierce battle. The fighting fish that broke the surface of the clear, blue-green waters was a large amberjack. An hour later, the secretary successfully landed his fish. At the dock, the amberjack weighed in at eighty-seven pounds, not a record, but big enough to merit a medal from the Long Key Fishing Club. Both the Key West and Miami press reported the catch, and the secretary returned to his busy schedule in Washington, pleased with his latest piscatorial triumph. A telegram received by Hoover on June 5, however, set in motion an extraordinary episode.[365] Florida in the mid-1920s was experiencing a great land boom. The stock market was going up like a Fourth of July skyrocket. Hundreds of outsiders came to Florida flush with cash and intent upon spending it to secure for themselves a place in the tropical sun. Miami grew at a tremendous pace and expanded its city limits some twenty-five miles to the south. The Miami Chamber of Commerce and the real estate boomers were ever on the lookout for publicity and more hype for their advertising campaign. Hoover's amberjack was likely appropriated into newly printed real estate brochures. At the very least, the big fish was intended as a featured part of their coming advertisements. Surely, the boosters argued, this large fish was caught in the new Miami suburbs. Perhaps an unconscious element in the speculators' actions was that they were unknowingly only months away from economic disaster. By year's end, the boom was bust.

The June 5 telegram that arrived at 6:07 P.M. was a request from the Key West *Daily News* asking Hoover to confirm the February reports that the capture occurred in Key West's jurisdiction.[366] Key West, mired in controversy over Miami's expansionist moves, smelled a rat, had seen the brochures, or had a mole in the Miami Chamber of Commerce. Only minutes behind the

Hoover off Long Key, Florida, 1926. COURTESY HERBERT HOOVER LIBRARY

Daily News, the Miami *Herald* wired Hoover at 6:15 P.M.: "PLEASE WIRE STATEMENT COD AS TO LOCATION OF EIGHTY SEVEN POUND AMBERJACK CAUGHT BY YOU FEBRUARY TWENTY FOUR OUR UNDERSTANDING THIS FISH WAS CAUGHT OFF SOUTHERN SUBURB OF MIAMI PLEASE WIRE AT ONCE."[367]

Hoover may have been dismayed by this outlandish capitalist competition, although he may have recalled his own days in Salem as an enterprising salesman for his uncle Minthorn's land speculation operation, which hyped the marvels of Oregon in advertisements throughout the nation. But at 6:30 P.M., the great amberjack controversy took a different turn when a telegram arrived from Jacob Rosengrowen, president of the Miami Chamber of Commerce. Rosengrowen pleaded with Hoover to confirm that the fish in question was caught in the new Miami annexation and said that his denial would "DO IRREPARABLE DAMAGE TO HUNDREDS OF MILLIONS OF DOLLARS OF PROPERTY AND WOULD INVALIDATE INVESTMENT IN ADVERTISING AND SELLING CAMPAIGN NOW ORGANIZED."[368]

Fifteen minutes later, at 6:45 P.M., another telegram arrived, this one from William Jennings Bryan, four-time Democratic presidential candidate, former secretary of state, and about to be star prosecution witness in the Scopes Monkey Trial in Tennessee. Bryan, who was always dependent upon his income, needed money and ended up working as the public spokesman for the South Miami Realtors Association. The leather lunged orator did not ask Hoover to lie. Rather, he stressed the importance of the amberjack catch to the real estate tycoons and confirmed that "THEIR CASH OFFER TO YOU IS MADE WITH MY KNOWLEDGE AND HAS MY SUPPORT."[369] On the heels of the Bryan telegram, at 6:50 P.M., came an offer from Rosengrowen of $5,000, held in escrow, in return for a statement from Hoover that his fish was caught in Miami waters.[370] Not to be outdone, at 7:30 P.M., the Izaak Walton League of America, fast friends of the secretary, wired that they didn't care where Hoover caught the fish; all that mattered was that he had caught it, and the amberjack's weight was such that the league was sending an official button.[371] Finally, the commandant of the Navy Yard Key West, at 7:56 P.M., fixed the exact location of the catch—fifteen knots, eight furlongs northwest of Key West.[372] Hoover had been close to the new demarcation line established by the Miami City Council, but he was roughly two miles on the Key West side. The last word, the bon mot, arrived at 7:56 from the Los Angeles Chamber of Commerce, who asked Hoover to hold tight until "FINAL ACTION ON LEGISLATION EXTENDING EASTERLY CITY LIMITS OF LOS ANGELES TO GULF STREAM."[373] The lesson for Hoover was that as he became more and more of a public figure, his privacy became more and more difficult to guard. On his next trip to Florida, he was successful in limiting press coverage of his vacation time, for little is known of his 1926 stay at the Long Key Fishing Club other than that he took along Mark Sullivan and Justice Harlan Stone. Again, Hoover did not hook a sailfish.

The tensions between Hoover's demand for privacy and his insatiable craving for publicity were exacerbated by his accomplishments and his presidential ambitions. Not only did the press and public want to know more about the leading candidate for the Republican nomination, they wanted to know more about him personally. What he liked to eat, what his hobbies were, how often he went to church, what his family was like, and where he vacationed were all questions he was asked and questions he skirted. For a reporter sent to interview Hoover, the human interest story was almost impossible to get. Hoover liked to talk about issues, programs, theory, and accomplishments, not about himself or his family. He rattled off data by the hour. In a sense, Hoover was pulled in two directions at the same time. His ambition, his accomplishments pulled him into the public spotlight, while the shy, retiring part of his character pushed him to seek secluded private retreats in the wilderness.

The opportunity to build the ideal mountain fishing retreat was not long in coming. Ray Lyman Wilbur, Hoover's friend since Stanford days, a fellow Bohemian and fishing companion, recommended that a group of like-minded individuals go in together and purchase eighty acres located deep in the wilderness of northern California. Wilbur had hunted and fished in Siskiyou County since World War I and was enthusiastic about an old ranch on Wooley Creek at the point where it was joined by Haypress Creek. A few miles farther downstream, Wooley Creek flowed into the Salmon River, and the Salmon was but a short distance from the famous Klamath. The Indians considered the creek an ideal place to camp because the woods opened onto a large meadow. Trout were abundant, and a salt lick at the edge of the creek attracted a large number of deer and other game. Wooley Creek was named for a miner and rancher who had originally homesteaded in the area.[374] A dilapidated log house and several outbuildings were still standing, probably built by a local Karok Indian named Jimmie Johnson around the turn of the century. Jimmie died of tuberculosis while still quite young, and his brother, a local guide named Elmer "Happy Hooligan" Johnson, took over Wooley Creek Ranch.[375] By 1925, the property was owned by a couple named Clarence and Villa Jackson. In April, on Wilbur's recommendation, Wilbur, Timothy Hopkins, Fred H. Smith, Alonzo E. Taylor, and Thomas M. Williams purchased Wooley Creek. A year later, in April 1926, Hoover lent his name, along with the other five, to the incorporation of the Wooley Creek Association, as the members mischievously dubbed themselves. The association proclaimed a dedication to good fishing, hearty fellowship, good cooking, deep thinking, and spiritual renewal in the wild.

In the fall, Hoover and Wilbur visited their Shangri-la. To reach the ranch, seven miles distant from the nearest road, the new owners rode horses over steep and twisting trails underneath the canopy of a dense forest of redwoods. Hoover soon appreciated the sanctuary afforded by the site, an almost inaccessible camp in one of the most remote regions of the United States.[376] Little traffic had traversed the region since the pack mule trains of the '49ers followed the creek through the Marble Mountains into the gold fields of Scott Valley. Perhaps the only other West Coast spot as isolated was the Olympic Peninsula in the state of Washington, and this was beyond Hoover's range. Northern California and southern Oregon were closer to Palo Alto and thus more convenient. For Hoover, the camp's only drawback was that he had to ride a horse to get there, but better one of nature's misbegotten creatures than the alternative—shank's mare. Wooley Camp captured Hoover's heart. The remoteness was a huge factor, but even better, it was one of the best places for steelheads anywhere on the northern Pacific coast. After looking over the meadow and flat land along the creek, the Association's members decided to build. The centerpiece was a forty-by-sixty-foot log cabin, a dining facility and clubhouse. Around the main building were six smaller sleeping log cabins, one for each of the partners. Construction work was possible only in summer, and it took a crew of three to five men two years to complete the project.[377] Hoover looked forward to years of fishing in this ideal camp, his privacy all but assured.

Just to the north of Wooley Camp in Oregon were the rivers of Hoover's boyhood. In the summer of 1926, he had agreed to address the Columbia Irrigation League in Seattle. It had been years since he had fished the McKenzie or the Rogue. It seemed a good time to visit his old home, family, and friends. A trip west also afforded him the opportunity to get out on the hustings and pitch his water conservation and utilization program in dozens of cities.[378] Hoover advocated maximizing water usage that included new hydroelectric power projects, waterway navigation improvements, flood control, land reclamation, and irrigation canals through a comprehensive and coordinated national plan. Each of the great river drainage systems was unique, but they all needed to be considered as specialized units integrated

Hoover's log cabin at Wooley Creek, built in 1927.
COURTESY KLAM-ITY KOURIER AND SISKIYOU COUNTY MUSEUM, YREKA, CALIFORNIA

into a gridlike network.[379] The secretary fully understood the complexities that arose because of a clash of interests and the conflicts created by jurisdictional disputes—international, national, state, county, municipal, and private. Within this diffuse voluntary system he wished to create, the role of the federal government was coordination, guidance, financial assistance, and oversight.

As Hoover's train wound its way west, he hammered home the salient features of his program night after night in an effort to garner support from groups interested in water projects—places such as Hammond, Indiana; Chicago; Omaha; Pocatello, Idaho; and Wenatchee, Washington.[380] On August 20, Hoover spoke in Boise, and the next morning, he left for Spokane on the Union Pacific Limited. Just beyond La Grande, Oregon, on the high desert plateau, a messenger handed him a note: "Hope I get to see you on the observation platform as your train passes through. Regards." The note was signed by Alva Cook, Hoover's boyhood friend from West Branch and later his onion weeding partner in Sherwood. Alva was living with his wife in Gibbon, Oregon, which had a post office but was no more than a "sheep-loading siding on the Umatilla reservations."[381] Alva was the Indian agent, and his wife ran a small supply store. Consultation with the conductor and engineer resulted in an agreement to halt the train for five minutes so that Bert and Alva might have a brief reunion. Both men seemed touched by their renewed acquaintance.

Hoover traveled on across the state of Washington to deliver his speech in Seattle. Blinded by the floodlights in the large stadium, Hoover remarked: "I couldn't see a face in front of me—the only thing I saw was the 'Mike.' It was about as inspirational as talking to oneself in the bathroom with the doorknob for an audience."[382] His business concluded, the tired secretary headed for Portland and the Willamette, the river valley of his youth, eager for the praise and attention his meteoric success would engender.

In Portland, Hoover, at an informal gathering on his friend W. B. Ayer's sunporch, lit up his morning cigar and told reporters that he was there to seek out old friends and visit his boyhood haunts. He expected some disappointment, however, as many had scattered and some had likely died.[383] Then, rod and reel in hand, he planned to disappear into the wilds of Oregon to fish for ten days. "I came here to discover if the surviving relatives of the fish I used to catch so easily with a worm will be as obliging about rising to an artificial fly."[384] The nostalgic Hoover had brought with him a fishing pole and the well-worn flies he had used when he had lived in Salem and fished the McKenzie and the North Santium. He also had brought his carefully selected collection of flies, the latest reels, jointed rods, and rubber hip boots. Pressed, he would not reveal where he was going and asked that he not be followed, as he deserved an uninterrupted vacation. Reporters, he said, were usually fair, and photographers were intrusive, but worst of all were telegram delivery boys. "Crawl up the highest peak, hide in the bottom of the Grand Canyon, go to boring a couple of holes in a fir stump on the farthest away homestead in Oregon, and if you've given a hint as to where you are goin', a messenger with a business telegram will find you."[385] Those listening anticipated that the conversation would turn to Hoover holding forth on the dozens of projects he was pushing, but instead he began by saying, "Let's don't talk economics—I hate the word anyway. Let's get away from trouble and chat about something pleasant."[386]

Enthusiastically, he took up fishing, a subject he had been elaborating on for some time in both his formal speeches and extemporaneous remarks. "When I was a youngster in Newberg, I tramped all over this part of Oregon fishing." Fishing, he claimed, "is where democracy comes in for its final test. All men are equal before fish." Recalling simpler times and man's uneasy relationship to modernity, Hoover noted: "I'm going back to the streams I used to fish as a boy and try out these modern appliances. Honestly, I believe I'd rather do it like I used to, with a worm, but they tell me the fish have changed too." Recognizing that the fate of men and fish are inexorably intertwined, he continued: "They are accustomed to modern conveniences now. They've been educated and refined, and along with all the rest of us, they've got away from the simple life of our ancestors."[387]

Warmed to his topic, Hoover invoked stories of his youth, what he called a "Court of Boyhood."[388] He remembered that the adults would not let the boys fish the Willamette unsupervised, and though they were restricted to Hess and Chehalem Creeks, the fishing was good. Speaking of the Chehalem reminded him of his old swimming hole and splashing about with his companions, the Edwards brothers, all of which triggered a long string of pleasant associations. He even fondly recalled his endless battle with fir tree stumps in those "happy Yamhill country days."[389] Someone in the group suggested that he write his memoirs. Hoover snapped back: "Memoirs are too often the assassins of people's character. I am not writing mine, never intend to. History should be allowed to say what it likes of a man."[390] Memoirs aside, the memory most embedded in Hoover's mind was his recollections of the smell of Oregon in the mornings. "The fine clear atmosphere with the aroma of fir trees . . . makes Oregon in the early morning the grandest place on earth, I think." Lapsing into his Mark Twain style rhetoric from his days in the High Sierras, he concluded: "When a fellow wakes up out here about sunrise he feels like running and taking a 14 foot jump. I could go out and climb a tree right off!"[391]

Lou, who had joined her husband in Portland, traveled with Bert in the early morning to Newberg, and the couple revisited the places of his boyhood. Hoover spent three hours talking with his old Sunday school teacher Vannie Martin. Sadly, in 1923, she had suffered a stroke that left her severely paralyzed, and she was essentially bedridden. Martin, who had been one of Hoover's surrogate mothers, a woman who had helped sustain him, told reporters that she had always believed in Bert's abilities and that he had become her hero.[392] The next day, the Hoovers looked over

Salem, the old house in the Highland Addition, and also the place where the Oregon Land Company office once was, the site of Uncle Cook's Friends Polytechnic College, and the buildings that had once housed Bert's favorite restaurant and ice cream parlor. Along with Oregon Sen. Charles McNary, a fellow Stanford alumnus, the Hoovers disappeared on a fishing trip into the heart of the Willamette Valley. The first stop was the McKenzie, where Bert, in a drift boat with Lou as a passenger, navigated the river's rough whitewater. Leaving the McKenzie, the fishermen traveled up through the Cascade Mountains to Diamond Lake—a tranquil alpine setting.

There the Hoovers were joined by their son Herbert, and all fished for large rainbow trout. Many big trout in the lake were the result of a stocking program begun in 1910, the kind of program Hoover ardently supported. That evening, the little party of fishermen drove the short distance south to Crater Lake Lodge, one of the West's magnificent hostelries. Crater Lake, nestled in the cone of an ancient collapsed volcano nearly two thousand feet deep, is the deepest lake in the United States. The seventy-one-room grand hotel built in 1915 straddled the lip of the "somnolent volcano" and looked out over the lake's deep blue water. Surrounded by the steep-sided cone, it was a magnificent panoramic view. A smaller, tree-covered cone rose near the lake's center to form Wizard's Island. Fishing in the lake was not considered good, as the trout were quite small because of the altitude and food supply. It was, however, a wonderful place to relax, dine, and take leisurely strolls—to soak up the natural beauty.

Leaving early in the morning, the fishing party drove to Grants Pass. Hoover stopped in Joe Wharton's wonderful fishing tackle store and then continued on to a second luxurious but smaller hotel, the Weasku Inn, on the wild, rushing Rogue River.[393] The inn, completed two years earlier, was a classic log lodge with high A-frame beamed ceilings. The main lounge was decorated in the primitive northwestern style; comfortable chairs and couches faced a huge stone fireplace. Stone fireplaces also graced each of the well-appointed guest rooms. Crater Lake Lodge and the Weasku Inn may have been in or near the wilds of Oregon, but on this outing, the native son was hardly roughing it.

The fishing here was terrific. Hoover spent the next week fishing the Rogue with his guide, Glen Wooldridge, and a new

Lou and Bert navigating whitewater in a McKenzie drift boat.
COURTESY LANE COUNTY HISTORICAL SOCIETY, EUGENE, OREGON

friend to whom his guide had introduced him, "Toggery Bill" from Medford.[394] Bill Isaacs owned the men's clothing store in Medford and had been fishing the Rogue since the turn of the century. He knew fishing, he knew the Rogue, and he had a delightful peeled and varnished log cabin with a huge stone fireplace, Big Stone Lodge, on the bank of the river. Toggery Bill was a Rogue River booster and one of the best fly casters in Oregon. In a regional contest for accuracy, he tied the national record by dropping his fly in the target zone ninety-eight times out of one hundred. His longest winning cast in completion was 120 feet, 20 feet farther than that of the second-place competitor.[395] At Bill's invitation, Hoover spent a night in his cabin.[396]

The secretary's luck held, for he arrived on the Rogue at exactly the right time. His first day of fishing was frustrated by a low water level on the lower river, which prevented the fish from moving upstream, but during the night, dam water was released over the fishway at Reamy Falls. The *Oregonian* reported that the result was astonishing: "Fish started coming over by the thousands, including small trout, steelheads and salmon. Steelhead

Hoover and guide on the McKenzie River.

PHOTOS BY C. L. STEVENSON. COURTESY LANE COUNTY HISTORICAL SOCIETY, EUGENE, OREGON

fishing in the Rogue River has now reached its prime, with limit catches reported yesterday and today by many anglers."[397] Popular flies included the Seth Green, Grizzly King, and Royal Coachman of varying sizes.[398] A satisfied Hoover dined that evening with Toggery Bill on salmon and trout. At the end of a week of successful fishing, he gloated all the way to Palo Alto. Once again, after a wonderful vacation in California, the Hoovers boarded the train for the long trip back to Washington, D.C. Lou once lamented: "Washington ought to be in California."[399]

Hoover's busy schedule prevented him from fishing at Long Key in January or February 1927. The war debt problem, import-export hassles, ongoing labor disputes, the continuing farm problem, plus all the kingdoms in the secretary's empire demanded his attention. On the horizon, an unforeseen crisis loomed, a natural disaster of unprecedented magnitude, one that would engage Hoover to the fullest. The spring runoff in the upper Midwest had sent the tributaries of the Mississippi River to record high-water marks; cities flooded from Pittsburgh to Omaha. The great drainage basin between the Appalachians and the Rockies was full to the brim, now worsened by repeated downpours through-out March. On into April, it rained incessantly. It had rained inter-mittently for more than forty days and forty nights. The raging, roiling Mississippi River was about to burst from its leveed chan-nel like some vengeful demon and spill out across the low, fertile deltas—in some places for as much as 150 miles or more.[400]

Years of levee building, channel straightening, and dredging had made the river more like a logging chute. The river's speed increased as it flowed south, and the bottom had silted so badly that the river was higher than the surrounding farmland. In the short run, this was not a significant problem, although the long-range impact was extremely destructive. But in times of increased water flow, it was a recipe for disaster. As the river rose, the chan-nel might act as a dam, actually holding back water and forcing the tributaries to spill their banks. At other times, the river became a racing torrent of whirling, surging, dirty water. Every-thing imaginable was trapped in its rush, disappearing then reap-pearing: old cars, whole buildings, entire trees, broken boats, oil drums, coffins, and numerous bloated carcasses of drowned animals—horses, mules, cows, sheep—all swept on to some unknown destination downstream.[401]

From St. Louis to New Orleans, black work crews struggled around the clock in the cold and rain to secure the levees. Many were held against their will at gunpoint.[402] As the water level continued to rise, it was apparent that it was only a matter of time before the levee system would fail.

The first breach on the Mississippi occurred at Dorena, Mis-souri, on April 18, followed by a devastating crevasse at Mounds Landing, Mississippi, on April 21.[403] Other collapses occurred up and down the swollen river. Throughout the Mississippi valley, millions of acres were flooded, and hundreds of thousands of people were refugees in need of food and shelter.

Even before the levees collapsed, the governors of the states along the river had asked President Coolidge to appoint Hoover to head a federal commission that would deal with the crisis.[404] All remembered Hoover's work for the Belgians and his long experience with the American Relief Administration. Coolidge, who had procrastinated in involving the federal government, was only too happy to slip this one to the "Wonder Boy." Hoover agreed that he was the man for the job, confident as always that he could do it. Ever the reformer, here was an opportunity for some real social engineering. In thinking through solutions to the crisis, he always considered long-term outcomes.[405] He was keenly aware that the publicity generated by his intervention would bolster his chances of winning the Republican party presidential nomination the following year. Hoover would be front-page news, paraded daily before the American public for several months. Both Hoover and the spreading flood shared a kind of inevitability. As was his style, he poured himself completely into the complicated and massive relief operation.

The "Master of Emergencies" was given wartime powers.[406] He set up headquarters in Memphis and used a special train to inspect the flooded areas, which spread out from both sides of the river in a huge arc. Looking at the task before him, Hoover declared the flood to be "the greatest peace-time calamity in the history of the country."[407] The resources of the federal government were immediately brought into play, but it took several weeks for deployment to begin to have an effect. A strange armada of eight hundred boats, including Coast Guard cutters, ensured that most survivors were not isolated for long. Thousands of people were trapped on sections of the levees, the only high ground, and hundreds remained on their rooftops or stranded in trees. In spite of the rescuers' best efforts, prolonged exposure took a toll. Sixty airplanes, some from the Army Air Force, twenty-seven seaplanes from the navy, and an assortment from nearly every government agency, made possible rapid transportation, emergency rescue, and aerial surveillance over the millions of flooded acres.[408] The American Red Cross, which had been expanding all through the 1920s, brought in thousands of nurses and volunteers. National Guard units across the Midwest were mobilized to erect large tent cities and assist with the cleanup. Farther south, the black workforce rounded up from the plantations did every kind of manual labor. Hoover reported, "We built wooden platforms for the tents, laid sewers, put in electric lights, and installed huge kitchens and feeding halls."[409] The radio, a new technology that Hoover had encouraged and regulated, was used to launch a Red Cross fund-raising drive with an initial goal of $5 million; $15 million eventually trickled in. Huge amounts of money came from other sources. The Red Cross expended its $16 million relief fund, the states' emergency funds spent $12 million, the federal government contributed $20 million, and help came from private business groups and relief organizations such as the Rockefeller Foundation.[410]

For three months, Hoover and his army of relief workers battled the flood. Most of Hoover's long-term goals—county health facilities, land reform, increased education, and a loosening of race relations—made little progress. In fact, by July and August, the job was not finished. Thousands were still homeless, and no crops had been put in. Coolidge decided that the $3 million dollars remaining in Red Cross coffers would suffice; no special legislation was necessary.[411]

Hoover, whatever the outcome, had effectively dealt with the emergency and put himself back in the national spotlight. The publicity generated by his relief efforts was immense. He was particularly pleased with a photograph taken of him in Opelousas, Louisiana, "beaming over newborn triplets named Highwater, Flood and Inundation."[412] The image of Hoover as the "Great Humanitarian," the man most qualified to lead the nation, was solidified in the public's mind. A witticism circulating a short time later was close to the truth: "The great Mississippi flood ruined the South and elected Hoover."[413] By early July, Hoover had wrapped up the relief operation and caught up on work in Washington; on the fourteenth, he left for the West Coast. On the way, he visited fish hatcheries and other Commerce Department operations, but he was especially looking forward to the annual encampment at the Bohemian Grove.

Hoover arrived in Yellowstone Park on July 18 and checked into the Lake Hotel. Horace Albright, the park superintendent, and Capt. C. F. Culler, the fishery's chief, joined the secretary for dinner.[414] Hoover had come to the park to look over the present fish hatchery, visit the collection stations at the head of the lake, and discuss the location for the new hatchery, the funds for which had been donated by William E. Corey, president of U.S. Steel. The generous gift had come a year before, when Albright was a lunch guest at the steel magnate's plush camp outside Yellowstone on Hebgen Lake. Corey complained at length that fishing had declined dramatically in the Madison River. Why, he wanted to know, hadn't the Park Service done something about it? Albright responded that the present hatchery was not up to the job. The Park Service could hatch the eggs but had no facilities that allowed the fry to grow to fingerlings. Yellowstone fry were shipped to other facilities that raised the trout and released them. Corey continued to grouse and then, out of the blue, asked how much a new hatchery would cost. Albright told him $27,500. Corey asked why they didn't go to Washington and get the money. Albright responded that the Park Service had tried but had been denied. Corey asked once more what the cost would be, and then announced, "I'm giving it to you; go ahead and build the hatchery." Albright was surprised but very pleased.

At dinner with Hoover, Albright, well aware of his guest's reticence, did not bring up the question of the planned hatchery's location. Neither did Hoover. The conversation drifted to fishing, and the Yellowstone men asked Hoover if he would like to try his luck in the morning. Hoover said he would. After dinner, Albright, Hoover, and their assistants walked along the shore of the lake. A beautiful full moon graced the summer evening; its reflection mirrored on the water's still surface. As they walked, Hoover "picked up a stick, or a limb of a tree, [and] stripped off its branches," but nobody spoke for more than half an hour.

Finally a discussion of the project began. Hoover listened to the argument that the Park Service wanted the new hatchery in a different location. As the sites were close to one another, the men carefully looked at both. Hoover asked a few questions as he walked all around the site. He crossed the road and revisited the old hatchery, and then returned to the proposed location. He said nothing. Finally, after several minutes of contemplation, he walked to the center of the clearing and stuck the stick in the ground—the decision had been made. On the way back to the hotel, one or two comments were made, but silence prevailed, and the men enjoyed the evening.[415] At the hotel, Hoover asked his host, "When do we start our fishing trip?" Albright replied that the hotel did not serve breakfast until seven, but Hoover protested that the delay would cause a late start. The hatchery chief said that he and his crew ate around six o'clock, as they were up early in order to check the wild trout traps and strip eggs from those fish that had been caught during the night. Would Hoover like to join them for ham and eggs?

Hoover arrived the next morning at the appointed hour and ate ham and eggs with the fish team, then the men prepared their gear and the boat to leave for the north end of the lake. All seemed fine, although Albright was astonished that the secretary "was wearing his customary blue-serge suit—double-breasted and a high collar, don't you know. He didn't look very much like a fisherman."[416] Albright suggested that Hoover don a pair of leggings he had brought along to protect his lower legs from the nettles and burrs in the bush; Hoover refused. Camp chairs were placed on the deck of the launch so that the fishing party could enjoy the sun and the scenery surrounding Yellowstone Lake. All tried to engage the secretary in conversation, but he would have none of it. The trip was more than twenty miles, and the boat was slow. After a while, Hoover pulled out a handsome tin box crammed with the best fishing equipment—everything from deep-sea lures to trout flies. Hoover asked Albright if he thought there was anything in the box he could use. Albright looked over the array of tackle and teasingly said he didn't think any of it was appropriate to Yellowstone. Hoover laughed and said that the box of tackle had been given him when he became the honorary president of the Izaak Walton League of America, and he wanted to try some of it out. Albright replied that he had brought along some tackle for Hoover, but after digging in the box, he found some excellent flies that would be of use on the lake. The jovial give-and-take exchange on tackle relaxed Hoover, and for the rest of the trip, he told fishing stories. By the time the boat landed at Clear Creek, all of the men were ready for a day of fishing. Hoover put on the leggings he had earlier refused, pushed his way through the thick brush, and worked the creek. Using his favorite flies, he soon reeled in eight trout.[417]

The next stop on the inspection tour was Pearle Island, at the south end of Yellowstone Lake, where the Forest Service ran a second collection station and maintained a cabin. On the way, Hoover continued his fishing stories. Casting from the shore of the island, he hooked several more trout. For lunch, Roy Ripley, who also piloted the boat, cooked the trout as the secretary wished—boiled along with potatoes in their jackets. While the fish and potatoes cooked, Hoover watched the egg-taking operation. After extraction, the fish eggs were deposited in ten-gallon wooden kegs, covered with tight wire mesh for protection, and stored in the lake water to ensure a constant temperature until they were loaded on the boat and taken to the hatchery for incu-

Hoover and Park Superintendent Horace Albright, July 1927.

COURTESY HERBERT HOOVER LIBRARY

bation. During lunch, Hoover, now on a roll, told the story of building the first levee around Lake Okeechobee in Florida after the great flood in the 1890s. The work was done with two-wheeled scrapers pulled by teams of mules—a massive undertaking in an age before huge, motorized machinery.[418] His audience listened in rapt attention. The fresh Yellowstone cutthroat trout may not have been roasted pumpkinseeds on a stick from the Wapsinonoc, but they were enjoyed by the hungry fishermen. After lunch, Hoover told the hatchery men how pleased he was with his visit. He asked if he would be welcome if he came back and spent the night. If his schedule permitted, he would like to fish, cook, and work out on the woodpile. The hatchery men said yes. On the way out the door, Hoover picked up an axe, took a hefty swing, and split a log in two. "I'm slipping," he said. "I was off center a bit but that's not bad since I have been away from an axe for twenty-five years."[419]

As the boat made the long trip back across the lake to the hotel, Albright mulled over his thoughts about the secretary. He concluded what many before him had, those who had the opportunity to come to know Hoover in a small group or in an informal setting: "I thought he was a shy man. And there were so many things that came out during that day that I just loved the fellow when I got back, despite the fact that I had been harboring a little bit of coldness toward him."[420] Hoover left Yellowstone well satisfied with the fishing and with the knowledge that his hatchery program was achieving modest success. His train wound its way through the fabulous mountain scenery of southwestern Montana and Idaho. He was bound for California and the Bohemian Grove.

For more than a week, Hoover relaxed among friends and enjoyed the Grove entertainment. On August 2, a messenger arrived at Cave Man Camp and handed him a telegram. The contents of the message were stunning. President Coolidge, on vacation in Custer State Park, South Dakota, had issued a press release that simply stated, "I do not choose to run for President in nineteen-twenty-eight." The door to the presidency suddenly seemed wide open for Hoover. The news of Coolidge's statement swept through the Grove like a prairie fire. Normally one had to be invited to visit Cave Man Camp, but on this day, throughout Bohemia, campers headed for Kitchen Hill. In his *Memoirs*, Hoover recalled: "Within a hour a hundred men—publishers, editors, public officials, and others from all over the country who were at the Grove—came to my camp demanding that I announce my candidacy. Telegrams poured in from all parts of the country in such numbers that the Grove operator had to send for more assistance."[421]

Ever cautious in dealing with Coolidge, Hoover and friends began to speculate, as did most of the nation, just what the wily

New Englander meant by "choose." Wisely, Hoover did not announce his candidacy, telling supporters that he would speak with the president when he returned to Washington. Before heading east, he squeezed in a visit to the Bureau of Fisheries facilities on Santa Catalina and San Clemente Island. For two days, he fished from early morning until late at night, ample time to contemplate the ambiguities of the statement "I do not choose to run for President in nineteen-twenty-eight." Working out of the prestigious Avalon Tuna Club, he hoped to land a sailfish. Pacific sailfish were much larger than their Atlantic cousins and were famous for coming completely out of the water and walking for some distance on their tails. Schools of tuna and swordfish were sighted. Hoover had a strike, but, perhaps distracted, he caught no fish.[422]

In September, back on the job, Hoover asked Coolidge for clarification, but Coolidge reiterated his earlier statement. He chose to leave "choose" undefined. The president likely meant what he said and did not choose to run, though he surely enjoyed thwarting Hoover's rampant ambition. Once Coolidge understood that Hoover was intent upon running, he "turned almost immediately against him."[423] In Coolidge's mind, Hoover's other great sin was that he was not a regular Republican, even though he had been registered since 1906 and had supported Teddy Roosevelt in 1912. That he had held high office in the Wilson administration, had been close to Wilson, and had spent a year at the Paris Peace Conference added to Coolidge's general suspicions.[424] On two more occasions, Hoover tried to pin down the president's intentions, and on both occasions, the president refused to say more. Republican hopefuls were hamstrung by Coolidge's lack of candor, but Hoover was the only real choice other than Coolidge. Gov. Frank Lowden of Illinois had been a candidate several times before and generated no real excitement, Vice President Charles Gates Dawes lacked political acumen, and Charles Evans Hughes was politically moribund.

In February 1928, Hoover again went to Coolidge and told him that a long list of prominent Ohio Republicans wanted to enter him in the primary against Sen. Frank Willis, who had put forward his name as a "favorite son."[425] To the point, Hoover asked the president if he intended to enter the contest. Coolidge said no. As he was not entering, Hoover continued, did he mind if Ohioans put forward his name? Laconic Cal responded, "Why not?"[426] Hoover's candidacy, his political future, rested on the president's two-word response. On February 12, 1928, without fanfare, Hoover wrote a letter of acceptance to those in Ohio who had asked that he run.[427] After years of circumspectly sniffing the nomination, Herbert Hoover had almost come out.

As usual, he masked his ambition with a series of qualifiers. "I have not engaged in any active campaign and will not unless I am nominated at Kansas City."[428] Even as late as May 1928, while his stalking horses beat the bushes for every available delegate, he told a Senate committee that his quest for the presidency was "not so much in my own mind as in the minds of others."[429]

In February, leaving the details of his budding presidential campaign to political lieutenants, Hoover went fishing. He and Lou, along with their son Herbert and good friends Mark Sullivan and Dr. Vernon Kellogg, boarded the Havana Special to Key West for a week of deep-sea fishing. The *Kilkenny*, docked at the Royal Palm Hotel yacht basin, waited.[430] After having missed a year of deep-sea fishing in the Keys, Hoover was eager to return. Maybe this time, his fourth trip, he would finally hook the big sailfish of his dreams.

The party arrived early in the morning, briefly stopped by their hotel, the Casa Marina, and boarded the *Kilkenny* for a full day's fishing. Sullivan and Kellogg did well, both reeling in thirty-pound kingfish. Hoover did hook a large king, but during the battle that ensued, his fighting fish was shredded by a shark. His consolation was a string of five dolphin. As the week progressed, the fishermen caught a wide variety of deep-sea denizens. In between fishing, Hoover worked on his answer to Sen. William Borah's questionnaire on prohibition and prohibition enforcement. The salt breeze, hot sun, and blue water coupled with fishing, friends, and good food allowed him to clear his mind and organize his thoughts on his presidential campaign. On the last day, as darkness followed the *Kilkenny* to port, a persistent but disappointed Hoover again had failed to hook "his sailfish."

As promised, Hoover did not campaign actively in the primaries, and he pledged to loyally carry out the policies of President Coolidge. He lost several primaries to state potentates—to Senator Willis in Ohio (who died during the campaign), to Sen.

James Watson in Indiana, and to West Virginia favorite son, Sen. Guy Goff—but he won six other primaries. In May, Hoover was clearly the Republican front-runner with the most delegates—the man to beat.[431] Only Coolidge could derail Hoover, but the president remained aloft from the political struggle, refusing to endorse a candidate and keeping his cards close to his breast—his role as a spoiler preserved. When Hoover looked over his shoulder, the shadow of Silent Cal hovered ominously.[432]

In mid-May, the height of the Appalachian spring in the mountains of Pennsylvania, Hoover returned to the Ogontz Lodge on Larry Creek for several days of fishing. Three of his best fishing companions, Larry Richey, Wilbur, and Sullivan, accompanied him, but Sullivan often fished with his friend simply because he did not have the heart to tell him no. [433] To the contrary, Richey was a fishing and hunting enthusiast, a first-class outdoorsman, who had worked for Hoover in various capacities since his days at the War Food Administration and was now a part of most fishing forays. The weather was glorious, and mountain cherry, laurel, redbud, and dogwood bloomed among the mixed forest of hardwoods and conifers.[434] If the budding oak leaves were the size of squirrel's ears, so the old folk saying goes, then morels were pushing up through the forest floor. Cardinals, brown thrashers, Baltimore orioles, and a panoply of migrating wood warblers fluttered in the trees. Hoover, up with the sun, put on his old brown suit, white shirt and tie, gray felt hat, and a pair of rubber hip boots. For breakfast, he consumed a stack of hotcakes covered with real Vermont maple syrup, a favorite. Then, alone, he followed the winding trail up the mountain stream for a morning of fishing.[435] Over his left shoulder was his well-worn khaki creel and in his right hand one of his favorite rods—one given him by the Izaak Walton League of America.

Near the headwaters of Larry Creek below the dam, Hoover found a pool, selected his flies, and whipped the water, looking for a strike. He caught a small native brook trout and placed it in his creel. A few minutes later, his solitude was interrupted by several reporters and photographers coming up the trail. He amiably agreed to have his picture taken in his fishing togs with boots, creel, rod, and reel. Reaching into his bag, he pulled out the small trout. "This is the evidence that I really am fishing," he commented.[436] "You might have thought we would get away from you fellows up here," he remarked, "but that looks to be impossible. There does not seem to be many places left in the world where a man can find solitude. Intrusion? Certainly not; it's part of your job."[437] Interview and photo opportunity over, Hoover returned to the stream after this brief interruption by the press. He must have realized that as a rising political star, his ability to escape into the wilderness had been dramatically curtailed. In the late afternoon, he returned to the lodge with his creel full. It had been ten years since he had been a guest of the Cookes and fished Larry Creek. He could thumb back through the record book and read his earlier entry. To conclude his visit, he signed his name to an entry written by J. Cooke: "Weather has been fine and fishing excellent. This year we have an election for President and 'who knows?'"[438] The fishing party left the Ogontz Lodge and traveled to the nearby Texas Block House Club for a day of fishing. The Texas Club was a large, rambling, two-storied colonial farmhouse, tucked into the base of the mountain. Here, too, the fishing was good. The following day, Hoover leisurely drove back to Washington amid the lush Mid-Atlantic spring.

The Republican Convention opened in Kansas City on June 12, 1928, and plodded along toward Hoover's nomination with no surprises. The highlight oration, delivered by Sen. George Moses of New Hampshire, was a firebrand attack on the Democrats and that vile institution Tammany Hall. Midwestern farmers, unhappy with Hoover's agricultural policy, were courted by Gov. Frank Lowden. A small group of farmer demonstrators tried to break into the hall, brandishing shovels and pitchforks.[439] But the opposition could find no answer to the question hurled at the convention by Hoover's many supporters: "Who but Hoover?" On the first ballot, the secretary received 837 delegate votes out of a total of 1,089. A scattering went to favorite sons, the closest competition coming from Lowden, who garnered 74 delegate votes. Sen. Charles Curtis captured 64. A number of hopefuls maneuvered for the vice-presidential slot; Senator Curtis from Kansas was chosen, which would help dampen the farm revolt. He was a prohibitionist, and he was well respected in the Senate. The ticket complete, Hoover resigned his office on July 14 and journeyed to Coolidge's summer retreat as a supplicant in need of both the popular president's blessing and his active support.[440]

Hoover on Larry Creek while at the Ogontz Fishing Lodge, Williamsport, Pennsylvania, May 1928. COURTESY AP/WIDE WORLD PHOTOS

It was doubtful that the "Little Fellow" would grant either of the "Wonder Boy's" requests.

In 1927, Coolidge had spent his summer vacation in the Black Hills of South Dakota. The summer White House was in Rapid City, and it was from there that Coolidge had released his cryptic bombshell concerning his political future. For his 1928 summer vacation, he and his wife, Grace, chose a new location, the Cedar Island Estate on the Brule River in northern Wisconsin, an isolated retreat far from the swirl of election-year politics. Central High School in Superior, though forty-five miles away, served as the summer White House. The Brule, fifty miles long, was a famous trout river connected to a series of spring-fed lakes that were part of the four thousand-acre Henry Clay Pierce Estate. Cedar Island, man-made, comprised three acres covered with huge pines and cedars. The grounds were beautifully maintained, clipped green lawns dotted with blue forget-me-nots, and along the banks of the Brule, to the west of the lodge, a tangle of cranberry bushes and wild roses formed a hedge.[441] The beds of forget-me-nots had escaped the confines of the estate and spread for thirty miles up and down the riverbank.[442] Here, in this tranquil setting, the Coolidges could relax and the president could fish.

The lodge boasted an enormous living room that featured polished hardwood floors, oriental carpets, cedar paneling, wicker furniture, and lavish draperies. The walls were covered with large landscape paintings and stuffed trophies of more than a hundred game species. Close to the massive fireplace made of imported stone was the centerpiece, a gold-inlaid maple grand piano. Off the living room were a sizable library, done in matching carved Italian oak, and eight imposing bedrooms, decorated to the hilt.[443]

To dine, Cal and Grace were required to walk from the lodge, across an arched cedar bridge that spanned the Brule, to the dining hall. At the end of the bridge was a natural spring, over which hung a long-handled tin dipper suspended from a notch on a tree. When Coolidge crossed the bridge, often three times a day, he took the dipper, filled it with spring water, and repeated the same phrase: "There's no clearer, better tasting water anywhere."[444] The dining hall matched the lodge in elegance. The high ceiling was punctuated by crystal-lined electrically lighted domes, which cast reflected light upon a fourteen-foot mahogany table that seated thirty guests. The walls were covered with large Swiss wood-carved panels of hunting and fishing scenes.[445] The dining hall also contained servants' rooms and dining room, butler's pantry and room, guest room, linen room, bathrooms, and a kitchen that was "larger than the average family home."[446] Verandas and patios graced the exterior of both lodge and dining hall.

Cool evenings at the end of hot days invited guests to dine outside or simply sit and relax. Large screened porches protected against Wisconsin's notorious mosquitoes. On the grounds were other amenities and operational support facilities: a stable, boathouse, office building, caretaker's house, superintendent's house, garage, laundry, dairy, fish hatchery, sawmill, and a house for the guides. The estate, though extraordinary, was not on the scale of the Biltmore House, one of the homes of the Vanderbilts in Asheville, North Carolina; nonetheless, it was a monument to the robber barons of the Gilded Age. Pierce, from St. Louis, had made his fortune in oil and as a New York financier.[447] The rococo style of the vast estate seemed far more appropriate to Teddy Roosevelt than to the ascetic tastes of the Coolidges, who, upon leaving the White House, planned to return to their $36-a-month duplex in Northampton, Massachusetts.[448]

Coolidge, who loved to fish, had at heart always been a bait fisherman. His presidency had touched off a national debate on the merits of fly fishing as opposed to bait fishing. Die-hards on both sides refused to give ground. Hoover received a letter earlier in the year that summed it up: "I will irrespective of politics vote for you if you fish for trout with the fly. But if you use dirty worms like Cal, goodbye."[449] Locals argued that not a worm had touched the Brule in three generations. On Cedar Island, fishermen did not use barbed hooks and usually practiced catch and release. People who were seen using bait were often yelled at by the river guides. The Chippewa guides supplemented their meager income by tying a beautiful locally developed fly made from woodpecker and jay feathers.

Coolidge as president stifled local opprobrium. Though he did sometimes use bait, he worked hard over the course of the summer to make the transition to fly fishing.[450] His instructor was a young guide named Steve Weyandt, who had mastered the Brule and the four Pierce Lakes at an early age and been selected by the Secret Service as a backup. Part of what recommended him was a record catch he had made: an eighteen-and-three-quarter-pound brown trout. Weyandt became Coolidge's guide when John Leroque, a Chippewa Indian, suffered a sprained back while cranking a car.[451] On one of their first days out together, Weyandt paddled the canoe up through the channel rapids into Rocky Lake and then on into another lake, named

President Coolidge and his dog with Chippewa guide John Leroque,
Brule River, Wisconsin, 1928.

PUBLISHED IN THE DULUTH HERALD. REPRINTED BY PERMISSION OF THE DULUTH NEWS TRIBUNE

Ghein's Slough. Coolidge was reluctant to try a fly—he had
rarely fished with flies before—but the patient guide gently
encouraged him. He rigged the president's split bamboo fly rod
with a 7-foot leader and attached a number 10 Royal Coachman,
a wet fly.[452] Trout fed on the clustered mayfly hatch, and numerous other insects skittered across the still lake water. Coolidge,
nervous with anticipation, desired to catch a fish. But after
numerous bad casts and one snag, the president sat in the bow of
the canoe and practiced.

At lunchtime, Weyandt paddled the president back to Cedar
Lodge. Encouraged, he asked that they return to Ghein's Slough
that afternoon and continue to fish. Responding to a partly overcast gray sky, Weyandt changed the fly to a number 8 Cahill wet.
Coolidge, after repeated casts, was improving, and on his second
good cast, a big rainbow took the fly. Taken unaware, Coolidge
did the right thing by jerking hard on the rod, setting the hook.
The fish leaped into the air, the gray day enhancing the rainbow's
vibrant colors. The battle commenced as Weyandt maneuvered

the canoe to keep the trout from running toward the shore. Coolidge's rod was nearly doubled over, but he kept the line taut and worked the fish. Just as Weyandt was ready to net the trout, Coolidge stood up to see his catch and nearly overturned the canoe. The tired fish swam toward the deep water of the lake. To land the trout, Weyandt beached the canoe, and Coolidge reeled in his fish from the shore. The president was jubilant at having caught a five-pound rainbow. Back at the lodge, Grace teased her husband about his success. That evening, the Coolidges dined on trout sumptuously prepared by the gourmet chefs in the magnificent Pierce kitchen.

Coolidge and his guide fished together frequently as the summer unfolded; most days the president alternated between flies and worms. He loved to bait his own hook, and when he had finished, there were so many worms on the hook that it was a wiggling mass the size of a golf ball—Cal was not a man to take chances. On the return trip, with five nice brookies in the live box, the president leaned back in his seat and enjoyed watching a mother mink and her litter romping on the bank.[453] The cool night air arrived with the coming darkness, which obscured the shoreline in shadow. The canoe glided through perfectly placid, clear lake water, leaving in its wake a wide, V-shaped ripple. In the twilight, the only sound came from the rhythmic dip of the canoe paddle. Coolidge was thoroughly enjoying his vacation. The first lady, who suffered from a number of maladies, had gained weight and felt much better. For the president, the long, quiet days fishing the tranquil lakes on the Pierce estate were "a lifesaver."[454]

After a series of campaign stops across the Midwest, Hoover arrived in Superior, Wisconsin, on July 16. Coolidge was not happy to have him as his guest, and Hoover was there only to paper over their relationship for the press and public and ensure that the two of them were photographed together. The next day, Coolidge and Hoover went fishing. Hoover had fished the Brule once before, in the summer of 1920 as the guest of Julius Barnes, a wealthy Duluth grain exporter and a member of Hoover's War Food Administration. He had fished at the Head of the Lakes for two days, and his guide had been Henry Denny, who also had guided Grover Cleveland and a long list of dignitaries.[455] The Chippewa guide Leroque, his back recovered, paddled the president. Weyandt was assigned by the Secret Service to Hoover. The day was warm and the night before it had rained steadily, a perfect day for fishing. Hoover told Weyandt that he was the guide, that he knew the lakes and the fish, and that he placed himself in his hands. Coolidge, ready, went on ahead while Hoover set up his rod and checked his gear. Weyandt rummaged through Hoover's fly box and was amazed at its completeness.

Hoover, at the guide's suggestion, dressed his fly line. Weyandt tied on a 7½-foot tapered leader and attached one of his favorite dry flies—a number 10 Royal Coachman.[456] Hoover asked him what he would use if the Royal Coachman did not do the job. Weyandt responded that he had several other flies in mind, but he would recommend a Beaver Kill. Hoover smiled. The Beaver Kill was in his tackle box, as were the flies with which he had fished years earlier in Oregon.[457] As the canoe maneuvered into the river, the trout were rising to the mayflies along the bank—a propitious sign. In the first lake, Weyandt sug-

Trout in the Brule River, Wisconsin. PUBLISHED IN THE DULUTH HERALD, JULY 11, 1929. REPRINTED BY PERMISSION OF THE DULUTH NEWS TRIBUNE

gested that Hoover try his luck. He later discovered that Hoover, "by practice casting before completing the cast, . . . managed a perfect shot almost every time. The hand tied bug sat upright on the surface as though just having hatched."[458] A large rainbow hit the fly, and Hoover reeled in the first fish of the day. The Republican nominee demonstrated his skills by making a perfect cast underneath an overhanging cedar tree limb. A fish hit the line hard, took the fly but not the hook, and slithered away. Unconcerned, Hoover continued to work the overhanging trees and pulled in six brook trout that measured from twelve to fourteen inches—a sweet catch. As Weyandt poled the canoe up the rushing whitewater rapids, Hoover remarked that the president was a reasonable bait fisherman but did little with a fly rod. The guide told him that Coolidge had greatly improved since coming to Wisconsin. Hoover took a wait-and-see attitude.[459]

Now in the biggest of the lakes, Hoover and Weyandt could see the president's canoe. Not far behind were the Secret Service men. The big lake was a good place to fish for rainbows and imported German brown trout. While Hoover was doping a Green Drake fly, a large trout broke the surface of the water and shot high up into the air. Surprised, Hoover yelled out, "Great balls of fire."[460] Determined to hook one of the big trout, he worked the interior of the concentric circle created by the fish's splash. He cast repeatedly, gently dropping the fly on the water. One minute the Green Drake was floating on the calm surface, the next it was gone. The trout took the fly and ran, often changing directions. Hoover kept the line tight, forcing Weyandt to paddle quickly in order to follow the fish. The trout repeatedly leaped into the air, rolled mightily in its efforts to free itself, but eventually tired. As the fish neared the boat, it made one more dash before Hoover was able to reel it in close enough to net. The big rainbow weighed more than six pounds and had taken twenty-five minutes to land. With the large, battling fish secured, it was time to catch up with Coolidge to see how he had done. The president too had done well—five trout, all around three pounds. The biggest was a beautiful red-spotted brown. Coolidge could hear Hoover's fish banging around inside the live box. "Is that a fish you have in that live box?" Coolidge inquired. Hoover responded, "It isn't an alligator."[461] After peering at Hoover's catch and praising it, Coolidge commented that the two fishermen had caught way more trout than they could eat. Hoover suggested that they let the big brown and big rainbow go. The president agreed, and they released the fish. As the canoes headed for the lodge, Hoover asked Weyandt how he cooked his trout. Rolled in cornmeal, lightly salted, and quickly fried in hot bacon fat, the guide replied, served with fried potatoes and hot biscuits.[462]

The next day was fiercely hot, but it was Hoover's last day to fish. When Weyandt arrived in midafternoon, Hoover offered him a glass of cold lemonade. Over lemonade, they laid out the day's fishing plans, got their gear in order, and waited until it cooled down in late afternoon. Hoover wished to fish the Brule rather than the lakes. Weyandt and Leroque, who had dropped by, dug through Hoover's tackle box, selecting flies. Leroque took the opportunity to ask about Hoover's abilities as a fisherman. "I've yet to see one better," came Weyandt's response. "He handles a rod like it had grown in his hand. He never seems to make a mistake when casting. It's the same when he's playing the fish. It's an education just watching the man fish. To sum it all up, John, Mr. Hoover is such a good fisherman he's irritating."[463]

When the sun reached the tree line, Hoover and Weyandt shoved off, floating downstream toward the falls. After dozens of casts, the wet fly still had produced no results. Weyandt suggested that Hoover spit on the fly, rub in the saliva, and run some up and down about a foot of the leader. The guide's technique was designed to add buoyancy, but Hoover must have recalled his childhood days on the Wapsinonoc, when he and the other small boys spit on the bait for luck. Nothing worked.[464] Hoover fished on down the river in the deep pools, in the riffles around the protruding rocks, changing flies often, but no trout would rise. Perhaps the fish were sated, having fed for days on huge hatches of mayflies and shadflies. Often the insects were in such profusion that they blanketed the surface of the lake. In the Brule's fast current, insects trapped in brown foam piled up in front of rocks and downed tree limbs. Small floating islands of bugs twirled in the river's eddies. In the face of the fish's stubborn refusal to bite, neither of the men employed the cardinal rule of all fishermen: "When all else fails, use a spinner." Instead, Hoover asked if might try one of the wet flies that Weyandt wore on his hatband. His favorite, one he went to often, and one that was a Hoover favorite as well, was the number 10 Royal Coachman.[465] The Royal Coachman was a classic fly, created by John Haily in 1878 and named by the founder of one of America's most famous fishing tackle suppliers, L. C. Orvis. This beautiful fly, a peacock green body with red floss, a brown hackle, and white wings, had the weight of history behind it. The secretary tied the Royal Coachman to his leader and began to whip-cast the pool. He soon caught and released about twenty trout as the canoe drifted, pulled on downstream toward the falls. Once again the Brule yielded delightful fishing.

Attracted by the roar of the falls, Hoover went to investigate while Weyandt prepared for the hard trip back against the current. At a divide in the river that created Hungry Run Island, a place the local Indians long before had cached food, Hoover tried several large dry flies. A big German brown trout struck his latest choice, and for more than half an hour, the fish attempted to win its freedom. Hoover had the trophy trout next to the canoe when it rolled into the swift current, snapped the leader, and fled as quick as a dart hurled in an Irish pub, into the deep recesses of a pool. The big one really had gotten away. Reconciled to his loss, Hoover rationalized that such a magnificent fish was better off free. That evening, Hoover said good-bye to Weyandt and gave him an autographed photo of himself and the president. Swearing that he would return to fish the Brule, he motored off to Superior and resumed the campaign trail leading to California. The fishing had been great, but Hoover had not received the president's endorsement of his bid for the White House.

From Superior, Hoover made the short trip to Duluth, and then worked his way south through Minneapolis, St. Paul, and on to Iowa. In Nebraska, he received a telegram that Lou's father had died of a stroke.[466] Hoover canceled most of his appearances and arrived in Palo Alto on July 20. Plans for the fall presidential campaign were on hold for several days, but the train set in motion left little time to grieve. This was particularly difficult for Lou, who had been very close to her father. On August 11, Hoover was scheduled to make a nationwide radio acceptance speech from the Stanford football stadium. He wished to get away to the wilds of northern California to fish, relax, and think about what he wanted to say.

A fishing trip also offered a political opportunity. Hoover understood that he was not a gifted public speaker, nor did he possess a charismatic personality. He had difficulty "putting himself over." In public, he faced difficulties common to many serious men who lack vibrant personalities and seek a high political office, difficulties faced by Robert Taft, Alf Landon, and more recently, Gerald Ford, Walter Mondale, and Al Gore. Lee Iacocca said of Walter Mondale what could have been said of Hoover: If you and six or seven people talked privately with Mondale, you would leave knowing there was no one else for whom to vote, but if you only heard him give a speech you would likely be unimpressed. Even though a Hoover, a Mondale, or a Gore might meet with hundreds of people in small groups, the difficulty with "having to be there" is that it does not translate into broad-based support—"so little time, so many groups."

For Hoover, a possible way to let the public come to know him better was to develop and manage his public persona through fishing. Those closest to Hoover were enthusiastic about the trip and its public-relations potential. T. T. C. Gregory, a San Francisco lawyer, treasurer of Stanford University, and a friend and political supporter of the candidate, invited the press to go along with Hoover to some of his favorite wilderness fishing holes. The newspaper writers asked to make the trip included some of the most prominent from the big East Coast dailies. In Palo Alto, Hoover told the assembled press that in the mountain stream, he could escape "jazz madness" and seek "relief from a frenzied existence."[467] Fishing was perhaps the only place, he speculated, where "the average busy man can be alone and not be criticized or suspected."[468] Success at fishing comes from working alone, he said, but finding a place where he would not be disturbed was getting harder and harder. Abandoning philosophical insights for history, Hoover remarked that fishing flies had been used since Izaak Walton's time, and those that proved to be productive were still in use and retained the same names, although many versions of the originals had been created. Plugging California to his East Coast guests, Hoover put forth the questionable assertion that flies were in use on the West Coast long before they were used in the East.[469] It is possible, however, that Spanish grandees fly-fished in California in the 1500s.

Hoover had been moving toward projecting himself to the public through fishing for some time, but it had been a sporadic effort. The mining engineer now more consciously began to tap a rich historical vein of associations. In 1927, he had published an article in *Atlantic Monthly* titled "In Praise of Izaak Walton." He mentioned Walton only in relationship to the point he wished to make: Walton did not have to deal with the frustrations of modern life, which included the rapid disappearance of game fish. Action was required, argued Hoover.[470] As he began to philosophize about fishing, to try to articulate the deeper meaning of angling, to become the "compleat angler," he more often reached back to Walton and to his image. Ironically, Walton, like Coolidge, had been at heart a bait fisherman.[471] In seventeenth-century England, the Anglican Church and later many other denominations that sprang from the rich religious compost of the Reformation forbade their clergy a long list of activities, but fishing they approved. After all, Christ himself approved of fishing and made Peter, Simon, and Andrew "fishers of men." Walton, however, established the genre of angling literature and "gave the sport its halo of letters."[472] The fisherman, according to Walton, was a man who appreciated books and art, and who saw "nature through the glass of culture, the townsman and the gentleman."[473] The inveterate Walton also speculated that the "good angler" was a hardworking man of the world, who successfully used his God-given talents but "still had room for other interests in his soul."[474] This was the image that Hoover wanted for himself, and the way he wanted others to see him. He relied on *The Compleat Angler,* quoting passages more frequently and using the book as a model to develop his own thoughts about the "usefulness" of fishing. As the popular poet Edgar Guest, a Hoover favorite, wrote, "There is much more to fishing than fish."[475]

The morning after his radio address in the stadium, Hoover, his son Allan, Ray Lyman Wilbur, Assistant Attorney General "Wild Bill" Donovan, longtime friend and western campaign finance manager Milton Esberg, and forty-one other guests, newspaper correspondents, photographers, and movie reel cameramen headed north from Palo Alto in a cavalcade of cars for five days of fishing on the Eel, Rogue, Klamath, and other rivers and lakes of northern California. The first stop and overnight was on Bull Creek Flat, a tributary of the Eel near Dyerville. No fish were caught, but dinner was served on rough wooden picnic tables in a redwood grove. As the evening chill penetrated the forest, all gathered around a large bonfire to talk and sing.[476] The

Rainbow Gibson, friend of Hoover, renowned fisherman, and owner of the Weasku Inn. COURTESY JOSEPHINE COUNTY HISTORICAL SOCIETY, GRANTS PASS, OREGON

second day of the trip started early; the caravan left for southern Oregon and the Rogue River. The plan was to arrive at Toggery Bill's cabin outside Medford for a buffet dinner featuring steelhead. On the edge of Grants Pass, the first three cars turned off for Medford, but the remainder of the procession, most of the journalists and photographers, missed the turn and drove into the town. Hoover for the first time met the new owner of the Weasku Inn, Rainbow Gibson, a man with whom he would become friends and who would on future trips to the Rogue act as a guide. Gibson's skill as a trout and salmon fly fisherman equaled that of Toggery Bill. That evening, Hoover and a few friends dined quietly on the banks of the Rogue.[477] Politics came up in conversation, although that violated the ground rules Hoover had established for the trip, and the candidate opined that the Solid South no longer looked like the Rock of Gibraltar. His mood was optimistic, and he would use the radio frequently to campaign in order to reach a wider audience.

At around six the next morning, in waist-high waders, Hoover and Toggery Bill waded out into the river to fish. When Hoover looked up, he was greeted by photographers and movie cameramen clustered on the far bank waiting for him to reach midstream. He called out to them, "Hurry up and take your pictures."[478] Managing his public persona never seemed more difficult. The photographers, hoping for better shots, close-ups, better light, and unusual angles, splashed into the Rogue. Several more enterprising journalists commandeered a boat and rowed out to where Hoover and Toggery Bill were fishing, threatening to overrun their lines. Under the best of circumstances, it would have been hard to catch a steelhead, as the run did not heat up until later in August; with the large number of determined photographers, it was all but impossible. Hoover made several casts, but nothing took his fly. Toggery Bill hooked a steelhead and offered Hoover his rod so that he might satisfy the throng of eager onlookers. Cameras were focused, shutters ready to click—the candidate refused. Obviously miffed, he headed for the cabin. A photographer on shore asked for a close-up but was curtly told, "You will not have one."[479] If Hoover were to fish, relax, and think, he would have to elude the press he had invited to come along. The outcome could be a public-relations disaster. Hoover found himself on the horns of a dilemma that he would never successfully resolve. Perhaps mistakenly, he would continue to try to split the difference, to walk the tightrope between protecting his privacy and allowing the public to know him better. He caught no fish, and by ten o'clock that morning, he decided to move on to Brown's Camp on the Klamath, where things might get better. Asked by reporters about the morning's events,

Hoover proclaimed, "A man should be alone when he is fishing or praying."[480]

An afternoon on the Klamath produced no better results than the Rogue, even though Hoover had a new gray fly made of raccoon hair.[481] Disaster struck while fishing when the power dam upstream released water. Hoover and Wilbur were soaked when they were caught in a three-foot rush of yellow water. The fishing ruined, the two men waded up Scott Creek in an effort to make a catch. When they returned to Brown's Camp, reporters, who had waited all day, immediately asked about the fish. Hoover responded: "No luck at all. I tried changing flies until I was tired. But it was no use. However, there is one consolation. No one else got anything either."[482] He had, though, seen a bald eagle and a kingfisher and gotten wet. It was, from his point of view, a good day.

The following morning, in a cold dawn, Hoover, Wilbur, and one reporter, Philip Kinsley, set out for Beaver Creek, a branch of the Klamath whose headwaters were high in the Siskiyou Mountains. If the steelhead would not bite, the hopeful fishermen reasoned, then perhaps the mountain rainbows would. To reach the site was an arduous undertaking, seventeen miles of rough road followed by eight miles of winding, narrow trails on horseback.[483] As they rode along, visible to the east through breaks in the trees was the domineering snow-capped peak of Mount Shasta. Hoover, before assembling his equipment, carefully studied the pools in the creek and decided on his flies—a red ant and the "tried and true" Coachman.[484] Without the throng of photographers and cameramen, the men had better luck with the rainbow trout.[485] Each fisherman reeled in small rainbows, but the fish were not big enough to offer a fight. The party worked its way down the creek in search of a greater challenge. By late morning, it was apparent that the big ones were not there or were not interested in what was offered. Still, between the three fishermen, thirty-five trout were in their creels. Tolerably pleased, they began the long, hot ride down the steep trail. Hoover rode out in front alone and enjoyed the quiet splendor of the day. Back in camp, he hid the small fish but served them that evening for dinner to prove that he had not again come up empty-handed.[486]

Undeterred by the string of bad luck, Hoover, a true fisherman and eternal optimist, suggested breaking camp and trying

Hoover midstream in the Klamath, Brown's Camp, California.
COURTESY HERBERT HOOVER LIBRARY

the McCloud and Pitt Rivers in the shadow of Mount Shasta. All agreed. The rolling cavalcade of cars wound through the mountains in the moonlight on their way to the headwaters of the Sacramento River, reaching their destination around nine o'clock that night. The Shasta Springs Hotel was another of the West Coast's famous lodges. There was no town; Shasta Springs was a railroad stop with a resort on the rim of a canyon. Glacier Falls tumbled down the side of the mountain, running between a gazebolike kiosk and the train depot. A standpipe had been driven into the springs, and a gusher of water shot into the air like a geyser. Southern Pacific trains stopped, allowing the passengers to stretch, sample the famous water, and shop in the gift store. The spring water, which percolated through the lava tubes honeycombed underneath Mount Shasta, supposedly had curative properties and was bottled and sold nationwide. A cable car carried hotel guests up the steep side of the mountain to the resort. The centerpiece of the resort was an impressive, huge, barnlike clubhouse, which had two tiers of windows set in the walls at different heights, as well as a cathedralesque window at the end of the long dining room, allowing natural light to pour in. From the exposed A-frame support beams hung lavish chandeliers. Across from the clubhouse was a long row of spacious white clapboard cottages. Several small streams graced the grounds and plunged over a moss-covered precipice into the Sacramento River, which was no more than twenty feet wide. At the point where the falls hit the river, a deep pool provided excellent trout fishing.

The secretary rose at five the next morning. His gait on the way to breakfast betrayed the previous day's long horseback ride.[487] Forgoing the Pitt and McCloud in favor of Medicine Lake, where the fish were said to be biting on anything attached to the end of a line, Hoover, his son Allan, his secretary George Akerson, and T. T. C. Gregory drove north around the base of Mount Shasta and then proceeded forty-seven miles northeast to the lake. On the lakeshore, they were met by a guide with a boat and commenced yet another "fishing venture."[488] Once again, the rumors of biting fish proved false. After a picnic lunch in a shaded grove, by early afternoon it was clear that Medicine Lake was another bust. Fishing was put aside for a driving tour of Mount Shasta and a relaxed dinner in McCloud, just north of William Randolph Hearst's castle, Wyntoon.[489] A sunburned Hoover returned late to be met by a gaggle of reporters who were worried that something had happened to the nominee. Realizing that he was safe, their next question was whether he had caught any fish. Only Allan had, his father reported, and he had caught but one.

Friends and press who did not accompany Hoover to Medicine Lake had their own tale to tell. A few of the anglers had descended to the pool at the base of the falls and fished with flies and salmon eggs. Only the bait fishermen achieved their desired ends. But the fishing was momentarily interrupted when two rattlesnakes crawled out onto the rocks to sun themselves. The venomous vipers were killed by a barrage of stones let loose by the frightened newspapermen. The appearance of the snakes, though vanquished, forced a general retreat back to the hotel grounds.[490] Few of the easterners had ever before encountered a rattlesnake. Their desire to explore the great outdoors suffered a serious setback.

The day's events retold, it was time to drive to Dunsmuir, where private railroad cars of the Southern Pacific awaited

Hoover and companions encircling a giant redwood. Left to Right: Stanford trustee Eland Carter, East Coast campaign manager John Q. Tilson, western campaign finance manager Milton Esberg, Hoover, and a journalist. COURTESY HEBERT HOOVER LIBRARY

the troupe for their return to Palo Alto. On boarding the train, Hoover, working what would become a standard line, told reporters that a burning campaign issue in northern California was "more and better trout and less time between bites."[491]

This small mob of hopeful fishermen, newspaper writers, photographers, and movie reel cameramen had traveled together approximately two hundred miles a day for five days and caught very few fish—a strenuous and potentially frustrating outing. Wilbur, however, reported that, to the contrary, Hoover "always enjoyed himself in the stream whether he caught a trout or not. He had been able to do what he wanted to do—get completely away from his acceptance speech for a while so that he could return and look it over with new eyes before it went into final form. He had the precious moments of solitude along the streams. He had gotten away from telephone and politics. He came back 'fit as a fiddle.'"[492]

Wilbur reported what Hoover had personally achieved, but more important, he also assessed how he thought the press had reacted to the madcap dash through the woods, rivers, and lakes of northern California and southern Oregon: "They had a chance to see Mr. Hoover in an entirely new light. Before, they had known him chiefly as the Secretary of Commerce in Washington, 'a high-powered government executive.' Now they found here a man thoroughly at home in the woods and mountains and along his favorite trout streams. They enjoyed his quiet humor, the stories he joined in telling about the camp fires, his genuine friendliness and informality."[493] If Hoover's occasional huffiness and insistence on privacy turned off the newspapermen or alerted them to the barriers the candidate repeatedly raised between himself and the public, none reported so in their papers. The fishing blitz had been a success; Hoover had momentarily satisfied the voracious appetite of the press and public for the human interest story. In the fishing camp, as reported by the press, the public discovered a warmer, more likable Hoover, a person who shared their love of the outdoors, a person they could better understand—Hoover the common man. What little the public knew of the private Hoover—that is, Hoover "at home" or "off the record"—came from glimpses into Hoover the fisherman. Fishing, coupled with Hoover's humble origins and rise to fame, fulfilled the demands of America's egalitarian myth, but these glimpses into Hoover's private life did not blossom into a full-blown open relationship with the public. Hoover was too guarded for that to ever occur; he revered too much the image of the impersonal, objective "manager," the man behind the scenes. Nevertheless, fishing was as central to Hoover's political and public persona as were sailing, stamp collecting, and the fireside chat to Franklin Roosevelt's image.

Hoover played to his audience through fishing, but in his own guarded fashion. Press and public clamored for more, but they were denied as this modern-day Izaak Walton refused to open up any further. Hoover hated, and therefore refused to participate in, any number of activities that the press and public expected from famous people: He would not hold up for the camera fish he had not caught, he would not kiss or pose with babies, he would not wear funny hats, he deplored costumes, and he would not allow newspaper reporters to accompany him fishing if he could avoid it. The rules governing his private life and the degree to which he would allow the press to intrude were established on the five-day outing in the summer of 1928. They would not change into the presidency or beyond.

In Palo Alto, the plans for the fall presidential campaign came to fruition. Hoover focused on his coming speech, writing draft after draft. On August 11, seventy thousand people packed the Stanford football stadium, and hundreds of thousands more tuned in on their radios as a coast-to-coast hookup carried the candidate's voice into living rooms throughout America. Hoover emphasized prosperity and prophesied that "given a chance to go forward with the policies of the last eight years . . . we shall soon with the help of God be in sight of the day when poverty will be banished from this nation."[494] Full employment, more leisure for the working man, and equal opportunity regardless of religion or color were themes he articulated, as well as relief for farmers through tariffs, public works projects, water resource development, child development, revision of immigration quotas, and support for one of the most contentious planks, the continued enforcement of prohibition. During his speech, he gave in to his love of statistics and his admiration for giantism: "Americans had built 3.5 million new homes, installed electricity in 9 million more, purchased 6 million telephones, 7 million radios and 14 million automobiles."[495] "Hail Columbia" Hoover concluded with tributes to his favorite sacred cows: honesty, efficiency, freedom of religion, and American individualism, calling his program "progressive constructivism."[496] During this comprehensive speech, delivered on his fifty-fourth birthday, Hoover never mentioned his Democratic opponent, Al Smith.

Hoover conducted a focused campaign, making six major addresses in different parts of the country. One of those was in West Branch, Iowa. All of his speeches were national radio broadcasts that reached huge audiences. On August 21, the orphan boy now turned presidential candidate returned to the place of his birth for a classic American trip in nostalgia. He was given a tumultuous welcome. A town of 745 residents accommodated a crowd of 15,000.[497] Relatives and old friends, including Mollie Brown Carran, his schoolteacher who had wished to adopt him after his mother died, all turned out to greet their hero. When he had spoken to students and faculty at the new West Branch High School in April 1923, Hoover had Mollie seated on the speaker's platform.[498] In recognition of the attention she had paid him, helping him succeed academically in the fourth grade, he presented his first surrogate mother with a framed autographed photo and signed notecard that read, "To the real founder of character, Miss Mollie Brown, from Herbert Hoover, Feb. 13, 1923."[499] In 1928, he again sought her out for special attention, and she was photographed sitting in the hammock on the porch of the Hoover home looking at the 1923 autographed picture. She seemed pleased that one of her pupils had climbed so high on the ladder of success. Hoover, genuinely drawn to his hometown and grateful for Mollie's help in coping with the death of his mother, was also grateful for the public-relations opportunity, a chance to reinforce the Horatio Alger myth that swirled around him—from the little Quaker schoolhouse to the White House, the poor orphan boy triumphant.

As the campaign progressed, it was clear that few substantive issues separated Hoover and Smith. The key to Hoover's election was to make no major mistake; he could count on peace and prosperity and his carefully crafted image to carry him to the White House. Smith had to overcome a number of negatives, even though his record as governor of New York was outstanding. His stand against prohibition hurt more than it helped, especially with women, a new block of voters that Hoover assiduously courted. The old bromide that women marched their men to the polls to vote them dry contained an element of truth. Smith's association with infamous Tammany Hall also hurt, especially in the South, as did the fact that he was from New York City—Main Street versus Broadway. His big-city cockiness and brown derby worn at a rakish angle did not go over well in rural and small-town America. The biggest factor for Smith was his Catholicism. Hoover denied that religion was an issue, but for many Americans, it was an important, if unspoken, factor.[500] For a small minority, people such as the evangelist Bob Jones, it was the only issue.[501] Those on the Christian right, "Prohibition and Protestantism," inveighed against "Rum and Romanism."

It was no surprise that on election night, November 6, 1928, Hoover won by a landslide. Eligible voters turned out in record number—over 67 percent. A lopsided popular vote recorded 21,437,277 for Hoover to Smith's 15,007,698. The electoral college vote more accurately captured the disparity: Hoover received 444 votes and carried forty states while Smith received 87 electoral votes and carried only eight states.[502] At home in Palo Alto on the Stanford campus, the Hoovers invited family, friends, and a few guests to listen to election returns. Edgar McDowell, a close friend of Allan Hoover's and a fellow junior at Stanford, was asked to help post returns on a large blackboard set up in the Hoover living room. A wire ran into the house on the ground floor, and other boys ran the returns from the ticker up to the next level for posting. Earlier in the evening, it was clear that Hoover would carry New York—a powerful portent of things to come. The outlook was so positive that little attention was paid to the boys working the blackboard. The phone rang with messages of congratulations and encouragement. T. J., Hoover's brother, stayed "very much in the background, but with a happy look on his face all evening long."[503]

A crowd of Stanford faculty and students was gathering outside the house, and in the distance a band was heard. McDowell's brother, who ran the Stanford concert series, had corralled that evening's performers, the John Philip Sousa Band, and brought them to the Hoover house. The crowd, led by Stanford cheerleaders, yelled, "Sis Boom Baa—Stanford, Sis Boom Baa—President Hoover." The Sousa Band commenced to play the Stanford hymn, "Hail Stanford Hail," and "From the Foothills to the Bay." The president-elect and guests were pulled onto the porches and verandas for the serenade. The concert ended with the rousing Sousa rendition of "Stars and Stripes Forever," followed by "The Star-Spangled Banner." Sousa was ushered into the house to meet Hoover.[504] Outside, the crowd became very quiet. Spontaneously, a song rose from the porches, the verandas, the hillside, and the street: "Where the Rolling Foothills Rise, Up Toward Mountains Higher." As the last verse of the alma mater drifted off, Lou Henry stepped forward. "I thank you all for coming here," she said.[505] Quietly the large crowd dispersed into the starlit night. It was a magical evening, a benchmark, for the crowd knew full well it was not just a victory for the Hoovers, it was a victory for Stanford, for California, for the American West, and for the new national class of professionals. Hoover was the first U.S. president born west of the Mississippi. Horace Greeley had been right: The power alignment was shifting.

The transition between Coolidge and Hoover posed no serious political problems, but it was a long time between November 6 and the inauguration in early March. After nearly three decades of intervention in Latin America, Hoover wished to place relations with countries south of the border on a new footing. To institute a "good neighbor policy" and ensure Latin Americans that they had nothing to fear from the "colossus of the north," he arranged an eleven-nation tour. It was also an opportunity to foster trade, stay out of Coolidge's way, and perhaps get in some fishing.

The USS *Maryland*, the mighty battleship that carried the diplomatic mission, left California on November 19. The ship had not reached the first port of call when three launches were lowered. One motored off some distance and then patrolled back and forth, guarding the fishing party. Zane Grey had written of the large fighting sailfish that swam off Cape San Lucas, at the tip of lower California; this was Hoover's opportunity to catch the fish that had eluded him for so long. He and Mark Sullivan, in the same boat, trolled with spinners but had no luck. The fishermen switched to silver minnows, anticipating a strike as the launch moved back and forth in a straight line. Hoover hooked a fifteen-pound dolphin and a five-pound Spanish mackerel, but none of the big fish—amberjack, marlin, tuna, swordfish, or sailfish. Sullivan hooked into a small, feisty dolphin that ran across Hoover's line, tearing his new reel from his rod.[506] Allan Hoover and George Akerson, in the other launch, caught nothing. Lou, who had spent a pleasant afternoon on deck knitting, lost a bet she had made that Allan would catch the largest fish.

For the Hoovers, who had circumnavigated the globe on numerous occasions, shipboard life was pleasant. Hoover enjoyed walking the decks, investigating the gun turrets and learning how a naval vessel ran. He also was happy to lie back in a lounge chair to read detective stores, westerns, and fishing adventures. Trap shooting, shuffleboard, and deck golf were popular, and each evening on the open deck, the sailors joined their guests to watch the latest Hollywood movies. Cecil B. DeMille contacted Hoover as he was about to leave Palo Alto and volunteered fifty films, which included *Felix in Jungle Bungle* and *Three Week Ends*, as well as movies featuring Tinsel Town stars such as Clara Bow, Emil Jannings, Marion Davies, and Janet Gaynor.[507] Many of the sailors brought their pets to the movies—a baby wildcat, a monkey, parakeets and parrots.[508]

Once the battleship reached El Salvador and the tour commenced, fishing opportunities vanished. Working their way along the Pacific coast, the president-elect and his entourage visited Honduras, Nicaragua, Costa Rica, Bolivia, Ecuador, and Peru. From Chile, they took the train to Buenos Aires and then to Montevideo and finally Brazil. In Rio de Janeiro, all boarded the battleship USS *Utah* for the voyage home to Hampton Roads, Virginia. The trip was a success. Many Latin American countries looked forward to a change in policy in Washington, especially a reduction in the U.S. military presence in Haiti and Nicaragua. Long days at sea gave Hoover time to contemplate cabinet appointments and think over his position on other key issues.

The Hoovers arrived home on January 6, then left for Florida two weeks later to take up residence in the opulent J. C. Penney mansion on Belle Isle. They were greeted in Miami by one hundred thousand people. From the train, through the station, and to the open-topped car that awaited them, the Hoovers were escorted by veterans, Boy Scouts, and Girl Scouts along a path carpeted with flowers.[509] A cavalcade of cars moved through the crowd-lined streets. At various intervals, mingled among the masses, were bands from throughout the state, delegations and clubs of every variety, and a trained elephant. Near the halfway point of the ten-mile route, Hoover mounted a reviewing stand, where he was given an oversize key to the city and a chest full of first-class fishing tackle. A second stop allowed him to pay tribute to William Jennings Bryan's widow. As the motorcade reached the bridges leading to Miami Beach, half a dozen planes flew low overhead. On each side of the causeway, a flotilla of boats joined the possession. In Miami Beach, the crowd included black delegations, farm organizations, sunburned bathers, and a troupe of costumed nightclub dancers cavorting on the roof of a gas station. A large sign read, "Come to Miami Beach and do as you damn please."[510] Momentarily, Hoover might have felt as though he were back in one of the mining towns of California or Nevada in the roaring 1890s.

Past the curious throngs, the motorcade drove across the Venetian causeway that connected Belle Isle to the mainland. The island, along with several others in the bay, had been artificially created by developers who had dumped tons of sand and dirt onto floating mangrove islands. On half an acre of beautifully

manicured grass, planted with a wide variety of blooming flowers, was the ostentatious J. C. Penney mansion.[511] Along with a
guest house and the mansion next door, the complex would
serve as the operations center for the president-elect and the
press.[512] The Penneys, in Europe, had volunteered the house, as
had their neighbor Joseph H. Adams. Adams also loaned his
yacht, the *Amitie,* and Jeremiah Milbank, a friend of Hoover and
eastern campaign treasurer, brought along his luxurious houseboat, the *Saunterer.* In Florida only forty-eight hours, Hoover
went fishing, leaving most of the reporters behind in Miami. The
Amitie and the *Saunterer* plied south forty miles to Angel Fish
Creek at Long Key. The Secret Service were on a Coast Guard
vessel that followed some distance off. Hoover and a few aides
drove to Long Key, where they boarded the *Amitie.* As a concession to the press, G. Edward Lowery, a magazine writer for the
Saturday Evening Post, joined the fishing party.

For the next few days, Hoover worked Hawk's Channel and
Tennessee Reef, flats and reefs that dropped off from Long Key,
as well as the edge of the Gulf Stream as far as ten miles out into
the ocean. Nearer shore in a small boat, he and Sullivan trolled a
famous spot, Trestle Bridge Number Two of the Florida East
Coast Railroad.[513] His heart was set on catching a big sailfish on
this, his fifth trip to the Keys. Nevertheless, his inaugural address
was in the back of his mind, and he had brought along stacks of
his favorite notepads, pencils, and one of his secretaries, just in
case his thoughts began to jell. While fishing, he ruminated on
the forthcoming speech. Up at dawn and fishing until dusk,
Hoover worked hard at his avocation, and he came close to
accomplishing his goal. He hooked two sailfish, but the first
broke his line and the second snapped his leader. Though he
landed no sailfish, he did catch two large barracuda, as well as
bonita, tuna, kingfish, and dolphin. Sullivan hooked into a large
sailfish, and after a fight that lasted an hour, he hauled in his trophy. Hoover refused to give up, and he and Sullivan fished until
eight o'clock that evening. The motorboat roared back directly to
Long Key, and twenty minutes later, the two men jumped aboard
the Havana Special, bound for Miami.[514] Hoover was excited
about Sullivan's catch and about how close he had come to his
goal. He returned to Belle Isle determined to clear his desk and
be back on the water as soon as possible.[515] His press secretary

announced that his boss wanted to get in more fishing and announced a drastically trimmed work schedule. On Sunday, he would attend church; on Monday and Tuesday, work; on Wednesday, meet appointments if necessary; and the rest of the week was reserved for fishing.[516]

Three days later, on the evening of January 30, Hoover was at sea on the *Amitie*, working over his burgeoning speech, making final decisions on cabinet positions, and preparing his tackle for a full day of fishing. The next morning, as he left Long Key, the old salts hanging around the dock concurred that the weather was perfect for sailfish—clear skies and calm seas prevailed. But after a long day on the water, he had again failed to catch his sailfish. The following morning, the sun was peeking over the horizon when Hoover, Milbank, Justice Stone, and Phillip Kinsley of the Chicago *Tribune* began to troll the edge of the Gulf Stream. Kinsley, the token journalist who would later relate the day's events to his peers, had accompanied Hoover on horseback up Beaver Creek six months earlier in California. One of the fishing guides cut bait from the flesh of bonita to look like a small fish. Mid-morning, after Hoover had trolled for more than a hour, a hungry sailfish took the alluring morsel. Hoover "let his line out rapidly and then as he felt the sailfish nuzzling the bait he made his strike. As his hook caught, the sailfish leaped out of the water, then began a long run to escape."[517] Having lost too many of these spirited fish in the past, he let this one run until it made a sharp turn. At that moment, he put on the brakes and began the process of wearing the fish down. He had to play it just right to keep from breaking the line or leader as before or ripping the hook from the sailfish's mouth. Half an hour later, his arms tired, Hoover had the big fish aboard the *Amitie*, suspended from a rope. Hoover was elated. The plucky sailfish weighed forty-five pounds and measured seven feet, six inches in length. After five trips to Long Key, two to San Clemente Island in the Pacific, and one attempt off Cape San Lucas at the end of the Baja Peninsula, the president-elect had finally met his goal. The sailfish was not a record, but it was big enough that Hoover could take pride in his catch.

Heading back to the anchorage off Angel Fish Creek, the fishermen worked the trestle bridge, catching amberjack, tuna, and triggerfish. At lunch, the conversation buzzed about landing the sailfish. His ardor increased, Hoover returned to the same fishing grounds hoping to repeat the morning's performance. Another big sailfish grabbed the bait, but insecurely hooked, it broke free from his line. That night, while Hoover was alone in his cabin, his inaugural address began to come together.

News from the fishing party that had remained behind somewhat diminished the day's accomplishments. Trolling along the edge of the Gulf Stream off Miami, Herbert Work, chairman of the Republican National Committee; Mark Wood, a leading Nebraska Republican; and Larry Richey, Hoover's recently appointed private secretary, found themselves in the middle of a school of large sailfish. Richey, who had fished with Hoover for years and was an accomplished fisherman in his own right, had landed three large sailfish in a little over two hours. Work, who confessed that he had been lucky, managed to catch two, and the neophyte from Nebraska hauled in one. All six sailfish weighed between sixty-five and seventy-five pounds. Displayed on the Miami fishing wharf, the sailfish were admired by strolling snowbirds.[518]

On Saturday, February 9, Hoover met with the Association of Captains of Chartered Fishing Boats at Miami, who presented him with a magnificent big-fish fishing rod. The president-elect spent about an hour swapping fishing stories with the captains.[519]

Later that morning, along with the Milbanks and the Rickards, he drove to the yacht anchorage north of Long Key and climbed aboard the *Saunterer,* his new rod in hand, for a weekend cruise to Florida's west coast. The houseboat slowly zigzagged through the Keys, crossed the Bay of Florida, and worked its way up the coast, finally plying the Caloosahatchee River to Seminole Lodge, the estate of Thomas Alva Edison, holder of eleven hundred patents.[520] Among those there to celebrate the great inventor's eighty-second birthday were Henry Ford and Harvey Firestone. Edison, who had no time for fishing, a complete waste of time from his point of view, teased the president-elect about his avocation. The elderly inventor achieved the solitude that Hoover did while fishing by pretending to be deaf.[521]

A few hours later, the *Saunterer* began to retrace its path down the Caloosahatchee for several days of fishing. On the return trip, Hoover hoped to land a tarpon, one of the only large

Hoover's first sailfish, January 30, 1929. COURTESY AP/WIDE WORLD PHOTOS

game fish that he had not yet caught. Though tarpon season had not yet arrived, it was reported that he still stood a good chance of finding the fish in Ponce de Leon Bay, farther to the south. The voyage was barely under way when a cool front brought strong winds and choppy seas. Fishing was ruined, and the *Saunterer* was forced to tie up. Two days at sea with little to do was too much for the active president-elect. He jumped ship downriver from Fort Meyers, driving back to Belle Isle across the Tamiami Trail in four hours. As he had scheduled no appointments, Hoover had two full days to rewrite his inaugural address. He did make time for a dinner engagement with Charles Lindbergh, who had spent the day fishing.[522]

On Friday, February 15, Hoover undertook a two-day tour of the devastation caused by flooding around Lake Okeechobee. The following Monday, he and Lou bade Florida good-bye and left for 2300 S Street in Washington, D.C. The vacation had been a success, the press reported; the president-elect was tanned by the tropical sun and well rested. "His battles with sailfish and other deep sea fish have hardened his muscle. He is in the best physical condition he has enjoyed in years."[523] Invigorated, Hoover was ready to assume the office of the presidency.

Back in Washington, the Hoovers packed for the move to the White House. Expectations in the country were high, the mood was upbeat, the economy was good after eight years of unprecedented growth. Those in the agricultural sector, who had not shared in the general prosperity, anticipated that they soon would. No international crisis was looming; peace prevailed. The reform-minded Hoover confidently expected to engineer solutions to most of the nation's problems. The Great Humanitarian, the Master of Emergencies, the Great Engineer would be the president to usher in the New Day. Hoover, however, understood that he and his supporters had oversold his abilities and his accomplishments. His prescience was expressed in an interview with Willis J. Abbot of the *Christian Science Monitor* just before leaving Florida: "I have no dread of the ordinary work of the presidency. They have a conviction that I am a sort of superman, that no problem is beyond my capacity. If some unprecedented calamity should come upon this nation. . . . I would be sacrificed to the unreasoning disappointment of a people who had expected too much."[524]

7

The Fisherman President

March lived up to its reputation for volatility. On Hoover's inauguration day, March 4, it came in like a lion. Cold rain fell on the couple as they traveled to the White House in an open-topped car. Later they stood in the downpour for several hours to watch the parade. Both escaped the fate of William Henry Harrison, who under similar conditions caught pneumonia and died. Undeterred, the hardy Hoover began his presidency as he had all of his previous jobs. He was a microburst of activity. He attacked on a broad front, dealing with dozens of problems simultaneously. Most oil leases on public lands were canceled, and a graduated tax reduction plan called for the greatest tax cuts on the lowest incomes. He intervened in corrupt patronage practices, made public all government tax refunds, successfully resolved a railroad strike, and called a special session of Congress to deal with agricultural problems.[525] Hoover moved aggressively to increase the size of many national parks, to create new ones, and to bring under federal protection millions of acres of land—especially in the West. Labor legislation, public education, child welfare pro-

grams, prison reform, public power projects, and a complete over-
haul of the Bureau of Indian Affairs were all undertaken.[526]

For Hoover to keep up this level of activity, and also to keep
from gaining weight, Boone, his White House physician, recommended more exercise. Hoover turned to medicine ball. He had
two courts set up in the backyard of the White House and invited
friends to play every morning before breakfast.[527] He would not
allow pictures to be taken of him playing medicine ball in the
backyard of the White House. Instead of just throwing the heavy
ball back and forth, Hoover invented a game with rules and a
scoring system. Hoover liked competition, and he liked to win.
On his fishing outings, he always tallied up who caught the
biggest and the most fish. The game of medicine ball went on
nearly every morning of Hoover's four years in the White House.
Only in extreme weather was a game canceled, and many times
he played in rain, sleet, or snow. Hoover, Stone, Sullivan, Wilbur,
Richey, and Boone were the regulars, and Secretary of War Hurley and Attorney General Mitchell often played, as did military
aides, guests, and other high-ranking government appointees.[528]
After a strenuous workout, the men ate breakfast and were off to
long days of hard work. The Protestant work ethic was alive and
well in the Hoover White House.

In the rush of reform, Hoover did not forget about fishing.
Before coming into office, he realized that the demands of the
presidency would limit fishing and camping trips to California
and Oregon. Wooley Camp was ready for use by 1927, but mired
in his work at the Commerce Department, running hard for his
party's presidential nomination, and distracted by an intense
relief effort during the great Mississippi flood, he was unable to
make use of his western Shangri-la. As president, it was even less
likely that he would be able to make the trip; time, distance, and
security negated Wooley Camp, the Rogue, or the McKenzie. He
also would be unable to attend the Bohemian Grove, as his presence would be disruptive, and providing security there was next
to impossible. Hoover always enjoyed fishing the Chesapeake,
but trout fishing, his first love, was possible in the mountains of
Maryland, West Virginia, or Virginia if the right location could be
found. A mountain lodge would provide the president with fishing, a secluded getaway, and in summer, a cool retreat from the
hellish climate of Washington, D.C.

In November 1928, Hoover instructed his private secretary Richey, along with George O'Malley of the Bureau of Fisheries, Col. Bill Starling of the Secret Service, and Horace Albright, now head of the National Park Service, to find a site within a hundred miles of Washington. It needed to be on a trout stream with a minimum elevation of twenty-five hundred feet, which would protect against mosquitoes and provide the longed-for relief from heat and humidity. Each member of the informal committee had a task. O'Malley was to determine if the stream could be racked so that when stocked, the fish would not escape. Hoover wanted a stream with rushing water for fly fishing and one in which deep holes could be dug for bait fishing. Albright was to ensure that the site was scenic and qualified for preservation, and Starling was to decide if the location could be protected by the Secret Service.[529] Richey coordinated and directed the committee.[530] Knowing Hoover's tastes, he would take the committee's recommendation to the president.

One of the sites that impressed the group was what is now Camp David in Maryland. Mount Weather, Virginia, was also considered. Land for Shenandoah National Park was being acquired atop a seventy-mile strip of the Blue Ridge range, and the streams there were evaluated. Throughout the winter, Richey trudged through snow and mud to look over a number of sites, but nothing seemed right. The persistent Richey, who went to great lengths to please his boss, was once described as a mother hen with one chick. Midwinter, William E. Carson, a friend of Albright's and head of the Conservation Department of Virginia, argued that the Rapidan River, between the twin peaks of Double Top Mountain, was the perfect choice. The site abutted the new park but had been previously overlooked. The committee skeptically journeyed to the valley. Because the site was not accessible by car, horses were necessary to traverse the rock-studded, rutted wagon road that crossed the ridge and worked its way up to the headwaters of the Rapidan, a distance of ten miles.

All of the horses loaned by local breeders for the trek were fine show animals. Albright recalled that his horse was one of the best mounts he had ever ridden.[531] With box lunches in saddlebags, the committee spent the day inspecting the valley, taking the horses up as far as they could climb. O'Malley judged the stream to be perfect, Starling thought the necessary protection could be provided, and Albright found the upper Rapidan Valley beautiful. An attractive wooded plateau lay between the confluence of Mill Prong and Laurel Prong, the streams that formed the Rapidan.[532] It was a fine location with adequate room for a number of cabins. The decision was all but made when the subject of rattlesnakes came up. Checking with the locals, it was learned that wild razorback hogs kept the rattlesnake population in check, but occasionally there was a stray copperhead or two.[533] In late March 1929, Richey told the president they had found the perfect spot. The President gave his tentative approval, but he and Lou wanted to visit the site, because in January they had looked at land along the Hughes River, twenty miles to the north, and been very disappointed. There, the landscape was dotted with huge dead chestnut trees that had succumbed to the blight rampaging through East Coast forests. Other hardwoods had been toppled, stripped of their bark, the rest of the trees left to rot.[534]

Lou planned on working out her own designs for the camp with the assistance of an architect. Through her association with the Girl Scouts, she secured the services of James Rippin, who had built several Girl Scout camps in New York and whose wife was the national director.[535] Like the house in California, she wanted the camp buildings to blend in with the environment and reflect the history of the Appalachians. Huge stone fireplaces, large open porches, and pine-sided, single-roofed cabins were central architectural features of their projected Boonesboro in the woods.

President and Mrs. Hoover planned their first visit to the Rapidan River on Saturday of Easter weekend. Their tasks included picking out a location for pitching army tents—temporary quarters while construction was under way—as well as reconnoitering the valley. The Wilburs were invited, a large picnic lunch was prepared, and all reporters and photographers were banned from accompanying them.[536] The press howled at being excluded but were reminded by the president, as they had been before, "that fish will not bite in the presence of the representatives of the press."[537] On Saturday morning around seven o'clock, a cold rain was falling. Hoover checked the weather by phone in Madison, Virginia, and it was raining there, too. By seven-thirty, the rain changed to a nasty drizzle mixed with hail and sleet. In Washington, March went out as it had come in—like a lion. The Hoovers canceled their outing.[538] The following Saturday, April 6, was the opening day of trout season, and the weather had improved. Again, the press was barred from accompanying the presidential party. Carson met the visitors at the proposed site and presented them all with Virginia fishing licenses and equipment, but Hoover did not fish. Instead, he spent the day exploring the valley on horseback, ensuring that the proposed building site was the best choice. The president affirmed the committee's judgment. The Hoovers were pleased and eager to begin the project. Sites were also selected for ten tents with wooden pallet floors and extended wooden porches that would serve as quarters for future overnight visits.[539]

To accommodate their dream camp, the Hoovers purchased 164 acres and carefully developed a building and landscape plan. They paid all expenses and pledged at some point in the future to transfer the land and camp buildings to Shenandoah National Park if not used by a future president or by the Boy Scouts or Girl Scouts.[540] Two platoons of marines, about a hundred men under the command of Maj. Earl C. Long, were assigned to provide security and to help construct the camp. To save the government money, Hoover decommissioned the presidential yacht *Mayflower*, which had been in service since Teddy Roosevelt's years in the White House.[541] The Filipino mess crew was transferred to Camp Rapidan to serve as kitchen staff; the cooking paraphernalia and the china came, too.[542]

In the spring and summer of 1929, the Hoovers visited their outdoor retreat as often as possible, supervising the construction as well as fishing, horseback riding, and sleeping in tents. Lou emphasized that all plantings must either be native to the area or be species that blended into the environment.[543] Only wood was burned winter or summer, and no live trees were cut for firewood. Dead wood was not in short supply because of the dead and dying chestnut trees. As the cabins were built, they were squeezed into the forest, disturbing the trees as little as possible.[544] The Hoover cabin was designed so that several trees came up through the deck. A "town hall" and a dining galley were planned, as well as additional guest cabins and a stable. Hoover quickly tired of having to ride a horse, a big black gelding named Old Billy, to the camp, and a five-mile surfaced entry road was

Temporary tents at Camp Rapidan, Virginia, August 17, 1929.
COURTESY QUEENS BOROUGH PUBLIC LIBRARY, LONG ISLAND DIVISION, NEW YORK HERALD-TRIBUNE
COLLECTION

begun. The marines also built their own tent encampment, a fire tower atop Fork Mountain, and a small airfield for planes that delivered mail as well as the morning papers and ferried important documents back and forth to Washington. Lou Henry decorated the "town hall," the main living area, with colorful handmade rugs in a southwestern motif.

Richey, who had accomplished the task of finding a perfect spot for the Hoovers, found one for himself as well. In Catoctin Furnace, Maryland, he discovered a piece of property that captured his fancy. In late March, the president's secretary purchased eighteen hundred acres of wooded mountain land along Hunting Creek and Fishing Creek, both fine trout streams.[545] As at Camp Rapidan, Richey installed tents as a temporary measure until cabins were constructed. These tents, however, had linoleum floors, wallboard sides, electric stoves, fans, lights, and telephones.[546] The Hoovers visited Richey's new camp in mid-April and in early May. Spring was in full bloom in the Maryland mountains. On a clear day, Big Round Top at Gettysburg was barely visible to the north. Hoover, in waist-high boots, waded the stream all afternoon and caught eight trout that weighed a little over a pound each.[547] Between the Maryland camp and the Rapidan retreat, the president was able to satiate his desire to fish for trout, though in both states the season was short. To ensure that Hoover could fish when the mood struck him, a third fishing ground was acquired: two miles along the waterfront on the Potomac River, between Glymont and Indian Head, Maryland.[548]

In June, the Hoovers journeyed back to Camp Rapidan. A hard rain turned the dirt road leading into the camp into a sea of mud. The cars, sometimes sinking to the running boards, took an hour and a half to make the last ten miles.[549] The party arrived around six o'clock, which left several hours of daylight for fishing. In the mountain twilight, Hoover and his companions, Boone, Kellogg, Richey, and Arthur Hyde, the secretary of agriculture, caught enough trout for a late dinner and the next morning's breakfast. Hoover slept well that night to the sound of a steady rain beating on the roof of his tent. The following morning, the men inspected the building progress of the cabins and then returned to the Rapidan to fish and to identify places where trout pools might be built.[550] Lou, with a Secret Service man in tow, rode to the top of the ridge and followed an old mountain trace that would soon be Skyline Drive. She picked an array of wild-flowers and plant specimens.[551] That evening around a roaring campfire, she challenged the men to identify her day's findings.

Throughout the rest of the summer, construction continued at a feverish pace. By mid-August, the "town hall," the Hoover's cabin, the galley, and several guest cabins were completed. The trout stream work, an ongoing project, was under way and well stocked with fish. Because of eels, the prongs needed frequent restocking. "We set many eel traps," Starling reported, "but caught very few of them."[552]

On Saturday, August 10, the president's fifty-fifth birthday, Hoover ended up with a fat baby opossum. The story of how he acquired the opossum is apocryphal. There are at least three different versions of the events, and within the versions, the details differ considerably. The most reliable version comes from Dr. Boone's diary and from an interview with Horace Albright.

Boone maintained that he was out riding along the crest of the Rapidan Valley in late July, when he passed a house where a boy was leaning on the fence. Boone stopped and asked the boy his name and where he went to school. The eleven-year-old said his name was Ray Buraker but that he didn't go to school because there wasn't any. There was a church and his father was the preacher. Their house was the church. Boone rode back to camp and related the story. Hoover asked Boone to go back and tell the young lad to bring him an opossum and in return he would pay $5. Boone rode back to the little cabin and related the president's offer. Nothing happened; no opossum was delivered.[553]

The day of the president's birthday, Boone, again out riding, stopped by Ray's house and asked if he had caught an opossum. The boy said yes, and Boone invited him to round up the critter and ride his horse back to camp. Ray, extremely shy, presented the baby marsupial to Hoover, was given the $5, met Charles Lindbergh, whom he had never "heared" of, and refused to join the birthday celebration. He did take several pieces of cake for his brothers and sisters after eating with the steward at the back of the galley.[554] On further investigation, it was learned that Ray could read a little, having been taught by his father. Many of the other children in the Rapidan neighborhood could not read at all, and none had ever been to school. Hoover put together both a local committee headed by Ray's father and a national committee to raise money for a mountain school. Ray was invited to the White House, had his tonsils removed in Washington, and went on a $20 spending spree in the city.[555] Word quickly spread among the mountain children that the president was paying $5 apiece for opossums. Several weeks after having received Ray's opossum, the Hoovers returned to Camp Rapidan to find clustered outside the gate several dozen children and a dozen opossums. The Hoovers pooled their dollars and distributed them to the eager children, after having them promise that they would bring no more opossums.[556] As the president and first lady became better acquainted with their mountain neighbors, they became more protective, for the national press loved to portray them as ignorant hillbillies. Hoover, since his summer in Arkansas while a Stanford student, understood their oppressive poverty, lack of education and medical care, and dismal diet.

Hoover on Old Billy, Camp Rapidan, Virginia.
COURTESY HERBERT HOOVER LIBRARY

The Hoovers formally inaugurated Camp Rapidan on August 17 and invited their Madison County, Virginia, neighbors to participate in the festivities as a way of thanking them for their many contributions. The Chamber of Commerce, which claimed that recent events had awakened Madison County for the first time since the founding of Jamestown, prepared to feed more than ten thousand guests. Hospitality demanded a memorable shindig. "From the Blue Ridge crest to the woodlots of the Piedmont, men went out to shoot squirrels to go into fifty 'oldtime washpots'

Hoover, elkhound named Weggie, and Lou Henry, Camp Rapidan, Virginia, August 20, 1932. COURTESY QUEENS BOROUGH PUBLIC LIBRARY, LONG ISLAND DIVISION, NEW YORK HERALD-TRIBUNE COLLECTION

(about fifteen gallons each) of Brunswick stew. Cattle and pigs were readied for slaughter. Three hundred loaves of bread and five hundred chickens were ordered."[557] Those who wished to sample the traditional mountain burgoo had to arrive early, for the chamber had ordered only five thousand tin cups. Though the crowd exceeded expectations, there was no shortage of food. People were encouraged to bring two picnic baskets, one for themselves and another for guests, and many did. A fifty-pound ham graced the dignitaries' table.[558]

One of those dignitaries, Virginia governor Harry Flood Byrd, arrived in an Army blimp, welcomed by two blaring bands and a company of Monticello National Guard dressed in colonial uniforms.[559] After depositing the governor, the huge airship slowly circled the field so that everyone could have a good look. Around eleven-thirty, the presidential caravan entered the fairgrounds with Secret Service men on the running boards of the cars. Shouts of "here he comes!" rippled through the crowd but were drowned out as the bands struck up "Hail to the Chief" and a twenty-one-gun salute ripped the air.[560] Hoover had planned to stay no more than half an hour, but warmed by the friendly enthusiasm of the crowd, he decided to stay for lunch. The Hoovers sampled the Brunswick stew, ham, fried chicken, and barbecued beef.[561] The table was laden with pies and cakes. The huge quantity of leftover food was trucked to the ever-hungry marine garrison, which now numbered nearly two hundred. In a very short speech, the president elaborated on one of his favorite themes:

> I fear that the summer camp we have established on the Rapidan has the reputation of being devoted solely to fishing. That is not the case for the fishing season lasts but a short time in the spring. It is a place for week-end rest— but fishing is an excuse and a valid reason of the widest range of usefulness for temporary retreat from our busy world. In this case it is an excuse for return to the woods and streams with their retouch of the simpler life of the frontier from which every American springs.[562]

Everyone was invited to visit the camp that afternoon, and hundreds of people accepted the Hoovers' invitation to tour the retreat. Until the end of his presidency in 1933, Hoover spent many weekends at Camp Rapidan, fishing, constructing trout pools, building dams, occasionally riding, sitting on the front porch, and contemplating in front of a roaring fire. Hundreds of guests and many government officials came to the camp, and much important business was transacted. The mountain school was built and a teacher hired. It remained open until most of the people in the area were resettled to make way for Shenandoah National Park.

On the diplomatic front, Hoover wished to invite British prime minister Ramsey MacDonald to Washington to discuss outstanding problems between the two countries. Issues included naval disarmament, defense, intergovernmental debt, reparations, and freedom of the seas.[563] Hoover thought an understanding would more likely be reached if he and the prime minister got to know one another in the relaxed atmosphere of Camp Rapidan rather than in the more formal setting at the White House—summit diplomacy in the woods. MacDonald, a Labor Party pacifist who had successfully campaigned for naval parity with the United States as a solution to the arms race, agreed to come to Washington.[564] Hoover adamantly believed that peace could be maintained through diplomacy and disarmament. He hoped that the United States and Great Britain might present a united front at the coming London Naval Conference to check aggressive nations such as Japan and began to downsize navies rather than merely slow growth. The president also wished to explore ways to settle international disputes through the use of public opinion rather than military action, sanctions, or binding arbitrations.[565]

MacDonald, the first British prime minister to visit the United States, arrived with his daughter Ishbel in Washington on October 4 to a tumultuous welcome. Hoover met his British counterpart at the White House and informed the prime minister that they were leaving for the country. MacDonald protested that he had not brought the proper attire, but Hoover loaned him what was needed.[566] Accompanied only by Mrs. Hoover, Richey, Boone, and a State Department representative, Hoover and his two guests rushed off to Camp Rapidan. Sequestered in the woods, the two men frankly discussed international problems. The hardwood trees along the stream had begun to change into their fall splendor of yellow, red, and orange. Saturday morning dawned cold and crisp, and as the day wore on, snow flurries blew through the camp.[567] Discussions took place inside in front of blazing fires. On Sunday, the weather warmed, and Hoover and MacDonald walked the trails along the Rapidan, stopping to continue their talks while perched on two logs. The details of their conversation were not made public, though back in camp, the press and photographers were allowed questions and pictures.

Both leaders thought the meeting a triumph. Though little of substance had been achieved, a mutuality of respect and outlook demonstrated a largely shared Anglo-American worldview, a basis for future cooperation. The two world leaders had generated a "spirit of Camp Hoover."[568] The press and the public responded enthusiastically to the classic American iconography staged by the president, the image of Uncle Sam and John Bull, relaxed, casually dressed, fruitfully discussing world problems,

Interior of the president's cabin, Camp Rapidan. From left to right: Abbe Rickard, Philippi Butler (secretary to Mrs. Hoover), Lou Henry, Dare McMullin, Filipino houseboy, and marine officer Earl C. Long.

COURTESY HERBERT HOOVER LIBRARY

all the while sitting on logs alone in the woods, fiddling with sticks or whittling. But unfortunately for the president, no diplomatic tête-à-tête or relaxed weekend in the woods could prepare him for the difficulties that loomed on the horizon.

Hoover had worried for some time that the stock market was excessively inflated and that at some point a correction would occur. In September, the market had faltered, but then it seemed to stabilize.[569] The MacDonalds had gone home, and Hoover, always a baseball fan, journeyed to Philadelphia to see one of the games of the exciting World Series. It was won brilliantly by the A's, four games to one over the Chicago Cubs. At the annual fall extravaganza, the crowd, after a recorded playing of "Hail to the Chief," rose cheering to give the president a standing ovation.[570] It was to be one of his last hurrahs while president.

The dust had hardly settled at Shibe Field when on October 23, 1929, a Thursday, the shaky New York stock market plunged. Sixteen million shares were dumped on "Black Thursday," and for a time, no buyers could be found. Later in the day, the market again stabilized. Over the weekend, Wall Street caught its breath, wishfully thinking the worst over. On Monday morning, when the bell rang to open the market, panic selling resumed. On Tuesday, the bottom fell out as twenty-three and a half million shares were dumped. By the time the market closed that afternoon, listed stocks had decreased in total value by about $18 billion since September 1.[571] For three more weeks, the bear fattened on the bull. Mark Sullivan, who spent a great deal of time with the president, helped lift his spirits as the two of them pored over a huge stock market chart one night in the White House. Contemplating what might happen if the market continued to plummet, Hoover pointed to Bethlehem Steel: "Well, suppose this drops another ten points?" Sullivan cleverly responded: "It can't; there's the edge of the chart." Both had a good laugh.[572] When the market finally bottomed out, however, comic relief could not assuage the fact that roughly $26 billion had been lost. Surprisingly, it was difficult to gauge the impact of the crash on the overall economy. Only a small number of Americans had invested in the market, and the massive correction was thought by some people, including Treasury Secretary Andrew Mellon and even John Maynard Keynes, to have had a positive effect—a cleansing of the system.[573]

The president reacted quickly to prevent a deflationary spiral, and for a while it looked as if the "Master of Emergencies" had stemmed the tide. He refused to panic, arguing that the economy was basically sound. In November, he held a conference of business leaders and asked them not to cut wages. The Federal Reserve eased credit and lowered the discount rate, and government construction projects were dramatically increased. This bold action helped restore a degree of confidence. By January 1930, the market had gained back 20 percent of its lost value. The average citizen looked forward to a bright economic future. There was no depression. Into the new year, it appeared that the economy had absorbed the economic shock triggered by the dramatic comedown. Few suspected that the October belly flop was just the initial plunge in a general economic collapse, taking down with it Hoover's and most Americans' hopes and dreams for a new day. Unknowingly, the nation teetered on the brink of economic disaster.

In February, Hoover returned to Florida to fish, eager for a week at sea. Accompanying him by train to Long Key were his favorite fishing companions—Kellogg, Stone, and Sullivan—as well as his doctor and secretary, Boone and Richey.[574] A small flotilla of boats assembled at the anchorage off the little island on the Gulf of Mexico. Around the *Kilkenny* and another Department of Commerce tender, the *Dixie,* smaller chartered fishing skiffs, the *Dolphin, Good Times, Goofus Boy, Hoo Hoo, Orca,* and *Miss Sally,* bobbed in the waves. At dockside, the fishing party boarded the houseboat *Saunterer,* ate breakfast, and put to sea. The small flotilla entered the Gulf, where two Coast Guard cutters assigned to protect the president took up position, one in front and one to the rear. Passing through a channel between keys, the vessels moved into the Atlantic and dropped anchor about a mile off-shore. Hoover and Stone climbed into *Goofus Boy,* and Sullivan, Richey, and Boone got into a second boat.[575] Ideally, the men pre-ferred two to a boat, as the stern of the small craft had room for only two fishing chairs. More boats allowed more time for fish-ing. A threesome meant sharing but also more fun.

When they reached the reefs, Hoover baited his hook with a large chunk of mullet and began to troll. He was in luck. It had taken him a long time to learn to catch sailfish, but this time, demonstrating his skill, he was patient and let out line as needed. Sailfish often took their time swallowing the bait. When the seven-foot fish broke water, Hoover knew it was hooked. The feisty forty-five-pounder took him half an hour to land.[576] The upper half of his shirt was soaked with sweat, and his arms ached.[577] The fish on board, Hoover sat back in his chair, relishing the physical and mental exhilaration of the battle. Stone also hooked a large sailfish, but as he reeled in his catch, it was stolen by a shark. Rain squalls periodically swept over the boat, drench-ing the fishermen, engulfing them for a few minutes in sheets of hard-driving rain. For Hoover, deep-sea fishing with a good friend was the height of sport. The visceral and mental aspects coupled with the aesthetic, the hues of blues in the sky and the infinite shades of green produced by the play of the sun on the water, were deeply satisfying. The threat posed by storms and not knowing what lurked beneath the waves produced a height-ened sense of awareness, a drama acted out on a primeval stage, exactly the kind of stimulating vacation the president needed

Hoover battles a sailfish, February 1930. COURTESY AP/WIDE WORLD PHOTOS

after months of fourteen-hour days. No one else caught any fish. At lunch on board the *Saunterer*, the table belonged to Hoover.

Just after sunrise the next day, the small fleet of fishing boats made its way north, sailing through Snake Creek and into Alligator Lake.[578] Hoover fished "for the ice box," as he liked to say, though he caught only four bonita, three barracudas, and one mackerel. Richey managed three barracuda and one mackerel. There were few fish for the dinner table. Stone fared the worst, catching nothing for the second day. He again claimed, amid skeptical glances, that hungry sharks had robbed him of success. Mrs. Hoover also came up empty-handed.[579] Kellogg and Sullivan, working the Gulf Stream, were the heroes of the day. Both had landed sailfish. Kellogg's catch, a fifty-two-pounder, succumbed after a tough fight. Sullivan's fish was a respectable thirty-five pounds. The sailfish competition among the members of Hoover's "Fishing Cabinet" heated up. The contagion also afflicted the wives, who joined the contest with verve.

On the third day, the fleet sailed out to the Gulf Stream in pursuit of sailfish. About eight miles off Long Key, south of the men's boat by half a mile, Mrs. Stone and the first lady let out their lines. Hoover, Sullivan, and Stone, on the *Miss Sally,* were barely in sight. Stone did not have to wait long before a sailfish grabbed his bait. The struggle lasted more than twenty-five minutes. This was his first catch since arriving in Florida, and he was elated to be in the competition. While Stone wrestled with his forty-pound fish, the women continued to troll. The *Dolphin* rocked in the wake of a Cuba-bound freighter when a fish struck Mrs. Stone's line. It was clear that whatever had swallowed the bait was big, as her rod bent in the shape of a horseshoe, the tip nearly touching the water. The three fishermen on the Hoover boat looked up to see "the big fellow break out of the water and dance across a wave on his tail."[580] Fishing stopped as they instinctively moved to the stern to watch the action.

It took Mrs. Stone more than two hours to subdue the big sailfish. The contest began in the late afternoon, continued as the sun dropped below the horizon, and ended with the moonlight shimmering on the placid mirrorlike surface of the ocean.[581] During the final fifteen minutes of the struggle, it was not clear whether she or the fish would prevail—both were exhausted. The first lady captured it all on her home movie camera while the men watched, fascinated, occasionally shouting words of encouragement. The huge sailfish weighed sixty-six pounds, the largest caught by any member of the Hoover party and the Long Key Fishing Club season record.[582] Mrs. Stone was awarded a prestigious gold button. Meanwhile, Richey and Boone successfully fished "for the ice box" near Trestle Number Two and returned to port at sunset. Several hours later, in the bright moonlight, the little flotilla pulled up to the pier. Both men were astounded by the size of Mrs. Stone's sailfish. At dinner later that evening, the table belonged to the victorious Stones.

Thursday brought another sun-filled Florida day. The president was busy in the morning with details surrounding the London Naval Conference, but by midafternoon, the fleet was once again under way to the edge of the Gulf Stream. After Mrs. Stone's fabulous catch, all looked forward to "getting into" a large school of sailfish. Most of the anglers faced disappointment, but for Mrs. Hoover, February 13 was her lucky day. She hooked a thirty-eight-pound sailfish, fought it for twenty minutes, and landed it successfully. Others brought in a variety of fish, but no other sailfish were caught. At dinner that evening, the first lady enjoyed her triumph in her own modest way. The others speculated that surely tomorrow, the last full day of fishing, the big sailfish would rise to the bait. Fishermen are by definition hopelessly optimistic.

Early the next morning, the Hoover vacation "armada" left Long Key, traveling south to Sombrero Light. Hoover, Stone, and Sullivan commandeered the fifty-foot sloop *Orca* for the day's fishing. By late afternoon, the party had caught one hundred pounds of fish. No sailfish were hooked or sighted. Hoover decided to send the larger vessels back to the anchorage so that everyone could enjoy a moonlight cruise in the small boats.[583] Darkness fell on the expectant anglers, but "the moon seemed reluctant to appear, sending millions of stars in its stead."[584] Tired and hungry, they headed back. After dinner, the conversation died down as all realized the vacation was coming to an end. On the decks of the *Saunterer,* the group of friends lingered late, quietly enjoying the gentle rhythmic rocking of the boat and the heavy tropical salt air, stirred by ocean breezes. In the morning, Hoover got in half a day more of fishing, though again the elusive sailfish were not feeding where expected. After lunch, he carefully packed his fishing tackle trunk and prepared to board his special express train headed north to a cold, snow-covered Washington.[585] In the president's private car, the tanned, tired anglers had much to talk about. As it was annually at the Bohemian Grove, care had been banished for six days but waited in the corridors of the capitol as a result of economic uncertainty.

Throughout the spring, unemployment continued to rise steadily. The trend was made more ponderous by a deplorable

Hoover displays his sailfish while Larry Richey holds the tail.
COURTESY HERBERT HOOVER LIBRARY

lack of reliable statistics. Past economic downturns were of little help, though the president's financial advisors sought to interpret the events of 1929 in light of the recession of 1921.[586] The prior economic downturn had been brutal, and unemployment had rapidly risen to nearly 12 percent. The good news was that it had been short, and the nation quickly recovered. Hoover assumed the present economic crisis would follow the 1921 pattern. In a speech before the Washington Chamber of Commerce on May 1, 1930, the president affirmed: "I am convinced we have passed the worst and with continued effort we shall rapidly recover."[587] By the end of the month, feeling cautiously optimistic, Hoover made his third trip to Ogontz Lodge on Larry Creek near Williamsport, Pennsylvania. In Washington, pressure to enact vastly higher import duties with the Smoot-Hawley tariff bill reached new heights. Escape from the rancorous debate into the serene woods was possible as Hoover gave the Memorial Day speech at the National Cemetery in Gettysburg. Surrounded by Secret Service and pursued by journalists and photographers, he mounted the podium and reiterated the need for moderation and a "calm vision" in the face of difficulties that "loom ominous"—exhibiting the same characteristics that so defined President Lincoln.[588]

That evening, a tired Hoover arrived at the Ogontz Lodge. Shortly after dinner, he climbed the stairs to the small, sparsely furnished bedroom, Gibson girl prints on the walls, and slept soundly under several quilts as the temperature dropped to a low of thirty-five degrees.[589] In the morning, after a huge breakfast that featured stacks of pancakes, the small fishing party started up the serpentine mountain trail in the cold air. Near the headwaters of Larry Creek, hemmed by House Lantern Mountain, Maneval Point, and Pulp's Rock, a spot where he had done well on his previous trips, the president cast his fly upon the waters.[590] The sun soon warmed up the woods and the hopeful fishermen. Relying on his favorite fly, the Royal Coachman, but going to a Cahill as a backup, Hoover reeled in eight nice brook trout, a pound to a pound and a half each.[591] Louis "Louie" F. Metzger, who had served as caretaker and cook for more than forty-five years, and who had cooked for Hoover on his last two visits, fixed the fish for lunch. Later that afternoon, the anglers were back at streamside, this time working the West Fork of Larry Creek. The trout were rising and taking the flies, providing enough food to grace the evening dinner table and for the morning's breakfast.

After sunset, the cold again settled in, but the crackling of a roaring fire made for a peaceful evening of quiet conversation—no politics. In the flickering firelight, "among the excellent prints on the wall of the main living room was a simple poster which drew the eyes of members of the party. It carried the inscription, 'For President—Herbert Hoover,' and bore a photograph of the President knee deep in a trout stream."[592] Revitalized after another good night's sleep and a big breakfast, Hoover summarized his visit in the Ogontz log book with his wry humor:

> May 30th–June 2nd, Windy; fair; few fish; much food good company; much sleep; no politics; U.S.S. [United States Senate]—not in session. Louis [Metzger] still the cook. May 31 U.S.S.—not in session. Louis still the cook. June 1 U.S.S.—not in session. Louis still the cook. I am glad to record the perfection of Mrs. Cooke's arrangements and Mr. Cooke's submissiveness thereto. It has improved the establishment materially since 1918. The time has come when the supply of fish should be turned over to Mrs. Cooke. Gratefully yours, Herbert Hoover.[593]

It was Hoover's last visit to the wooded hills of central Pennsylvania. The increased demands of his increasingly troubled presidency cut deeply into his time for fishing. The whirlwind on the banks of the Potomac awaited the president's return.

With the onset of summer, though trout season was over, frequent trips to Camp Rapidan provided a modicum of relief for the overworked president. On most weekends, he took people with him, bent on finding solutions to problems. Walking the trails, building dams and trout pools, and horseback riding took up his spare time. His dislike for the equine species had not changed, not even for Old Billy, but a horse was the only way the large valley could be explored, and Dr. Boone continually encouraged him to exercise by riding. Hoover often rode with guests, and one of his favorites was Jay Darling.

Hoover was an admirer of Jay "Ding" Darling's political cartoons in the Des Moines *Register*. They had met once at the Hotel Fort Des Moines when Hoover was secretary of commerce. Occasionally Ding received word through intermediaries that the secretary admired his cartoons. After the inauguration, he continued to receive secondhand reports. One day in 1929, Darling got a phone call from the president asking him to come to Washington for the weekend as his guest. The cartoonist asked if the president had anything specific in mind. No, said the president, he just wished to know what he was thinking. The weekend was a success; the two men enjoyed one another and discovered that they had much in common. Darling loved to hunt and fish and was an adamant conservationist and member of the Izaak Walton League. Both men had grown up in Iowa. Future invitations were forthcoming, and Ding and the president became good friends. Darling participated in the early-morning medicine ball games at the White House and was a guest at Rapidan on several occasions.[594]

One Sunday morning, when the two men were out riding, they decided to escape from the Secret Service escort that always shadowed the president. Darling remembered that Hoover had often publicly said that the only way a president could be alone was in prayer or when fishing. This was an opportunity not to be missed. The moment presented itself when a side trail up ahead meandered off into the woods. The two riders exchanged knowing glances, spurred their horses, and bolted down the trail. After some distance, they galloped up another partially hidden trail that wound to the top of the ridge. An abandoned fire tower proved a safe haven. Hoover and Darling hitched their horses in the bush, then, like two mischievous boys, climbed to the observation platform, where they could laugh as they watched the escapade below—frantic Secret Service men "scouring the countryside" in search of the president. Hoover's day off also included building a fire over which to cook their lunch, constructing a dam, and catching a number of trout. Darling recalled that it was "the only time in life that I ever saw that man happy and unrestrained."[595] For years they periodically reminded each other of that fun-filled day on the Rapidan.

Hoover had always been known for fast driving, as had Lou. Now the presidential motorcade beelined between Washington and his mountain retreat—not at excessive speeds, as his growing number of detractors claimed, but with determination.[596] But the image of Hoover scurrying between the capital and Rapidan became a metaphor for his perceived ineptness, for his failed attempts to hold up the economic house of cards.

In 1930, the American banking system was chaotic and poorly regulated. Thousands of banks were undercapitalized, and throughout the 1920s, more than five hundred banks a year failed.

Many were rural midwestern banks done in by the festering farm problem. The Federal Reserve System was partially designed to rescue failing financial institutions, though it often did not do so. The problem worsened by August 1930, as a serious drought spread ominously across the Midwest.[597] Even the weather seemed to conspire against the president. More bad news arrived in November. Republicans took a shellacking in the congressional elections, losing control of the House by a few votes and maintaining control of the Senate by only one.[598] At the end of the month, the bank failure rate was a little above normal but not a source of grave concern. Then in December, without warning, a calamity struck. First in Kentucky and then in the surrounding states, small banks weakened by years of financial struggle went down, as a midwesterner might say, "faster than salts through a widow woman." The calamity worsened when a large New York bank joined the list of casualties. By year's end, the number of failed banks reached 1,352, more than double the normal rate.[599] As with the market crash a year earlier, the panic subsided, and in its aftermath, a slight recovery occurred. The financial system had now been hit by lightning twice, and though damaged, it had survived. What else could possibly go wrong?

The Hoover administration and the American public did not have long to wait to discover the answer to the question. The complicated and flimsy European economic system, based upon the settlement of World War I at Versailles, had staggered through the 1920s in spite of itself, sustained only by a large infusion of American dollars. U.S. loans to Germany were used to pay reparations to France, which used the money to repay World War I debts owed to the United States. With the stock market crash and the banking crisis, the United States quit lending money and called in some outstanding loans. The system collapsed when the cash cow dried up. Without American loans to meet its obligations, Austria's leading bank collapsed in May 1931.[600] The reverberations were like a tsunami that washed away the international financial system and left devastation in its wake. By the end of the year, each country scrambled to save itself from drowning. Though Hoover took many weekend trips to Camp Rapidan, they were hardworking sessions that sought solutions to an economic quandary no one understood. There was no time for fishing.

As the nation moved into the economic labyrinth of the Great Depression, the toll on the president was terrific. Since his days as an ambitious young hustler at the Oregon Land Company, Hoover had known only outrageous success; he had faced great difficulties and learned how to overcome them. His attempted solutions to each wave of the economic crisis drew him farther away from things in which he believed and things that had worked in the past. The British abandonment of the gold standard left Hoover puzzling over the worth of currency, which was the basis of international trade and credits. He feared that all might drown in the uncharted waters. The president vetoed several bills passed by the House and Senate that authorized direct federal welfare payments, as he also feared the dole. Critics asked how he could refuse to spend government money on relief for Americans in need after having done so for foreigners when he was head of the American Relief Administration.

The answer lay in Hoover's view of the difference between the United States and Europe. The dole might create a permanent underclass as existed in England and on the Continent, perpetuating poverty. It would rob its citizens of incentive. People would look to Washington for solutions to their problems rather than to themselves. America was based upon upward social mobility. Unemployment statistics purported to measure the number of people who were between jobs, not to measure some permanent condition. He believed at first that American individualism, American exceptionalism, and cooperation would rise to the occasion and smite the ogre of recession. When voluntarism failed, Hoover reluctantly proposed new solutions. Since the depression did not come all at once, it was easy to think that each crisis heralded the end of the downturn, and that things would get better. But unforeseen economic exigencies multiplied. In his frustration at his inability to stop the economic slide, Hoover yelled at his secretary, Theodore Joslin: "This job is nothing but a damned twenty-ring circus, with hell breaking loose everywhere."[601]

Hoover finally did break away from his ideological moorings when he created the Reconstruction Finance Cooperation (RFC) in 1932, a government agency that provided funding for the undercapitalized private sector. But freed from the shackles of his scruples, Hoover still failed to follow through with direct taxpayer dollars for relief. His critics asked him to explain the difference between loaning money to people at the top as opposed to those in need at the bottom. Hoover's ambivalent answers did him no good politically. He sacrificed short-term necessity to long-term principle.

To the American public, this penchant for principle made him appear callous, hard-hearted, impersonal, and unconcerned about their welfare. What good were principles to those who were unemployed and starving? But nothing could be farther from the truth than the accusation that the president didn't care. Hoover knew full well the suffering of the unemployed and bore the burden heavily. He had not forgotten his desperate search for a job in the mining camps of Nevada. Feeling personally responsible, he could not look at breadlines or talk with apple sellers on the street. He shut himself away in the White House and at Camp Rapidan and worked harder—often eighteen-hour days. Night after night at dinners in the White House, the Hoovers entertained between twenty and fifty people. Often the president stared at his plate as he ate rapidly and said nothing. He and Lou responded to hundreds of individual appeals that reached the White House, ensuring that legitimate requests received assistance. They also supported dozens of relatives and friends in need. The first lady hired additional secretaries to handle the volume and spent a good deal of her own money.[602]

Matters were further complicated because Hoover's relationship with the press had steadily deteriorated. Few in the press corps gave him the benefit of the doubt. His aides suggested he use the radio for weekly reports to the American people on efforts to curb the downturn. Aides and friends encouraged him to make himself visible to the public, to demonstrate faith in the future through his presence. But he refused to get out on the hustings and be a cheerleader for the things in which he believed.[603] The American people needed leadership, a president who would share himself with those he led. What they got instead was a chief executive officer, a man who in public was uncomfortable with himself. Hoover's greatest failing was his refusal to attempt to build a covenant with the average American. William Allen White, the "Sage of Emporia, Kansas" in a letter to a friend in February 1931, succinctly characterized the problem of Hoover's personality and the demands of presidential leadership:

From forty to sixty per cent of the power of the presidential office is not in administration but in morals, political
and spiritual leadership, quite apart from party responsibility. He is after all, President of the Nation and a servant
of God as well as head of the Republican party, and as
President of the nation and servant of God, he has much
more to do than to run a desk as a head of the greatest
corporation of the world. He has to guide a people in the
greatest adventure ever undertaken on the planet. For
without leaders the people grow blind and without vision
the people perish.[604]

By 1932, the handwriting was on the wall. Hoover had isolated himself from the press, from the Congress, and from the
American people. The 1932 Republican Convention was more
like a funeral. Ironically, the Hoover force's challenge at the 1928
convention, "Who Else but Hoover," was relevant in 1932, if for
dramatically different reasons. The delegates dutifully offered
up Hoover's body to be cremated by the electorate. Worse, in the
general election, Hoover would face the charismatic Franklin D.
Roosevelt, governor of New York, a natural campaigner and
gifted orator.

After the uneventful convention, the battered president, seeking rest and seclusion away from the eye of the public and the
press, gave up the "battle on a thousand fronts" to go fishing,
something he had not done in more than a year.[605] He boarded
the *Sequoia* in Washington on Sunday afternoon, August 14,
accompanied by Secretary of War Patrick J. Hurley; California
banker friend Henry Robinson; journalist and longtime friend
Will Irwin; and Clarence M. Woolley, president of American
Radiator. Together they sailed down the Potomac to Piney Point,
where Secretary of Agriculture Arthur M. Hyde joined them. The
weather was perfect—blue skies, sunshine, moderate tempera-
tures, and a slight breeze. That night, a bright moon lit the pathway of the *Sequoia* to its anchorage at the mouth of the Potomac.

Early Monday, the houseboat made for a famous Chesapeake
fishing spot called the Southeast Middle.[606] All morning, Hoover,
Hyde, and Robinson fished from the deck of the inspection boat,
but they caught few fish. They decided that a new spot was warranted, and Solomon's Island held potential. The anglers climbed

Hoover reels in a rockfish on the Chesapeake Bay, August 14, 1932.
COURTESY AP/WIDE WORLD PHOTOS

into a smaller speedboat and trolled not far off the island's shore. They were rewarded with a "good mess of fish," including twelve sea trout, one weighing nine pounds, and Atlantic croakers.[607] After a late lunch, the *Sequoia* steamed on to Tangier Island, where a well-known fishing guide, John Crockett, was brought on board. Tall and lean, Crockett was dressed in blue coveralls. He had been working his crab traps when the Secret Service, in a speedboat, pulled up beside his small craft and asked if he would join the president.[608] He agreed. Those on board the *Sequoia* had many questions for Crockett on crabbing and fishing along Maryland's Eastern Shore. Asked about the best fishing grounds, Crockett suggested a spot three miles out toward the center of the bay.

The small fishing village on Tangier Island was founded in the early 1600s. Isolated for hundreds of years, the villagers spoke a dialect close to Elizabethan English. Hurley, Irwin, and Woolley went ashore to look around. Word quickly spread that the president would visit the island, but he did not. Instead, Crockett and Hoover took one of the motorboats and went off to fish, discreetly followed by the Secret Service. After a brief tour of Tangier, the men returned to the *Sequoia* to rendezvous with the president. The fishing improved: About forty hardheads, blue- fish, and trout were caught. Crockett's judgment was vindicated. When he returned to Tangier, reporters asked him about Hoover as a fisherman. He responded that he and the president had dis- cussed how to fish. "Mr. Hoover," he said, "is a good fisherman. He caught more than anybody else. He is a very pleasant man. I'll be glad to go out again if he comes down here any more."[609]

Regardless of the fishing success, Hoover wished to try his luck on the Patuxent River, across the bay and farther north. The *Sequoia* anchored for the night at the mouth of the river. A fresh fish dinner was served on the open decks on a beautiful, breezy, moonlit summer evening. Determined to have a full day of fish- ing, the president was up before dawn the next morning and casting from the deck of the boat. The right spot had been found; Hoover was reeling in rockfish and hardheads. He slept well, ate well, sat in the sun, and relaxed a little as he tried to ignore what awaited him in Washington. He enjoyed himself so much that he opted for another day at sea. The fishing remained good as the boat cruised north. But sadly, the outing was coming to an end. Late Wednesday afternoon, the *Sequoia* docked at Annapolis. When the president walked down the gangplank, he was sun- burned and chipper. Under escort of the Maryland State High- way Patrol, the president's motorcade sped back to the capital.

Hoover did little campaigning in August and early Septem- ber, arguing that attention to business took precedence over the election. The workaholic president redoubled his effort to find solutions to the nation's economic ills. Though he had developed innovative approaches to stimulate the economy, he now backed away from them and turned to more orthodox solutions, a bal- anced budget and a tax increase.

But on September 12, an election in Maine, a traditional Republican stronghold, was handily won by Democratic candi- dates. Hoover now realized that his presidency was imperiled; if he were to win, he would have to "carry the fight right to Roo- sevelt . . . crack him every time he opens his mouth."[610] In Hoover style, he marshaled what he considered to be the facts and went on the attack. When he targeted the numerous inconsistencies in Roosevelt's proposals, he gleefully assumed that he was scoring points with the electorate. As Election Day neared, an exhausted Hoover continued to defend his record in speech after speech. Desperate to avoid defeat, his fallback position became, "if it had not been for my efforts things would be worse." This further revealed his desperation. The massive number of unemployed lacked Hoover's imagination. Presidential style was a key election issue, one that Franklin Roosevelt won hands down. Roosevelt, a born aristocrat, radiated confidence. His public persona was warm and affable, and it was obvious that he loved to campaign—to "bloviate," as Warren Harding would have said. Roosevelt, demonstrating his arrogance, speculated whether it would be appropriate, if he beat Hoover by ten million votes, to request that he assume the presidency immediately. Justice Oliver Wendell Holmes, on meeting Roosevelt, judged him to possess a second-class intellect but a first-class temperament.[611] If the justice was corect in his analysis, in 1932, temperament trumped intellect.

On November 8, the voters overwhelmingly demonstrated that they wanted a president who was willing to experiment and who visibly exuded confidence. Hoover carried six states and lost half a dozen more by less than 3 percent. Nevertheless, he was beaten by Roosevelt by about one and a half million more votes than he beat Al Smith in 1928.[612] Hoover's presidency began on a wave of genuine enthusiasm and ended in overwhelming rejection by the voters. The orphan boy from Iowa found himself orphaned once more. The tragedy of Herbert Hoover was that what was needed he could not give, and what he could give was not needed. He was incapable of reinventing himself. Not Lou, not his family, no one was able to lighten his burden. The country needed someone at whom to point the finger of responsibility, and it chose Hoover. The Great Depression became his cross to bear, and he was crucified upon it.

For the Hoovers, the election loss was a terrible disappointment, but the four-month interregnum proved a longer agony. Hoover hoped to keep working on solutions on which he and Roosevelt could agree. The president-elect, however, wanted nothing to do with the pariah in the White House and correctly saw Hoover's pleas for cooperation as a Trojan horse. To relieve the tension and escape the White House, the Hoovers, in December, decided on a ten-day holiday cruise and fishing trip to Geor-gia and Florida. An added relief was being able to cancel the dreaded annual New Year's Day reception at the White House to which the public was invited. For years, on the first day of a new year, presidents and first ladies stood in reception lines for hours and shook hands with thousands of people. On New Year's Day 1929, more than six thousand people plodded through the White House to meet the president and first lady.[613] The lines of well-wishers stretched several blocks down Pennsylvania Avenue. At the end of the day, the Hoovers' hands were red, sore, and swollen. The tradition ended in 1932, when the planned vacation became the pretext for cancellation.

To ensure a pleasurable trip, the Hoovers invited close friends: the Rickards, Stones, and Sullivans, as well as Sen. and Mrs. War-ren Austin of Vermont. Richey, Boone, and Mrs. Hoover's secretaries, Dare Stark McMullin and Mildred Hall, rounded out the holiday travelers. A special train left Washington on the evening of December 23, bound for Savannah, where the well-stocked *Sequoia* and *Kilkenny* waited in port. Reports from the coast claimed the fishing prospects were good, as sea trout were running near Savannah. Hoover's appetite was whetted. All aboard the president's train were glad to escape the claustropho-bic political atmosphere of Washington; a holiday mood might be possible after all. The next morning in Savannah, the Hoovers were pleased to be met by a large, cheering crowd.[614]

A famous fishing guide, Guss Ohman, the sixty-year-old mayor of Daufuskie Island, South Carolina, joined the party at dockside. Like Henry Denny, Hoover's guide on the Brule in 1920, Ohman also had guided President Grover Cleveland. Nick-named the "King of Daufuskie Island," he had scouted the waters between Savannah and Ossabaw Island for several days before Hoover's arrival. On board, he assured the president that the fish were "biting like hungry tigers."[615] By midmorning, with the promise of a warm, sunny day, the small flotilla of boats was under way, led by the Coast Guard cutter *Minamar* and headed for Ossabaw. The tricky water passages meant navigating a com-plex series of rivers, narrows, and sounds: down Thunderbolt and Skidaway Rivers, past the Isle of Hope, through Skidaway Narrows, down Burnside and Vernon Rivers, past Possum Point, across Green Island Sound, through the Hell Gate, across

Ogeechee Sound, and into Ossabaw Sound.⁶¹⁶ At several prese-
lected spots, Hoover fished from the speedboat lowered from the
Sequoia, but he had no luck. The only fish caught, a sheepshead
and a drum fish, were reeled in by the guide. The anglers were
disappointed with the fishing but enchanted by the phosphores-
cent waves that broke over the hull of the *Sequoia.*

The small flotilla finally reached the beautiful sea island,
ghostly visible in the Christmas Eve twilight. Ossabaw, the third
largest island along the Georgia coast, was the twenty-five
thousand-acre resort of Dr. H. N. Torrey and his wife, Nell Ford
Torrey, of Detroit, heiress to a glass fortune. She and her husband
had purchased the island in 1924 for $150,000. The fifteen-
bedroom, red-tile-roofed, Spanish revival manor house was close
to a number of historic "tabby" buildings. Nearby were the old
clubhouse, built in 1876, a frame house, a barn, an oyster house,
and three surviving slave cabins. Tabby construction used ground
seashells as a major ingredient in the adhesive plastered between
the outer logs of the buildings.⁶¹⁷ Both sides of the long driveway
leading to the mansion were lined with huge oak trees covered
with hanging Spanish moss and mistletoe. Local legend maintained that the hull of "Old Ironsides," the USS *Constitution,* was
hewn from the island's mighty oaks.⁶¹⁸ The Torreys' Christmas
Eve guests were treated to a classic southern oyster roast. After
dinner, gifts were exchanged. A huge pile had been trucked from
the hole of the *Sequoia.* Then the Hoovers and their friends
returned to the boats, the passageways festooned in evergreen
bunting, to be rocked to sleep by the gentle waves.

Early Christmas morning, the flotilla weighed anchor for
Bear River. As Christmas Day was also a Sunday, Hoover and his
guests did not fish. Instead, they sunned on the boat's deck and
enjoyed a leisurely cruise down the Florida Passage to Sapelo
Island, another millionaire's tropical paradise. Howard Coffin,
the owner of the sixteen-thousand-acre island, was the founder
of the Hudson Motor Company. He had become rich by manu-
facturing a four-cylinder roadster that sold for $900. In 1912, he
purchased Sapelo Island for $150,000. Coffin and Hoover had
become friends when both were members of Woodrow Wilson's
War Cabinet. At the end of World War I, Coffin purchased Sea
Island and a portion of St. Simon's Island. Forming a partnership
with his favorite cousin, Bill Jones, the two enthusiastic entrepre-

neurs organized Sea Island Investments and became the premier developers of the Georgia islands. Both were ardent conservationists who attempted to preserve the historic buildings on the islands and protect the environment. Sea Island succeeded and became a world-famous resort. On Sapelo, Coffin built his mansion atop the foundation of a destroyed manor house. It was Mediterranean in style, tile-roofed, and featured indoor and outdoor swimming pools surrounded by Italian statuary.[619] The descendants of slaves that lived on the island spoke Gullah or Geechee, and many worked in the oyster and shrimp canning factory established by Coffin. He was one of the first "scientific oyster farmers." The stock market crash and ensuing depression were major blows to his fortune.[620]

The *Sequoia* and its attendants arrived at Sapelo Island in late afternoon. That evening, the Coffins served a lavish Christmas dinner and provided musical entertainment by a group of black singers that performed spirituals and chanteys first sung in the 1600s. A ninety-eight-year-old black man named Old Liverpool was introduced to the president. The man then related several stories from his youth that revolved around island life and the institution of slavery.[621] The guests returned to the boats late that evening, but in the morning, the flotilla hurriedly headed south, as Hoover was eager to fish. The chances of catching sailfish were much greater if the party fished the edge of the Gulf Stream. By midday, the boats stopped at Fernandia on Amelia Island to refuel. Hoover ordered the speedboat lowered into the water and took the opportunity to fish the surrounding bay. Mrs. Hoover, the Stones, the Austins, and Sullivan followed in a boat lowered from the *Kilkenny*. The fishermen trolled the Spanish Main for several hours but had no luck.[622] That night, the boats dropped anchor off the mouth of the Nassau River near Black Hammock Island.

The following morning, the dash south continued past Jacksonville. The flotilla stopped in St. Augustine only long enough to receive the mayor and a delegation of prominent citizens. The fishing party wished to reach Daytona by nightfall, but slower speeds were required to keep the boats from running aground in the shallow channels of the East Coast Canal. By nightfall, the flotilla was still twenty miles north of Daytona; it would take another two days of sailing to reach Palm Beach. Frustrated over the slow pace of the boats and having caught no fish, Hoover contemplated going ashore and catching a train. But the president acquiesced and used the time to clear up outstanding work and relax. In the mornings, the men gathered on the top deck of the *Sequoia* to play medicine ball. On Wednesday evening, the boats had not reached their anchorage at Lake Worth and attempted to run the narrow passage in the dark. All four boats ran aground on an unseen mud bank.[623] Finally, on Thursday afternoon, the flotilla reached Palm Beach and Lake Worth, the base of operations for the remainder of the trip. Hoover worked with the boatmen and guides to ready the equipment for the coming early-morning foray.

Seven miles to the southeast of Palm Beach, the sailing sloop *Orca* and the cabin cruiser *Miss Sally* worked their way along the edge of the Gulf Stream. In the first boat were Hoover, Austin, and Richey, and in the second, Stone, Sullivan, and Boone. The two fishing boats were flanked at a proper distance by the Coast Guard cutters. The fishermen attached their baited lines to aerial kites, which were kept aloft by the speed of the boat and the wind. The kites allowed the baited hook to drag along just below and occasionally on the surface, popping up and skip-jumping along the waves. This method presented a more tempting morsel for sailfish and other denizens of the sea, such as amberjack, barracuda, dolphin, shark, and tuna. The kites also prevented the fishing lines from crossing one another and tangling. After little more than fifteen minutes of trolling, Hoover had a strike. For thirty minutes, he battled a seven-foot, six-inch sailfish and landed it successfully. The day was off to the right start. A white flag was run up signaling that a sailfish had been caught.[624]

The president took no break, baiting his hook and immediately beginning again to fish. Richey had no nibbles, but Hoover soon hooked a fighting dolphin, a big, golden-hued beauty. Boone, on board the *Miss Sally*, tied into a large sailer and was thrilled to bring in a fish almost eight feet in length. Back on the *Orca*, Hoover had another strike. The taut line and bent rod suggested he had a large fish on the end of his line. The *Orca*'s captain, Herman Gray, reported that the fifty-five-minute battle was one of the most exciting he had ever witnessed. According to Boone: "The sailfish leaped entirely clear of the water repeatedly in an effort to shake the hook from his mouth, but the President managed to draw him close to the boat within fifteen minutes. When Captain Gray leaned over the side to gaff him, however, the fish started a new battle that lasted twenty-five minutes more."[625] The sailfish measured seven feet, eight inches. Austin hooked a seven-footer, but as the crew was pulling the fish aboard, a shark lunged from the water and tore the fish in two. By lunchtime, the hungry fishing party flew four white flags from the masts of two boats, although only three and a half fish had been landed.

For most of the afternoon, nothing happened; the sea was choppy and the boats bobbed up and down in a brief rain shower. Later, Hoover described the perils of deep-sea fishing: "These boats have a habit of suddenly descending to the floor of the sea, then rising up to the sky in a fashion that takes your breakfast overboard. You spend the whole day hanging onto the boat with your right hand, and with your left hand dragging a dead fish in the far-away behind the boat."[626] While choking down their lunches in the rough waters, Hoover and Richey decided to attach their lines to one bigger kite. As the kite flapped in the breeze and the sloop gingerly rode the rough swells, sailfish struck both lines at the same time, and both went taut.[627] For forty minutes, this double dynamic duo battled—man against fish, fish against man. Both Hoover and Richey stood pumping their bent rods and fighting to maintain control of the lines. In the end, the two skilled fishermen prevailed. Richey's fish, hooked in the tail, splashed ferociously as it neared the boat. Two more white flags were run up.

The *Orca* team was doing well, with a total of five big sailers and two dolphin. Meanwhile, those on the *Miss Sally* had fished for nearly eight hours, with Boone landing just one sailfish mid-morning, and Sullivan catching an amberjack. Suddenly, persistence paid off. The men on the *Miss Sally* hit a bonanza when the fishermen wandered into a school of biting sailfish. During the next several hours, Boone caught two sailfish weighing more than eighty pounds and just under eight feet long, Stone landed two, and Sullivan hauled in one, all of similar size. In the light of the fading winter sun, the fishermen returned to port after eleven hours of fishing. Eleven white flags flew from the masts of the two boats—a stellar achievement. The *Orca* led the way. Hoover and Richey slipped a paddle between the rigging near the sloop's bow to proudly hang the day's catch. All were pleased but Richey, who was upset that Boone, a less experienced fisherman, had caught three large sailfish while he caught but one. He vowed to better his take the next day.[628]

Shortly after their return, the tired president and his fellow anglers greeted representatives from the Palm Beach Sailfish Club. The club made Hoover an honorary member, and in return, he presented the club with his seven-foot, eight-inch sailfish, which they promised to stuff and display.[629] After a hearty dinner, all retired early. Of the seven trips Hoover had made to Florida to deep-sea fish, this was his best day's fishing. He had mastered the art of sailfishing. The politically battered president was grateful for the reprieve.

On the last day of the year, the ocean was still choppy, though calmer than the previous day. Around seven-thirty in the morning, the two fishing vessels wended their way back to the Gulf Stream. The men had switched around so that Hoover, Richey, and Stone now fished from the *Orca,* and Sullivan, Boone, and Austin from *Miss Sally.* Perhaps the sailfish school still lay in wait. After trolling for more than an hour, Hoover got the first strike, his "duel with the swift swordsman of the sea" lasting forty-six minutes before he managed to subdue the fish, which were more than seven feet in length.[630] Once again a white flag was run up the halyard. Luck held aboard the *Miss Sally,* as Sullivan took a hard strike not long after Austin landed a whole sailfish. Sullivan's fish was a real battler, and the struggle left him exhausted. The fish was barely on board when his luck nearly turned to tragedy—Sullivan collapsed. Boone later recalled: "I had to lay him in the bottom of the boat and we left the other fishermen of our party for me to return Sullivan to the *Sequoia.* Happily, I did not have to send him to a hospital, as we were able to resuscitate him, and after a few hours he seemed to be all right. I think the exertion of the hours he put in to haul in his hooked sailfish, bright sunlight, and the heat, all contributed to his cardiac embarrassment."[631]

Meanwhile, those on the *Orca* continued to catch sailfish. Richey was luckless and terribly disappointed, but Stone was successful. Soon after an early lunch, Hoover's line straightened, and he was again engaged in a fray with a big sailer. The contest lasted forty-five minutes, and to his surprise, the iridescent

Hoover brings in his catch on the Orca, December 30, 1932.
COURTESY QUEENS BOROUGH PUBLIC LIBRARY, LONG ISLAND DIVISION, NEW YORK HERALD-TRIBUNE
COLLECTION

finned fighter was the largest he had ever landed. A whopper, more than eighty pounds in weight and seven feet, eleven inches in length, the fish was but an inch short of winning a prestigious diamond button from the Palm Beach Sailfish Club. The club had made only eight diamond awards in the past four years.[632] Hoover was satisfied and returned to port early, the almost magical fishing trip was at an end. The *New York Times* reported, "So far as Mr. Hoover is concerned, 1932 went out in a blaze of glory, it was a day made to order for the President—a day on the fishing grounds teeming with the gamest sailfish seen in these waters in years."[633] The president discreetly arranged to trade fish with the Palm Beach Club, substituting the seven-foot, eleven-inch monster, and spent the rest of the afternoon cleaning up paperwork. He looked forward to a quiet New Year's Eve among friends and was especially pleased that his fishing companion and confidant, Mark Sullivan, had not suffered a heart attack.

For the competitive Richey, who refused to be outdone, the day had just begun. After leaving the *Orca*, he rented another, smaller boat at an exorbitant rate and, in the rain, set out to better the record. He returned later in the day, having caught five large sailfish. "Experts on the dock decreed that there was no catch of five in a single day by a single person on record, as far as they knew, off Palm Beach. Larry was overjoyed."[633] Aboard the *Sequoia*, New Year's Eve toasts, nonalcoholic, were to the usual— a happy New Year, long life, good fortune—along with others that commemorated catching twenty sailfish, six of them by Richey and five by Hoover. The president acknowledged Richey's fishing achievement and declared him the better fisherman and the winner of the yearly deep-sea-fishing contest. For Richey, down five to one in the bottom of the ninth inning, it was a miraculous comeback.

After midnight, the New Year brought a precipitous drop in temperature along with a cold rain. The Hoovers canceled a planned holiday cruise and instead dressed warmly to attend church services at the Royal Ponciana Community Chapel. The following frigid morning, the unpopular president was pleased to find a small crowd at the railroad station to see him and the first lady off. As the train slowly pulled out of the Palm Beach station, Hoover smiled at the absurdity of the send-off. A black jazz band, a type of music he detested, was playing Roosevelt's campaign song: "Happy Days Are Here Again." The crowd smiled, and Hoover smiled back.[635]

Returning to his desk in the White House, Hoover tried to devise ways to foist his program of recovery on Roosevelt. He was maniacal in his efforts to obtain Roosevelt's allegiance to gold, one he correctly suspected as being weak. The depression had worsened as the country entered the twilight zone of the interregnum. As March 4 approached, the economic crisis deepened. The president and the president-elect both refused to budge from their radically differing philosophical positions. Nothing would happen to counter the latest banking crisis until Hoover was out and Roosevelt was in. Invited to tea at the White House the day before the inauguration, Roosevelt had again clashed with Hoover. By the following day, March 4, the feelings of distrust and suspicion that had fermented throughout the interregnum had hardened to enmity. As the two men silently rode together in a opened-topped limousine toward the Capitol, the nation was in near paralysis. Cold winds, dark clouds, and scattered rain reflected the mood of the country. Banks were closed in thirty-two states and operated on a limited capacity in the remaining sixteen. The New York Stock Exchange and the Chicago Board of Trade were closed. Thirteen million unemployed looked to Washington for relief and leadership.[636] What Roosevelt had done for himself at Campobello, he was now challenged to do for the nation.

Shortly before the swearing-in ceremony, the sun broke through the clouds, warming the large crowd packed in front of the Capitol. In his inaugural address, Roosevelt proclaimed that the nation had "nothing to fear, but fear itself." Afterward, the Hoovers were driven to Union Station, where they were greeted by a crowd of loyal supporters. Aboard the train, Hoover and his wife remained on the rear platform of the observation car. Waving to the crowd as the train pulled from the station, the ex-president had tears in his eyes.[637] Hoover's immediate destination was New York City and an opulent ten-room suite on the thirty-third floor of the Waldolf-Astoria, the couple's frequent East Coast headquarters. Lou wished to return to her beloved house in California, but Hoover found Palo Alto too far from the corridors of power. He did not tell his wife, but he also disliked the house on San Juan Hill on which she had expended such effort. He found academic life both claustrophobic and insular. Washington was impossible because of Roosevelt and because he would be drawn into incessant political squabbling. With a few friends and advisors, and without Secret Service protection, the train carried the Hoovers north to an unknown future. In Philadelphia, Lou boarded another train for the long trip to California and home. Hoover promised to follow as soon as he finished setting up shop at the Waldorf. Defeated and disgruntled, he would begin his wilderness years not in the canyons of the West, but in the canyons of New York City.

8

Fishing for Fun
and to Wash Your Soul

In New York City, Hoover was hurried through a crowd of well-wishers and sped off in a police-escorted motorcade to the Waldorf-Astoria. When he arrived in his new headquarters on the thirty-third floor, he was in a deep funk, the nation's depression moving through his psyche like a lengthening shadow. He professed to be unaffected by his fall from power, but he was unable to let go. Bob Greene's insight that "celebrity is embraced by most upon whom it is bestowed" aptly described Hoover's frame of mind.[638] While he moved in, he reviewed the relief organizations for which he still bore responsibility and signed the papers giving his and Lou's beloved Camp Rapidan to the government for use by Roosevelt and future presidents. It must have galled him to picture "that man" enjoying the retreat in which he had spent so many happy weekends. Franklin and Eleanor visited Camp Rapidan in early April, but Roosevelt could not manage the terrain on his crutches and had to be carried to the Hoovers' cabin.[639] Though the camp was in a lovely setting, Roosevelt chose a more accessible site and built his own Shangri-la, later named Camp David.

An additional and unexpected blow fell on the ex-president on March 12, 1933, when his forty-nine-year-old secretary, French Strother, died, "the victim of pneumonia contracted on Inauguration Day."[640] Strother's death was especially hurtful, as Hoover and his secretary had planned a series of books defending his administration and his attempts to pull the nation out of the depression. A deflated Hoover traipsed to New Jersey for the funeral.

The Strother funeral over, Hoover left for California to join Lou in Palo Alto. In the coming months, he planned to work on building his library on war, revolution, and peace; motor through the High Sierras; attend the Bohemian Grove for the first time in five years; and fish his favorite western rivers. These activities seemed a cure, but finding something meaningful to occupy his time was a challenge for an unemployed workaholic used to having dozens of balls in the air simultaneously.

In the first week of April, the Hoovers, along with his former treasury secretary, Ogden Mills, and his wife, took a pleasure trip to Nevada. The political outcasts drove through the High Sierras, walked the streets of Reno in the early evening, and took the historic Virginia and Truckee Railroad, owned by Mills, to Carson City and Virginia City. At Lake Tahoe, they stayed in the Zephyr Cove resort, also owned by Mills.[641] For Hoover, who had surveyed the boundary line between California and Nevada in the summer of 1893, this was a nostalgic trip. Lake Tahoe brought back memories of his time at Tallac House and his attempts to capture the beauty of the landscape in letters to his sister, May.

Hoover enjoyed the Nevada trip, but he continued to struggle with the withdrawal symptoms associated with his fall from grace. In Palo Alto, he paced back and forth in his den, played solitaire, read stacks of eastern newspapers, railed against Roosevelt and the New Deal, and drove around California in an effort to work through his disappointments and imagine for himself a future. Yosemite, Grass Valley, the High Sierras, the redwoods, oceanside drives, even a short fishing trip to Yellowstone Park and time on the Madison River did not fill the gnawing void. At age fifty-eight and possessed of abundant energy, he was not about to accept a cloistered retirement at Stanford. In a ten-week stretch in April, May, and June, the troubled Hoover drove eight thousand miles.[642]

One night, camped at the northern end of the Sacramento Valley, Hoover and his son Allan awoke in a sweat. They looked at each other and asked, "Why should we sit up here sweltering when we can go to Palo Alto?"[643] Even though it was the middle of the night, the two got up, got dressed, and started down the Sacramento Valley Turnpike. The flat, open stretch of deserted road tempted Hoover to open up his big sixteen-cylinder Cadillac. Hurtling down the highway, Hoover looked in the rearview mirror and saw a flashing red light gaining on him. Soon he could hear a siren.[644] Dutifully, he pulled off the highway and fumbled for his license, handing it to the stern police officer. The patrolman looked at the license, then examined it more closely in the illumination of a headlight. Returning to the car window, he placed a foot on the running board and asked Hoover, "Tell me are you that guy?" The ex-president, with a slight grin, said, "Yes, I guess I'm that guy."[645] The policeman then asked, "Well, does it make you feel any better to drive sixty miles an hour down this Valley Pike in the middle of the night?"[646] Hoover reflected for a moment and replied, "Well, under the circumstances I think it does."[647] The highway patrolman stepped back from the running board, looked Hoover in the eye, and with a wave of his arm said, "Drive on, brother."[648]

On July 1, Hoover and two of his favorite fishing companions, Ray Lyman Wilbur and Harlan Stone, along with Wilbur's son, Ray Lyman, Jr., arrived at the Desert Inn on Pyramid Lake in Nevada.[649] The twenty-mile-wide, green-water, natural lake was famous for its huge trout, some weighing as much as forty pounds. In fact, the record for the world's largest cutthroat trout was established here in 1925 by a Paiute Indian named Johnny Skimmerhorn, who hauled in a fish that weighed forty-one pounds.[650] As in so many other places, commercial interest had greatly reduced the trout population by the 1930s, although big fish could still be caught. In the winter and spring of 1888-89, one hundred tons of fish from Pyramid Lake had been iced down and shipped by rail to fish markets nationwide. After a brief slowdown, the depletion of the lake's fish hit a new high just before World War I, when each week, ten to fifteen tons of these behemoth trout were shipped to feed hungry miners in other parts of Nevada and California.[651] Hoover was lucky to fish Pyramid Lake in the early 1930s. Ten years later, like so many of the West's natural resources, the giant cutthroats were gone.

Though it was possible to fish Pyramid Lake from a boat, most fishermen preferred to wade out a long distance in the shallow waters. Some accepted the dangers of casting for big fish while submerged chest-deep in the lake. Boats were scarce, but on one day of their trip, members of the fishing party managed to round up two, complete with Indian guides. Ray, Jr., ended up in the boat with Hoover and a guide that spoke very little English. He later described the experience: "For four hours were out on the lake and he [Hoover] was trying to fish and there was practically no conversation at all the whole time. I was a little embarrassed to talk, and he wasn't the kind to break the ice and help out, so it was sort of uncomfortable but very interesting."[652] The reticent young man might have recalled the old story about a fishing trip taken by two Quaker gentlemen named Ernest and Ephraim. The brothers had risen early, packed their gear, and pushed off into the lake just as the sun broke the horizon. Five hours later, Ernest moved his legs, and Ephraim snapped, "Ernest, did you come here to fidget or fish?"

Hoover preferred to fish Pyramid Lake from the rock jetties that jutted from the shoreline. He caught the smallest trout recorded in the first week of July, a dinky two-and-a-half-pounder. That same week, a Dr. Miki from California reeled in a twenty-two-and-a-half-pound cutthroat.[653] Hoover nevertheless was happy with the outing and with his companions, and ever eager for a bigger catch, he planned to return in a few weeks for several more days of fishing. Instead, the wished-for fishing trip was set aside as he and Lou traveled to Chicago and spent ten days at the World's Fair. Hoover used the opportunity to meet with a number of midwestern Republican party leaders to draw up a declaration of party principles and to found the Committee on Monetary Policies—an organization dubbed the Sound Money Club, one dedicated to reintroducing the gold standard.[654] Hoover, working behind the scenes, was inching his way back toward the great game of high-stakes politics.

In mid-July, the former president planned to visit the Bohemian Grove, but he was deeply worried about the reception he

Hoover fishing Pyramid Lake, Nevada, July 1933.
COURTESY HERBERT HOOVER LIBRARY

would receive. He had not been to the Grove encampment since 1927, the summer when Calvin Coolidge had issued his famous statement that he chose not to run again for the presidency. The news had spread like wildfire throughout the Grove, and a stampede of admirers had descended on Cave Man Camp to encourage Hoover to run. Five years later, after losing the presidential election during the worst depression in American history, Hoover feared he would be shunned by members who judged his presidency a failure. The byzantine ethics of Bohemia seemed unpredictable. Whatever its shortcomings, Hoover loved everything about the Grove and ardently desired to be readmitted into its inner circle of power brokers. Friends who shared Cave Man Camp with the ex-president would be supportive, so in late July, an apprehensive Hoover drove from Palo Alto to the annual gathering of the power elite underneath the towering redwoods on the banks of the Russian River. At first he stuck close to Cave Man Camp, eating his meals with a few close associates. Walking the trails that honeycombed the encampment, he barely recognized his old friends.[655] But at the end of the first week, at Low Jinks on Saturday night, Hoover received a standing ovation from a gathering of more than a thousand men, who thus gave him his welcome home.[656]

From 1933 until the early 1960s, Hoover rarely missed "the greatest men's party in the world." Cave Man Camp became one the Grove's heavy-hitter campsites, a center of Republican party presidential politics, a place where nominees, aspirants, and potential future candidates, like Thoroughbred racehorses, were invited and carefully looked over.

At the end of the encampment, a semblance of his dignity and confidence recovered, Hoover returned to Palo Alto and increased his political activity, struggling to find ways to rebuild the shattered Republican party and find a role for himself. In deference to the overwhelming popular support for the New Deal, he said nothing in public of his loathing for the policies of the new administration.

Immediately after leaving the Grove encampment, Hoover, along with Esberg, Wilbur, and other friends, drove to Wooley Camp for two weeks of fishing. The formaer president had not been to his secluded mountain hideaway since the camp was completed in 1927. He was met by an American Indian guide known as "Happy Hooligan" and made the seven-mile trek by horseback to the cabins nestled on Wooley Creek, the most isolated of all Hoover's fishing spots. A strenuous day's fishing began with wading the creek, then, if enough daylight remained, he would work on down the Wooley into the Salmon River. After an overnight under the stars, Hoover might find himself the next day on the Klamath. Even though Wooley Camp was isolated, one of its joys was its closeness to other good fishing and camping spots, many owned by friends, such as One Mile Lake, Happy Camp, Brown's Camp, Smith's Fork, and Medicine Mountain.[657] But the rugged terrain of the Marble Mountains made even such short distances arduous undertakings.

In October, Hoover and several fishing companions once more headed for their favorite rivers in northern California and southern Oregon. Hoover, Esberg, Ding Darling, and Nicholas Roosevelt, an Oyster Bay Roosevelt and Hoover's ambassador to Hungary, journeyed first to the McKenzie River, then on to the Rogue River, and finally on to Brown's Camp on the Klamath River to fish and enjoy Esberg's spacious lodge. On the way, Hoover's sixteen-cylinder limousine pulled up in front of a small-town grocery store near the Oregon border. Apprehensive that he would be recognized, Hoover scrunched down in the backseat and pulled up the collar on his coat, hoping the driver would quickly pick up the needed items and they would be on their way out of town. Fate, however, did not favor Hoover's wishes. "As we waited," Ding later wrote, "I noticed a typical country newspaper editor with a green eyeshade, pencil over his ear, sleeve guards, and a sheaf of proof sheets in his hand pause and, from the sidewalk, make an inventory of the big black limousine, the license number, and the passengers. He then hurried away up the street."[658] The editor disappeared and returned with a crate of attractive fresh pink pears and handed them through the window to Ding.

Hoover still might have escaped had it not been for the school across the street letting out. The students immediately saw the limousine and flocked to the car, assuming someone famous was inside. Dozens pushed all forms of paper through the window to secure the former president's autograph. Hoover looked at Ding and snapped, "Now look what you've done." Ding responded declaratively, "I haven't done a damn thing."[659] More and more people arrived. A moment later, a "sweet-faced little old lady in a lace cap and shawl" pushed her way to the front of the crowd, stuck her land into the limo, and said, "Is that really you, President Hoover? We all love you and I just want to go home and tell my family that I have seen you and shaken your hand."[660] Hoover kept his head down, but he did momentarily grasp the old lady's hand. The driver returned and the big limo drove off, leaving behind a street full of admiring people.

Ding, upset at Hoover's attitude, asked, "Did you see that sweet little old lady, who only wanted to shake your hand?"[661] Hoover admitted that he had. Ding snapped, "Well you didn't act like it."[662] There was little conversation the rest of the way to the Rogue, and after dinner, Hoover retired early. By morning, Hoover was fully recovered from his dreaded encounter with the public. After several days of good fishing, time with Toggery Bill, Rainbow Gibson, and guides Glen Wooldridge and Connie Briggs, it was time to head for the McKenzie.[663]

Near Blue River, Oregon, Hoover and his friends stayed at a fishing camp christened Holiday Farm Resort. The neat, white-shingled cabins, which each had two bedrooms with twin poster beds, a large sitting room and study, and ample porch space, were tastefully landscaped and far enough apart to offer privacy. The porch on Hoover's favorite bungalow protruded out over the McKenzie River. The resort was run by Pat and Vivienne Wright, who offered excellent food in part of an old farmhouse that had been converted into a dining room.[664] Hoover especially loved the charms of Holiday Farm, a place to which he returned nearly every year until 1958, although on this first trip the fishing was not so good.

On Hoover's frequent visits to the McKenzie, he also often stayed at the lodge of W. E. Travis, a friend who had made his fortune in the bus business. Fred Harris, a man who worked for Travis and who had spent his life on the river, served as Hoover's guide. This relationship would last for twenty-five years. Milo Thompson, who was especially adept at handling a McKenzie River boat in boulder-strewn whitewater, also fished with the ex-president, as did Howard Montgomery of Leaburg and Prince Helfrich of Blue River.[665]

On the October 1933 trip, the fishing was also poor at Brown's Camp on the Klamath. On the third disappointing day, a local teacher named Elsie DeAvilla dropped by the camp and asked whether Hoover would visit her Honolulu school the next morning. This isolated country school on Lumgrey Creek had received the strange appellation "Honolulu" because several hundred Hawaiians had once panned for gold along this stretch of the Klamath.[666] When the gold petered out, many of the Hawaiians had remained in the area. In the depth of the depression, gold seekers returned as desperate people camped along the creeks and rivers of northern California in an effort to eke out a living. As in the past, few succeeded, and some sank to levels of penury. DeAvilla pleaded that the children would be thrilled if the former president of the United States paid a visit to their one-room school. Hoover was unable to respond to the invitation because he was out wading the river in pursuit of steelheads, but Esberg, moved by her request, took it upon himself to assure her that Hoover would call on her students.[667]

Later that evening, after a good meal, Esberg tactfully broke the news to Hoover, who was none too happy at having his fishing trip interrupted. "I won't do it," he emphatically responded.[668] For years, Hoover had announced on principle that a man was not to be disturbed when in prayer or when fishing. Even in the wilds of the Marble Mountains, however, he could not evade favor seekers, people who did not recognize his principle. It was not the first time that the needy directly sought his help, nor would it be the last, even though he was sequestered in the woods, seemingly out of reach. Darling and Roosevelt joined with Esberg in arguing that the school visit was an obligation. Petulant, Hoover said little the rest of the evening. The next morning, however, he relented and agreed to tour the school and meet its pupils. The reluctant ex-president, the teacher, and the poor mountain children mingled surprisingly well. Hoover commented that the children appeared underfed. The teacher responded that they were and hesitantly revealed that she used part of her salary to buy food for her students' lunches. A "soup kittle" bubbled on the stove each day, and those who could brought vegetables and other ingredients to add to the pot. The "kittle" provided every child a hot, nourishing meal, something many likely would not get at home.[669]

Upon leaving, Hoover revealed what he had learned to his fishing companions, stressing that the teacher used a portion of her small salary to supplement the children's meager diet. One hundred dollars, he said, would provide ample lunches for all of the children for a year. The hook baited, he now reeled in his catch with a suggestion to which his companions could not say no: "If you . . . will help out, I'll underwrite the balance."[670] Esberg, Darling, and Roosevelt ponied up. The problem solved, Hoover was back in the water fishing by early afternoon. Years later, in the late 1950s, he had not forgotten the Honolulu school, which remained one of his favorite charities. His willingness to intervene immediately, after a full investigation established need, and to accept long-term personal responsibility, even when it impinged upon his retreats into the wilderness, were among his outstanding characteristics. Darling, who also related this story in his memoirs, concluded that "Herbert Hoover never, to my knowledge, wanted anything for himself, but there was no limit to his energy and devotion if he could be of service to others."[671] Service to others was the road of ambition that Hoover trod.

The morning after the Honolulu school visit, necessity forced Ding to excuse himself from the fishing party and return to work at the Des Moines *Register.* All week, the fishing had been poor as a result of the low water level maintained by the power company, and fishing on the Rogue River the week before had also been disappointing. But the next day, a release of water raised the level substantially, and Hoover, Esberg, and Roosevelt all caught fish.[672] To compensate Darling, Hoover shipped him a portion of his catch and asked that he share his bounty with Gardner Cowles of *Look* magazine.[673]

On the way back to Palo Alto on October 17, the three Republican fishermen checked out the New Deal firsthand with a visit to the newly created Civilian Conservation Corps (CCC) camp on the Klamath at Oak Knoll, California.[674] Hoover always had been suspicious of the CCC, thinking of the organization as if it were a kind of "private army" of potential mercenaries similar to Hitler's SA. After his visit, he wrote a friend, "I find that the military officers in one of these camps think that they are laying plans for a new military arm of the government."[675]

Back home but a week, Hoover again left on a fishing trip, this time a two-week cruise on the yacht *Samona II,* owned by Willitts J. Hole, a wealthy businessman, rancher, and art collector. The cruise was a quest for the giant Pacific sailfish that inhabited the waters off the coast of Baja California. Hoover had fished off Cape San Lucas twice before, once when secretary of commerce and again when president-elect, but on both occasions he had failed to catch a sailfish. Guests on this excursion included Arthur Hyde, former secretary of agriculture; H. S. Mudd, a Cal Tech engineer who had helped construct the California aqueduct, one of the engineering marvels of the century; and W. L.

Hollingsforth, a Hoover associate from the War Food Administration.[676]

Hole welcomed his fellow fishermen aboard his 147-foot yacht late Wednesday afternoon, October 25, in Los Angeles. Newspaper reporters, photographers, and newsreel cameramen recorded the departure. A crew of twelve ran the vessel and saw to the needs of the guests, who wanted for nothing, as the *Samona* was well stocked with food, liquor, and fishing gear. The men unpacked, rested, and turned out for a first-class dinner.[677] With prohibition at an end, Hoover could sip his favorite evening libation, a dry martini or two, accompanied by macadamia nuts and yellow cheddar cheese. At dinner, a fine wine could be served. That evening, after an excellent meal, the conversation focused on everyone's expectations of catching huge, fighting sailfish. Mexican waters off the 760-mile-long Baja peninsula were famous for big fish, including sailfish, bluefin, yellowfin, bigeye, dolphin, and yellowtail. Magdalena Bay in the fall yielded wahoo, tuna, striped marlin, and most important, the sought-after sailfish.[678] To the north of San Jose del Cabo, at the tip of the peninsula, the Golden Gate banks and the nearby Jamie banks sheltered marlin, dolphin, yellowfin tuna, black sea bass, grouper, and pargo.[679] Hoover and his fellow fishermen were a bit early for the best billfish, whose season peaked in late winter and early spring, but their anticipation was justified. Zane Grey had made this area, as well as Long Key in Florida, famous for the huge fish he caught on light tackle. As the evening wore on, stories of previous fishing successes, disappointments, and absurd situations bounced about the table. The warm, friendly environment filled with "the spiritual uplift of good will, cheerfulness and optimism that accompanies every fishing expedition" created anticipation of a marvelous two weeks at sea.[680]

The next morning, the *Samona* landed at the first port of call, Ensenada, in order to obtain the necessary Mexican clearance papers. Hoover met with a friendly press corps for more than an hour. All day and night, the yacht steamed south while the fishermen lounged, read, and napped. When the sun came up on the second day, the Bonitas Islands lay off the bow to the port side. It was time to fish. The *Samona* lowered two boats, one for Hoover and Mudd and the other for Hyde and Hollingsforth. The sea was rough and the sky overcast, not ideal fishing conditions, but Hoover landed a large cabrilla, a type of sea bass, which put up a thirty-minute battle. Both Hoover and Mudd caught rock bass, while Hyde and Hollingsforth hooked large yellowtail tuna and several bass. The propitious start was a good omen. After lunch, the yacht headed to Santa Maria Bay in search of larger game fish. The afternoon proved productive; Hollingsforth reported "84 for four rods, mostly sierra mackerel, but some barracuda, a few yellowtail and one cabrilla," plenty of fish "for the ice box."[681]

On Sunday, the time between bites increased dramatically, and by midday, the yacht pulled anchor and sailed farther south to Cape San Lucas, cruising past beautiful mountain scenery on a smooth sea in the warm sun.[682] The *Samona* sailed all night and by early morning had reached its destination in front of a rugged coast, broken here and there by lovely sandy beaches and fronted by deep blue water. Up early, Hoover and Hole were off in pursuit of swordfish. The Chief, as Hoover was frequently called by those who had known him for a long time, hooked a large swordfish, which he fought for more than an hour before it finally broke free. At sixty years of age, an hour's fight with a big fish tired Hoover more than it had half a dozen years earlier in Florida. Both fishermen continued to troll for trophies, but on the way back to the yacht, they settled for a variety of smaller fish. Meanwhile, Hyde and Mudd landed hammerhead sharks, which weighed roughly 150 pounds each. All of the men were disappointed at not having caught a swordfish. The four friends continued to fish all afternoon in heavy seas without result. The next day, Hoover hooked another large swordfish, but it too freed itself and plunged off through the choppy swells.

Tuesday was also a bust. No big fish were caught, although lots of smaller species were hauled aboard. On Wednesday, the situation dramatically improved. Hyde hooked a large sailfish and fought hard to land a 164-pound, nine-foot battler. Hoover lost a second big sailfish, and later in the day, Hollingsforth fought a large marlin for more than half an hour before his line snapped.[683] A week into the trip, Hyde held the honor of catching the largest fish. In the late afternoon, the *Samona* made for Los Frailes Bay. After sailing south all night, the fishermen tried trolling from the rear of the yacht but caught no fish. Arriving at their destination, the party lowered the motorboats and spent the afternoon fishing the bay for bait with which they hoped to lure swordfish. The next morning, Hoover and Hollingsforth began the hunt. Hoover had just finished letting out his line when a large swordfish grabbed the bait. The sword swam off rapidly, the reel spinning at a furious speed. The line held taut for a few seconds but then snapped. Neither fisherman despaired at losing the large fish; they had stumbled into a school. Quickly Hoover baited his hook and again let out his line. Over the next several hours he was rewarded with two swordfish of almost equal size, both weighing in at close to 120 pounds.[684]

Excited by their success, the four friends fished all afternoon. Mudd hooked a big swordfish, but it managed to shake free. Again smaller fish were caught for bait and "for the ice box." That evening the party dined on the day's catch and then lolled on the deck, exhausted from days of hard fishing. Time seemed to stand still as they relaxed in the heavy tropical air under the light of a bright moon and listened to Mexican music floating through the ship's sound system. No one spoke as each man basked in the tranquility of the evening. In the background, barely audible, was the muffled reassuring sound of the yacht's twin diesel engines, a small reminder of man's efforts to prevail in the vast, indifferent ocean. Deeply religious, Hollingsforth turned to Mudd and quietly recited the eighth Psalm, which starts and ends with the same stanza:

> O Lord, our God, how glorious
> Is thy name in all the earth![685]

By morning, the *Samona* reached Cape San Lucas at the tip of Baja California—a famous spot pregnant with possibility. As the sun came up on what promised to be a perfect day, the two smaller boats set out across a placid sea. When the boats returned to the *Samona* for lunch, Hoover and Hyde were proud to have each landed a 140-pound marlin. Mudd also was successful, having caught a 111-pound, nine-foot sailfish. That afternoon, Hollingsforth and Mudd went after smaller fish and landed a number of large sierra mackerel, amberjack, and a 51-pound rooster fish, a beautiful tunalike fish with two dark, angular stripes near its upper body and a large, separated dorsal fin reminiscent of a rooster's comb. Hoover and Hyde continued to pursue big game fish. Later that afternoon, the Chief brought in a second marlin, one that weighed 120 pounds. It was a good day of fishing.

That evening, a full moon rose over the eastern part of the bay. "The moon was so big, the clouds and the shore line so bold and impressive that, in the slightly hazy atmosphere, one could not but yield to enchantment . . . each of us sensed something of exaltation."[686] Bathed in the beauty of the descending night, the spent sportsmen all retired early.

Sunday morning, shortly after dawn, the four anglers ventured back on the water. Lady Luck favored Hoover as he tied into a large 130-pound sailfish. This one did not break the line, because he used his tried-and-true method of letting the fish run before he set the hook—snap on the drag and strike. Hoover wore down the battling sailer and successfully landed the big fish. His fish ended up being the highlight of the day, for no other big game fish were caught. Hollingsforth wrote in his trip diary, "Of all the fishing thrills surely the greatest is in the taking of a big marlin, coolness and strength are called for, there is a suspense and uncertainty, a wild excitement in the dashes and spiral leaps of the fish, that provide an experience unequaled in sport."[687]

At half past six, with the burnt orange sun sinking fast in the November sky, the fishing party embarked for Tosco Bay, where they hoped to catch some sierra mackerel to take back home.[688] The fishing banks were productive, and all caught a good supply—Hollingsforth was content with eighteen. With the fish iced down in the yacht's locker, it was time to head for home—a two-day cruise on a calm sea in magnificent weather.[689] Once again the *Samona II* cleared customs at Ensenada and then sailed on to Los Angeles, where the fishermen met their wives and the press. That evening, all attended a farewell dinner at the home of the Holes, where they viewed the couple's renowned art collection and reflected on their two-week trip. On reflection, the contented fishermen rated the Mexican adventure one of the best fishing trips that any of them had ever taken. Hoover wrote to Ding, judging the Baja as "the place where the fish either come from or go to. The sizes vary from 1 foot to 11 feet long and the limit is only human exhaustion. I tell you this so that you will know that I can catch fish and second that there are fish in the West."[690]

In 1933, after leaving the presidency, Hoover spent more days fishing than ever before, but all of his successful angling and his return to the Bohemian Grove were no cure for his anxiety or his growing enmity toward Roosevelt and the New Deal. At Christmas, friends found him defensive, fearful of the future, and self-pitying.[691] In 1933, Hoover stumbled blindly in the wilderness.

The New Year brought a partial revival of Hoover's spirit as he forced himself to undertake a new project. He began to write a book titled *The Challenge to Liberty*, a volume that eviscerated the philosophy of and policies initiated by the New Deal without ever mentioning the Roosevelt administration by name. To complete the volume, Hoover passed on deep-sea fishing in Florida, and then sent the draft manuscript out to friends for review. While waiting for their responses, he took off on an extended automobile trip to witness firsthand the destruction done to the Republican party by his defeat and the overwhelming political success of the New Deal. Not surprisingly, he found the party in debt and disarray, and the leadership depressed. In Kansas, he met Gov. Alf Landon, who was already maneuvering for the Republican presidential nomination in 1936. Hoover campaigned for a new national chairman in an effort to improve Republican fortunes.

In early May, the Chief managed the first of half a dozen trips to one of Richard Hanna's cattle ranches, the Circle S near Mill Creek. Hanna, a wealthy San Francisco businessman, owned a Ford trimotor aircraft that was available to shuttle guests between their point of departure and Corning, California, the closest airfield to the ranch in Vina.[692] Hoover declined the airlift, driving to the ranch with Lou, their son Allan, and Lawrence Sullivan, a journalist and longtime friend. That evening after dinner, Hoover, always attracted to young people, engaged in a conversation with Hanna's daughter Elizabeth on the art of fly fishing. He was charmed by her enthusiasm for the sport and appreciative of her skill at tying flies.

The following morning, Lou, Mrs. May Hanna, and Elizabeth left for Morgan Springs to ride horses.[693] The men set out for the isolated campground on Deer Creek, south of snow-packed Mount Lassen. The day before, the guides, Albert and Merle Apperson, in two Model T Fords, had hauled in a supply of food, sleeping bags, and other camp equipment. They took no tents as the hardy outdoorsmen planned to sleep on the hard ground under the stars. The fifteen miles of mountain road that led to the creek, Hanna claimed, were the roughest in California, a grueling drive over rocks that took hours and often shredded tires. Deer Creek was even more inaccessible than was Wooley Camp. Only the old Model Ts had a wheelbase high enough off the ground to prevent hang-ups. The two flivvers, loaded with fishing gear and baggage, jostled along at a snail's pace, pitching their occupants in different directions. Hanna's veracity as to the difficulty of the drive was confirmed. When the road finally ended, the would-be fishermen still had a mile and half to go, on a steep trail that wound down to the creek. The guides waited in a clearing with saddled horses, that mode of transportation that Hoover so disliked.

Once encamped, the fishermen's perseverance was amply rewarded, as the fishing was good. Merle Apperson, who served as cook, knew how to fix trout—crispy brown on the outside and moist on the inside. The weather held—no rain. That night, the stars gleamed through the tall redwoods, inducing a sense of awe. This was the kind of outing Hoover loved. The wild forests and streams of Tehama County were an instant hit.

On his return to Palo Alto, Hoover sent Elizabeth an assortment of exquisite Japanese flies and a book titled *Fishing with a Hook,* written by Dame Juliana Berners. Originally published in 1496, it was reissued in a handsome edition in 1933. Written by a prioress, the book was the first mention of artificial flies in English literature.[694] Hoover bought a number of copies and sent them to fishing friends. Beginning during his years in London, Hoover had assembled a substantial library of books on fishing and the outdoors, many privately published in limited numbers. Favorites included an early edition of Walton's *The Compleat Angler,* Grover Cleveland's *Fishing and Shooting Sketches,* Sir Edward Grey's treatise *Fly-Fishing,* and Zane Grey's *Tales of Fishes* and *Tales of Fishing the Virgin Sea.* Hoover also loved all of the ephemera circulated by fishermen: cartoons, prayers, poems, anecdotes, and amusing stories. He often appropriated this material, successfully incorporating it into his store of fishing lore. One of his favorites was about a fisherman who was walking along the bank of a stream, having caught nothing, when a boy walked by with a string filled with good-size trout. The fisherman eagerly inquired, "Where did you get those fish?" The boy responded: "You just walk down the lane marked 'Private' till you come to a sign saying 'Trespassers Will Be Prosecuted.' Just beyond is a stream marked 'No Fishing Allowed,' and there you are."[695]

In June, Hoover was able to escape to Wooley Camp for a quick three days of fishing. But his resurrectionist activities so crowded his calendar that he spent July commuting back and forth between the Bohemian Grove and Palo Alto. This summer his two sons, Herbert Jr. and Allan, became members of Cave Man Camp.[696] Near the end of the encampment, Hoover gave a lakeside talk in which he preached the "gospel according to Palo Alto."[697] These lakeside talks, preaching to the converted, would become well-attended annual affairs often delivered on a Sunday afternoon. Finally, in the afterglow of the Grove, he was off for a few days in Yosemite and a week of fishing at Wooley Camp with Herbert Jr., Allan, and friends. The Grove and the trips to Wooley Creek, the Hanna Circle S Ranch, and the McKenzie now became regular items on the Hoover agenda as the ex-president established new routines. Years later, he explained in a draft of his memoirs: "As I was known to like fishing, I soon had invitations from friends all over the country who had fishing camps or boats. Gradually I established a route among them by plane or automobile, according to the season."[698]

In October 1934, *The Challenge to Liberty* was published. Largely through the influence of William Allen White, the book was selected by the Book-of-the-Month Club, made the best-seller list, and by December had sold eighty-five thousand copies.[699] Reviews were mixed, depending on the political persuasion of the magazine or newspaper in question. Both Hoover and Scribner's were disappointed, having projected higher sales, but the following year a second edition went to print. This disappointment, however, was overshadowed by the pounding Republican candidates received at the polls in the 1934 off-year elections. The new Congress had only 147 Republicans: 27 senators and 120 House members. The House Democratic majority was so large that many were forced to sit on the Republican side of the aisle. In 1934, a Republican comeback seemed a long way off. Hoover disparagingly prophesied that the party might lose three or four more elections before the political tide turned. This was one of his few predictions that proved to have the ring of truth.

At Wooley Camp. Back row: unidentified man, Tom Williams, Timothy Hopkins, Ray Lyman Wilbur. Center: Hoover. Front row: Fred Smith, J. P. Mitchell, Allan Hoover.

COURTESY SISKIYOU MUSEUM, YREKA, CALIFORNIA

As he had the previous year, Hoover chose political activity over angling for big game fish in Florida. Though he would not admit it, like Landon, he was angling for the 1936 Republican presidential nomination. Vindication was a powerful motivating force. The old guard and many progressives in the party just wished that the pariah from Palo Alto would go away; he was in their eyes the excess baggage that would keep the Republican airplane from ever getting off the ground. To their chagrin, Hoover proved his persistence. Seizing the initiative, he invited Landon to the Grove, where the two of them might become better acquainted. Landon tentatively accepted, but later, for legitimate reasons, he was unable to attend.[700]

In March, Hoover managed a three-day fishing trip to California, and in April, he was back in Yosemite. In early May, to Hoover's delight, the Supreme Court dealt the New Deal a first blow by finding the Railroad Pension Act unconstitutional. Jumping back into the political fray, Hoover at the end of the month received more good news. The Supreme Court dealt a second stunning blow to the New Deal by unanimously finding the National Recovery Act (NRA) unconstitutional. Republican prospects seemed enhanced and sent an electrical charge through the party.

Just before leaving on a cross-country jaunt that would end at the Waldorf in New York City, the Chief squeezed in a quick trip to fish the Rogue River. On the way, he managed a day's fishing on the Snake River in Idaho.[701]

While in the East, Hoover branched out into new fishing territory with a four-day trip to Vermont and New Hampshire. He, his son Allan, and Richey took the Twentieth Century Limited from New York City to Albany. The next morning, the threesome motored through the Green Mountains, over Mendon Mountain, and into Ottauquechee Valley, then on to Plymouth, Vermont, where they visited the Coolidge home. They stood in the room where Silent Cal's father had conducted the presidential swearing-in ceremony and paid their respects at the president's gravesite. By late afternoon, the expectant fishermen arrived in Bernard at the fishing club on Lake Lakota. A newspaper reporter awaited Hoover at the club lodge and was greeted with the comment: "How did you get up here? I thought you fellows were to be kept away from this place."[702] The enterprising reporter did not get his story.

As it was already late in the afternoon, the gear was quickly unloaded, and Hoover headed for the lake. Garfield Miller, a White River Junction automobile dealer and prominent Republican, manned the oars. Hoover stood in the stern of the small rowboat to cast. When his Silver Doctor fly plopped onto the water, it made a series of tiny ripples on the surface of the tranquil lake. Switching back and forth between a number of flies, including a Brown Hackle, Hoover lured the hungry trout to rise to the temptation. In two hours, he caught his limit.[703] One fish on his stringer was especially nice, a trout over fifteen inches long that weighed more than two pounds. The two boats that carried Richey, the younger Hoover, and guests did well, but the Chief caught the largest fish. That evening in the rustic lodge, all dined on the fresh catch, joined by the governor and former governor of Vermont, Charles M. Smith and Stanley O. Wilson. The assembled Republican leadership denied politicking, insisting that the trip was nothing more than a fishing outing capped off by an evening social affair.[704]

At six-thirty in the morning, Hoover was back on the lake. By noon he had caught twenty-two brookies, getting the trout to bite again on the Silver Doctor and Brown Hackle.[705] After lunch, the fishermen left for the Lake Mitchell Trout Club in Sharon, Vermont. Standing nearly all afternoon in the boat, Hoover landed eighteen trout, five or six that measured twelve inches in length. Satisfied with a good catch, the fishing party drove to Corbin Park near Newport, New Hampshire. At dinner, Hoover was joined by Republican governor Styles Bridges and ex-governor Huntley Spaulding, who had worked for him in the War Food Administration. After dinner, while the Republicans assembled on the lodge porch to discuss economics and fishing, but supposedly not politics, four deer grazed in the meadow. That evening, a happy Hoover often smiled, his face reddened by a day in the hot sun.[706]

Corbin Park was another of those luxurious estates that survived from an earlier era, a private game and fishing preserve of twenty-five thousand fenced acres, approximately five miles wide and ten miles long.[707] Austin Corbin, a successful financier, had acquired the land for the park in the 1890s, stocking the grounds with a menagerie of wild game: deer, elk, boars, moose, caribou, mountain goats, beavers, bison, pheasants, trout, bass, and pickerel. All thrived in this protected environment. Teddy Roosevelt came to hunt in the park, as had Richey, who stalked wild boars in four feet of snow in twenty-below-zero weather.[708] In the morning, Hoover donned his fishing garb: khaki pants and coat, a gray felt fedora with black band, and the obligatory collar and tie.[709] At streamside, he slipped into his hip boots and began to wade. Sticking with the productive Silver Doctor and Brown Hackle, the Chief reeled in another nice string of trout. After lunch, with the fish packed on ice, Hoover, Allan, and Richey left for New York City.

Throughout the remainder of the summer and fall, fishing took second place to politics. Hoover redoubled his activity, meeting with dozens of Republican groups in dozens of states. As always, he campaigned indirectly, hoping to stir up enough

Hoover fishing in Bernard, Vermont. Garfield Miller of White River is rowing. COURTESY QUEENS BOROUGH PUBLIC LIBRARY, LONG ISLAND DIVISION, NEW YORK HERALD-TRIBUNE COLLECTION

enthusiasm for his undeclared candidacy that the party faithful would turn to him at the convention and offer up the nomination he so coveted. On into the winter and spring of 1936, Hoover kept up his frenetic pace, but in May, after the California Republican voters scotched a bid by William Randolph Hearst for party control, he combined business with pleasure. Larry Richey invited the Chief to come and fish with him at his country house in Catoctin, Maryland. Hoover, who now made numerous political trips east, was delighted at the opportunity. It was also a chance to meet with Maryland Republicans in an effort to persuade party members to send an uncommitted delegation to the coming national convention in Cleveland. In springtime, the Appalachian hardwood forest was awash in blossoming trees and flowering plants. Migrating birds flittered in the scrubs and bushes. The trout in the clear, bubbling stream were plentiful, and the Chief, among friends, relaxed in the warm environment in between meetings with party leaders. The well-stocked creek yielded a large number of ten-inch rainbows.

Committed to his shadow candidacy, playing the role of the shy maiden who demanded she be properly courted by well-intentioned suitors, Hoover forced the hesitant Republican National Committee to invite him to address the 1936 convention in a midweek evening slot, a time guaranteeing a national radio audience. The hopeful candidate fantasized that he would deliver a great speech, one that would sweep away the opposition and win for him the coveted nomination. Hoover's speech, a combination of his classic liberalism and a virulent attack on the New Deal, was received enthusiastically by those in the packed hall. Regardless of his oratorical success, the following evening the convention delegates dutifully nominated Landon without a serious challenge.[710] Hoover once again had established himself as an important voice in the party, but Landon did not wish his services during the coming campaign, so that his would be a voice infrequently heard. With his vindication plans on hold and his future role in politics in doubt, Hoover went fishing.[711]

On July 1, the Chief packed his tackle and gear and took the train to Oregon. The first stop was the Upper McKenzie and the Blue River, high in the Cascade Mountains.[712] He was joined the following day by one of his favorite fishing companions, Arthur Hyde. The two fishermen were the guests of W. E. Travis, the bus magnate, at his ample lodge near McKenzie Bridge. On the Fourth of July, Hoover, like millions of his fellow Americans, spent the day fishing, catching a number of rainbows.[713] The "big one," however, got away when a three-pound trout broke the leader. Hoover remarked to friends, "It'll be 10 pounds when I get east."[714] Later that day, he pulled in a Dolly Varden that had swallowed a rainbow trout he was trying to land.[715] Days spent wading and casting in the cold, rushing water affirmed Hoover's love for the McKenzie. Though he also loved deep-sea fishing, despite all the excitement involved in hooking those battling sea monsters he remained loyal to his first love, the isolated wilderness rivers and lakes of northern California and Oregon, especially the McKenzie River, where he had fished as a young man. As Steve Raymond explains in *Steelhead Country:* "I think, over time, that almost every fisherman develops something akin to a monogamous relationship with a favorite river, a river he loves and knows more intimately and desires to fish above all others."[716]

The holiday over, it was on to the Rogue River, where Hoover and Hyde were guests of another friend, Frank M. Madison of San Francisco.[717] Summer steelhead, eighteen inches and larger, swam in the upper reaches of the river. Big rainbows lurked in the deep pools, riffles, and back eddies. The fishing was good, and Hoover declared the McKenzie and the Rogue the best fishing in the West. The trip at an end, the Chief boarded the train in Medford and headed south to home.

Back in California only a few weeks, Hoover decided to skip the Bohemian Grove encampment in order to accept an invitation from W. D. Thornton, a mine operator and friend who lived in New York City. He would spend two weeks fishing on the Madison River in Upper Yellowstone. The luxurious fishing camp included a number of well-constructed log cabins located just outside the national park. Thornton and three friends, known as the "Four Horsemen of the Madison," had all grown up in Butte, Montana, and for twenty-five years returned annually to enjoy fishing the river. Surprisingly, none of the anglers were fish eaters. They gave their catch to friends, neighbors, and nearby railroad men.[718] The Madison, a river Hoover had fished briefly in 1933, was one of America's spectacular streams. Two weeks offered him the opportunity to explore a beautiful and diverse natural paradise, one he had glimpsed as secretary of commerce on a short visit to Yellowstone Park in 1927. The majestic Madison, named by Lewis and Clark, starts in the park at the confluence of the Gibbon and Fire Hole Rivers and flows on west, through Hebgen Lake, and north for 140 miles to form a part of the headwaters of the Missouri River. Because of the volcanic underlay of geysers and hot springs, the water in the Madison often exceeds eighty degrees in temperature. The high temperature has a negative effect on fish in certain stretches of the river, but brown, rainbow, and cutthroat trout survive and are in abundance, as are the native whitefish.[719]

John Colter, a member of the Lewis and Clark expedition, mountain man, and explorer of the American West, was likely the first white person to stumble into Yellowstone. Later, he told all who would listen, usually downing a number of whiskeys as the tale unfolded, fantastical stories of a land with bubbling mud pits, hot springs, huge geysers, weird moonscapelike geological formations, crystal blue deep-water lakes, broad trout-filled

Hoover and an unidentified park ranger fishing in West Yellowstone,
Montana. COURTESY HERBERT HOOVER LIBRARY

rivers, and lovely valleys surrounded by snow-capped mountains. His disbelieving listeners, while transfixed by his engaging surreal tale, labeled his fantasy land Colter's Hell.[720] But as God was his witness, Colter told the truth about the strange land hidden away in the northwest corner of Wyoming.

Hoover eagerly fished the rivers and lakes that made up the park and thoroughly enjoyed exploring the geological oddities.

One day, accompanied by a ranger, the two men horsebacked up to a mountain lake and caught two nice stringers of trout. Along the Madison, Hoover and three of the "Four Horsemen" had day after day of successful fishing. At the end of his stay, he pledged, as do all impassioned visitors, that he would return to Yellowstone as soon as possible. Unlike most vacationers, it was a pledge Hoover kept.

Back in Palo Alto, Hoover surveyed the progress of the Landon campaign, which he judged lame and unlikely to win. With time on his hands, he decided on a driving tour up the coast to Coos Bay, Oregon, with Lou and their Palo Alto friends Mr. and Mrs. W. C. Van Antwerp. New fishing challenges were in order, and from Coos Bay, the foursome crossed the Cascade Mountains to Bend, Oregon.[721] There they planned to fish the Deschutes, a river Hoover had never before angled, an intriguing stream that tumbled down the northeast face of the Cascades through steep canyon walls and emptied into the Columbia River. At South Twin Lake, Hoover waited nearly two hours for the guide, Fay Robideau, to return from an earlier excursion. The guide had accompanied two Stanford students, who hauled in their limit of trout.[722] The two young Hoover chauffeurs, seeing the other boys' fish and observing trout jumping in the lake to feed on a hatch, decided that they too wished to fish. Robideau outfitted the boys with tackle, loaded them into a boat, and bade them adieu. The guide then rowed Hoover and Mrs. Van Antwerp upstream for many miles, an arduous task, so that they could float back down, fishing all the way. Robideau skillfully handled the boat while Hoover, standing, whipped the waters with his favorite flies in an effort to coax the trout to rise. The fishing party did not return to dock until seven o'clock that evening; it had been a wonderfully scenic trip, but they caught few fish. Meanwhile, the two drivers, novice fishermen, had both caught their limit of rainbows.

Hoover was enchanted by the Upper Deschutes and asked why no one had built a resort. The answer grated on the former president: "Well, you know how things have been, for the past few years."[723] Flirting with the possibility of a new river mistress, Hoover declared the Deschutes "better than the McKenzie."[724] No cabins were available for an overnight stay, so the Hoovers and their guests spent the night in Bend, where the Chief spoke at a Republican district rally. In the morning, all consumed a trout and pancake breakfast at the Butte Inn. Hoover obligingly signed autographs, and then they left to catch the train for Palo Alto in Klamath Falls.[725]

While Hoover maneuvered to participate in the Landon campaign, he revived his interest in mining. He visited the Jumbo Gold Mine in Humboldt County, Nevada, in the heart of the Awakening Mining District ironically located in the Slumbering Hills.[726] The Chief was impressed with the mine's potential, and when he said so publicly, it touched off a mini-gold rush. People impoverished by the Great Depression, people from all over the country who had wound up broke in California and Nevada, flocked to the site hoping to strike it rich. The boom lasted only a few years, though the Jumbo continued to produce sporadically until 1951.[727]

In mid-September, Hoover again traveled to New York City. Unlike his wife, who had wished that Washington were in California, Hoover edged ever closer to a decision to move East. While in New York, politicking, conducting business, and attending an American Relief Administration reunion, he again had the opportunity for a new fishing experience. Friends invited him to fish the waters off the tip of Long Island at Montauk, New York. Hoover, along with Richey, investment banker and longtime friend Lewis L. Strauss, and George LeBoutillier, vice president of the Pennsylvania Railroad, arrived at the Montauk Yacht Club on the last day of the fishing season. As LeBoutillier and his guests wandered the clubhouse, boxes were being packed everywhere. A hard northeast wind delayed the start of the excursion. To kill time while waiting for the wind to die down, the fishermen toured Montauk Point and picnicked aboard the yacht *Mongoose*.[728]

Around one o'clock, weather conditions had improved and the yacht set sail, but the rough seas forced the party to stay in Block Island Sound instead of fishing the open water for swordfish. Bluefish were the quarry, a fish once accurately described as "an animated chopping machine," as they will attack anything living.[729] Traveling twice a year in migrating schools, they are ferocious eaters that consume huge numbers of menhaden, herring, and mackerel. They weigh about five pounds on average, though the big ones weigh about fifteen pounds, and some have even been caught that weigh over forty. Bluefish strike hard, put up a good fight, and are very difficult to handle because of their extremely sharp teeth.[730] They have been known to bite off surfers' toes and fishermen's fingers. Removing the plug or spoon from the mouth of an aggressive bluefish can be tricky business.

Trolling the bay, Hoover caught the first blue, a scrapper. Throughout the afternoon, the party hooked four more, but two managed to escape after netting.[731] At dockside, someone recalled that Hoover's nemesis, Franklin Roosevelt, had fished Block Island Sound for an entire weekend with Vincent Astor in 1933, sailing in his yacht *Nourmahal,* and had not caught as many fish as Hoover. The Chief, in an upbeat mood, smiled broadly in response to the story.[732] The three bluefish, "as sweet as corn right off the stalk," were prepared by the chefs aboard LeBoutillier's private railcar and eaten for dinner on the trip back into the city.[733]

In October, Hoover attended one of the subway World Series games in Yankee Stadium. The Bronx Bombers beat the Giants in six games. In spite of his commitments to politics and fishing, he now spent much of his time on a new project, the Boys' Clubs of America, becoming the chairman of the National Board of Directors. The clubs had been around for a long time, but Hoover now wholeheartedly endorsed the mission of providing opportunities for urban boys. Beginning in 1936, he dedicated thousands of hours to building the organization and raising substantial amounts of money. New boys' clubs sprang up like mushrooms in dozens of cities.

November brought the awaited election. The Landon-Knox ticket was soundly thrashed by Roosevelt. Poor Landon carried only two states, which was one of the worst drubbings in U.S. political history. Hoover pawed through the wreckage and calculated his chances of regaining control of the Republican party.[734] His mother had been an evangelist for Quakerism, and her son now went on the road as an evangelist for what he defined as true Republican values. To paraphrase Reinhold Niebuhr, he was a tutor "of mankind in its pilgrimage to perfection." If the party were ever to defeat Roosevelt, Hoover postulated, it would have to stand right of center, not attempt to "out–New Deal the New Deal."[735]

The election over, the ominous threat of war in Europe claimed more of Hoover's attention, and he began to contemplate a fact-finding mission to survey the situation for himself. These things, however, would have to wait while the Chief went fishing in Florida for two weeks in December. Staying in Palm Beach with Richey, Van Antwerp, and his old friend Mark Sullivan, he chartered a boat and hired Capt. Herman Gray, the guide he had used in 1932, a Florida conch who knew the waters surrounding the Keys well.[736] Craig's Camp on Key Largo served as an anchorage and a source of supplies, especially ice. It was early in the Florida winter fishing season, and the men caught few fish. Several days aboard the yacht *Virago*, owned by George F. Getz, the former treasurer of the Republican National Committee, were also disappointing.[737]

Returning to California, Hoover spent Christmas with his family, but in early January, he was already planning trout fishing trips for the coming year, spending a part of the day in his office with an expert on fishing flies. In February, Hoover spoke out forcefully against Roosevelt's plan to further the New Deal, "schemes of good and new for titipu," by packing the Supreme Court.[738] If Roosevelt increased the number of justices in the Supreme Court, then he diminished the chances that the New Deal legislation would be declared unconstitutional. Before spring arrived to melt the ice from the trout streams, releasing the hungry fish to search aggressively for food, Hoover and Richey, along with Sullivan and Van Antwerp, were back in Florida. As guests once again of George F. Getz, the fishing party was determined to land the game fish they had failed to catch in December.[739] The *Virago* cruised the Keys for two weeks, working out of Craig's Camp. This time the fishing was excellent.

In March and April 1937, the Supreme Court battle reached new heights, swirling around Washington like a hurricane. Added to the political hubbub surrounding the court-packing controversy were the militant efforts of the Congress of Industrial Organizations, funded by John L. Lewis and the United Mine Workers, to unionize the automobile and steel industries by staging sit-down strikes in plants across the country. Violence erupted frequently and Chicago strikers were killed. Hoover said little publicly, but to friends he fumed that Roosevelt failed to govern or to maintain order and enforce the law.[740] To the chairman of the Republican National Committee, he advocated a midterm leadership convention that would set out the party's principles, from which policy would be deduced. In Hoover's thinking, Republican compromises with the opposition spelled defeat.

Regardless of the political problems fomenting around him, Hoover made time to fish. He accepted the invitation of George Warren, head of the Fish and Game Commission of New Jersey, to join him for a fishing trip to the Pequest River in late April. The Pequest originated in the swampland of the New Jersey meadows, and on its downhill course to the Delaware River, passing south of Jenny Jump Mountain, it became one of the best freestone trout streams in New Jersey, with pools, pockets, riffles, and runs. The trout were large, on average twelve to fourteen inches, and fed on frequent hatches of assorted bugs.[741] Overhanging trees made casting a challenge, but Hoover and Warren, entering the river around Vienna, both caught their limit of ten. Hoover, who had not fished before in New Jersey, was so impressed that he returned two weeks later on May Day, and landed a seventeen-and-a-half-inch rainbow—a real beauty. Again the two fishermen caught their limit.[742] The Chief was genuinely pleased to discover a trout stream within easy drive of the skyscrapers of New York.

Throughout the summer, the economy worsened. Hoover kept up his crusade for a midterm convention, smelling Republican opportunity in the forthcoming elections of 1938 and 1940, as well as the possibility of the presidential nomination for himself. In July, he found time to return to the McKenzie, spending four days standing in the bow of a specially designed McKenzie River boat. His guide, Fred Harris, deftly navigated the fast water while Hoover reeled in the trout. Staying in his favorite cabin at Holiday Farm was always a treat. Later in the month, at the Bohemian Grove, the Chief luxuriated among the like-minded denizens of Cave Man Camp, reassured by the wide acceptance of his ideas. A few days before attending the Grove encampment, he had received from Will Thornton a letter, a package of flies, and an invitation to fish the Madison River in Montana. In his thank-you note, he wrote, "The flies have come and the movement is in my bones."[743]

A week after leaving the redwoods behind at the Grove, a reinvigorated Hoover packed his fishing gear for two weeks on the Madison River and a side trip to the Bighorn Mountains in north-central Wyoming. He invited his son Allan to accompany

Hoover and New Jersey game commissioner George Warren on the
Pequest River, New Jersey, May 30, 1938. COURTESY QUEENS BOROUGH PUBLIC
LIBRARY, LONG ISLAND DIVISION, NEW YORK HERALD-TRIBUNE COLLECTION

him and told Lou she would have to cancel his birthday party, a
yearly family extravaganza planned for the next day, saying, "I
hear they are biting good up in Yellowstone. I think I'll be gone
for about two weeks. Good-by."[744] Getting off the Union Pacific
Overland in Wells, Nevada, after sleeping the night on the train,
he picked up his car, spending his sixty-third birthday with his
son and a Stanford student chauffeur on a leisurely drive to West
Yellowstone.[745] The Chief loved to fish the Madison and its lakes.
The river was easy to wade, and between Hebgen Lake and Ennis
Lake, called the fifty-mile riffle, there were no overhanging trees,

no fallen timber, no boulders, no slow pools, and no "tumbling runs."[746] The fifty-mile-long riffle moved grandly at five miles per hour over a bed of gravel and small stones in an open prairie setting. The headwaters of the river, inside Yellowstone Park, were also easy to wade and contained pools especially suited to dry-fly fishing. Toward evening, herds of deer, elk, antelope, and buffalo moved along the banks of the river. Occasionally a fisherman spotted his competitor, the bald eagle, diving for fish.

After a few days with the Madisonians, Hoover and Allan drove across Yellowstone Park, stopping to talk with Superintendent Edmund Rogers and to take in sights such as Old Faithful.[747] Continuing across the open spaces of northern Wyoming, the Hoovers aided a stranded motorist who had run out of gas.[748] Later that afternoon, the two travelers arrived at the sprawling ranch of Frank Horton, a Republican National Committee member. The ranch, near the Clear River and nestled in the lodgepole pines of the Bighorn Mountains, held out the promise of several days of good fishing. Dr. O. Glen Saxon, a Yale professor who headed the research department of the Republican National Committee, had arrived a few day earlier.[749] The next morning, Hoover, his son, and Saxon disappeared into the mountains and returned with a nice catch. The Chief hooked four trout, one a fine six-pound rainbow.[750]

Reporters, who had driven out from the little town of Buffalo, descended on the ranch. Hoover, dressed in his fishing togs—a well-worn brown suit, old shoes, and a white shirt, but surprisingly, no collar and no necktie—sat on the porch in a rough-hewn ranch chair to field questions. His opening remark was the same as he had uttered dozens of times in the past: "I talk politics at home and other places, but not on fishing trips. And I'm here to fish. I caught four good ones. That's enough for anyone in one day. There's no use in catching too many at once."[751] Asked repeatedly to comment on the proposed 1938 midterm meeting, he dodged the question but admitted that the idea was floating around. He consented to be photographed, quipping that he doubted taking his picture would cause a national crisis. He laughed off the suggestion that he put on a ten-gallon hat and pick up his fly rod.[752] After another day of fishing in the mountain streams, father and son, accompanied by Saxon, drove back to Yellowstone to fish the Madison.

On the way, not far from the national park, the car came up quickly on a middle-aged woman hitchhiker, who was trudging along the hot, dusty road carrying nothing but an overnight bag. Hoover pulled up alongside the woman and asked her destination. "Yellowstone," came her reply. The Chief motioned for her to get in the backseat, and the big car sped off down the road. A few minutes later, Hoover, his curiosity piqued, asked what a woman was doing hitchhiking on a hot day in the middle of nowhere. She answered that she was an evangelist with the Big Sister League in Los Angeles. Her mission was to work the tourist camps of the West, "saving fallen souls." Her gospel, she said, was simple and to the point: "First, Soup; second, Soap; and third, Salvation." When asked how she managed to fund her revivalist efforts, she solemnly responded, "The Lord always provides." At the tourist camp in Yellowstone, she got out of the car, and Hoover asked her if she needed money to continue her work. Shaking her head, she thanked Hoover for the ride and again said, "The Lord always provides."[753] "This will help you buy some soup and soap," he said, pushing a bill into her hand. The woman stretched out the crumpled bill and examined both sides carefully, finally saying, "Don't you have any hard money?"[754] The former president said nothing, dug through his pockets, and came up with approximately $3 in silver. The woman started to walk away, turned to thank him, then disappeared through the gates of the camp. Hoover drove on, but a few minutes later he looked at Saxon with an amused expression on his face and said, "Glen, she must be one of the few in the country who still believes in sound money."[755]

The Thornton camp was fun. Horseplay, practical jokes, ribald humor, tall tales, and blue stories abounded, encouraged by expensive liquor, good cigars, and good food. Hoover enjoyed this type of tomfoolery and in the proper setting liked to tell off-color jokes. His favorites were the kind starting with "One day, a priest, a minister and a rabbi . . ." The Chief euphemistically called these stories "Eskimo jokes." He also held "farmer's daughter" and "traveling salesman" jokes in high regard. Jim Howell, a San Francisco businessman in charge of getting everyone up in the morning, amused the early risers with his unorthodox techniques. Those who lingered were suddenly awakened by exploding firecrackers under their bed. Malcolm Gillis, relieving himself in the bathroom, was bushwhacked by Howell, who attempted to attach a string of lit firecrackers to his pajamas. Howell partially succeeded, as Gillis fled the cabin in a burst of speed amid gales of laughter and exploding ladyfingers.

After a hearty breakfast—for Hoover, fried trout and a stack of pancakes with real Vermont maple syrup—the seven fishermen worked the river's riffles. For years, Thornton had been the most successful of the fishermen. But when Hoover arrived, Thornton's daily catches sharply declined, and Hoover reeled in the most fish nearly every day. The others accused Thornton of revealing his secret locations, though he blamed his lack of success on the low water level, noting that all of the fish he caught had "corns on their tummies from crawling over the rocks" in the streambed.[756] Another Madisonian swore that the water was so low "the fish had dust in their eyes."[757] The fishermen agreed that only one thing was certain—all of the fish caught were Republicans. In this playful environment, Hoover also came in for his share of ribbing as he slipped on the rocks in the river, filling his waders with water. He was pummeled with advice on "how to handle heavy Dutch socks after they have been at the bottom of the creek."[758] In the evening after dinner, the men relaxed, talked, smoked, and enjoyed a brandy or cognac in front of a roaring fire. Two of the guests, Howell and Thomas H. O'Brien, an executive with the Inspiration Copper Co., spent their evenings tying flies especially suited to particular pools and runs on the river. They were quite successful with their mimicry of the insects that hatched on the Madison.[759]

After several more days in this enjoyable setting, Hoover and Saxon left for Oregon, and Allan Hoover returned to his huge vegetable farm near Bakersfield. The two sportsmen fished their way across the divide in typical Hoover fashion. They fished in the mornings, then took a break for a picnic lunch, and then drove on to the next trout stream of choice, fishing until dark. On the western slope of the mountains, somewhere in Idaho, the two men stopped at a tourist camp that consisted of a number of cabins strung out along a good trout stream. Saxon went to register but was told that the only available accommodations were two cots in a room up over the office. He and Hoover talked it over, deciding that they had no choice other than to take whatever was offered. Saxon used his real name in the register but signed in Hoover as Mr. J. B. Smith from Palo Alto.

As the two ate breakfast at six o'clock the next morning, the woman owner commented that Saxon's friend sure looked a lot like President Hoover. Saxon concurred that there was, in fact, a striking similarity between the two men, and that she was not the first on their trip to notice the resemblance. It was a common mistake, he said. Leaning forward to pour coffee, the woman looked more carefully and exclaimed, "Why, you are Mr. Hoover."[760] Flustered, she announced proudly that both her daughters attended Stanford. Asked about fishing, she walked across the room and took from a drawer a map and some fishing flies, telling them she tied her own flies. Then she spread out the map on the table and marked the best fishing spots on the river—places that harbored five-pound rainbows. She dug through her book and, as Saxon noted, "shyly selected several of her flies and hesitatingly offered some of each kind to both of us. Suddenly she stopped short and said with a scorn such as only a fly fisherman has for those who bait their hooks with worms, 'I hope that you don't use worms like President Coolidge.' He took all the flies and shook his head and said with a poker face, 'No, I never stoop to such lowdown tactics, but this fellow Saxon, here, does—and don't give any of your flies to him—he wouldn't appreciate them.'"[761] The hand-tied flies were put to good use that morning in the swift current of the Idaho stream.

Hoover and Saxon drove on west that afternoon, both realizing that there was yet time to wrestle with the stacks of mail and unattended business that awaited them in Palo Alto. They were like two vagabonds in pursuit of adventure on the open road, fishing for fun and to wash their souls. A tanned and smiling Hoover told a reporter in Yakima, Washington, "We hope to find more fishing in Oregon."[762] They did. The two men worked their way down the Willamette Valley, first fishing the McKenzie, then the Rogue, and finally moving west over the mountains to the Klamath. Along the way, they mended Republican fences and garnered IOUs.

Throughout the fall, Hoover battled Landon and the congressional Republicans, nearly all of whom opposed a midterm convention. His lack of success remained for him a mystery, as he would not accept that his principles could no longer gain the support of the American people.[763] In November, the Republican National Committee rejected the midterm convention proposal, ending Hoover's bid to reassert his leadership of the party. Regardless, those that supported "their Chief" continued to play Sancho Panza to this ideological Don Quixote. A month later, Hoover's hopes revived when at last a long-awaited invitation to visit Belgium arrived.[764] Perhaps the road to the Republican presidential nomination lay somewhere in the heart of Europe rather than in the heartland of America.

Hoover undertook the European trip to bolster his image and his ego. Demonstrating his standing in the international community might well awaken memories in the United States of his past achievements. Possibly the trip could set the stage for his political comeback, as Europeans appeared likely to resolve their differences once again through war. Parrin Galpin, a longtime associate and head of the Belgian American Educational Fund, pondered the predicaments his boss might encounter on a foreign visit as former president of the United States. What if he was asked, Galpin queried, to toast the president of the United States? "Well," Hoover responded, "I can certainly do that." Galpin, still worried, pressed on. But what if he was asked to comment on Roosevelt's foreign policy? "Oh," Hoover said without cracking a smile, "I think I can keep silent in seven languages."[765]

As Hoover well knew, Europeans remembered him differently than did Americans, and he was welcomed by large crowds who turned out to see the "savior of Europe." A different lexicon of words associated with his name emerged in several European languages. "Benevolence" and "charity" could be expressed in Finnish by the word *Hooveri*, and from the American Relief Administration child-feeding program in Germany came *Hoover Speisung*—"Hoover supplies."[766] To his delight, upon his arrival on February 16, he was wined, dined, toasted, and paraded through fifteen European capitals, garnering numerous honors on a triumphant march that included twelve honorary degrees. Would Hoover, on his return to the United States, be able to exchange these honors for political capital? Returning home, he fulminated over the supposed excesses of the New Deal, praised British prime minister Chamberlain for his efforts to secure a peaceful resolution to Europe's mounting problems, ruminated against any U.S. participation in foreign wars, and began the rudiments of his presidential campaign by establishing a front organization called Republican Circles—a discreet effort to enlist potential national convention delegates in western states.[767]

Hoover arrived in Chicago on May 15 after being on the Republican "rubber chicken circuit" in the spring.[768] He was only too glad to accept the invitation of George Scott, president of American Car and Foundry, to join a two-day fishing party of business luminaries headed for northern Wisconsin, where they were members of a private club whose vast acreage straddled the border between Marinette, Wisconsin, and Pembine, Michigan. Among the wealthy businessmen were Col. Frank Knox of the Chicago *Daily News*, Alf Landon's 1936 Republican running mate; Sewell Avery of Montgomery Ward; D. A. Crawford, president of the Pullman Company; and George Murnane, a New York financier. On Sunday, Hoover boarded the Chippewa, the Milwaukee Road's streamlined express, and sped through the Wisconsin countryside, arriving in Pembine around five o'clock. Hustled into a limousine by the chauffeur, he was driven straight to the Coleman Fishing Club. The fishing camp consisted of a number of palatial lodges owned by individual members. The Scott lodge, built before the turn of the century and dutifully maintained, was constructed of pine logs cut from some of the largest trees ever to grow in northern Wisconsin. A number of the logs were one hundred feet in length.[769]

At dinner, Hoover held forth on the state of the union. He spent nearly all of the following day fishing the South Pike River, where he caught his limit. That evening, he and the other guests consented to an interview by the local press.[770] Coming in off the river, he slipped out of his hip boots, put down his creel, and ambled out onto the huge front porch of the lodge to sit and talk. Recently Hoover had begun to dress more casually than in the past, including an open collar, but this evening he donned a tie, though tucked into the front of a blue chambray work shirt. His old dark gray oxford suit coat was offset by a favorite hat, a light gray fedora with a black band, which emphasized the fullness of his face. On his feet, protruding from his high-water khaki pants, he wore a new pair of ankle-high, black and brown, lace-up basketball shoes. Hoover, at sixty-four, at long last looked like a fisherman.

Hoover and Col. Frank Knox at the Coleman Fishing Club, Pembine, Wisconsin, May 1938. COURTESY CONANT STUDIO, MARINETTE, WISCONSIN

Relaxed and in a jovial mood, he lit his briar pipe and opened his remarks with a line from his stock repertoire: "Newspapermen and photographers respect a man's privacy only on two occasions—at prayer and when he is actually fishing."[771] While everyone was chuckling, W. C. Janson of the Marinette *Eagle-Star* took the opportunity to present Hoover with three Michigan Coachman flies he had tied.[772] The former president, pleased, said he would try them out in the South Pike in the morning. Fishing dominated the conversation, and Scott slipped into the lodge and returned with his collection of prize flies, which were passed around for all to see. Knox walked up the concert steps onto the porch, admired the flies, lit his own pipe, and joined the conversation, which soon switched to the Japanese war in China and international affairs in general. The Chief shared his conclusions on his recent European trip. The discussion finally wound down, and H. A. Conant and his son Howell, excellent photographers from Marinette, asked if they could take photos. Hoover agreed and the Conants took a number of shots. In the middle of the photo shoot, George Murnane arrived in his fishing outfit: "waist-high boots, two hats with mosquito netting and visor, and all of his fishing accessories dangling from the back of his belt."[773] Hoover declined to have his picture taken with Murnane. He looked the financial analyst up and down and cracked, "New York is the only place they could sell an outfit like that."[774] The next day, the new flies proved productive, as Hoover again caught his limit.

The former president was back hard on the political trail for a week, but he broke off his pursuit of delegates to join George Warren for two days of fishing on the Pequest. He was in luck and hauled in his limit of twelve- to fourteen-inch trout. This short respite, however, brought no relief from rough-and-tumble politics. Hoover's speeches on foreign policy linked European difficulties to planned economies and totalitarian leadership. The same threat to liberties that destroyed European countries, he said, emanated from Roosevelt and the New Deal. In Seattle on June 29, Hoover continued his attack, asserting that "the democracies of Europe that held to sound economic policies tightened their belts, balanced their budgets and refrained from interfering with private business, had recovered from the depression 18 months after 1932, had restored their national income to points higher than 1928."[775] Again badgered by reporters who wished to know his political plans, the noncandidate quipped, "Fishing and politics don't mix."[776] A few days later, the *New York Times* suggested that the reason politics and fishing did not mix was because both endeavors were the same. Politicians fished for votes and "some are sharks. Some seem to live in darkness and have no eyes. The big ones eat the little fellows up."[777] The editorial went on to harpoon Hoover's often repeated line about "prayer and fishing." To the *Times*, Hoover's privacy was in no danger. Since he was not in office and not a candidate, he could fish in seclusion, but it was understandable that he might pray for the Republican party while fishing. The article concluded that the final fate of politicians was also the final fate of fish: "Sooner or later they swallow the fly or get the hook."[778]

Hoover had stopped briefly in Seattle to attend a reception at the Olympic hotel given in his honor by prominent northwestern Republicans.[779] But he was on his way with Wilbur and Hyde to fish in British Columbia. Wilbur had fished the famous Fraser River the summer before and was impressed with the size and fight of the river's trout and salmon. At Stuart Lake, after an extended battle, he had reeled in a whopper on a Leonard rod—a Kamloops rainbow trout that weighed twenty pounds and was thirty-three inches in length.[780] Wilbur claimed it was the largest one ever caught in British Columbia.[781] When he returned to Stanford, he regaled Hoover with tales of the Fraser and the huge Kamloops trout that swam in the Thompson River. He was successful in convincing his friend that a fishing jaunt to the wilds of British Columbia was a necessity. When leaving Palo Alto, Wilbur was asked by a reporter how long he, Hoover, and Hyde would be gone. Stanford's president replied, "Until the fish stop biting."[782] In actuality, the three fishermen spent two weeks guided by their host, Al Hager, a Vancouver fish company owner and Stanford alumni, fishing the streams and lakes of British Columbia from Lillooet to Fort St. James, a small settlement far to the north on Stuart Lake.

In Lillooet, Hoover was given the opportunity to shoot a ranch-raiding, thousand-pound, silver-tipped grizzly bear holed up in a canyon. His experience with rabbits as a boy in Iowa had cured him of a desire to hunt, and he declined the invitation to pursue the ferocious beast.[783] Fishing on the Fraser River was very good, but the next three days spent on Canim Lake produced an even finer catch. The first day, Canada's Dominion holiday, very few fish were caught because of the cold, rainy weather. On days two and three, the weather and the fishing improved, and Hoover and his companions landed eighty-five rainbows of varying size. This was a large number of fish, but far below the legal limit of fifteen per person per day. Hyde hauled in a rainbow that weighed sixteen and a half pounds, a fish he had stuffed.[784] After the men ate their fill, the remainder of the fish were iced down and sent by overnight train to Vancouver, where they were given out to the city's needy.[785]

Traveling north to fish the Cariboo district around Prince George, the party continued on to Stuart Lake. Fort St. James, on the lake, was the site of the first trading post in British Columbia, the place where Carrier Indians met white traders in 1805. The Indians descendants, now called the Stuart Lake tribe, performed an impressive ceremony inducting Hoover into their ranks as a chief. He was honored for his humanitarian work in feeding starving peoples during World War I and so was given the Indian name Chief Bread Giver. The former president was led to an Indian throne accompanied by local dignitaries, several Canadian mounted police, and an honor guard of eighteen members of the Canadian Legion. An eagle-feather bonnet was placed on his head by Chief Louis Billy, who addressed the crowd through an interpreter. The speech over, Billy knelt down, took off Hoover's shoes, and slipped a pair of moccasins on his feet. Chief Billy concluded the ceremony by offering a blessing that the Great Humanitarian might catch many fish in Trout Creek.[786] Hoover, who usually detested these kinds of affairs, genuinely enjoyed his induction into the Stuart Lake tribe.[787] The Chief had now come full circle, from chief engineer to Indian chief. As to the blessing, it proved propitious: The fishing party caught lots of lake trout.

A few days later, in Medford, Hoover politically worked southern Oregon Republican leaders and then caught a plane to Oakland. Airline service in the West had expanded exponentially,

At Stuart Lake, British Columbia, July 1938. A. L. Hager, R. L. Wilbur, and Hoover. COURTESY HERBERT HOOVER LIBRARY

A. L. Hager, Hoover, and Wilbur, at Stuart Lake.
COURTESY HERBERT HOOVER LIBRARY

and the Chief now took to the air with greater frequency, forgoing driving his sixteen-cylinder Cadillac at high speeds on long trips.[788] For the remainder of July, however, he drove back and forth between Palo Alto and the Bohemian Grove, ensuring that he did not miss the best shows. His annual lakeside evangelistic talk focused on the importance of principles in the Republican party. During these summer sojourns in California, Hoover on occasion escaped his busy schedule to spend time with T. J. and his family at the ocean-side ranch. Less frequently he made the drive to Santa Monica to spend a few hours with his sister May; the relationship between him and his sister remained strained.

Responding to an invitation to join the "Four Horsemen" in Montana for a third time, Hoover on July 14 wrote to Thornton: "I have been fishing up in British Columbia, and I recommend now that you move your base of action. The enclosed pictures are somewhat indicative."[789] Hoover's recommendation was partially in jest, but fishing on the Madison and in Hebgen Lake had steadily declined, especially on the lower Madison. The State Fisheries Department made a major restocking effort in 1937 and 1938, predicting that the addition of one million Loch Leven fry promised great improvement. The fisheries superintendent assured Thornton that "there were untold numbers of young fish in the Madison, Duck Creek and the South Fork."[790] With an eye on the August primaries and the hope of good fishing, Hoover flew to West Yellowstone to spend two fun-filled weeks.[791]

The coming 1938 fall election, Hoover maintained, was as important to the nation's future as was the election of 1860. The Republicans looked forward to picking up seats in Congress as well as gaining control of a number of governorships. Hoover financially aided Thomas Dewey in New York and spoke up for other New England candidates, ending up in Woods Hole, Mass-achusetts, on October 13. On Naushon, an island in the Elizabeth chain, he spent three days as the guest of William Cameron Forbes, former governor-general of Haiti and the Philippines and Hoover's ambassador to Japan, fishing for black bass and striped bass in the island's ponds as well as pursuing bluefish in the bay.[792] While quietly fishing, Hoover mulled over last-minute political plans. Then it was back to California and a trip up the West Coast to Oregon, where he crammed in a few more days fishing, delivering a last hard-hitting speech in Spokane forty-eight hours before the election.

Hoover had been right to smell blood. For the first time since 1932, the Republican party shrank the huge Democratic majority, as gleeful Republicans picked up sixty-seven seats in the house and an additional seven in the Senate.[793] One of the few disap-pointments was the defeat of Dewey in his New York gubernato-rial race against the popular Herbert Lehman. For the Grand Old Party, 1938 was a banner year, and 1940 promised to be even big-ger. Hoover envisioned himself as the 1940 Republican nominee. He was genuinely excited about his possibilities, but it remained to be seen if he would get out in front and actively campaign for his nomination. If the past was any guide, he would remain behind the scenes and attempt to indirectly bring about his nom-ination by somehow igniting the delegates' inner light, a strategy that held little promise for success.

In Europe, the tragic events of Kristallnacht followed closely upon the heels of the U.S. election. On the night of November 11, the Nazis undertook a nationwide pogrom against the Jews, burn-ing synagogues, smashing Jewish store windows, looting Jewish shops, and beating Jews who defended their property or were found in the streets. Hoover spoke out forcefully against the Nazi persecution of the Jews on a national radio broadcast, but he clung to nonintervention and neutrality to prevent America from becoming embroiled in another European war.[794] American participation, Hoover argued, would end our prized liberties and would be the death of economic freedom.

The new year brought political opportunities for the former president, ones that were closely tied to the burgeoning crisis in Europe. In February, Hoover stepped back from the troubled world and spent three weeks deep-sea fishing in Florida. Arriving in the Sunshine State on the twenty-fourth as the guest of Jeremiah Milbank, the Hoovers boarded the *Saunterer* at the Gulf Oil docks in Stuart.[795] Located between West Palm Beach and Fort Pierce, Stuart boasted good fishing and was more secluded than marinas farther to the south. The *Saunterer* plied the inland waterways and worked Hobe Sound while the Hoovers and the Milbanks fished, soaked up sun, and relaxed. Then, midway through the vacation, the yacht sailed south to Palm Beach and into the Gulf Stream for three days of "outside" fishing. Later, a reporter from the Stuart *News* asked the Chief about his catch. Hoover commented that he had caught a battling seven-foot sailfish, adding that "it was just about seven feet long for all practical purposes."[796] The reporter, who had not done his homework, wanted to know whether it was his first sailfish. Hoover curtly responded, "Hardly, I have been fishing Florida waters off and on for almost sixteen years."[797] Lou interjected that she thought "the most exciting thing was the big shark we hooked. It was a monster, measuring more than 11 feet long."[798]

The vacation ended with more successful "inside" fishing in Hobe Sound and one near fatal mishap. Lou and Kitty Milbank rented bicycles and rode along the road that fronted the sound. The two women stopped for a minute, and Lou looked down to see a small reddish thing moving along the pavement. Kitty warned, "Don't pick that up; it looks like a little reptile of some kind." "Oh, no it's beautiful," said Lou. "I want to pick it up."[799] As Lou was about to reach down and grab it, a car sped by, and the creature slithered off into the grass. The car saved the day, for the beautiful red thing turned out to be a poisonous coral snake.[800] On March 6, after another good time with the Milbanks in the tropics, the Hoovers boarded the train for the long trip north. Lou did not like Stuart, agreeing with Elizabeth Hanna, who called the place a "little hole in a slough."[801]

After being back in New York City for only a few days, Bert and Lou left for California, where Hoover met with members of Republican Circles, an organization ostensibly created to strengthen the Republican party in the western states, but which was, in reality, a front organization for Hoover's campaign for the 1940 nomination. Traveling to Oregon for a political appearance, he arrived in time for the opening day of trout season. Hoover, once again staying at McKenzie Bridge as a guest of W. E. Travis, waded the river in "tin pants," and even though the river was extremely crowded, he managed to reel in five nice redsides.[802] On Sunday, he abstained from fishing, as always, but consented to shoot the swift, dangerous Martin Rapids in a McKenzie River drift boat rowed by either Milo Thompson or Fred Harris. Asked by reporters to describe his experience, he responded with two words: "most thrilling."[803] That evening, at a banquet in the Eugene Hotel, a sunburned Hoover spoke "off the record" to three hundred Republicans. The Eugene *Register-Guard* speculated that "somehow we have a hunch that that tight little, right little dinner meeting . . . may bring out more arguments over the relative merits of the red upright, the flying caddis or the yellow bucktail than can be started by discussing Roosevelt policies."[804]

That scenario might have prevailed, but while Hoover fished on Saturday, the world situation inched closer to war. Hitler violated the Munich agreement, and his legions seized what remained of the Czech state. After Hoover's speech, in which he again warned that U.S. participation in a new war would mean fascism in America, anxious questioners put aside fishing and wanted to know what Hitler's action meant. The former president's conclusion was that any resulting war would "be small if at all."[805] A few days later, in a thank-you note to Travis, he put politics ahead of fishing: "I would have imposed upon you longer had it not been for the accursed conscience that I have that I should keep on talking against the New Deal as long as anybody will listen to me."[806] Regardless of Hoover's concern for the New Deal, dark clouds continued to gather over Europe.

In May, Hoover was buoyed by his continued opportunities to secure the 1940 nomination. He lunched frequently with Thomas Dewey and simultaneously worried that Dewey was the likely nominee. He worked hard to heal his long rift with Alf Landon and the liberal wing of the party. Robert Taft, who had once

Hoover and Maine governor Lewis O. Burrows with a good catch,
May 1939. COURTESY HERBERT HOOVER LIBRARY

worked for Hoover and was new to the Senate in 1938, was also a
potential candidate. The more candidates, the Chief reasoned, the
greater the chances for an open convention.

At the end of the month, right after Memorial Day, Hoover
and Larry Richey were off to fish in Maine. "As Maine goes, so
goes the nation" was the conventional wisdom, and Hoover
hoped that at the coming convention, Maine would go for him.

He was the guest of Gov. Lewis O. Burrows in Portland, and though he gave no speeches, he did have breakfast with a group of leading Republicans before plunging into the woods. Lake Kennebago, surrounded by mountains of the same name, was a beautiful body of water. In the deep, cold, placid lake, both brook and brown trout grew large. After six hours on the lake, the first few in a persistent drizzle, Hoover returned to the dock with ten fish, one a four-and-a-half pound squaretailed brookie. He told reporters that "it had been a perfect afternoon. The only reason I stopped was that I had my legal limit."[807]

Hoover was also accompanied by Herbert Welch from Haines Landing, Maine, a world-champion fly fisherman, who judged Hoover a "swell fisherman."[808] Carroll Huey, the local guide, agreed with the assessment rendered by Welch. Richey, who remained an outstanding and competitive fisherman, caught only three trout, while Governor Burrows landed but two. Burrows complained that he could not let Hoover beat him in his own backyard. He returned to his cabin, retrieved a number of surefire flies, and headed back out on the lake until after dark.[809] He did well, but not well enough to surpass the Chief. That night, Hoover slept soundly in a lakefront log cabin, serenaded by the cacophonous croaking of frogs and the occasional hooting of an owl.[810] He awoke in the morning to the cry of the loon, ate a hearty breakfast, and proceeded to catch his limit. On Wednesday, necessity forced Hoover and Richey to board the train in Portland bound for New York City.

Throughout the summer, Hoover stayed in the West to expand Republican Circles, though he did find time to spend a number of days at Bohemian Grove. The first part of August was dedicated to fishing and political meetings in Colorado and Wyoming. An old friend and supporter, Frank L. Fetzer, a Denver lawyer, arranged for Hoover to fish the Gunnison River while on a loop through the western part of the state. The fishing party also included Nelson Markham, a noted fisherman and guide; several prominent area Republicans; and Ben Allen, a longtime associate serving as Hoover's press secretary. Colorado Gov. Ralph Carr started out with the group but was called back to Denver to deal with a violent miners' strike, which turned so ugly he was forced to call out a contingent of the National Guard.[811]

A real beauty caught by Hoover on Kennebago Lake, Maine, May 29, 1939. COURTESY QUEENS BOROUGH PUBLIC LIBRARY, LONG ISLAND DIVISION, NEW YORK HERALD-TRIBUNE COLLECTION

When the party arrived at Hendersonville late in the afternoon, the fishermen piled into canoes for a three-mile run down Black Canyon to Sportsman's Lodge, a well-appointed six-hundred-acre private resort that served as a base camp. As the canoes navigated the swift river, the setting sun lit up the finger-like clouds on the western horizon in fiery oranges and reds while casting purple shadows on the canyon walls. Hoover commented that he had only once before in his life seen a comparable sunset. At the landing in front of the lodge, he waxed eloquently on the fishing, the mountain scenery, the canyon, and the marvelous river.[812] Momentarily desiring anonymity, he confided to Fetzer that he wished that he and Mrs. Hoover might unexpectedly drive through the gate and spend time enjoying the surroundings and together do some fishing.[813] In the descending darkness, canoes were dragged screeching and banging across the gravel. The equipment unloaded, the men gathered together

Hoover refuses to hold up a fish he has not caught, Gunnison, Colorado, August 1939. COURTESY HERBERT HOOVER LIBRARY

the day's catch. The Chief had caught four rainbows, including one over fourteen inches in length. Fetzer had landed six rainbows, all over twelve inches, and the others had bagged three or four fish each. Together, they had a fine mess of trout. All might have caught a few more had it not been for a heavy release of water from Taylor Reservoir.[814]

That evening in the lodge, the hungry diners gathered on the porch for cocktails. Fetzer took the opportunity to present

Hoover with "Colorado Guest Fishing License Number One." He remarked that in scripture, Jesus had asked Peter and his brother James who they were, and both had replied that they were fishers. Jesus then said, "Come with me and I will make you fishers of men."[815] While all gathered were fishers, said Fetzer, the Chief had for much of his life also been a fisher of men. The solemnity of the moment was broken as Hoover read aloud the information typed on the license: "Weight 180, to which the Chief commented 'Umph, that is 190 plus'; Height, 5 feet, 8½ inches, with another 'Umph, that is two to three inches shy'; Color of eyes, blue, and another 'Umph.'"[816] Fetzer teasingly suggested that perhaps the license belonged to someone else. For dinner, the lodge served up steaks and salads, along with a fine imported French Chablis. "The conversation," said Fetzer, the Denver lawyer, "was scintillating and we all enjoyed an intimate visit with the Chief quite apart from the rest of the world. He is never at a loss for an interesting story or an anecdote, or a philosophic observation on circumstances and events around him."[817]

Early the next morning, Hoover waded into the chilly water of the Gunnison, cast his favorite fly to midstream, and turned to witness Markham baiting his hook with a minnow. Their eyes met, and though Hoover said nothing, it was obvious to Markham that he was a "dyed-in-the-wool" fly fisherman.[818] The two men enjoyed each other's company, and both caught a number of large rainbows. The trout were packed in ice and taken along on the trip back to Denver to be eaten for breakfast. On the way, the men made a stop in Salida at the drugstore of the Republican county chairman. Hoover ordered a lemonade, sat down in a booth, and conversed with the locals as he slowly sipped his drink.[819] Asked how the fishing was, he reverted to his stock lines: "Good, but the big ones got away. Besides nobody believes a fisherman. If you tell them you caught ten, then the man next to you says he caught eleven."[820] Hoover surely wanted the 1940 nomination, for his willingness to press the flesh, to linger with the voters, was indeed unusual behavior for the crypto-candidate.

For the next two days, Hoover worked his way up through the major cities on the eastern slope of the Rockies, arriving in a rainy Cheyenne late Sunday evening. He talked with guests until one o'clock in the morning, slept for an hour and twenty minutes, and then awakened to catch the two-fifty Monday morning flight to California, a true red-eye express.[821] Surely, as the plane winged its way through the darkness above the vast expanse of the American West, Hoover realized that he was closer to vindication than ever before. The editor of the Calhan, Colorado, *News* savored the potential moment when he wrote, "Wouldn't it make the gods of chance laugh with glee if the man who was unhorsed and rolled in the dust of a bitter defeat by the peoples of a great nation should be the one chosen by those now dillusioned [*sic*] followers of chimerical panaceas to lead them back to sanity and self respect?"[822]

Back in the Golden State but a week, the ambitious Hoover flew to West Yellowstone, stopping to stump in Idaho Falls before pushing on to fish and to continue to campaign for his brand of "pure Republicanism," the updated gospel according to Palo Alto. The Chief spent the weekend at the Thornton camp, fishing for trout in the Madison River and grayling at Grebe Lake.[823] On Monday, he undertook a four-day jaunt in Wyoming, speaking to Republican gatherings. While in Jackson Hole, he had his first opportunity to fish the icy rushing mountain streams of the Grand Tetons. The Hoover fishing luck held, and he did well. On Friday, he returned to the Madison for most of the next ten days, making only one political excursion to Helena. As in the past, the time with the "Four Horsemen of the Madison" was filled with fun, relaxation, and lots of good fishing.

Hoover arrived home in Palo Alto in late August, just in time to witness the European crisis spill over into war. The former president spoke for millions of Americans when he stated that the first week of September was "one of the saddest weeks that has come to humanity in one hundred years."[824] Ironically for Hoover, a man of peace who hotly contested any U.S. intervention, the coming of war held out the possibility of his rescue from public and political oblivion. President Roosevelt's policy of limited emergency aid to Poland opened the door for Hoover to reenter the relief arena. A successful relief drive promised major press coverage, the kind of publicity that was sure to strengthen his chances of obtaining the presidential nomination he so ardently sought. Hitler's timing suited Hoover's ambitions.

In mid-September, President Roosevelt sent emissaries to Hoover to feel out the possibility of his entering the administra-

Hoover fishes the Gunnison River at Sportsman's Lodge near Cebolla, Colorado, August 1939. COURTESY HEBERT HOOVER LIBRARY

tion to head European Relief, but after several discussions, it was clear that the two old enemies had radically different ideas on the subject. The Chief thought he was in a strong position to negotiate because he assumed that the Republicans would win the 1940 presidential contest; any appointment under Roosevelt would be short-lived. In reality, Hoover had missed his one chance for meaningful participation in the coming war, though his chances of working successfully with the administration were always a long shot. Throughout the fall, he dedicated himself to aiding Poland, but in November, he squeezed in a trip to fish Lake Mead in Nevada. Mead was an artificial lake created by Boulder Dam, originally named for Hoover, who had been responsible for its creation. Secretary of the Interior Harold Ickes, with Roosevelt's approval, had renamed the engineering marvel Boulder Dam shortly after coming to office. Despite the irony, the Chief now fished the lake in a rowboat and hauled in a number of good-size trout and bass.

Hoover, far right, fishes Lake Mead, Nevada, November 1939.
COURTESY HERBERT HOOVER LIBRARY

This year, 1939, turned out to be one of Hoover's best for fishing, a high-water mark that capped a decade in which he fished as many as a dozen times a year from coast to coast and in the waters off Mexico as well as in the interior of Canada. Hoover proved himself an excellent fisherman, one of the country's finest, almost as good as two other fishermen he greatly admired—Zane Grey and Ernest Hemingway. He was sixty-five in 1939, and in the coming decade, his fishing would be slowed considerably as a result of his advancing age and activities associated with the war. But though he cut back, he pursued other kinds of fishing in which he could continue to excel. His need to do well at whatever he undertook propelled him in challenging new directions. His desire to fish, to seek relaxation and renewal in the outdoors, remained strong.

On November 30, the Soviet Union invaded little Finland, and Hoover went to the aid of the Finns as he previously had the Poles. The demands of running two large relief organizations kept Hoover from his yearly winter trip to Florida. In fact, the relief campaigns so consumed his efforts that he had no time for politics or fishing. The relief situation was further complicated when Hitler conquered Denmark and Norway in March and then went on to subdue Luxembourg, the Netherlands, Belgium, and France in May and June. One dizzying tragic event followed another. Poland might be conquered in five weeks, but to see France, a great empire, conquered in six was nearly beyond comprehension. The world appeared topsy-turvy, run over by events. The political situation at home also was further complicated when a relatively unknown former Democrat, Wendell Willkie, came streaking out of nowhere to become the leading candidate for the Republican nomination.

On June 1, just three weeks before the convention, and with the battle for France winding down, the Chief traveled to Connecticut for the second time to meet with his old friend and fellow Polish relief commissioner, former senator Fred Walcott. The two men drove to a fishing camp just across the Connecticut border near Sheffield, Massachusetts, which was owned by another longtime Hoover associate, George H. Quinion. Tucked in the Berkshires, Schenob Brook began in Twin Lakes. The frigid mountain waters ran north, eventually winding their way to the Housatonic River.[825] On the stretch of the brook near the headwaters, deep holes provided for great dry-fly fishing. The brook flowed through a swamp fed by dozens of bubbling small springs.[826] Once the brook was more established, it remained a challenge because of the amount of underbrush and low-hanging trees that lined the banks.[827] Hoover released several trout that day, and Quinion was impressed by the care the Chief took in handling them: "He had respect for all wild life, and fish especially. When he let a fish go, that fish could swim away and survive."[828] Quinion noted that when many other sportsmen released a fish, it floated downstream and was likely to die. By handling the fish with dry hands, some of the fish's protective covering was removed, and a week later the fish would develop a fungus. But not so with Hoover, who "always handled a fish with wet hands."[829] Fly fishermen who respected fish, fishermen like Hoover, said Quinion, used hooks without barbs so that they might "shake the fish off without even touching it." The Massachusetts trout responded well to Hoover's choice of barbless flies, thereby making for a nice catch.

At the last minute, Hoover wrangled an invitation to address the Republican National Convention in Philadelphia, but after

George H. Quinion, Hoover, and Fred C. Walcott.
COURTESY HERBERT HOOVER LIBRARY

two years of hard campaigning in which he had spoken before thousands of prominent Republican leaders, he arrived in Philadelphia on June 23 with no organization and no plans on how to proceed. Officially he was not a candidate, so those delegates who might have wanted to support him were prevented from doing so. He continued to cling to the will-o'–the-wisp illusion that a great speech would turn the convention toward him, a "Cross of Gold" speech like William Jennings Bryan had given at the 1896 Democratic convention. To the contrary, Hoover's opponent, Wendell Willkie, left nothing to chance—his partisans packed the convention galleries, hotels, and streets, demanding that their candidate be nominated. Thousands of telegrams of support poured in from Willkie Clubs across America. Hoover, as the hour of his vindication grew late, did little, knowing there was little he could do. His speech, which was barely audible because of problems with the sound system, did not receive a thunderous response. The Willkie tidal wave, without the support of much of the party's leadership, washed all before it. Hoover vehemently maintained that the sound system had been tampered with, but regardless of what went wrong, one fact clearly stood out: Hoover had lost his last chance for electoral vindication. He was severely disappointed, but perhaps he intuitively understood that though he was many party members' favorite Republican, and the leading spokesman for Republican principles, the party saw him as unelectable. He was anathema particularly to younger Republicans, who flocked to the Willkie Clubs.

Hoover and Walcott near Schenob Creek in the Berkshires in Connecticut, May 26, 1940. COURTESY HERBERT HOOVER LIBRARY

If Hoover understood that his popularity could not be translated into votes, he was loath to admit it. His dream, a political
battle in which he defeated Roosevelt and again became president, was not to be. The Chief would never again hear "Hail to
the Chief" played for him. On Friday afternoon, he left Philadelphia for New York, where he took up the new task of finding
ways to add Belgium to the list of countries receiving American
aid. The next day, he and his son Allan arrived at La Guardia
Field to board a flight to California. A bevy of reporters surrounded them and asked Hoover what he thought of the Willkie
nomination. The Chief, masking his letdown, snapped his fingers, saying, "I have no doubt that he will be elected just like
that."[830] Pressed for more details, he replied, "I'm going fishing;
I'm not going to talk politics now."[831]

Hoover began his recovery by spending several days at
the magnificent Ahwanee Hotel in Yosemite National Park.[832]
Yosemite had been a favorite place of the Hoovers since their college days at Stanford. The Ahwanee, whose Indian name meant
"deep grass valley," was completed in 1927. It was one of the
grand hotels of the West, built to blend in with the environment
at a cost of more than $1 million. The rock edifice was impressive
from the outside, and inside it was a marvel of contemporary
design, with one hundred guest rooms with baths. The huge,
twenty-five-foot-high ceilings of the great lounge and dining hall
were set off with exposed beams stenciled in Southwest Indian
motifs.[833] The eclectic interior successfully wove together American Indian designs with those from other parts of the globe.
Navajo rugs, Near Eastern rugs, colored and decorated tiles,
stained-glass panels at the tops of windows, pottery, oriental
porcelain lamps, woven baskets, and English country furniture
came together to produce a warm yet monumental effect.[834] At
the Ahwanee, Lou rode the numerous horse trails and took walks
identifying plant life while her husband fished. After several
days in the High Sierras, the couple returned to Palo Alto.
Hoover left almost immediately for his favorite rivers to the
north.

On the McKenzie River at the Holiday Farm fishing camp,
the failed presidential candidate mulled over the future while fly
fishing, and then went off to more fully recover among friends in
the cloistered, receptive atmosphere of the Bohemian Grove.

From the Grove, Hoover traveled to the Madison for two more weeks of fishing pleasure in and around Yellowstone Park. In early August, Willkie had invited Hoover to accompany him on a fishing trip, but the two men's conflicting schedules precluded the arrangement.[835] Willkie, vacationing at the fabulous Broadmoor Hotel in Colorado Springs, another watering hole for the rich and famous, asked Hoover to come over from West Yellowstone to confer. It was a clumsy meeting, made more difficult when the candidate invited the president's son, Elliott Roosevelt, to join them for dinner and for press photographs on the hotel lawn. Hoover, however, agreed to deliver several national speeches for Willkie and confided to Edgar Rickard that "he was satisfied with his party's candidate, a man of immense charm and equal candor."[836] As promised, in late October, Hoover gave three campaign speeches, encouraging Willkie to mount a head-on attack against Roosevelt. He privately despaired at the lack of organization that surrounded the candidate and permeated his campaign, a ragtag affair that reflected Willkie's "grab bag mind."[837] Throughout the fall, the Chief quietly lobbied for recognition of one of his new relief agencies, the National Committee on Food for the Small Democracies (NCFSD), an effort to provide aid to Poland, Finland, Luxembourg, Norway, and Belgium.

The November election again brought defeat to the Republican party. The Willkie bubble burst when Roosevelt beat the maverick Hoosier by five million votes. Roosevelt, like Joe Louis, was the undisputed champ, now a three-time winner. For Hoover, his party's defeat meant that the wilderness years were not at an end. To accommodate himself to the new political landscape, he considered selling the fashionable Washington, D.C., home on S Street that he and Lou had owned for so long. A ten-room suite, 31-A at the Waldorf-Astoria, was now home, a comfortable if self-imposed exile from the nation's capital. Lou, who had moved many times before, found a way to conduct their elaborate lifestyle in their new cramped quarters, of which several rooms were used for Hoover's secretaries and for office space. In December, the Hoovers left cold, snowy New York to spend Christmas and New Year's with the Milbanks in Florida, where they cruised and fished on the *Saunterer*. On this trip and their previous one to Florida, the Chief did far less deep-sea fishing. Hooking a large battling sailfish, a big marlin, or a huge shark that fought for half an hour or more was exhausting. The price of success was a sore back, leg cramps, or arms that ached. Instead, he spent more time on the inland waterways in pursuit of smaller species, including the elusive fighting bonefish.

Suntanned and refreshed, Hoover headed north to make a big push to overturn the British blockade and feed the hungry in occupied Europe. That same month, he also decided upon another major change in his life, reluctantly severing his twenty-year relationship with Larry Richey. Hoover explained to Wilbur, "I have had to part with Larry as his neuritis has become so bad that he is not of use—he cannot stand this climate."[838] Richey was stunned by his boss's decision, but he received a three-and-a-half-year severance package that partially assuaged his hurt feelings.[839] He was now, however, a hen with no chick. To his credit, he recovered, and he and Hoover remained friends and continued to fish together occasionally. New to Hoover's staff was Bunny Miller, a diminutive woman who had been seriously injured in a horseback-riding accident as a girl. A Stanford graduate, she had assisted Lou for a number of years but now was assigned to aid Hoover in writing his memoirs, a three-volume project he haphazardly undertook.[840]

Spring found Hoover working hard to prevent American intervention into the war, all the while fighting a rear-guard battle against Roosevelt's Lend-Lease proposal. He lost on both issues but spent May 23 and 24 fishing with Walcott and friends in the mountains of western Massachusetts. That same summer, the Hoovers lived in California. As part of Stanford's fifty-year anniversary celebration, the Hoover Library Tower opened in June. This building housed an amazing collection of primary documents from around the world.[841] After a weeklong commemoration seminar, Hoover decided a long vacation was in order. Fishing trips to the McKenzie in Oregon and the Madison River in Montana, as well as time at the Bohemian Grove, took up much of the summer. In between, Hoover continued to work for food aid to the five hungry democracies.

After leaving West Yellowstone and just before returning to New York, he and Lou managed a fishing trip together in New Mexico. Bert, as Lou still called Hoover, flew to Salt Lake City to meet her. She arrived on the Union Pacific Overland from Palo

Alto. Then, as they had done so often in the past, the contented couple set off in their big car for New Mexico via Colorado. Lunch was a picnic on the side of a flower-filled mountain meadow. That night, they stayed at the Hotel Belvedere in Montrose, Colorado, and the next day took dusty, rutted backroads to explore old mining towns such as Ouray, Silverton, and Durango.[842] The second night out, they stayed in Trinidad, Colorado, a city hosting a Red Men's Lodge convention. Peace and quiet was shattered by the noisy comings and goings of dozens of families, the sound of brass bands, and incessant parades. The tired couple persevered and the next day pushed on to Vermejo Ranch, a secluded 1890s-style complex owned by William B. and Winifred Coberly, their in-laws and friends, and tucked forty miles off the main road into the mountains. At Tercio, the Hoovers were met by a truck that guided them twelve miles deeper into the mountains over a series of treacherous roads. The Coberlys gave Bert and Lou the grand tour of the spread, and the rest of the day was spent getting everything ready for the next day's ascent. The upper ranch, at ten thousand feet, was nearly atop the mountain. That evening at dinner, Lou, now joined by Allan Hoover and his wife, Coby, marveled at the authentic New Mexican cuisine: the best real Spanish food, she called it, a dinner of "flat enchillades [*sic*], tamales, chili con carne, frijoles and perfectly wonderful tortillas. Everything was cooked exactly as it should be. And as I did not realize could be found anywhere any more!"[843]

Mr. Coberly had modified a truck into a camper he christened the Oxcart. The seats in the interior of the Oxcart could be folded down to make a bed that slept three. Lou commented that it resembled a covered wagon. A table pulled out from the rear of the contraption to reveal a pantry that contained a wide variety of canned food and a panoply of camping paraphernalia—a kind of super survivor bus. Early in the morning, after a hearty breakfast, all clambered aboard the vehicle for the bumpy trip up the mountain. The upper ranch was a log cabin with ten rooms, each of which opened onto one long, covered porch. After lunch, Lou reported, "The ox-cart scattered us all over some miles along a creek . . . and we all fished." The lone anglers were in sight of each other as the stream ran through an open valley near the timberline. The distant view of snow-capped mountains was impressive, but the trout were small because of the altitude. The next day, the fishing party followed the creek down to a long, narrow lake in which the trout were much bigger. That afternoon, it began to rain, and when it continued, the party decided to head for the cabin. The narrow, muddy road ran through a treacherous pass with a drop-off of several hundred feet on one side. To avoid the possibility that the Oxcart might slide over the cliff and tumble into the lake, the passengers wisely got out and walked. The driver calculated a quick exit. Several hours later, a muddy, wet, cold, and hungry crew welcomed the roaring fire and hot meal that awaited their return to the cabin.[844]

The next morning, the party split up and spent most of the day fishing. Lou and Mrs. Coberly fished in small ponds created by beaver dams and did quite well, catching eight- to ten-inch trout. On the last day in this splendid isolation—no newspapers, mail, telegrams, telephones, or radios—the two women rode horseback to the top of the mountain and picked wildflowers. Lou remarked, "I have never seen lovelier ones, and there were simply carpets of them everywhere." But when the Oxcart returned them to the lower ranch late that afternoon, the outside world awaited the Hoovers. Bert caught the Santa Fe Silver Chief in Trinidad, while Lou, Allan, and Coby took in the sights on their long return drive to Palo Alto.[845]

Hoover had spoken out, warning for some time that Roosevelt's policy toward Japan amounted to "sticking pins in rattlesnakes."[846] On December 7, 1941, the rattlesnake struck. The war Hoover had opposed for so long was upon the America people. In a press statement the next day, he frankly stated that he had opposed the president's policies, but "American soil has been treacherously attacked by Japan. Our decision is clear. It is forced upon us. We must fight with everything we have. We will have victory."[847] In January of the New Year, victory seemed a long way off, as the defeat at Pearl Harbor was compounded by a series of stunning Japanese military successes. Bernard Baruch, who had worked with Hoover in the Wilson administration, suggested to Roosevelt that he call in Hoover and put him in charge of war mobilization. Baruch had discussed the idea with Hoover before his meeting with Roosevelt, and Hoover expressed interest. Roosevelt caustically responded to Baruch's suggestion,

"Well, I'm not Jesus Christ" and "I'm not going to raise him from the dead."[848] Despite the pleas of those inside and outside the administration, Hoover continued to be shut out. Roosevelt, however, did allow the War Department to brief the former president on a regular basis.

Busy with his food aid projects, Republican plans for the 1942 election, and his writing, Hoover did not travel to Florida to fish. In a series of conversations with Hugh Gibson, a diplomat who had worked with Hoover in World War I and remained within the Hoover circle, the two men began to speculate on how to secure a lasting peace. For Hoover, the best place to think was on a trout stream, and the best place to write was in a lodge or hotel, or on the deck of a boat. The Chief's favorite cabin at Holiday Farm was a perfect spot for such an undertaking. From April 18 to 25, Hoover and Gibson fished the McKenzie River and laid out their ideas on a fair, just peace plan. It was a plan, unlike Versailles, that engaged the countries of the world constructively. The two writers maintained the belief that the Allied cause would prevail, even though the first five months of 1942 registered a series of stinging defeats. Working together steadily, the two friends, whose writing styles were radically different, managed to hammer out a draft.[849] Before *The Problems of the Lasting Peace* was released in hardback and selected by the Book-of-Month Club, essential portions were serialized in *Reader's Digest*.[850] Hoover and Gibson hoped to reach as many people as possible with their ideas. The work done, Hoover made three short fishing trips in May.

On May 13, Hoover met former senator Joseph S. Frelinghuysen for a day of fishing and an overnight stay on a trout stream in western New Jersey. Midmorning on May 18, George Warren picked up Hoover at the Waldorf, and the two men were off for a successful day of fishing on the Pequest. The following week, Gibson, Rickard, and Hoover joined Walcott on May 23 and 24 for three days of fishing on Schenob Brook and Twin Lakes. The Berkshire Mountains were at the height of spring, and the brookies were eager to take the fly. Hoover wrote to Walcott two days later: "That was indeed a fine outing, and one that brought me back to the city refreshed and filled with joy—about fishing! I do want you to know of my gratitude for a few hours' respite in these difficult days."[851] Renewed by his brief plunge into nature,

Hoover battled with those who opposed his views of the postwar world. Opposition came from Roosevelt and from Henry Wallace, the ultraliberal secretary of agriculture. Within the Republican party, Wendell Willkie, author of *One World,* led an international-ist crusade against what he described as the isolationists in the party.[852] Hoover withdrew from his latest battle to spend time at the Bohemian Grove. In the past, he had been forced to miss a summer or two at "the greatest men's party in the world," but starting in 1942, he would attend every Grove encampment, at least for a few days, until his last appearance in 1962. The glory years at Cave Man Camp still lay in the future.

Nearly every August, Hoover set aside as much time as possi-ble to fish, usually a driving trip to Wyoming that included stops in local streams in which he had not before cast a fly. As usual, he mixed business with pleasure. The Chief and his son Allan left Palo Alto on the fifth and drove to Klamath Falls, Oregon, for sev-eral days of fishing. Then it was on to Weiser, Idaho, to inspect mining property jointly owned with Lawrence Requa.[853] Weiser, named after Sgt. Peter Weiser of the legendary Lewis and Clark expedition, was a town that hugged the bank of the Snake River and an excellent place to fish. Just outside Weiser, the Snake River rushed north through Hells Canyon, the deepest gorge in North America.[854] Hoover had fished the Snake before and had visited Weiser on several occasions, but he seemed uninterested in the huge white sturgeon that inhabited the river. The largest fresh-water fish in America, the Snake giants occasionally grew to more than twelve feet in length and over one thousand pounds. Twenty-pound chinook salmon, steelhead, and rainbows from twelve to sixteen inches in length also challenged the fly fisher-man.[855] Though Hoover was in Weiser on business, and on his numerous visits was in town only for a few days, it is hard to believe that he passed up this marvelous opportunity to fish. The town's hotel, where Hoover sometimes stayed, was a short walk-ing distance from the riverbank, yet there is no record that he fished.

For a number of years, the Requas lived in a small log cabin near the mine, with no indoor plumbing and no kitchen. The couple ate their meals in the miners' boardinghouse.[856] The Hoovers stayed there, too, and enjoyed the primitive facilities as well as the mining-camp atmosphere. Their business concluded,

Hoover and his son left Weiser and made the long drive across Montana, stopping to fish, picnic, or take in a view whenever the mood struck them. A few days later, they arrived at their destination, Thornton's camp on the Madison River. This was not the final stop on this outing, for Albert C. Mattei, a San Francisco friend, joined Hoover and Allan for several more days of fishing in the Grand Tetons near Jackson Hole. Hoover once commented on these spectacular mountains, which seemed to leap straight up from the prairie floor, "If I wanted to escape the world, and one has tendencies that way these days—I would build a cabin where I could look at the Tetons and in a dead spot from radio reception."[857]

From September 1942 until May 1943, Hoover did not fish. It was the longest time he spent away from rod and reel since he had left the presidency. His efforts to push the ideas expressed in *The Lasting Peace,* to persuade the Republican party to hold a conference on postwar policy, and to force Washington and Downing Street to allow food aid to pass through the blockade into occupied Europe consumed his time and energy. Hoover, like some latter-day Joshua, blew his trumpet before the walls that surrounded Roosevelt's Washington, but they did not come tumbling down. Undeterred by the strength of the ramparts, Hoover puckered up and continued to blow warnings of dire consequences unless policy changes were soon undertaken. He was encouraged in his opposition by Republican success in the November off-year elections. The party scored its biggest gains—forty-four seats in the House and nine in the Senate—since Hoover's sweep into office in 1928. Roosevelt controlled the House by a mere 7 seats, 216 to 209, escaping by only a few seats the restraints placed on Woodrow Wilson in 1918.[858]

In May, Hoover managed to escape to Massachusetts to again fish Schenob Brook with Walcott, Richey, and C. K. Davis, CEO of the Remington Arms Corporation. Shortly thereafter, he and Lou left for California to spend the summer. On the way, the Hoovers spent several days with George Snyder at his fishing camp in the mountains outside Salt Lake City, and then went on to visit Jeremiah and Kitty Milbank, co-owners of mining properties in Pioche, Nevada, in the Wilson Creek Range. In the local grocery store, Kitty Milbank hit several jackpots while playing the iron bandits. Pioche, a boomtown after the Civil War, was as wild a mining town as any—saloons, dance halls, whorehouses, gun-fights, and mayhem predominated. Around 1875, gunmen were imported at the rate of twenty per day, and not one of the first seventy-five people buried in Boot Row died of natural causes.[859] Hoover sometimes ate in the local café, where silver-dollar cakes were a favorite. Perhaps he recalled his own days in the Sodom and Gomorrah-like mining towns of western Nevada.

After much soul searching, the Hoovers decided to give their San Juan Hill mansion to Stanford to serve as the home of the university's president.[860] Lou had lovingly designed and built the large southwestern-style house, so for her to part with it was obviously a difficult decision. Hoover, however, was eager to return to the action of the East Coast. California, especially Palo Alto, was in his view too far from the centers of power. A good part of the summer was taken up with sorting out a huge accu-mulation of treasures, storing belongings, and moving to a rental house on campus. Fishing may have taken a backseat in 1943, but Hoover did not miss the Bohemian Grove encampment. While Hoover was secluded at Cave Man Camp, Lou took the opportu-nity to hike the hills behind her Stanford home and to explore the redwood forests and coast of the state she loved so much. In mid-August, the Hoovers left for New York City, where the Chief plunged back into a wide array of political battles, determined to finish off any chances that Willkie might have for the 1944 Repub-lican presidential nomination. For the first time since 1920, he did not think of himself as a potential nominee.

On a Friday afternoon, January 7, 1944, Lou left 31-A with Bunny Miller to attend a concert that featured one of Lou's old friends, the harpist Mildred Dilling. Afterward, Lou suggested that they walk back to the Waldorf, as the late afternoon air felt refreshing. They had walked only a few blocks when Lou decided a cab was in order. Bunny hailed a taxi, and the two women rode back to the Waldorf. When the elevator reached the thirty-first floor, Lou did not invite Bunny to have dinner with her. She simply said good night and entered the apartment. On her way to her bedroom, she was greeted by her husband and Edgar Rickard, who were leaving for a dinner engagement. Hoover gathered up his things, then walked to Lou's bedroom to say good night. There he found her passed out on the floor, barely alive. Hoover and Rickard gently lifted her onto the bed, and Rickard hurried to the phone to summon a doctor. Before the doctor arrived, Hoover walked into the living room, looked at his old friend, and said, "She's gone."[861] Lou Henry Hoover, a few months shy of her seventieth birthday, had succumbed to a massive stroke. Three days later, on January 10, fifteen hundred mourners jammed St. Bartholomew's Episcopal Church to attend her funeral services.[862] After the services, Lou's coffin was loaded onto a train for the long trip back to California. As the train rumbled along, hour after numbing hour, Hoover may have recalled previous cross-country trips that had been exceedingly difficult: his seven-day trip to Oregon as a young orphan boy; the return of President Harding's body to Washington, D.C., in the summer of 1923; and his and Lou's trip to Washington after his stinging defeat in the 1932 election.

Lou had lived an uncommon life—one of adventure in many parts of the world. She was an accomplished scholar, geologist, mother, wife, first lady, and outdoors woman, a progressive woman of the American West. She drove fast, rode hard, could shoot straight, and was able to handle a large fighting sailfish. After forty-four years of marriage, Bert had lost the love of his life, his confidant, and his best friend. Throughout their ecstasy and agony, she had sustained him. Her untimely death was a heavy blow for a private man who opened himself to almost no one. Typically, he demonstrated the fortitude he had learned after the death of his parents by saying little and moving on with his life, regardless of the pain.

Two weeks later, a disconsolate Hoover was back in New York, where he and Rickard undertook a final wrap-up of Lou's affairs. The vacation fund, "Seeing Cairo," which had sent the Rickards and Hoovers on a grand tour of Europe just before the outbreak of World War I, was closed, and the money donated to the Hoover Institution Library. That same week, an invitation arrived at 31-A from a couple Hoover had befriended who had suffered great adversity and had spent much time at the Waldorf Astoria—the duke and duchess of Windsor. The duke, serving as the governor of the Bahamas, invited the deflated Hoover to join him and the duchess for several days of relaxation. Hoover accepted the invitation and combined his trip to Nassau with an excursion in Florida with family. Rarely sick, he spent his time in Florida recovering from a nasty case of the flu rather than fishing.[863] Two weeks in the sun, relaxing in royal company revived his fighting spirit, and he returned to the Empire State ready to pick up the cudgel for the array of causes in which he believed.[864] Although Lou's death was a loss from which he would never fully recover, hard work had always been Hoover's solution to life's difficulties The historian Richard Norton Smith wrote that Hoover "stayed young by working, as well as by nurturing the animosities of a lifetime."[865]

Several days before Hoover left Florida, the evening of February 12, 1944, the Tates, friends of the Roosevelts, arrived at the White House for dinner. It was a small dinner party, and the president was in an ebullient mood. The conversation flowed from topic to topic: oil resources in the future, the Berlin to Baghdad railway, and the origin of the shad. In the midst of speculation over the shad, Roosevelt queried whether any of his guests knew how, as he put it, "my distinguished predecessor Mr. Hoover" fished. The guests were delighted, as they knew that the president loved to do imitations of friends and enemies alike, mimicking the voices and gestures of his targets. As background to his story, Roosevelt recalled that Hoover had built a camp at Rapidan, Virginia. On weekends, Hoover drove to the camp, Roosevelt maintained, "at 80 miles an hour, pushing all the people off the road as he went."[866] Eleanor Roosevelt, giving her husband the green light, interjected, "Now, Frank, that is a mean story." "I know it," said Roosevelt, who appeared to delight in telling it.[867] The camp, he pointed out, was built on a stream in a valley, and the Bureau of Fisheries stocked the stream. Roosevelt, now grinning mischievously, stressed that a truck from the bureau arrived just ahead of Hoover and released a dozen trout into the stream, "pet trout: all of them had pet names."[868] "There was a bridge across the stream and the trout were dumped under the bridge," he said. "Just above and just below the bridge nets were placed so that they could not get out; then an arm chair was brought out and President Hoover would come and sit in the arm chair while someone handed him a rod and fixed a fly on the hook which he would then cast and pull in the trout one by one." The president's story, punctuated with hand motions and pantomime, was "quite malicious and very funny."[869]

Now onto his Republican predecessors with a vengeance, Roosevelt tapped his repertoire of hilarious Calvin Coolidge stories. Hoover now and then enjoyed a good Roosevelt story, but he would have been furious at the president's antics had he known what had occurred, although both men's hostility toward one another was unbridled.

Throughout the spring of 1944, Hoover involved himself in a plethora of politics in preparation for the upcoming Republican convention. Nevertheless, he found time for a number of fishing trips. The Chief now made up for the fishing time he had sacrificed in the last few years. The trout season was open but a week in New Jersey when George Warren swung by the Waldorf at eight o'clock in the morning on April 22, picked up Hoover and Gibson, and returned to fish the waters of the Pequest.[870] It was a rainy two-day affair, and the fishing was poor. Warren invited Hoover to come back soon. "I am not going to feel satisfied," he wrote, "until we can have one of those fine days that make trout fishing on the Pequest a real pleasure; I have had many of them and want you and Mr. Gibson to know what it is like."[871] Hoover replied that they would try their luck again soon.

May 6 to 8 found Hoover visiting his friends the Milbanks at their opulent home in Port Chester, New York. The city sits astride a long, narrow bay that opens into Long Island Sound. It was a good place to pursue bluefin tuna, Spanish mackerel, and bonito. A week later, Hoover, Gibson, and Walcott joined a number of other men who met in Bridgeport, Connecticut, and then drove to the inviting streams and lakes of the southern Berkshires, where they spent their weekend working their way north to Schenob Brook. One of the fishermen was Fred Erlich, a New England champion fly-fishing expert. The fishing was so good that Hoover and Walcott put together another trip the first week in June.[872]

The Chief was relaxed and ready for the Republican convention. In his speech to the delegates, he stressed postwar problems and the future of the party. Thomas Dewey, an austere-looking provincial New Yorker who wore blue serge pinstripe suits, managed to overcome the feuding Republican factions, especially on foreign policy, and won the nomination. Hoover, not an ardent Dewey backer, once more picked the wrong candidate and was shunted aside. As the Democrats again chose to run against "Hoover and the Depression," Dewey distanced himself as far as possible from the icon of economic ruin. Hoover left Chicago, openly accepting of his party's choice, and traveled west to Palo

Alto and the Bohemian Grove, a place were he could confidently express his considerable reservations.

August was always a fishing month, and Hoover availed himself of two opportunities: time in the mountains outside Salt Lake on his way to check on his mining operation in Pioche, and a two-week family outing to Cresent Lake, Oregon. A. C. Mattei and his wife joined Hoover, Allan, and Coby at the lake resort. The fishing was great, and the alpine lake was beautiful in the shadow of Saddle Horn Mountain. Having no real part in the 1944 election, Hoover found time in September to fish Silver Lake, California, as the guest of Nate F. Milnor, president of the California Fish and Game Commission. The lake, on the Silver Fork of the American River southwest of the bigger and more famous Lake Tahoe, was at an elevation of seventy-two hundred feet and only about a month away from winter. The High Sierra lake was abundant in trout, and the fishing was good. At night, the temperature dropped to a point that required a roaring fire, a Hoover favorite.

Back in New York, Hoover's fishing expeditions were over for the year. He decided it was time to make some additional changes in his life. He completed the transfer of his interest in Wooley Camp to his son Allan; he had not been there for a number of years and at age seventy was no longer up to the seven-mile horseback ride in to the camp. Wading cold, rushing trout streams also was no longer possible, as he feared he would lose his balance and be swept away. In *Fishing for Fun and to Wash Your Soul*, he elaborated on the difficulties associated with wading streams:

> If you are fishing mid-stream, you must have those special waterproof pants which reach from inside hobnailed shoes to your armpits. You must carry an iron-pointed staff to prevent your being washed downstream. When that happens, the waterproof pants fill with water and you sink. If you have the good sense to hold onto the iron-pointed staff, you possibly save your life. But you will need to buy a new rod and reel.[873]

In a stream for any length of time, Hoover's legs turned blue with cold and his knees stiffened. Recovery mandated vigorous rubbing, as his circulation did not return as rapidly as it once had. In 1945, Walcott wrote to Hoover about a fishing trip to Norfolk with Vannevar Bush. "We waded around in ice-cold water up to our knees, but when we did get to the bank of the stream, we managed to catch a few good-sized trout. It was hardly worth the risk of stiff knees," he complained.[874] From now on, Hoover fished from the bank of the river or lake or from a boat. Advancing age had brought an end to another one of his favorite ways to fish.

For the next few years, Hoover's fishing routine included occasional new opportunities, as well as spring trips to the Pequest and Schenob, mountain trout fishing on the way to inspection tours at Pioche, a summer trip to Holiday Farm on the McKenzie, and bonefishing for long stretches in Florida. Summers, of course, also included time at the Bohemian Grove.

9

It's the Old Horse
for the Long Race

The opening months of 1945 were tumultuous. The U.S. Army was slugging it out with the Germans in the snow-covered, frozen Ardennes forest; the Marine Corps was locked in hand-to-hand combat with the fanatical Japanese on Iwo Jima underneath the cone of Mount Suribachi; and the Big Three—Roosevelt, Churchill, and Stalin—were reshaping the world at Yalta on the Crimean Peninsula in the summer home of the former tsar. Victory was just a matter of time, although difficult battles still lay ahead. Hoover used what leverage he had to try to shape feeding and occupation policies planned for both Germany and Japan. On April 12, to Hoover's surprise and dismay, Franklin Roosevelt died in his sleep of a massive cerebral hemorrhage.[875] Hoover's great nemesis, eight years his junior, was dead. In spite of his hostility toward the late president's policies, Hoover recognized Roosevelt's political genius. If Roosevelt had been focused on Hoover and the Great Depression and used the economic tragedy to win the presidency four times, Hoover continued to focus his animus on Roosevelt and the New Deal. The two presidents were inexorably intertwined. The story of one was in many ways the story of the other. With Roosevelt's death, the world of Washington just might open to Hoover once more. The idea of his vindication was resurrected by this new possibility.

A week after Roosevelt's impressive funeral, the Chief was in New Jersey fishing the Pequest River with his friend George Warren. This time, both the weather and the trout were more accommodating.[876] On May 9, Hoover went fishing with Kingsland W. Macy, Suffolk County Republican leader. He had received this fellow fisherman's enticing invitation in mid-April, when Macy wrote: "Talking with a mutual friend the other day I was pleased to learn that you had lost none of your interest in trout fishing. I took twenty speckles the other day at 18 pounds 7 ounces. If you would be available some day in May and cared to do so, it would be a great pleasure to have you join me for a day's sport." Hoover responded that the "last paragraph of your letter especially impresses me, and when I get some obligations off my shoulders, I will be ready." Macy wrote again to set the date, telling Hoover that on a weekday, they would have nearly four thousand acres to themselves. The Chief was interested and quickly learned that Macy wished to escort him to the South Side Sportsmen's Club of Long Island in Oakdale, New York.

The well-heeled private club was a protected environmental jewel within thirty miles of the Manhattan skyline, only an hour-and-a-half drive from the Waldorf in traffic. The Connetquot River and bay shoreline had been a popular fishing spot for a very long time, well back into the seventeenth century. A mill was built on the river in 1701, and in 1820 a man named Snedecors constructed a stagecoach inn on the Old South Country Road.[877] The inn quickly became popular with fishermen, who stayed overnight, sometimes hung around for weeks, and took the stagecoach back and forth to the city. In 1866, at the end of the Civil War, an "assembly of good fellows," wealthy New Yorkers who had a difficult time finding rooms in the inn, pooled their money and bought a thirty-eight hundred-acre wooded tract along the Connetquot River. The inn became the clubhouse, and by the turn of the century, it had a distinguished membership that included swells such as Teddy Roosevelt, J. P. Morgan, and the Vanderbilts.[878]

The "mighty Connetquot," only eight miles long, fifteen feet wide, and three feet deep, flows from its headwater springs into three large ponds and then on into the Great South Bay. Its size is misleading, however, for it is a fine trout-fishing river. Native brookies, recognized regionally for their particular beauty, ranged from five to five and a half pounds, and local scuttlebutt claimed a river record of six and a half pounds. If so, this was the largest brook trout ever caught in New York State. In the 1880s, the South Siders built a hatchery and introduced German brown and rainbow trout to the river. The record brown weighed a whopping sixteen point one pounds, but locals swore they had glimpsed a fish as large as thirty pounds. Over the years, the browns and brookies hybridized, producing tiger trout. The tigers looked more like their brook trout parents but were bigger like their brown trout ancestors. They averaged ten pounds and were scrappy fighters.[879] Trout that swam the seas came back as steelhead.

Macy, who went by the nickname "King," provided the tackle and picked up Hoover at the Waldorf at ten in the morning for the day's excursion. The Chief had a great time and thoroughly enjoyed the cloistered confines of the elite South Side Club. King was impressed by Hoover's ability to successfully cast regardless of the impediments nature placed in his path—overhanging trees, brush, and partially submerged stumps. The two fishermen did not record the number of fish caught, but in his thank-you note to King, Hoover graciously remarked that the club was "the grand-est fishing place I know."[880]

Rumors repeatedly reached Hoover throughout the spring that his name kept coming up in White House discussions on what to do about the growing food crisis in Europe. Famine hov-ered over the European wreckers' yard, a charnel house of deep-ening despair. Hoover lunched with Henry Stimson, secretary of war, and Stimson talked to the new president, Democrat Harry Truman. Finally, Truman sent a formal invitation for Hoover to come to the White House on May 28. The president sought Hoover's opinion on food relief for Europe, the domestic food situation, and his ideas on how the war with Japan might be brought to an end. In his conversation with Truman, Hoover was not shy, nor was he lacking an opinion on any of these subjects. The two men talked for fifty-five minutes. Truman slid a pad of paper across the desk to Hoover and asked that he write it all down. Hoover left the White House in an upbeat mood. Truman might not pay any attention to his memorandum, and he may have invited the former president to Washington as a way of distancing himself from Roosevelt, but the president had listened. That "big job in Europe" he so arduously desired might be in the offing.[881] Throughout the war, Hoover had been forced to sit on the sidelines like some frog in an icebound pool. He had frustratingly been unable to contribute his considerable organization skills to the assurance of an Allied victory. Hoover hurriedly compiled his memorandum and sent it off to Washington.

With the war in Europe over, the United Nations meeting in San Francisco and the fearsome battle of Okinawa winding down, Hoover went fishing with Walcott and friends in the Berkshires. He decided not to take the train so that he might enjoy the early summer countryside on a drive through the Connecticut River valley. Hoover's selection of flies must have matched the hatch, for the fishing was good. Back in New York, Hoover kept up a steady drumbeat of opposition to Communist takeovers in Eastern Europe and the Communist subversion of the coalition government in Poland. He now saw the Yalta agreement as a form of appeasement and worried about the upcoming meeting of the Big Three—Churchill, Stalin, and Truman—at Potsdam.

But while worrying, he undertook three fishing trips and squeezed in his two weeks at the Bohemian Grove. From June 17 to 24, he was back in British Columbia with Milbank, fishing the Fraser River and mountain lakes to the northeast. After his trip in 1938, events had forced him to cancel several planned outings, but the lure of twenty-pound trout and fifty-pound salmon pushed him to return. In early July, he rendezvoused with George Snyder in Salt Lake, and then drove to Pioche to inspect the mine. On the drive through Nevada, his secretary Bunny Miller played the iron bandits without the same success achieved by Kitty Milbank on earlier trips.[882] In Pioche, Hoover was met by Rickard, who accompanied him back to Palo Alto. Hoover stopped for three days of fishing at Silver Lake, California. Rickard did not join the fishermen, as he heartily disliked the sport, but he did note that Hoover caught a dozen nice trout.[883]

While the Big Three wrestled with the world's problems in Potsdam, Hoover was ensconced at the Grove playing the armchair critic. Shockingly, Churchill was defeated in a general election while at Potsdam and was replaced at the conference table by Clement Atlee. For Hoover, this was another victory over one of his lifetime opponents, but it was a Pyrrhic victory, as the Labourite Atlee headed a Socialist government.[884] The Chief's Sunday afternoon lakeside talk blasted postwar America and the direction it was headed. For Hoover, the world continued to hang daily on the lip of disaster. The day after he left the Grove, Paul Tibbets, in a B-29 named the *Enola Gay*, dropped an atomic bomb on Hiroshima, Japan. Hoover denounced the new weapon as deplorable and called its use unjustified.

On August 11, the Chief traveled to Long Beach to participate in the celebration of his seventy-first birthday, hosted by the Iowa Association at its huge annual picnic. The long war now over, Hoover spent five days with Allan and Coby, fishing Diamond Lake, Oregon, another alpine body of water high in the Cascade Mountains. The last weekend in September, Hoover finished out his fishing year as the guest of his writer friend and fellow Republican Clarence B. Kelland, casting in the sound off Port Washington, Long Island. The fishing was not good, but the company was enjoyable.[885] Back in 31-A, Hoover eagerly plowed through each day's mail, hoping he would hear from the Truman White House. The European food situation continued to deteriorate. Surely the president would be in need of his services and accept the advice of those who advocated his return to government. The weeks turned into months, and still he heard nothing.

Convinced that he would again be ignored, Hoover headed south to Palm Beach and Miami in search of bonefish, sailfish, and sunshine. He was accompanied by his son Herbert's wife, his granddaughter Joan, Richey, Sullivan, and Miller. The sailfishing off Palm Beach was deplorable, so Hoover, along with his family and friends, moved farther south. They checked into the Flamingo Hotel and boarded a rented houseboat, a yacht named *Nicoya*, and set sail for the Keys, a place Hoover knew well and one that rarely disappointed expectant fishermen.[886] Craig Key served as a base and anchorage. Hoover fished the shoals along the small islands to the south halfway to Key West. These isolated spots were reached in a fishing boat that towed behind it one or two fourteen-foot flat-bottomed skiffs equipped with outboard motors. Hoover and his guide, Slim Pinder, often accompanied by Miller and a second guide, searched the shallows for bonefish. When the skiff reached a likely spot, Pinder shut off the motor and poled in closer to the flat. To be able to catch these silvery shadows, it was necessary to see them. They often gave themselves away when their tails broke the surface while feeding, but the fish had to be approached with extreme stealth. If they saw the boat or its shadow, they spooked in an instant and darted away in a flash. Bonefish rely on their amazing speed and protective coloration to survive. "Think of the most nervous person you know and multiply that behavior by 20 and that is the life of the bonefish."[887]

After a successful approach, the guide would cast a shrimp-baited hook three or four feet in front of the wily creature and hand the rod to Hoover, who then attempted to lure the fish to the bait.[888] The moment the bonefish took the shrimp, he brought the rod up with both hands in a quick, sharp motion that usually set the hook. Hoover was patient and loved the careful procedure involved in catching his elusive prey. He often did his own casting, depending on the location of the fish. In the 1940s, few people fished for this skittish fighter. Hoover was also one of the few who, along with Zane Grey, sometimes ate bonefish, filleted and broiled under a hot blue flame.[889] The Chief was a pioneer fisherman, an early enthusiast of the bonefish, as he had been for sailfish in the 1920s—just half a step behind the more famous Zane Grey.

In Miami, the eleventh annual fishing tournament was in progress, and Hoover and his secretary decided to enter. They each selected a fish for competition: Hoover's bonefish weighed ten pounds, three ounces, and Miller's nine pounds, five ounces. The contest was open until late April, but the two big fish stood a good chance of winning. Unexpectedly, Hoover's romance with the bonefish was interrupted on February 25 by a call from Secretary of Agriculture Clinton Anderson. The secretary, who had earlier in the month received Hoover's public support for an expanded food program for Europe, now phoned and asked if Hoover would fly to Washington and accept the chairmanship of the Famine Emergency Committee. Hoover agreed to consider the offer, and Anderson sent a navy plane to Miami to pick up the Great Humanitarian.[890] The "bones," as Hoover affectionately called bonefish, would have to wait while he rounded up food for a hungry world. In Washington, Truman asked him to fly to Europe, assess the damage, and report back on what the continent needed. Hoover at once agreed and returned to Florida in a jubilant mood for another week of fishing. His exile, the wilderness years, were truly over. He was back in government and again useful.

On March 17, Hoover climbed aboard an unpressurized C-54 aircraft nicknamed the *Flying Cow* and commenced a mission that had been expanded to include Asia.[891] At seventy-three, and with a bad cold, he found it to be the toughest assignment of his life. Hoover arrived home on May 10, having successfully acquired substantial amounts of grain to feed Europe, to discover that his bonefish had won for him second place in the Metropolitan Miami Fishing Tournament. The prize was a Heddon bait-casting rod, Coxe casting reel, and a hundred yards of 18-pound nylon line.[892] Bunny Miller did not place but received a citation for her fish, which was only a few ounces shy of a medal.[893] For Hoover, recognition of his fishing accomplishments, though pleasing, took a backseat as he wrestled with the international food crisis.

Relief activities engaged Hoover well into July and included a grueling trip to ten Latin American countries, but regardless of his crowded schedule, he found time for a welcome break at the Bohemian Grove. In August, he spent nearly three weeks at Holiday Farm, fishing the McKenzie and working on his memoirs. His old friend George Quinion persuaded him to join a few fellow fishermen at the home of C. K. Davis for a weekend of bass fishing near Bridgeport, Connecticut, in late September. Hoover brought along his former undersecretary of state, William Castle. It rained nearly all weekend, but the weather did not discourage Hoover, who caught fish and enjoyed the company. Quinion invited Hoover back to his camp on the Schenob year after year, but this fall trip was the last the Chief would make to this area he had come to love. Responding to Quinion in May 1950, he reiterated a decision he had made several years before: "I am afraid that my days of wading about streams are over—sorrowful as I am at not being able to accept your cordial invitation."[894]

In December, Hoover and his family returned to Florida to vacation and fish. A. C. Mattie and his wife, along with Richey and Miller, joined the fish fest. With so large a fishing party, Hoover hired three guides, Elmo Capo, Frank Karcher, and Paul Page. It proved to be one of the best family outings ever, with a total of seventeen sailfish reeled in. Another ten were hooked but fought their way to freedom. Hoover hoped that his granddaughters Peggy Ann, age twenty, and Joan, sixteen, would have the thrill of catching a sailfish, and he was not disappointed. Peggy Ann proved a demon angler, catching a tremendous number of fish: three sailfish, three jacks, a twenty-pound tarpon, two snook, grunt, grouper, two mackerel, two bonito, eight barracuda, two snapper, and a dolphin.[895] Joan did well, too, catching two sailfish, a sixty-eight-pound grouper, two dolphin, a bonito, two bonefish, a twenty-pound tarpon, a snook, some grunt, and some bottom fish.[896] The Chief, focusing on the "bones" while nursing a sore right arm, caught eight fish that weighed more than seven pounds, including some ten-pounders.[897] His catch was particularly impressive, because he was casting with his left hand and using a left-handed reel. A bad case of shingles in his right arm prevented him from using it to either cast or reel in line.[898] Everyone else did exceptionally well, too.

As he often did while fishing, Hoover kept a running tally of the catch and devised a contest based on points for catching certain types of fish. The points were tied to dollar amounts. For example, the reward for a sailfish was $5; for a pompano, $4; and for a kingfish, grouper, or snapper, $3. If someone caught a bonito or barracuda, he or she was fined.[899] On the last day of fishing, when the tallies were in, no one paid or was paid. For Hoover, it was all just good competitive fun. In a letter to Clarence Kelland, he summed up the trip: "Yes sir, I just went away with my children and grandchildren on a grand fishing trip. We caught the choicest and most of anybody in Florida."[900]

Home from the reefs and shoals of the Sunshine State only a few weeks, Hoover was soon off to Europe on a food mission for President Truman. The Chief pushed for a restored Germany that would rejoin the family of nations. Part of that restoration included resurrecting the Children's Feeding Program, with soup kitchens that fed 3.5 million schoolchildren a hot meal every day.[901] As a conservative Republican, Hoover carried great influence with the isolationists in congress, who were reluctant to appropriate the large sums of money necessary for reconstruction in Germany and Japan. His testimony before Congress was critical in obtaining the necessary funds. On April 27, however, he and Gibson managed to slip away from their busy lives for a Sunday of fishing with George Warren on the Pequest.[902] Over the years, Hoover and Warren had become good friends, two men who thoroughly enjoyed the outdoors. They had fished together since the spring of 1937 and caught many fine trout. But this April trip, a week after trout season opened, was Hoover's last visit to the Pequest. His crowded schedule and advancing age necessitated a cutback.

Hoover's long-suffering self-esteem received a boost when the Republican-controlled Congress passed a bill that changed the name Boulder Dam back to Hoover Dam. Truman signed the bill on April 30, 1947. The name change signified a change in Hoover's fortunes. In the public's estimation, his star had risen considerably. Hoover, the only American to have a depression named for him, had finally regained a large portion of his reputation. In early May, he found the courage to speak to the Gridiron Club for the first time since February 1933, perhaps the lowest ebb of his entire career. In his remarks, he briefly reviewed his recent trips to secure food for Europe, told a few appropriate jokes, and ended with a tribute to the man who had brought him back into the spotlight—Truman.[903]

Hoover's transformation took another big step on May 18, when he was a guest on the CBS radio show "Invitation to Learning" to discuss fishing.[904] He began his presentation with an explanation of the importance of Izaak Walton and *The Compleat Angler* to the piscatorial art. In the past, he had published half a dozen or so articles on fishing since *Disappearing Game Fish* appeared in 1927. That same year, he published an article in *Atlantic* titled "In Praise of Izaak Walton," but his references to Walton were oblique. In this radio talk, he took the time for a deeper explanation of Walton's meaning, philosophizing on the restorative qualities of fishing—the spiritual side of his avocation.[905] While he linked himself more closely with the famous Anglican angler in spirit, much of his talk relied on his previous stock remarks on fishing. Still, Hoover had accelerated the development of his image as a weathered philosopher-fisherman, and Walton was to be his touchstone.

In July, Hoover and Richey left New York on the Twentieth Century Limited for Chicago, where they changed trains for Pioche, Nevada. The two friends set aside a couple days for fishing at Snyder's camp in the mountains outside Salt Lake and had brought some of their fishing gear on board the streamliner. Because the All-Star game was in Chicago, the train was swarming with New York sportswriters. Bill Corum of the New York *Journal-American* was intrigued by two long, tubular cases carried by Richey and asked what they contained. Richey explained that the cases held a new, innovative fiberglass fly rod, only the second one ever manufactured and a gift to his Chief.[906] Hoover, who loved technological innovations, was enthusiastic about the new rod and was only too glad to answer Corum's questions. He pointed out that the fishing rod was extremely flexible, and if practical, "it will be easy to make them in mass production and then youngsters can have a fine rod at small expense."[907] Always concerned with young people, he went on to note that "good bamboo rods, now extremely scarce, run into far more money than most boy fishermen can afford."[908] Hoover planned to try out the rod on the trout in Utah. Regretting that they could not stay in Chicago for the All-Star game, the two fishermen headed for their Union Pacific connection. The fiberglass rod met expectations.

After two days on business in Pioche, the Chief and Richey drove to Hoover Dam to tour the facility and bask in the political triumph of the name change. The two rolling stones ended their summer with a three-week stay at the Bohemian Grove. Hoover passed up the McKenzie River for a long visit to Herbert, Jr., in Pasadena before taking the train back to New York City. In September, President Truman again asked for Hoover's services to help establish and serve on the Commission on Organization of the Executive Branch of the Government.[909] Hoover agreed and enthusiastically undertook his new assignment, though in early October his workaholic ways earned him three days in the hospital, a place he had been only a few times in his long life. His busy schedule did not allow him to escape his new commitments until January 14 of the New Year, when he left for Florida to commence his annual assault on the "bones."

When in Florida, Hoover traditionally had lived on a rented yacht anchored off Craig's Key or Bill Thompson's farther south in Marathon.[910] But the refurbished and expanded Key Largo Anglers Club offered superior accommodations. The new docking facilities were able to handle fifty large boats and provided ten cottages on shore as well. The club had come into existence in the early 1930s and had changed ownership several times. Guests arriving by plane or train were picked up in Miami by the Aerocar, a car pulling a lavishly equipped trailer. The nearby Ocean

Reef Club bested their competitor by employing the latest marvel of technology to transport their guests—a half airplane, half helicopter tabbed the Auto Gyro. In 1946, the Camray Corporation bought the Anglers Club and selected Clint Campbell and his wife, Kay, to develop the facility.[911] They did, adding a dock, an eleven-hundred-foot breakwater, a swimming pool, a skeet range, and a new clubhouse with milled cypress sliding.[912] The stately clubhouse, with a large veranda, was set on a sloping, manicured lawn of green zoysia grass.[913] The cottages were enlarged and refurbished. The club, located at the northern tip of Key Largo, was an idyllic spot for a fisherman like Hoover, with easy access to Card Sound, the Atlantic, Biscayne Bay, the mainland shore, and Miami. Ready for business in 1947, the club limited its membership to less than one hundred. Hoover was one of the first members of this exclusive winter fishing haven, and he selected a spacious cottage with six rooms and six baths. Other notable members included James L. Knight, Miami *Herald*'s vice president and general manager; Benjamin F. Fairless, chairman of the board of U.S. Steel; Richard Joshua Reynolds, Jr., of the tobacco family; and Vining Davis, chairman of the board of the Aluminum Company of America.[914]

The Chief had been in this new fishing paradise only a few days when he came in contact with a guide named Calvin Albury. Albury had been casting from a boat near Hoover's and pulled in a couple of big bonefish. Hoover was impressed with the guide's fishing ability, as well as his size and stature. Albury was six feet, four inches tall, black-haired, and spoke with a lilting Conch accent, greeting people with a wide smile and "heyloo."[915] Like Hoover, he maintained a rigid schedule. He was an early riser, up by five o'clock. After he had coffee and read the paper, he was off to fish. Dinner was served promptly at five in the evening, fish at least five nights a week, followed by family time until the six o'clock news. Often he had an appointment as a guide for nighttime tarpon fishing, but if not, it was television and talk until nine. "Nine o'clock," said Abury, "begins the deep of the night. Every hard working man should be in bed by nine to get a good start on the morning."[916]

The next day, Hoover sought out Albury: "Well, I've always wanted to fish with you. I'm going to be your victim for the next week."[917] The curiosity was reciprocal, for Albury harbored doubt about a fisherman who dressed in a suit, white shirt, and necktie. The first day they fished together, Hoover landed a twelve-pound bonefish, the largest he had ever caught. Albury's question as to Hoover's fishing ability had been answered: "He was one of the tops."[918] At the end of their week together, often fishing Hoover's old haunts off Long Key, both Hoover and Albury realized they had developed an affinity for one another.[919] It was the beginning of a relationship that would grow and would last fourteen years.

Elated with his new base of operations in Florida, Hoover headed north in early February to the massive amount of work that awaited him on the commission to reorganize the executive branch. Trout season opened in mid-April, but the Chief was too busy throughout the spring to fish. In June, Hoover spoke before the Republican National Convention. He preferred Robert Taft to Dewey but was sure that when Dewey was nominated for a second time, he would win. Unlike previous campaigns, Hoover had no plans to participate in this one. He remained at his desk until it was time to travel to California for three weeks at the Bohemian Grove. On the way back to New York, he spent a few days at Snyder's fishing camp outside Salt Lake and went on to inspect mining property in Pioche. His seventy-fourth birthday was celebrated in his hometown of West Branch. A huge turnout welcomed Iowa's favorite son back to the place where he had spent his earlier years, to hear a talk he titled "The Miracle of America."[920] The celebration over, Hoover traveled back to Washington and New York to continue his work for the commission. Once again, fishing would have to wait.

Throughout the fall, Dewey conducted a carefully crafted campaign based on the assumption that if he made no mistakes, he would win. Almost everyone seemed to agree with the candidate's assessment, and so on election night, November 3, 1948, Hoover held a soiree, inviting thirty-five old friends to 31-A.[921] Early eastern returns suggested that the chilled champagne might be uncorked before ten o'clock, but as the evening unfolded, the euphoria turned to concern, then worry, then disbelief, and finally despair. The impossible had happened. In the middle of the night, Truman surpassed Dewey and won the election. No one left the Waldorf on a happy note. Hoover, worried that the work of the commission would now be pushed aside, was reassured by Truman that he would ask Congress to pass the recommendations. His two-and-a-half-million-word report would see the light of day. Hoover's job was nearly over.[922]

Sitting in the commission boardroom, smoking a pipe, he told United Press reporter James C. Austin: "I'm going fishing. It's a grand excuse. If you are in public office—and I used to be—and you say you are going fishing, you are not questioned further."[923] He continued his monologue with the thought that "whatever your associations are, you are in the presence of optimism, gladness and joy, and, of course, fish. Your catch is the most expensive food you ever obtained. But," he pointed out, "if you just want fish, you'd be better off just going to the fish market. There's a certain value just in communing with nature—and you certainly do a lot of communing while you're trying to catch a fish."[924] Though he was about to leave for Florida with his sons and granddaughters, he said, "My favorite fishing is first, for brook trout, because you always find him in beautiful surroundings. Secondly, I like sailfish, because this one makes it a test of endurance. My third favorite," he continued, "is the bonefish, because you literally have to hunt him down in shallow water. He gives more resistance for the weight than other fish."[925] When asked by the reporter if he fly-fished, Hoover grimaced and set out to educate Mr. Austin. "There's one thing you must understand," he said; "there are three distinct social levels in trout fishing. The real aristocracy use only a dry fly. A step lower socially are those who use wet flies. And the lowest of all are the bait fishermen."[926] Hoover reminded Austin that Coolidge had fished, and that he used worms until there was a hue and cry from the nation's fly fishermen. "Of course," Hoover added, "Mr. Coolidge was a fundamentalist in economics, religion and fishing."[927]

The San Antonio *Texas News* was frustrated with the United Press release. The editor liked the piece but wanted to know more, even though he recognized Hoover's right to keep the details of his fishing private. Almost in frustration, he asked, "Does Mr. Hoover use a gut leader or one of the newer nylon kind? How many flies does he cast at one time and does he tie them with a knot or use a swivel?"[928] The kind of information the *Texas News* demanded was almost impossible to find out.

Back in the sunny warmth of Key Largo, the Chief chased bonefish with Albury for three weeks. Hoover still found time to work on his memoirs, sitting and writing on the glassed-in after-deck of his rented yacht. From his elevated perch, he could talk with friends who passed by, see other boats arrive and what was being caught, and look out at the sea and sky when the mood struck him.[929] He also wrote when the mood struck him, and he always took pencil and paper along with him in the skiff. Often he spent hours bobbing in the small boat, scribbling away. But he wrote at a furious pace on land or sea and kept Bunny and one other secretary busy typing his daily longhand drafts and retyping his revisions. Most chapters went through dozens of rewrites. A friendly critic once said that he beat the life out of any sentence he wrote. His deadline with Macmillan was fast approaching; the first volume, *Years of Adventure,* was to be released in 1951. To ensure that the book was published to his standards, Hoover ponied up a $70,000 subvention.[930]

On July 11, 1949, Hoover left the Waldorf for California and the Bohemian Grove. At the end of the encampment, he traveled to Pioche to inspect the combined metal operation—ore from Guatemala was blended with ore that was locally mined. There he met his business partner, Jerry Milbank, along with his wife, Kitty, and daughter, Nancy. Like Hoover, the Milbanks loved the high desert. Mornings were taken up with business, but afternoons were given over to long, scenic drives and picnics. In the evenings after dinner, good conversation was the rule, but on this trip, Nancy Milbank taught Hoover to play canasta. The Milbanks had been enthusiasts of the game since it had been imported to the United States from Brazil in the early 1940s. On this occasion, Jerry and Kitty were partners and played against Hoover and Nancy. Kitty recalled: "Nancy showed him just how to play and what to do—deal twelve or fourteen cards to each person, and so forth—and he was bored to death the first game. They lost everything. The second game they won completely against Jerry and me, and Mr. Hoover looked at Nancy and said, 'Nancy, this is not such a bad game after all.'"[931] From that evening on, he was utterly taken with the game, eventually made up new rules, and missed few opportunities to play at a penny a point. Coby Hoover claimed that "the saddest thing that ever happened was when he took up canasta. Because we used to just love after dinner conversation, it was just so much fun and he would really get started after dinner. Then when canasta came into his life, it was canasta."[932] Hoover, however, was not alone. Canasta became a national craze, one of the few things that pulled people from their televisions or interrupted an evening pasting Green Stamps into redemption books.

When the inspections were completed, Hoover and the Milbanks drove to Salt Lake for several days of fishing with George Snyder. Hoover returned to Stanford for a special celebration of his seventy-fifth birthday, as "the first President since James Buchanan to reach the age of 75."[933] To attend, he canceled his fishing trip to the McKenzie River; Holiday Farm would have to wait. Upon his arrival at his alma mater, he was not pleased to see a huge red-and-white sign hanging on the side of Encina Hall, the dormitory in which he had lived as a student, proclaiming in bold letters, "Hoover Slept Here!"[934] But the accolades he so desired poured in from around the world.[935]

Before journeying East, Hoover visited his sister May and slipped her a check for $500 to help cover the costs of a recent operation. Her husband's alcoholism had progressed to the point that he rarely worked, so the Leavitts were dependent on the Hoover brothers' largess.

In February and early March 1950, Hoover was back fishing in Florida for three weeks. He and Albury successfully worked the crystal-clear greenish blue waters of the saltwater flats and inlets. The two anglers left early each morning. Hoover routinely walked down to the boat carrying his old brown canvas bag and said, "Good morning, Calvin." Albury responded, "Good morning, Mr. Hoover. How are you?" To which the Chief cheerfully replied: "Well, I'm happy to be alive and to be here. If we catch something, that's just a little extra bonus; if we don't get anything, I'm not going to feel bad about it. I'm just happy to be alive and to be here."[936] When all was ready for departure, the Chief asked, "Where shall we fish today, Captain?"[937] Albury or one of the other guides suggested various places, and Hoover would comment on past successes: "That was always a good place. I caught fish there two years ago."

When the chosen spot was reached, Hoover took out a large dollar pocketwatch and set it where he could easily see it. If he

Hoover, Calvin Albury, and two nice bonefish, Key Largo Anglers Club, ca. 1950. COURTESY THE HOOVER INSTITUTION

had not caught anything in fifteen minutes, it was time to try somewhere else. If he did catch a nice-size bonefish, he would stay fifteen minutes more.[938] Often he returned to the bigger boat for lunch, but on other days he brought everything along to make a sandwich.[939] Sitting in the front swivel seat, he placed a piece of bread on each knee and constructed a sandwich for himself and his guide—first mustard or mayonnaise, then lettuce, pickle, and ham or chicken. The two men sat quietly eating their sandwiches, washed down with cold iced tea or lemonade poured from a thermos as the boat rocked in the gentle waves under the hot Florida sun.

Hoover sunburned easily, so he used a variety of suntan lotions he called "dope." In addition, he wrapped up to protect himself from the merciless sun. His canvas bag contained a sweater and a raincoat, along with a bottle of water and an ample supply of pipe tobacco. The guides laughingly said that when he ran out of tobacco, he smoked matches. Nearly every day Hoover caught nice-size bonefish, although he occasionally scared them all off when he banged his pipe against the side of the skiff to clean out the bowl.

After a long day on the water, Hoover returned to the main boat, *Captiva,* by about three, cleaned up, and went back to his writing. He was insistent about punctuality, so dinner was served every evening at eight o'clock sharp.[940] He appeared dressed in a blue blazer with gold buttons, white pants, black silk socks, and white shoes. Cocktails were served at seven or seven-thirty, depending on how long Hoover wanted to spend socializing. He usually drank two martinis—he always said one and a half— accompanied by cubes of Colby cheese, which he called rat cheese, saltine crackers, and macadamia nuts. After dinner, canasta was de rigueur. Breakfast was served promptly at eight and lunch at one, whether the Chief was there or not; often he was out fishing. An orderly productive daily routine characterized his yearly fishing trips to Florida.

Hoover left Key Largo on March 4, 1950, and did no more fishing until his trip to Salt Lake and Pioche in August. Before traveling to Utah and Nevada, he spent three weeks at the Grove. Cave Man Camp had a special guest that summer: Gen. Dwight Eisenhower. Hoover's lakeside talk, usually reasonably lighthearted, struck a somber note, as the world again was mired in crisis.[941] A series of events heightened the Cold War. In June, North Korea invaded South Korea, and America was again in a hot war. The year before, Russia had successfully tested an atomic bomb, and China fell to Mao and the Communist party. Sen. Joseph McCarthy's committee hearings sought out homegrown Reds in key government positions. In December, in a national radio address, Hoover stirred up debate by advocating a "fortress America." He opposed sending an additional four army divisions to Europe—a move recommended by President Truman. From his perspective, the Four Horsemen of the Apocalypse were saddling up for another ride. His solution was to withdraw behind an established line of defense and use airpower and atomic weaponry as deterrents.

Hoover did little fishing in 1951, but on his annual outing to Florida, he was determined to boat a bonefish that would beat his Key Largo record of nine pounds, eight ounces and his Miami tournament record of ten pounds, three ounces. The competition was fierce. A Texan, Mrs. Maco Stewart, reeled in what might have been a world-record fish, a whopping sixteen-pounder. She caught the fish in early morning but did not officially weigh it in until six o'clock in the evening.[942] In the interim, the fish had shrunk some four pounds in the hot Florida sun. J. G. Ordway also came within a few feet of landing a trophy bonefish. As he pulled the fish from the water, a shark struck, biting the bonefish in two. The head and remaining body weighed nine pounds.

One afternoon, out with Albury in pursuit of his monster bonefish, Hoover lost his temper. A jet plane from the recently opened air force base at Homestead, flown by some young jet jockey, dove on the skiff—so low, Albury claimed, that he could have hit the bottom of the plane with his sixteen-foot pole. As the plane pulled up, the guide reported:

> The smoke and fumes came all up in our face and just about smothered us to death. Mr. Hoover's hat went off of his head and I guess it went for four miles down the flats before it ever fell. There were black oil marks all over the boat as the plane went over—you know, the kerosene or whatever it is they burn coming through there, that hadn't been burned—and all over Mr. Hoover's clothes, all over the boat, all over my clothes and all.[943]

Albury continued: "Mr. Hoover sat there for about three or four minutes and he never said a word. Finally he turned around to me and he said, 'I wish he'd stick that flying blow-torch so far in this mud flat that it would take them twenty-five years to find it.'" Albury paused, "That's the only time I ever saw him real mad."[944] The Chief's annoyance was compounded, for on this trip he did not break his record. Politics mingled with pleasure as day after day Hoover read the record of congressional hearings. From the Key Largo Club, he offered: "The day I read the Pentagon Generals' attempt to fool the country I never got a bite. Even the fish were repelled by that fishy four division story."[945]

Summer found Hoover back at the Bohemian Grove and then at Snyder's ranch and Pioche. The mining operation was growing and making money. In August, he returned to Holiday Farm to fish the McKenzie along with his son and daughter-in-law Herbert, Jr., and Peggy, and Bert Mattei and his wife. After a week on his favorite river and a trip to Newburg, Hoover hung up his fishing gear until March 1952, when three weeks at the Key Largo Anglers Club kicked off an extremely active year of fishing. In May, he spoke at the Gridiron Club, mostly on fishing, and in July, he spoke at the Republican National Convention, delivering a forceful attack on the erosion of life in America. His candidate, Robert Taft, failed miserably in his effort to stop Eisenhower. Ike was nominated on the first ballot. "We All Like Ike," an Eisenhower campaign slogan, was not a sentiment shared by Hoover, Taft, or Gen. Douglas MacArthur. Asked by the press for his thoughts on the Eisenhower-Nixon ticket, Hoover assured the fourth estate that he would vote Republican but, he tersely said, "I am going fishing."[946] He was off to the West in pursuit of trout at Snyder's camp in Utah and, of course, to attend the Bohemian Grove, where he was free to rail against what he saw as the gathering forces of darkness, both foreign and domestic, that threatened to shatter the American dream.

In early August, Hoover managed a week at Holiday Farm on the McKenzie. Later that month, he accepted the invitation of Nate Milnor to spend a long weekend, August 22 to 24, on Silver Lake, a luxury estate near Yosemite where he had fished on numerous occasions. This visit was different, however, because the Chief came close to losing his life. After a good day of fishing, catching three- to five-pound rainbows, and a good dinner, Hoover, Mattei, and Milnor had retired around nine-thirty in order to get an early start in the morning. All three were sound asleep when a fire at the back of the lodge was ignited by a faulty butane tank.[947] A young neighbor, Bill Jenney, age twenty-one, was reading in bed when he gazed out the window and saw the cabin engulfed in flames. He sprang up, raced the quarter mile to the burning cabin, and awakened the five occupants. All of the hallways were cut off by flames except a door that led to the boat landings. The seventy-eight-year-old Hoover slipped on two topcoats over his pajamas, picked up his suitcase, and exited the burning lodge.[948] Spryly, he leaped from the porch and fled to two boats moored at the dock. At Hoover's direction, the men piled into the boats, pushed off, and drifted out into the lake. Milnor rowed one of the boats while towing the other. Hoover, calm and cool, commented, "I've taken care of refugees all my life, but this is the first time that I've ever been a refugee myself."[949] The wind shifted and blew the flames out toward the lake; the cabin was consumed in ten minutes. Had the wind blown in the opposite direction, the entire Milnor ranch would probably have been destroyed in a ferocious forest fire.

The next morning, Mattei summed up the traumatic experience for the press: "It was a narrow escape and I can't give enough credit to that fine boy, Bill Jenney."[950] Hoover added, "I'm very grateful to be alive."[951] In a thank-you letter to Milnor four days later, Hoover wrote: "While our visit seemed to have a bad end, it made friendship even deeper. I trust you are fully recovered from the shock and only a good story lingers in your mind."[952]

The Chief certainly had a new story to share with his fishing friends at the Key Largo Anglers Club and the Bohemian Grove, but a week later, his fishing enthusiasm undeterred, he had rod and reel in hand at the Hannas' Circle S Ranch. It was his last visit to the Circle S, and the fishing was not good. So before returning to New York City, he drove to Holiday Farm near Blue River and spent a week on the McKenzie chasing redsides. He was back at the Waldorf in time for another of his favorite activities, the October fall classic, as he called it—the World Series. The Bronx Bombers beat the Brooklyn Bums four games to three. During the "fall classic," Hoover received a supposedly innovative new fishing reel from his old friend E. J. Sullivan in Casper, Wyoming. When Hoover examined the reel, manufactured by the Zero Hour Bomb Company, he exclaimed: "Let all mankind stand aside while I take this apart and see its innards. It is probably the only improvement on fish attack in 50 years."[953] But with fishing over for the year, Hoover looked forward to the coming election. In November, the Republicans returned to power after a twenty-year hiatus, as Eisenhower won in a landslide over Adlai Stevenson. The Chief attended Ike's inauguration on January 20, the first since his own in 1928, and rode in an open-topped limousine at the front of the parade. He stood in the cold January rain throughout the swearing-in ceremony without an overcoat or hat.[954]

Two weeks later, a tired Hoover, suffering from a lingering cold that he had developed a few days after the inauguration, left for the tropical climes of the Flamingo Hotel and the Key Largo Anglers Club. The second night in Florida, aboard the yacht *Sunset*, the Chief's temperature began to rise. His son Allan called his Florida doctor, Nicholas Tierney, who rushed to the docks. Below deck, Tierney found Hoover dressed but bundled up in blankets, with a 104-degree temperature.[955] He had pneumonia. An ambulance carried Hoover off to a crowded St. Francis Hospital, where he spent the next five days recuperating. On his last day, shortly before being dismissed, the hospital superintendent, Mother Magdalena, popped into Hoover's room and asked if there was anything he required. Hoover asked, "Sister, can you make a good dry martini?"[956] "You bet I can," the nun responded.[957] On the way out the door, a recovered Hoover sipped his favorite cocktail from a plastic cup and told reporters, "I feel like I have just been released from jail."[958] A sixteen-day assault on the "bones" was about to commence. As the *Sunset* pulled into the docks at the Key Largo Anglers Club, Albury was there to help Hoover plan the coming attack.

As much as Hoover admired the latest technology, when it came to catching bonefish he remained committed to his "old proven methods."[959] His numerous guides, James Blocker, Don Bowers, Harry Jepson, Floyd Majors, and Calvin Albury, all encouraged him to use the new spinning reel and a single hook, but he refused. Instead, he relied on a Penn 109 casting reel with a 20-pound-test line. At the end of the line was a three-way swivel, to each eye of which was tied a ten-inch piece of wire. Don Bowers, who occasionally fished with Hoover, explained, "That made a spreader rig—about ten or twelve inches . . . and then you'd put a hook on each end of that wire, see, and then a shrimp on it—no sinkers." Other oldtimers used an Ambassador reel, but with a single hook on it and a small sinker. Hoover liked the double-hooked rig, in spite of the problem of backlashes, as he often caught two fish at the same time, which he found to be even more exciting sport than hooking just one. Albury vouched for Hoover's successes: "Mr. Hoover was one of the luckiest persons in the world when it came to fishing. And Mr. Hoover landed more double-headers . . . than any other fifty people that have ever been fishing."[960] Warming to his topic, he continued: "One morning I made five casts, and Mr. Hoover hooked and landed nine fish out of five casts. The Chief, elated, responded in his self-effacing manner, 'Well, I believe that you could find them in a rain barrel.'"[961] "I'll tell you," Albury said, "Mr. Hoover was the best I've ever seen. I've fished a lot of people—I've been fishing for thirty-five years and I've fished a lot of people, but when it comes down to catching bonefish I don't believe there's a man who ever picked up a rod and reel who could beat him."[962] One day, Albury claimed, Hoover slowly reeled his spreader contraption through a mixed school of tarpon and bonefish. "He got a seven-pound tarpon on one hook and a nine-pound bonefish on the other."[963] Obviously, as Hoover knew, sticking with the tried and true had its momentary rewards.

Several weeks later, in cold, blustery New York, Hoover was inducted into the Old Guard of the Bohemian Grove Club; it was the fortieth anniversary of his joining on March 18, 1913. The banquet celebration and induction ceremony was held at the Waldorf, and the packed room was festooned with redwood boughs flown in from California. In his acceptance speech, he emphasized the importance of "old guards" to the nation generally, perhaps recognizing his own role, one that Richard Norton Smith characterized as "Counselor to the Republic."[964] For Hoover, honors bestowed upon him by the Bohemian Grove were cherished; after all, it was "the greatest men's party in the world."

On June 7, 1953, Hoover faced a misfortune. May, the youngest of the Hoover siblings, was the first to die, succumbing to a number of maladies that had afflicted her for some time. Her family honored her wishes and held no services—her body was cremated. Hoover had wished for a service for his sister and offered a mausoleum, but his request was rejected.

In early July, Hoover was back in his beloved Oregon, ensconced in his favorite cabin at Holiday Farm. He had arrived

Hoover and his longtime guide Fred Harris in a McKenzie drift boat, July 1953. PHOTO BY LES J. ORDEMAN. COURTESY OREGON JOURNAL

with his family and the Matteis in their private plane. On his first day, among the towering pines, inhaling the earthy scent of the forest, he walked into Meyers General Store in Blue River and bought his Oregon fishing license for $5.[965] He wore his usual formal fishing garb: an old gray suit, gray shirt, red-and-white-checked necktie, silk socks, and tan oxfords.[966] On his head was

Hoover, the pipe-smoking septuagenarian sage, McKenzie River, July 1953. PHOTO BY LES J. ORDEMAN. COURTESY OREGON JOURNAL

his familiar gray fedora with a black band. The license procured, he and Mattei drove a short distance upstream to Blue River landing. There they met their guides, Fred Harris and Milo Thompson, as well as several photographers and reporters: Donald J. Sterling and Les Ordeman from the Oregon *Daily Journal* and Burt Glinn of *Life* magazine. Sitting in a McKenzie River drift boat, Harris put together Hoover's bamboo fly rod and rigged his line with two flies: a Brown Hackle and a red-bodied beetle-like lure.[967]

On the McKenzie, in spite of his advancing age, Hoover stood in the drift boat as Fred Harris piloted upstream. The Chief braced himself in a "notched thwart" and cast out roughly forty feet of line. He sat down in the rocky riffles, and then fished again in the deep pool sections of the river. As the day warmed, he shed his coat, put on sunglasses, and tied on a bandanna to protect his neck from the sun.[968] Mattei caught the first redside as his guide tacked upstream at a forty-five-degree angle.

Fishing was not good; the river was muddy because of upstream construction and a stiff breeze that rippled the surface of the water. The boats pulled to shore under the shade of some overhanging trees. Mopping his forehead, Hoover lit his pipe.[969] As he cooled down and relaxed, the Izaak Walton-like sage recalled his days on the McKenzie: "When I was a boy living in Salem we used to fish on the Santium with worms. We'd figure if we didn't get 60 or 70 fish a day it wasn't a good day."[970] Hoover went on to tell of his experience with his first three flies, a story he had told many times before. The two fishermen, the guides, and the journalists traded fishing stories while lounging in the cool shade. The wind at last subsided, so the party, now rested, pushed off for several more hours of fishing. At seven o'clock, in the gathering twilight, that magical halfway house that trans-forms reality, the drift boats made Hawthorne's Landing, six and a half miles downstream. Hoover caught one fish while Mattei landed his limit of ten. Harris confided that Hoover, too, would have caught his limit, but his failing eyesight made it "difficult for him to strike a rising fish."[971] No matter, it was a marvelous day on a magnificent river.

For the first time at the Bohemian Grove, on the first Saturday night, July 18, Hoover attended the Old Guard outdoor dinner that preceded the Cremation of Care. On the last Sunday of the encampment, he delivered his sixteenth lakeside talk. The next day, he, Clarence Kelland, and Stanford friends left for a three-day stay at the Ahwanee Hotel in Yosemite. August was no longer devoted to fishing. Three weeks at the Grove and three days in Yosemite were enough.

January 1954 found Hoover again in Florida at the Flamingo Hotel docks. There he entertained his old friend Joseph P. Kennedy before sailing down to Key Largo on the *Captiva*. For two weeks, he and Albury searched the Keys for bonefish. On some days, Hoover brought along guests. One of those, William L. White, the famous journalist and son of William Allen White, fondly recalled: "When you went bonefishing you didn't discuss politics, science or anything else. You fished in silence for bonefish. This I got rather quickly—small talk was not allowed."[972] But Hoover occasionally broke the silence with a short treatise on the art of fishing: "When a fish strikes, then you strike back; when the fish runs, you rest; and when the fish quits running, then you go to work."[973] These little commentaries were just interjections, not invitations to conversation. Hoover carried a roll of Lifesavers in the breast pocket of his coat. If the fishing was slow, he popped one in his mouth and momentarily broke the silence: "Well, we'll take a pill and see what happens."[974] If nothing happened, it was time to move on.

On February 2, the Chief returned to New York, but he was back in Key Largo for two more weeks of fishing by mid-March. He continued to write, devoting more time to a book that would never be published—his magnum opus, a searing exposé on Roosevelt and the New Deal. In the protected but friendly confines of the Anglers Club, Hoover learned to relax. He began to open up more to other people in the club and to participate in social events. Hoover had found a home away from home, a place where he felt welcome and could still retain his privacy. That winter, to his great satisfaction, he won the club contest for the largest bonefish. His good friend Richard Berlin, president of the Hearst Corporation, wrote to him in June and asked if he would write a short article on bonefishing for *Sports Afield*.[975] Hoover responded, "Sometime when I am older and have finished my present job of writing 5000 words a day, remind me again!"[976]

In July, he pushed aside his work and, for a week, checked into "his cabin" at Holiday Farm and fished the McKenzie. In cleaning out things in California, he sent Larry Richey a box of fishing tackle from his huge accumulation. Richey, who confessed that he could not possibly have enough tackle, thanked his old friend: "Mrs. Hoover's reel I can use for big rock fish and blues, and your reel will have to take on sail fish and marlin, and of course the real big reel will have to go for the King of the Sea, that is, some of those big blue and black marlin off Peru which I hope you and I can make next year."[977] Hoover spent the last three weeks of July under the redwoods at the Grove. When he returned to Palo Alto, he was surprised to find an invitation from Eisenhower to join him on a fishing trip to Colorado, near Fraser northwest of Denver.[978] Ike offered his aging predecessor a number of dates, and Hoover selected early September. In accepting the invitation by telegram, Hoover wrote, "IT WOULD BE A GREAT PRIVILEGE TO SPEND A DAY OR TWO WITH YOU IN OR NEAR THE WOODS. I AM PROHIBITED FROM WADING ROUGH STREAMS BUT I CAN FISH IN ANY OTHER WAY AND AM PRETTY GOOD AT CAMPING WITH RESERVATIONS ON COOKING."[979] Eisenhower wrote back, describing the fishing camp on Nielsen's ranch: "There is a small stream on which we catch ten and twelve inchers, and of course there is always the chance for the occasional big fellow of something on the order of sixteen or seventeen inches."[980] The president opined, "I assure you that you don't need to be especially terrified at the prospect of living on my cooking for a couple of days. My culinary reputation is pretty good—but my repertoire is limited. It is only after about four days that my guests begin to look a little pained when they come to the dinner table."[981]

On August 10, Hoover celebrated his birthday in his home-town of West Branch, Iowa. Eisenhower, who for some time had wished to warm up to Hoover, sent a heartfelt letter con-gratulating him on his eightieth birthday and expressing his admiration for his long years of public service.[982] Ike "genuinely admired Hoover, not only for his public spiritedness but for his worldview."[983]

In West Branch, the former president was cheered by twenty thousand people, who jammed into the tiny town to honor him. His speech, in which he emphasized the strengths of America and warned of socialism at home and the growing Communist threat from overseas, was preceded by an old-fashioned Iowa picnic. Mounds of fried chicken and big ears of roasted fresh-picked new corn were fed to two hundred special guests by a cadre of women volunteers from the local Methodist church.[984]

The hoopla over, the Chief was back in New York but regularly commuted to Washington, D.C., to work on the second Hoover Commission, charged with the further reorganization of the government. Hoover's workaholic ways persisted; he still put in twelve- to fourteen-hour days regardless of his advancing age. Despite this unrelenting schedule, he still found time on August 14 to accept a tribute from the New York Yankees by throwing out the first ball at the yearly old-timers' game in Yankee Stadium. On August 30, he flew to Des Moines to speak at Hoover Day at the Iowa State Fair—one more event in a long list of public outpourings that recognized his many lifetime accomplishments. Ike, too, came to the fair to participate in the festivities. At the end of the president's speech on foreign policy, he told the crowd, "Now, my friends, Mr. Hoover and I have a very important date with a few finny comrades up in the high Rockies, and it is about time we were getting along."[985] In a VIP room under the grandstand, Jack Calhoun, general manager of the Kirkwood Hotel, asked Ike how the fishing was in Colorado. He had good luck, the president said, flashing the famous Eisenhower grin, "but it might be that Colorado authorities had just been stocking bigger fish."[986] Hoover did not seem amused by the former general's humor.

Later that afternoon, regardless of any doubts either man may have had about the other, they flew to Denver and drove off into the mountains to fish. St. Louis Creek, at ten thousand feet, was just across the Continental Divide, a cold, fast-running stream surrounded by snow-capped mountains. The weather was perfect. At night the temperature dropped to below freezing, and during the day it climbed back into the low sixties. Lovely rustic cabins with large fireplaces were near the creek, which made for comfortable evenings—a marvelous escape to an earlier time. In front of the fire after a hard day outdoors and a good meal, "we get repose," Hoover wrote, "from the troubles of soul that this vast complex of civilization imposes upon us in our working hours and our restless nights. The quiet chortle of the streams is soothing to our 'het-up' anxieties."[987] The fishing was poor, even though the creek had been specially stocked for the president's visit. Ike charcoal-grilled large porterhouse steaks for his guest, although Hoover preferred fish to beef.

Eisenhower and Hoover grilling steaks after a day of fishing in Colorado, September 1954. COURTESY QUEENS BOROUGH PUBLIC LIBRARY, LONG ISLAND DIVISION, NEW YORK HERALD TRIBUNE COLLECTION

Despite Ike's efforts, the Chief was not about to warm up to his host. He assumed, as he had on numerous occasions in the past, that efforts to please him by those with whom he disagreed were really efforts to co-opt him ideologically. From Hoover's perspective, Eisenhower had not only failed to dismantle the New Deal, but he also was a poor fisherman and took far too much time in preparing breakfast and dinner.[988] Hoover's friends claim that he once ate a five-course meal in ten minutes. To Ike's credit, he did make small, thin "silver dollar" pancakes that pleased Hoover's palate.[989] In short, however, Eisenhower was too much for the prickly, fidgety Hoover, who liked, and was used to, having things his way.

The fishing over, the Chief arrived in early morning at LaGuardia Field on board the president's plane, *The Columbine*. As he walked down the gangway, he sported a ruddy tan. A crush of reporters asked if the fishing had been good. Hoover responded: "You don't go fishing to catch fish. You buy those. You go to get away, for the company and the scenery."[990] The next question: How had he and Ike gotten along together in Colorado? Hoover replied that the trip was fine. He and the president had enjoyed one another, but they had been hounded by swarms of reporters and photographers. Hoover invoked his line on the sanctity of "prayer and fishing," chiding the press for an invasion of privacy.

His complaint, coming from the nation's octogenarian fishing guru, touched off an editorial-page blitz across America. Most editors sided with Hoover and privacy, but some said forthrightly that if you chose public life, the public had a right to know—even famous fishermen lived in a fishbowl. Many quoted Hoover's various comments on fishing, now a part of the American lexicon of fishing anecdotes. A few took a tongue-in-cheek approach. The Birmingham, Alabama, *News* explained that all good reporters had read Ernest Hemingway's *Big Two-Hearted River* and, in imitation, demanded the most minute details "minutely reported."[991] The White Plains, New York, *Reporter-Dispatch* commented, "If Herbert Hoover catches the fish, and Dwight Eisenhower handles the cooking, the resultant chowder could be just what this country needs."[992] To journalism's credit, the reporters in Colorado attempted to contribute to a spirit of merriment around the evening campfire. They were in such profusion along St. Louis Creek that they were able to form a chorus that wrote and sang their version of "The Battle Hymn of the Republic:"

> What did General Eisenhower have to eat
>   today?
> Was it trout, or was it meat, or was it
>   curds and whey?
> What did Mr. President give to his
>   honored guest?
> Buns or tack or toast?
>
> He's always cooking up fish chowder,
> The recipe by Eisenhower.

Silence fills the cooking hour
And no news from Hagerty.[993]

Of all the commentary, the one Hoover likely found the least amusing was the gaffe by radio personality John Raleigh. Raleigh reported that Dwight Eisenhower and Herbert Heever were fishing in Colorado. To smooth over his faux pas, he reminded his audience of "Harry Von Zell's classic boner in referring to Hoover as 'Mr. Heever Hoobert.'"[994] Unfortunately for the tongue-twisted Raleigh, he muffed the historical reference, for Von Zell had actually said "Mr. Hoobert Heever."[995] Raleigh realized his mistake, paused, and tried again—"Mr. Hobart Hoober." Finally, "he stopped trying to be funny, took a deep breath," and enunciated clearly, "Mr. Herbert Hoover."[996]

In November, after the Republicans lost control of Congress in the midterm elections, Hoover traveled yet again to Europe at the invitation of Konrad Adenauer. He praised Germany's accomplishment since the war's end, noting that Germany and Europe should provide for their own defense.[997] Hoover received his eighty-first honorary degree, this one from Tübingen, and was lauded for the many times he had provided food for Germany.[998]

In December, tired from his overseas trip, Hoover return to the sunny Keys. He and Calvin Albury had a serious date with the "bones." As the two fishermen sat hour after hour in their small skiff in the hot sun, the sea, Key, and sky all blended together hypnotically. Zane Grey called this trancelike state "bonefish oblivion."[999] During long spells of inactivity, Hoover remained vigilant, alert to the slightest tug on his line. Albury marveled at the unique techniques Hoover developed. The Chief held his rod in his right hand and used the thumb and index finger of his left to grasp the line about twelve inches above the reel.[1000] In this way, he could feel the fish and set the hook far faster than if he relied on the tip of the rod. Quick as a flash, he brought the left hand down and began to play the silver speedster on the end of his line. Once hooked, bonefish run. They are famous for winding the line around coral and sponges in an effort to throw off the hook. Hoover furiously wound the reel in an effort to take up line when a bonefish charged the boat at a terrific speed and then cut a series of sharp figure eights. Snags occurred frequently. With the slack out of the line and the rod bent like a bow, fighting "bones" often swam round and round the boat—"as many as twenty-six times," swore Albury.[1001]

Sitting in the swivel chair at the front of the boat, Hoover went round and round with the fish. In the middle of the struggle, Hoover often took out his handkerchief and tightened the drag on his reel.[1002] These terrific battles might last half an hour or more. When the fish was spent, he reeled it in. Hoover, too, was often spent and took a long break before his next cast. "No one," said Zane Grey, "will ever believe how powerful a bonefish is until he has tried to stop the rush and heard the line snap. As for cunning, it is utterly baffling. As for biting, it is almost imperceptible. As for tactics, they are beyond conjecture."[1003]

Starting in 1954, Hoover went to Florida twice each winter. The first session, usually in late December or early January, was reserved for family and a few close friends. He enjoyed his grandchildren, teaching them how to fish and telling them stories. The younger Hoovers, however, much preferred to fish the Gulf Stream rather than sit in a boat for long periods of time in the hot sun coaxing bonefish to bite, but on occasion they did accompany their grandfather on his forays. One winter, Andy Hoover caught a forty-two-pound sailfish, which was entered into the Metropolitan Miami Fishing Tournament. The second trip each year was usually in March but sometimes slipped over into April. Friends invited by Hoover rotated in and out every four days or so. Family also showed up during the second session.

In New York, Hoover was consumed with his work on the commission. On February 4, he was shocked to learn that his older brother, Theodore, at age eighty-four, had died during the night of a cerebral hemorrhage at his ranch at Rio Del Oso.[1004] The two brothers had been extremely close throughout their lives and supported one another since they were orphaned in Iowa some seventy years earlier. Bert and Tad had gone far together, beating the odds against their eventual success. Theodore seemed comfortable being dragged along by and living in the shadow of his more successful younger brother.

Throughout the spring, Hoover labored long and hard on the completion of the second Hoover Commission final report. He ran into major opposition from several commission members, but with the submission of a hostile minority report, the work was completed in May. Hoover's long years of government service, begun as war food administrator in the Wilson cabinet, had come to an end. He was now free to return to writing books, a task he undertook with a vengeance.

In July, Hoover made his annual pilgrimage to California and the Bohemian Grove. In the 1950s, Cave Man Camp became one of the most prestigious, famous for its rich and powerful guests and its food. A top camp was expected to provide gourmet fare. Restaurateur George Mardikian, owner of Omar Khayyam's, a popular Armenian eatery in San Francisco, each year supplied the food, drinks, and waiters to the Hoover camp. Invitations to dine, converse, and politick were prized by those in the higher ranks of the Fortune 500, as well as by those who resided in other Bohemian camps. Eventually Mardikian became a guest of Cave Man Camp, and then a member, but he continued to supervise the details of the food service, always as a labor of love supplying the best and freshest foods available, an act of gratitude for a man he ardently admired. Before immigrating to America in the 1920s, Mardikian, near death, had escaped from a Turkish prison with the aid of the Near East Relief Commission—one of Hoover's many relief operations. In America, he climbed the ladder of success to become founder and owner of Omar Khayyam's.[1005] Through the restaurant, where Hoover sometimes dined, the two men became acquainted. Sometime after World War II, Hoover asked Mardikian to become the purveyor to Cave Man Camp. Partially in jest, Mardikian occasionally told Hoover: "Chief, many years ago, in the form of relief to the destitute people of Armenia, you cast bread upon the waters of the River Arax. Now, I am in charge of your meals here at Caveman's Camp. So I am seeing this bread comes back to you, in the form of *daron abour, bulgur pilaff* and *shish kebab.*"[1006]

Though Hoover ate quickly, he liked to eat well, usually simple foods simply prepared. In the fall of 1955, Mardikian wrote a detailed article on what he served the Chief at the Grove. "Maybe the article," Mardikian maintained, "will give you one or two new ideas about dishes and menus for your table. But even if they [the recipes] don't do that, I'm sure they'll give you a new and warm and human insight into the grand old gentleman whom all the world is regarding as one of the greatest of living

Americans."[1007] Mardikian began with the Chief's morning cup of hot coffee laced with equal measures of cream and sugar. Breakfast included three kinds of melons, cubed and chilled—white casaba, Persian, and crenshaw—followed by scrambled eggs and crisp bacon. Hoover crumbled the bacon and mixed it with his scrambled eggs. Other breakfast favorites included "lovely, firm, flaky grilled trout" or wheat cakes with butter and sprinkled with granulated sugar. Hoover regularly ate a piece of toast spread with butter and a hunk of orange blossom comb honey on top. A typical lunch included abalone chowder, braised stew beef with fettucini, buttered peas, and a fresh peach for dessert. Before dinner, while Hoover sipped his martini, Mardikian served razor-thin slices of aged hickory-smoked Kentucky ham. Dinner started with a bowl of navy bean or split pea soup and a salad, although Mardikian claimed he never saw "the Chief finish one yet."[1008] The entree, roast duck with bulgur pilaf and gravy, was accompanied by a bowl of chilled applesauce. Red wines from the Napa and Livermore Valleys were Hoover's preference. Dessert was ice-cold watermelon served with sharp American cheddar cheese, followed by a slice of pumpkin pie.[1009] Life was very, very good in 1950s America, under the redwoods at the "greatest men's party in the world." Mardikian sent off his article to 31-A for Hoover's approval.

In Newberg, Oregon, on August 10 for his eighty-first birthday, Hoover attended the dedication ceremonies of his boyhood home. Touring the house, Hoover was genuinely moved when he walked up the stairs and down the hallway into his old room. Tears welled in his eyes, and he stammered, "This was my room."[1010] Newbergers turned out by thousands to salute the Chief. He visited the graves of his aunt and his irascible uncle, Dr. Henry John Minthorn, as well as that of Evangeline Martin, his old Sunday school teacher who had given him so much love and encouragement. On the platform for his speech were old classmates and Oregon friends.[1011] Hoover defended America and its way of life, advocating that we needed to "occasionally mention something good about ourselves."[1012] The celebration over, Hoover retreated to Holiday Farm for a week of fishing on the McKenzie.[1013]

On September 10, 1955, Mardikian received a classic Hoover response in regard to his innocuous article on Hoover's eating habits at the Grove. Bunny, answering for her boss, put the kibosh on the project: "We are going to have to invoke one of the oldest and firmest rules of the Bohemian Club and the Bohemian Grove—and that is, that the Club, the Grove, the members, the friends or guests, and all of their words or activities are never put into print."[1014] She went on to explain the serious difficulties that might arise from the publication of such an article: "There are . . . a few statements that will bring the wrath of devoted friends of the Chief a-flying!"[1015] Bunny explained that Mardikian's revelation that Hoover ate comb honey on his cakes at the Grove would surely upset those "who regularly supply him with delicious maple syrup."[1016] At the Waldorf, she said, Hoover ate corn cakes, not wheat cakes. "Iowa thinks," she emphasized, "that the Chief only eats corn cakes."[1017] Even worse, "his New York doctors would have a fit that he ate butter at all (and after all he is on a holiday and a vacation—and we should not give him away!)."[1018] The admission that Hoover consumed gin and wine, she purported, would send the WCTU into a tizzy. Then Bunny returned to hammer home the main point: "This nice little article runs completely against all of the rules from the founding of the Bohemian Club—and the Chief has always abided by them." She concluded with a suggestion that must have left Mardikian bewildered: "Should you care to write an article on some other subject—such as his Americanism—or something of that sort, you know the Chief and certainly I too will try to be as helpful as possible."

Mardikian responded a few days later, recognizing the sacredness of the Bohemian Club rule but suggesting a revision, arguing that the article was about Hoover's Americanism.[1019] On September 26, Bunny sent a note to Hoover attached to a draft telegram: "We did not succeed. What now?" Hoover scrawled a reply underneath: "Well, I guess you . . . have to edit it completely—also get Bill [Bill Nichols of *This Week* magazine] to help." The telegram was sent. "Many thanks for your letter. I just think that the article is too personal and I know that the Chief will be distressed should something like it be published as it is not the type to which we ever can give our consent to. Kindest regards."[1020] Outmaneuvered by Hoover's stubborn obstinacy in regard to his privacy, Mardikian threw in the towel. "Please forget the whole thing as there will not be any article written concerning the Chief or his eating habits."[1021]

It was December 21 when Hoover escaped the cold of New York City and the confines of his Waldorf apartment for his yearly island retreat to Key Largo. To a friend, he wrote, "I have decided to go fishing for the holidays in Florida because out in the skiff on the blue water, and with no radio, television, telephone or tabloids with their scoops of murders, and with only a bone fish for an objective, one can recover some stability from the jars and shocks of the times."[1022] On Christmas Eve, he and Bunny entertained friends, fishing guides, and the crew of the *Captiva*. All received autographed photos and inscribed copies of Hoover's books. A few days later, fishing the tidal flats, he caught two bonefish at the same time.[1023] Perhaps hooking "the double" presaged good luck in the coming New Year. Hoover welcomed the New Year by attending the celebration at the Anglers Club, but he went home early so as to get an early start fishing the next morning. In mid-January, he returned to New York and began to sketch out what would become a four-volume history of his many relief efforts, a book he titled *An American Epic*. But he returned to Florida in March for several more weeks of fishing.

It was common knowledge among the guides at Key Largo that Hoover was famous for telling them where he wanted to fish rather than listening to their advice on choice locations. One morning when Don Bowers was acting as his guide, Hoover said, "Don, what about going over to Hoover Point?" This was a spot on the other side of Card Sound, on one of the Arsenicker Keys. Don replied, "Well, Mr. Hoover, there ain't no water there now." Hoover rebutted, "Well, let's go and look."[1024] Bowers started the motor and sped across the sound. As they approached Hoover Point, the boat began to scrape the bottom and then suddenly ran aground. Bowers looked at Hoover and said nothing. Hoover admitted, "Well, I guess you're right. There isn't enough water here for any fish."[1025] Bowers claimed that all the guides liked the Chief but understood that they "just had to show him."[1026] When dealing with Hoover, there was no other option. Occasionally, however, the Chief's hunches were right. Another guide, Floyd L. Majors, was fishing with Hoover when the allotted fifteen minutes without a nibble ran out. The Chief asked him to try a certain flat.[1027] Majors protested, "But, it's low tide and that flat's high and dry."[1028] Still peeved at Hoover for doubting his word, and sure that when they arrived at the designated spot they would find nothing, Majors complied with Hoover's request. Coming up on the flat, it was clear that much of it was out of the water, but along the bank appeared the telltale signs: "bonefish tails . . . insolently waving in places where no bonefish should be."[1029] Majors concluded that Hoover was not just a good fisherman, he also was lucky.

Home in New York, he was back to writing six days a week. Neil MacNeil, a *New York Times* night editor, friend, and Hoover's literary executor, was amazed to discover that "in the morning the secretaries would come in and find a lot of work. What happened was the old boy would get up at night, put in two or three hours at his desk, and leave all this new work for them to do in the morning—enough to start them all off and keep them going again—and then he'd go back to bed. Then he'd get up for breakfast."[1030] Hoover wanted to finish his numerous projects and fully realized that it was unlikely he would live much longer, that time was running out; "he was an old man in a hurry."[1031] In June, he left for California and spent a week at Holiday Farm, but here, too, he spent half of each day writing in pencil on foolscap. Even at the Grove, he continued to devote a good deal of time writing. As women were not allowed on the premises during the encampment, one or two of Hoover's secretaries arrived at the gate each morning to receive his daily output and bring him his typed corrected drafts.[1032]

Hoover's lakeside talks at the Bohemian Grove often opened with humorous stories, ones that were just enough off-color to please his fellow campers. In the summer of 1956, one that brought an enthusiastic response was his tale of a midwestern traveling salesman who was forced to spend the weekend in a motel. Digging through the room for something to read, he only found a Gideon Bible in the drawer of the nightstand. Opening the Bible, he saw a note in female handwriting saying, "Dear friend: If you are far from home and lonesome, read Numbers 22 and 31."[1033] The salesman followed the instructions and read the suggested passages. Again at the bottom of the page was another note: "Friend, if you are still disconsolate and lonesome, read

Ecclesiastics."[1034] Once more, at the bottom of the page was a note sending the poor salesman on to yet another book of the Bible. At the bottom of this page was a final note that read, "Friend, if you are still lonesome, call Mabel at 3-3562."[1035] His audience warmed, Hoover went on to make some of his oft-repeated remarks on fishing, and then, becoming serious, he stressed the role and abuse of academic freedom in America's institutions of higher learning.

After leaving the Grove, Hoover retreated to Palo Alto to work on his speech for the Republican National Convention, which opened the third week of August in San Francisco. He used the opportunity, his sixth speech before a national convention, on the one hundredth birthday of the Republican party, to reiterate Republican values and warn against the Communist menace.[1036] The convention over, he traveled to Oregon in the Matteis' private plane for another week of fishing at Holiday Farm. In New York, his work pace continued, but in October, he took time off for a World Series game at Ebbets Field. Midmonth, he held a Bohemian Club afterglow party at the Waldorf for previous summer guests. In late October, Hoover organized his last international relief effort, founding First Aid for Hungary, a group that managed to provide significant aid to Hungarian refugees fleeing for their lives from the Soviet juggernaut that crushed their attempt to throw off communism. Some medical aid even reached Budapest before the Iron Curtain came thundering down again.[1037] In November, he was pleased to see the Eisenhower-Nixon ticket roll to victory. Writing and relief dominated the remainder of the year, but a few days after Christmas, the Chief was back at the Anglers Club in Key Largo for his annual dance with the bonefish.

In the winter of 1957, Hoover and Calvin Albury spent a good deal of time fishing the Keys strung along both sides of Caesar Creek. This was not really a creek at all, but a narrow saltwater channel between Biscayne Bay and the open Atlantic, separating Elliott and Adams Key to the north from the Rubicon Keys and Old Rhodes Key to the south. The flats and the patch reefs were a fishermen's paradise. The crystal blue waters teemed with a host of marine species. The waters were so clear that one could see the schools of fish to a depth of twenty-five feet or more. Mangrove snappers, groupers, cero mackerel, and yellowtails were easily

Hoover and Albury with a trophy bonefish, Key Largo.
COURTESY HERBERT HOOVER LIBRARY

caught on shrimp bait—"fishing for the ice box," as Hoover always said. In closer along the banks of the inlets were the skittish bonefish. With an early start, there was time on the way home to work the dozens of inlets sprinkled throughout the isolated bay between Totten and Old Rhodes Key. Day after day, Hoover and Albury returned to this horn of aquatic plenty in search of "bones" and also simply to enjoy the unspoiled natural beauty of the Keys. The flora and fauna were quite alien to

Hoover and his granddaughter Lou Henry Hoover, who caught a nine-and-three-quarter-pound bonefish in April 1957. COURTESY QUEENS BOROUGH PUBLIC LIBRARY, LONG ISLAND DIVISION, NEW YORK HERALD TRIBUNE COLLECTION

Hoover, who had spent his boyhood in Iowa and Oregon, yet he had become utterly entranced. For Hoover, alone in a boat with Albury, skimming across the Florida waters in the embrace of Mother Nature was exhilarating. Hoover harbored a deep love for the Keys, a place he had come to know as well as or better than many of the old Conchs and guides, a place that rivaled the other spot from which he derived spiritual sustenance—the McKenzie River in Oregon. This shy man was always at peace with the world in the cathedral of nature.

In the spring of 1957, Hoover was in luck. He caught a thirty-four-pound wahoo, one big enough to enter into the Metropolitan Miami Fishing Tournament. Not to be outdone, Larry Richey hauled in a forty-four-pound dolphin.[1038] For Hoover, the best catch of the season was made by his granddaughter Lou Henry Hoover, who snagged a nine-and-three-quarter-pound bonefish on April 3, a few weeks before the season ended. Lou Henry's bonefish was duly entered in the Miami tournament.

Back in New York, Hoover wrote for long hours every day, often continuing far into the night. If hungry, he might send a bellboy at the Waldorf out to the Horn and Hardart automat for some baked beans.[1039] As he plugged away on the first volume of *An American Epic*, he became caught up in the story of his relationship with Woodrow Wilson. Neil MacNeil, proofreading a draft copy of the manuscript, argued that the story of the relationship was an important subject in and of itself. Including it in the volume on aid to Europe disrupted his relief story. What was needed was a separate book. Agreeing, Hoover set aside *An American Epic* and wrote the *Ordeal of Woodrow Wilson*.[1040] A great admirer of Wilson, Hoover was attracted to the former president's commitment to change, moral idealism, and desire to "engineer" a solution to Europe's ongoing political problems. Hoover's account of the war leader's character and their close relationship became a best-seller.

Added to the Chief's literary burden was his continuing work on a book he tentatively titled *Freedom Betrayed*, which was soon called his *Magnum Opus* by those who were involved in its research and writing. The *Opus* was an exposé of Franklin Roosevelt and the New Deal, so specific and full of accusations that upon Hoover's death, it was decided not to publish the book for reasons of libel and reputation.[1041] It remains today secreted in the

Hoover Institution, unavailable to even the most friendly of researchers. The depth of Hoover's animus was displayed one night in the Waldorf when an overnight guest awoke and trudged to the bathroom. Coming down the hallway on the way back to bed, he noticed a light shining in one of Hoover's work spaces. Surprised, the guest stuck his head in and asked his sleepless host what he was doing. The aging Hoover snapped, "I'm making my Roosevelt book more pungent."[1042] In the last years of his life, he was driven to complete what he considered his political legacy.

In June, Hoover headed west. He and the Matteis made a final trip to Holiday Farm and the McKenzie River. It was also his last trip to his beloved Oregon. Hoover may have thought he would return, but circumstances and then later his health prevented it. For more than sixty-five years, Hoover had been a fly fisherman, ever since the late 1880s, when a kindly fisherman had given him three flies: a Royal Coachman, a Gray Hackle, and a Professor. He began to fish the McKenzie as a boy but did not return until he was the secretary of commerce. After the presidency, he fished the river dozens of times, catching innumerable fighting redsides, a fish he loved grilled for breakfast. Once, asked by a reporter about his longtime relationship with the river, he said the McKenzie "was my own special jewel of a river."[1043] In *What the River Knows: An Angler in Midstream,* Wayne Fields wrote, "Surely every cast represents the desire to be hooked to something, but I still cannot say what is the object of that longing."[1044] On the McKenzie, Hoover thought he knew. Oregon would continue to live in his mind.

Later in the summer, at the Grove, Hoover was surrounded by an all-star cast of guests. Cave Man Camp had reached a pinnacle of prestige.[1045] Its members included Vice President Richard Nixon; Roy Howard, president of Scripps-Howard; journalist and travel writer Lowell Thomas; and restauranteur George Mardikian. It also hosted distinguished guests such as Stanley C. Allyn, president of the National Cash Register Company; Secretary of the Treasury Robert B. Anderson; *Newsweek* editor Henry Hazlitt; and R. Douglas Stuart, chairman of the board of Quaker Oats.[1046] One afternoon, member Peter Grimm invited a friend from another camp to come over for cocktails with the luminaries. The friend had never met Hoover, and Grimm introduced him. The two got along well and struck up a conversation. As the cocktail hour was coming to an end, the guest approached Grimm to thank him for his hospitality, remarking, "I have never met so much brass in any one place in all my experience—governors, generals, admirals—what a remarkable lot of men here. But, there is one man here more famous than anyone else and I wish you would tell me who he is."[1047] Among the large, milling crowd, the guest pointed out Mardikian. Grimm asked, "What makes you think he is the most famous man here?"[1048] The guest stammered that he had to be, "for as these visitors, each in turn came up to greet Mr. Hoover, he had a pleasant word for each, but remained seated. When this man came in Mr. Hoover stood up to shake hands with him."[1049] That, my friend, said Grimm, "is George Mardikian, the commissary of our camp."[1050]

In August, Hoover returned to New York and his writing. He did not fish again until mid-January, when he arrived in Florida. As always, Hoover and Albury went after the bones, but in 1958, they set a record—thirty days of fishing in a row without a break, some days spending as long as eight hours on the water. The two fishermen had become so close that Hoover no longer liked to go out with other guides if Albury was not available. When Albury came down with a bad case of the flu, various guides offered their services, but Hoover said, "No, Calvin isn't going to be sick forever. He knows my ways and I know his, and I'll sit here and wait until he gets back."[1051] Albury was out for three days. Hoover busied himself with writing. When the guide returned, Hoover asked, "Well, do you feel like you could go out for a couple of hours?"[1052] Albury replied, "We'll make the day," but Hoover said, "No, I don't want you to stay out there all day if you don't feel like it."[1053] By three o'clock in the afternoon, both were to ready to call it quits.

One afternoon on a hot, breezeless bonefish flat, Hoover pulled out a gold-plated pipe lighter but was having trouble with the flint wheel. It was a British lighter, and the wheel turned up to light the wick rather than down. Hoover, hot and impatient, tossed the lighter to Albury. "Here, you take this thing before I throw it overboard."[1054] Albury kept the attractive lighter and discovered that it had been a gift to Hoover from Winston Churchill.

On another trip south to Marathon, with Floyd Majors as a guide, the *Captiva* pulled up to Bill Thompson's vessel. The yachts had been docked for only a few minutes when Hoover

Hoover and Richey with thirty-four-pound wahoo, March 1957.
COURTESY AP/WIDE WORLD PHOTOS

appeared on the aft deck, swatting mosquitoes and yelling, "Let's get out of here!"[1055] He was only too aware that if the swarming insects were that bad during the day, at night they would attack in waves. Majors joked that before spraying, "there wasn't enough air space to support all the mosquitoes at one time and they flew in different shifts. Apparently the day shift was doing reconnaissance on Mr. Hoover's yacht immediately after she docked."[1056]

On occasion, Hoover would break off his pursuit of the bones and go after another, larger fish that shared many of the bonefish's characteristics—permit. One blustery March morning, after several days of unsuccessful fishing, Richey suggested fishing for permit. Majors agreed, but this necessitated a trip to Harbor Key, sixty miles to the south in rough seas. From the guide's perspective, permit were the king of sport: "When an angler has convinced himself that he's the master of other forms of light tackle fishing, when he's ready to graduate from bonefishing, then it's time to think in terms of permit. You might consider achievement in this class as a sort of doctorate in angling."[1057] Majors continued: "Other aspects of permits are their express-train speed, great stamina and a satanic cunning which enables them to find any sponge or obstruction to wind your line around, thereby disengaging the hook."[1058] Hoover, in utter disregard for the weather, determined that permit fishing it was. On the way south, they picked up crawfish bait at No Name Key. The second day at Harbor Key, the storm subsided, but Hoover stayed on the *Captiva* to write. Herbert, Jr., and his wife, Margaret, decided to fish. Guided by Majors, Margaret was successful in landing one of the large silvery, satanic creatures, one that weighed twenty-five pounds or more. On board the yacht, Bunny Miller asked whether the fish was good to eat. Majors told her they were "the very best. They're like an over large pompano."[1059] That evening at dinner, all were satisfied with Margaret's express-train catch.

But as exciting as permit fishing was, Hoover remained loyal to the bonefish. To glorify the sport, he had designed and manufactured a beautiful Steuben glass trophy—a bonefish replica mounted on a pedestal with a brass plaque that read, "The Herbert Hoover Bonefish Trophy." The impressive prize was awarded each year at the close of the season to the Key Largo angler who caught the largest bonefish.[1060]

Home from Florida for only a few weeks, Hoover entered the hospital on April 20 for a gallbladder operation. The operation was a success, and he was able to "escape" after a two-week stay. While he was recovering, President Eisenhower called and asked whether he was in good enough condition to represent the United States on July 4 at America Day at the Brussels World's Fair. Ike would provide the presidential airplane. Hoover's doctors huddled and concurred that he was up to the trip. The "Savior of Belgium" returned to a jubilant welcome. Once again he was the toast of the Belgians, wined, dined, and applauded by a small grateful nation that had been twice traumatized by war in half a century.

Fresh from his overseas trip aboard the *Columbine,* Hoover arrived at the Bohemian Grove with new stories to tell from his latest adventure. The encampment on the Russian River ended on a Saturday, but each year Mardikian hosted an afterglow luncheon at his El Rancho Silverado in the Napa Valley north of Rutherford.[1061] Wives were included, and a gourmet lunch was served outdoors under the canopy of large oak trees. A specialty was the fruits grown on the ranch, especially strawberries, melons, and peaches. The afterglow luncheon, with Cave Man Camp in attendance, served as an early celebration of the Chief's birthday.

On August 12, Hoover flew from New York to Quebec City, Canada, to spend a week on Murray Bay at the home of Richard Berlin, a longtime friend and the head of the Hearst empire. The Berlins had invited Hoover many times before, but he had never been able to find the time. Murray Bay, at the confluence of the Murray and St. Lawrence Rivers, was one of the most scenic and famous places in North America, often called the "Newport of the North." President William Howard Taft had a magnificent summer home on Murray Bay, as did other rich Americans such as the Kennedys, Cabots, and Clarkes. The rich built their fabulous homes on Pointe-au-Pic on the Chemin des Falaises. The Donohue home, next door to the Tafts, was designed and built by the famous architect M. Charles Warren.[1062] When asked by friends, "Where is Murray Bay?" Taft replied, "Murray Bay is a state of mind."[1063] "Big Bill" was also fond of saying that the Charlevoix region was "as intoxicating as champagne, but without the headache of the morning after."[1064] Picturesque Old World-Style villages hugged the banks of the St. Lawrence River, framed by the Laurentian Mountains in the background. The social crème de la crème of Canada and the United States arrived in Murray Bay aboard large, gleaming white pleasure boats called "floating palaces." With the silk stockings' arrival, a gala summer social season was under way. The water level in the bay, a combination of salt and fresh water, was subject to the tides. Trout and salmon were in abundance—the fishing was good. Near the mouth of the Saguenay River, pods of whales could be seen.[1065] At Ciel sur Terre, Hoover relaxed and enjoyed the wonderful scenery and gracious hospitality of his host. During his weeklong stay, he fly-fished on several occasions and caught a number of trout. Although this was his first fishing trip to eastern Canada, the Murray River trout were the last he was to catch. At eighty-four, after a lifetime of fly fishing, he retired from a sport he loved and had mastered.

Back in 31-A, Hoover burned the midnight oil in his effort to complete the first volume of *An American Epic.* While laboring on the book, he had the satisfaction of seeing Congress pass recommendations made by the second Hoover Commission. He spent Christmas in New York with family and friends, and as always, he had the largest tree possible dragged into his apartment. The "Great Engineer" fastidiously directed its yearly trimming, insisting on "proper" placement of favorite strings of lights. He was maniacal about his method of putting tinsel on a Christmas tree. Mounds of gifts arrived, including presents from amorous widows, and mountains of food, liquor, and cigars. Hoover generously shared the yearly tribute with his staff and his friends.[1066]

In January, with the holidays over, it was time for Florida and bonefish. The year before, he had fished thirty days in a row, and he had every intention of repeating the performance. Day after day, Hoover, Richey, and Albury chased the bones. The Chief also spent long hours each day writing. On their twenty-second consecutive day of fishing, the three men got an early start. Albury cast out the line, handed Hoover the rod, and said, "Here, . . . strike him; he's on it."[1067] The Chief took the rod, placed it across his lap, and sat there. The reel spun rapidly as the bonefish made a freedom run that successfully shook off the hook. Then Hoover handed the rod back to Albury, who wound in the line. Finally, the former president turned and said, "Calvin, I don't mind telling you I'm a tired old man, and the best thing for you to do is take me back and put me out."[1068] Richey encouraged his old friend to hang in there and continue to fish, "Chief, you'll feel better in a few minutes."[1069] Hoover, however, clearly recognized that it was the end of the fishing endurance contest. "Larry," he said, "there isn't anybody knows when Herbert Hoover is tired any better than Herbert Hoover does himself. You'll do me a great favor if you'll crank up that outboard and take me back home."[1070] Albury did as requested: "I cranked up and took him back in and put him out."[1071]

Richey was baffled by his hero's behavior. "Well, I never saw the Chief give up like this before."[1072] Albury countered: "Mr. Richey, you have to remember that Mr. Hoover is an old man. Mr. Hoover is eighty-six [actually eighty-four] years-old, and you just remember all the fish that Mr. Hoover has caught in these twenty-two days." He had landed 196 big fish. "Those fish," said Albury, "ran from eight pounds up to eleven or eleven and a half pounds."[1073] "Yes," Richey agreed, "he's caught a lot of fish but usually he can hold down his end of the deal with anybody when it comes to a long stay at fishing."[1074] "Yes, but that's hard on a person like that," Albury reminded Richey, "putting in seven and eight hours a day out in that boat all day long in the hot sun. And with him fishing hard like that, catching so darned many fish like that—why it beat the old man out. He was just beat out—that's all."[1075] Albury had it right, the old man was beat out, and if he wanted to continue to fish, he would have to slacken the pace. Hoover, however, bounced back. Later that season, Albury marveled that he could still walk the gunwales of the skiff. "You know," he said, "Mr. Hoover was as sure-footed as a mountain goat—it just seemed like his feet were glued to the deck."[1076] They were, and his heart was still into fishing.

In March, again displaying his disregard for severe weather, Hoover decided to go out in the midst of a gale, even though all the signs pointed to poor fishing. The wind was blowing from the south, and the tide was falling.[1077] Majors was the guide again that day and suggested a sheltered area on the leeward side of a key as protection. "Weather?" Hoover protested. "This little breeze will keep us cool."[1078] The Chief recommended the windward side of Long Key, where the fishing had recently been quite good. As the wind was blowing at twenty knots and the sky promised even worse, Majors was concerned about transferring between boats in rough waters, "a feat for the nimble, not for aging statesmen." As the skiff bobbed, rain squalls lashed Hoover and Richey, and the fish were uninterested in the bait. At last all agreed it was time to quit. The little skiff bounced back to the cruiser, only to discover that the anchor had dragged, allowing the boat to turn broadside into the wind and wash up on the flat, fast aground and in need of a rising tide. Another cruiser

Painting of Hoover and Albury on wall of Key Largo Anglers Club.
COURTESY HERBERT HOOVER LIBRARY

piloted by Clyde Allen picked up Hoover and Richey. Majors stayed with his boat, but it was two o'clock in the morning before the tide set the cruiser free. The next morning at the Anglers Club, red-eyed and tired, the guide inquired about the fate of his two passengers, worrying that Hoover might have contracted pneumonia or worse. Bumping into Richey, he asked after the Chief and was surprised when Larry told him that "it had all been great fun. In fact, a little excitement made the trip more enjoyable." Richey continued, "And by the way, I'd better be getting ready to fish, for the Chief was planning for another assault on the 'bones.' Just as soon as he finished his breakfast."[1079]

When Hoover arrived home from the tropics, he resumed his writing frenzy. The first volume of *An American Epic* appeared on schedule, and he pushed ahead with the remaining three volumes. He continued his work with the Boys Clubs, arguing that juvenile crime was reduced significantly when boys were afforded opportunities other than the street.[1080]

In the summer of 1959, back at Bohemian Grove, one of the guests at Cave Man Camp was Oregon Gov. Mark O. Hatfield. Hatfield had written his master's thesis at Stanford on Hoover, and as a rising star in Oregon politics, he was being looked over as a future Republican leader. The Grove was an exciting place for an aspiring young politician to spend a week. Hatfield found the conversation, the food, and the entertainment impressive. Though the bar was always open at Cave Man Camp, rarely, if ever, did it result in drunkenness. After dinner, all gathered around a huge roaring fire. Sometimes there was music; one evening John Charles Thomas, a Metropolitan Opera star, sang selections from Gilbert and Sullivan. Always there was much talk and often storytelling. Ike was winding down his second term, and the Republicans were abuzz over who would be the Republican nominee. Nixon was the odds-on favorite, but the vice-presidential spot engaged heated debate.

Hoover rarely visited other camps, but rather greeted and talked with those who visited him. Hatfield vividly recalled that "Hoover was often seen with his martini glass in one hand and smoking his pipe, holding forth on a number of topics."[1081] In the

Hoover and Oregon Gov. Mark O. Hatfield, Bohemian Grove, July 1959. PHOTO BY FRED CLARK. COURTESY HERBERT HOOVER LIBRARY

privacy of the redwood grove, said Hatfield, "Hoover let down his formidable guard, left his mask at the gate, and was jovial, witty, warm, accessible, and 'authentic'—he showed outstanding leadership."[1082]

At lunch one day, Hoover asked Hatfield if he knew how to eat a peach, a question Hoover asked every new camp attendee. Hatfield said no, and Hoover offered the following: "Hold the peach between your forefinger and thumb, cut around the midship of the peach all the way to the freestone center, then twist in opposite directions and pull it apart. Then use a spoon to eat the peach that has become a kind of peach cup."[1083] Hoover concluded the lesson with a summation of peach-eating rules: "This is the only way to do it. You don't waste any of the juice, you don't waste any of the fruit by cutting the skin. You save all of the goodness of the peach."[1084] Hatfield was impressed and added this story to his storehouse of Hoover lore.

At his lakeside talk, Hoover fretted over unreliable European allies and the spread of communism in Asia and the Third World. He left the Grove for another wonderful day at El Ranchero Silverado with the Mardikians and then returned to New York to throw out the first pitch at the New York Yankees' Old Timers Game.

On August 9, he was a guest on "Meet the Press." When Chet Huntley asked what he considered his greatest contribution, he unhesitatingly answered, "I should think, taking it all together, the various relief operations which I directed, stretching over a period of nearly forty years."[1085] Bob Considine, in the wrap-up, asked, "On the eve of your 85th birthday, how do you feel?"[1086] Hoover answered, "I feel physically perfect," and then added, "About 68 I should think."[1087]

Throughout the fall, he was occupied with his writing, the Boys Clubs, the Hoover Institution, and baseball. He also produced a steady stream of short articles on fishing. In November, Larry Richey and Joel Boone, Hoover's White House physician, visited Camp Rapidan, a place where they had spent many a weekend, and a place filled with memories, a place loved by the Hoovers. Over the years, the camp had deteriorated badly, so the National Park Service had removed a number of the buildings. Richey reported, "The streams were filled with sparkling water and the sun was shining, and it is still a very beautiful spot."[1088] On December 29, just before Hoover was ready to leave for Key Largo, his longtime secretary, friend, and fishing partner, Larry Richey, died. For Hoover, this was a tremendous loss; the chick had lost its mother hen.

In the hot Florida sun, Hoover and Albury continued to work the flats for that mythic granddaddy bonefish—the whopper. Hoover had caught the largest bonefish of anyone in the Anglers Club, a twelve-pounder, and he also had taken the largest permit, a thirty-six-pound bundle of fighting fish.[1089] Regardless of his success with rod and reel, at eighty-five, Hoover could no longer stay out on the water as long as he might wish, nor could he fish as many days in a row as he had in the past. But as he aged, he developed a near total disregard for the weather. It took a howling gale, a northwester, to keep him off the water. He confided his attitude to Albury: "If other people can go, I can go too. I'm not going to stay home because it's cold or it's windy. If others can go and fish," he emphasized, "I can go and fish too."[1090]

The highlight of the Key Largo season came one morning, March 2, 1960, while Kay Campbell was typing in the Anglers Club office and James Blocker was catching up on paperwork. The complex was sent into a dither when the receptionist ran into Kay's office and announced that President Truman, escorted by two highway patrolmen, was at the front desk. "I thought she was joking," said Campbell, "so I continued typing. I looked up and there was President Truman."[1091] Somebody at the bar saw Truman and said, "Gosh, what's that Democrat doing in this Republican club?"[1092] Kay introduced herself and escorted Truman, who she said looked as if he had just stepped out of *Esquire*, to the Hoover cottage. Blocker ran ahead to inform the Chief of his distinguished visitor. Hoover, who was writing, exclaimed, "Oh, my gosh, give me a couple of minutes. I've got to get my shoes on."[1093] He scurried around, found his shoes, and then spent an hour talking with Truman. The president explained that he and Mrs. Truman were driving to Miami from Key West, and he wanted to stop, chat, and pay his respects. The odd couple continued to delight in their friendship.

In the summer of 1960, the Grove was again stimulated by persistent political banter. It was an election year, a time of quadrennial madness, and a member of Cave Man Camp, Richard Nixon, stood to gain the nomination. Hoover, who had wished

Nixon at Cave Man Camp, Bohemian Grove, 1961.
COURTESY HOOVER INSTITUTION

not to speak to an eighth national convention, was finally persuaded to do so. He left the Grove and flew to Chicago, where on
July 25, for the fourth time, he gave a "farewell address." This
one, however, was in fact his last. Assessing the hopefuls, Hoover
thought that Nixon would make a fine president and that Henry
Cabot Lodge should have the second place on the ticket. The
negative assessment was that he thought John F. Kennedy, the
son of his close friend, would win the presidency. Back at the

Grove, many Republicans dismissed Hoover's harbinger of political disaster, as victory seemed in the air for the GOP. With campaign speeches to write and books to finish, Hoover returned to his workaholic schedule, but he did make time for the World Series in October. The second volume of *An American Epic* was published. November brought the awaited presidential election, and the contest was extremely close. Kennedy slipped into the White House, winning the election by a nose.

A tired Hoover greeted the warmth of the sun when, in January, he stepped off the plane in Miami. He met briefly with the president-elect and accepted an invitation to the inauguration. Then it was off to bonefish, this time with Lewis Strauss and his wife as guests. Several days into their Florida stay, Floyd Majors took Strauss out to fish. Coming back in the late afternoon, Majors backed his cruiser toward the anchored yacht. The gangplank was extended and all looked ready, but a sailor on the yacht's ladder was making some last-minute adjustments. Majors stopped about six feet short of the extended gangplank. Strauss, his glasses covered with salt spray, stepped on the transom of the cruiser and then again stepped, expecting the board to be beneath his feet. Instead, he plunged into the ocean in between the two boats. Majors claimed that the admiral "completely disappeared," but "when he popped to the surface the quick-thinking sailor already had a long handled boat hook overside, and reaching over the yacht's rail he got the hook under the floundering victim's jacket collar. By this time everyone aboard was lining the rail, the crew having spurted from their quarters like drops from a lemon."[1094] Relieved, Majors reported, "Aside from the wetting, no harm was done and I'm sure Admiral Strauss never bore a grudge though I doubt that any Admiral ever boarded a boat under more ignominious circumstances."[1095]

The year 1961 was apparently one of mishaps, for when Hoover accepted the invitation to Kennedy's inauguration and flew to Washington, D.C., a blizzard forced the closing of National Airport. Hoover's plane, unable to land, was forced to return to Florida.[1096] Disappointed, the Chief went fishing. In March, near the end of his stay, he delivered a short speech, a compilation of his best fishing anecdotes, to welcome on board the new Anglers Club flag officers.[1097] The celebration was a five-day affair with parties nearly every night. The climax was the

Saturday night costume party. Virginia Green, a longtime club member, remarked, "[Hoover] was a man who never liked cocktail parties and would never go to cocktail parties anywhere else, but during the Commodore's party . . . he went to every cocktail party. He spoke to everyone there and it must have been tiring for him, but he wanted to do his bit for the Club."[1098]

At the Bohemian Grove that summer, Richard Nixon and Cave Man Camp analyzed the close presidential election, looking for an answer to why Nixon had lost. Some blamed Mayor Richard Daley of Chicago and his political machine, suspecting foul play or a ghost vote, but others felt the television debates were a deciding factor. Hoover concurred with the analysis that on TV, "Nixon looked like a made-over stiff," though he shared that view with only a few close associates.[1099] Hoover's problem with Nixon was the same one he had with Eisenhower—they were both middle-of-the-road Republicans who accepted much of the New Deal as a permanent part of American life. In Hoover's view, this was heresy. But Nixon was in the right place to gain a sympathetic ear. Cave Man Camp, for all of its luminance, knew with certainty the agonies associated with bitter defeat. As for Nixon's future, perhaps he could rebuild his shattered career by capturing the governor's mansion in Sacramento.

Hoover flew back to the Waldorf to a waiting stack of mail. Much of the correspondence was from young boys and girls from across the country. He enjoyed these letters and always found time to respond to them all. Many asked serious questions, others wanted his autograph, and a few asked his advice on fishing. He wrote to one young inquirer, a fellow angler: "Nowadays I mostly fish for bonefish with a shrimp for bait. I put them back in the water so they can grow bigger. Bonefishing around the Florida Keys is especially adapted to older gentlemen who can no longer clamber among the rocks and brush. Keep this in mind when you are eighty-seven."[1100]

Throughout the remainder of 1961, Hoover did no fishing. Instead, he pushed as hard as possible to finish all of his book projects. The third volume of *An American Epic* was published, and his work progressed on the last volume as well as on two other small books: *On Growing Up* and *Fishing for Fun and to Wash Your Soul*. Bill Nichols of *This Week* magazine contributed editorial advice on the last two volumes.[1101] Overworked and in need of a rest, the Chief arrived at the Key Largo Anglers Club on January 15, 1962, after an inauspicious beginning. After taking off from New York, the plane could not retract its landing gear and was forced to jettison fuel and return to LaGuardia. There the Hoover party boarded another plane and arrived safely in Miami.[1102]

Settled in, Hoover and Albury fished nearly every day, but they cut down the number of hours on the water and took an occasional day off. Hoover hoped to win the bonefish contest, and by mid-February, he was the front-runner, having caught a nine-and-three-quarter-pounder.[1103] He also hauled in the largest tarpon, but though his chances of winning with both entries were good, the contest was open until the end of April. There was still a long way to go. Mixed with fishing and writing was a steady stream of family and guests. A "boat load," said Bunny Miller, who also described their serene life in the tropics: "We live aboard the boat, we fish—after bonefish and big ones—we go sightseeing for we have a car with us, we cruise about—and life is not strenuous or dressy."[1104] On one of those trips, Bunny and Hoover toured the Art Deco pastel cube motels and hotels packed in close to Miami Beach, places with names that were meant to sound exotic and enticing. Hoover asked his FBI driver, Vincent Antle, if he knew "where they got all those names."[1105] "No Chief," said Antle, "I really don't know where they got all those names."[1106] "I do," Hoover told him. "They had a tape recording in an insane asylum."[1107]

One morning in early March, Hoover, Bunny, and Don Bowers, acting as guide, decided to go after the bonefish, typically disregarding warnings of strong winds and choppy seas later in the day. When they anchored the cruiser and stepped into the skiff, the sun shone and the water was calm.[1108] Bowers poled the skiff in close to shore on flats in which the water was only two or three feet deep. The fishing was good on the west side of Card Sound. Bonefish wagged their tails in the sunlight as they fed on small crabs nestled on the bottom. Around noon, as the storm front began to move in, the wind picked up and the seas churned.

Several miles away, another fishing party, consisting of Harry and Nydia Bruno and a guide named Dick Friday, was also bonefishing. Bruno, a New York public-relations man, had been lucky: He hooked a nine-and-a-half-pound bonefish and anticipated an even bigger catch. Then the storm hit. Friday suggested they seek a spot that was more sheltered. Bruno described the scene: "We bucked the waves at fairly high speed, and then the motor quit cold. Over went the small anchor and we hoped it would hold until we could find out what the trouble was."[1109] The guide tinkered with the engine, cleaned the spark plug, and attempted to choke the engine—all failed. The only course of action was to haul in the anchor, allowing the wind to carry the boat across the bay to the relative safety of the far shore. Being pushed up against the mangrove trees at the edge of the swamp for a night was preferable to being caught in the open and capsizing. The waves coming over the bow had soaked the boat's occupants, and the storm was increasing in ferocity. In the distance, the stranded fishermen "heard the high hum of an outboard motor and saw another boat about a mile away."[1110] Friday said he thought it was the boat owned by Don Bowers, but it was traveling in the opposite direction, toward the safety of the ship channel. Miraculously, it turned and headed for the Bruno boat—the party had been seen. The Hoover boat offered help, and Bruno asked them to send a message when they reached their cruiser asking that a rescue ship be sent to fetch them. Hoover said, "We will not leave you here."[1111] Bowers threw a line to Friday in order to tow them in. In the process, the boats nearly swamped on several occasions. When the two skiffs reached the cruiser, Hoover, now eighty-seven but still a "sure-footed mountain goat," had little difficulty climbing the ladder in the storm-tossed seas. Safe at the Anglers Club, Bruno thanked Hoover, who replied, "Think nothing of it. I am glad we were able to help."[1112] Amazed by the entire experience, and especially impressed by Hoover's composure, Bruno went back to New York and wrote up the adventure for *Outdoor Life*. Hoover and Bowers thought the article overblown, but both enjoyed the write-up.[1113]

At the commodore's party on March 2, Hoover gave another of his anecdotal speeches. A favorite story he told that evening was one from when he was president in 1929. A fishing club in Maine (Hoover's sense of decorum caused him to always omit where the club was located) sent the first salmon caught each year to the White House. The salmon was accompanied by a club member, and each year a photograph was taken of the president with the fish.[1114] Hoover claimed that "these photographs lined the walls of the Club."[1115] On one occasion, when the salmon arrived at the White House, it was sent to the kitchen, where the chef cut off the head and tail and was about to stick it in the broiler. When the mistake was discovered, the cook, attempting to save the day, sewed the head and tail back on and finished the job with stuffed cotton. On the White House lawn, the president carefully displayed the fish horizontally lest the fishy situation be revealed. The club member arrived and the flashbulbs popped. But as the press continued to take photos, cotton began to disgorge from the salmon's mouth. Hoover attempted to cover the emerging cotton, but the last round of photos demonstrated that something was wrong with the fish. Hoover concluded, "The Fishing Club did not use those later editions."[1116] Throughout the five days of celebration, Hoover was congenial and accessible. He truly enjoyed himself.[1117]

Hoover's doctors warned him that this was likely his last trip to Key Largo. Though the source of his growing discomfort was not yet discovered, he intuitively understood he had reached the end of his fishing days. On April 3, 1962, Hoover and Albury made their last excursion together. That afternoon, when they returned to the dock, Hoover took off his wristwatch and gave it to Albury. A moment later, he handed him his rod and reel. "Here's a little memento for you," he said. "If I ever get back, I'll use the rod and reel; if I never get back, it's yours. You keep it and do whatever you want with it."[1118] The next morning, Albury went over to say good-bye. Hoover walked up to meet him, put his arm on Albury's shoulder, and tears began to stream down his cheeks. "Well," he said, "maybe if it's the Good Lord's will, I'll see you again. I regard you as being one of the best friends I have on earth."[1119] Albury responded, "Thank you, Mr. Hoover, and I feel the same way."[1120] With that, Hoover got into the waiting car and headed off for the Miami airport, his fourteen-year relationship with Calvin Albury and his long years of Florida fishing at an end.

Later that summer, he attended his beloved Cave Man Camp for the last time. At night, under the redwoods, the temperature dropped into the low forties. Everyone piled on blankets, and only the brave edged out of bed to add wood to the fire. Hoover had a potbellied stove in his cabin, and when he arose at three o'clock in the morning to write, he could often be seen outside in

Hoover and Bunny Miller, Key Largo Anglers Club, ca. 1962.
COURTESY HERBERT HOOVER LIBRARY

his nightshirt picking up an armload of wood to stoke the fire.[1121] One of the Armenian waiters was concerned that Hoover arose in the middle of the night and made his own fire. Nick, as he was called, stayed up all night in order to help Hoover. One night, the Chief finally said, "Nick, I stay away for 50 weeks. I come here to escape civilization, for two weeks. I want to make my own fire. Now, you go back to your cabin and stay in bed!"[1122] Hoover attended Mardikian's afterglow party and then returned to the Waldorf.

On August 10, a fading Hoover flew to Iowa to dedicate the Herbert Hoover Presidential Library in the little town of West Branch, an event attended by forty-five thousand people. Among the numerous dignitaries was his good friend Harry S. Truman.[1123] It was to be his last address upon a very long American road, fittingly the road on which it had all begun. A few days later, in New York, doctors discovered abdominal cancer. It was the beginning of the end.[1124]

Over the next two years, Hoover battled a number of converging disorders, but through perseverance, he completed his book projects. *Fishing for Fun and to Wash Your Soul* was published in 1963. Hoover was gratified to see in many reviews that his

FISHING

IT is the chance to wash one's soul with pure air, with the rush of the brook, or with the shimmer of the sun on the blue water. It brings meekness and inspiration from the decency of nature, charity toward tackle makers, patience toward fish, a mockery of profits & egos, a quieting of hate, a rejoicing that you do not have to decide a darned thing until next week. And it is discipline in the equality of men—for all men are equal before fish.

Herbert Hoover

"On Fishing," by Herbert Hoover. COURTESY HERBERT HOOVER LIBRARY

name was linked with his touchstone Izaak Walton. In the foreword, he summed up his eighty-five years of angling: "Fishing tis
the chance to wash one's soul with pure air, with the rush of the
brook, or with the shimmer of the sun on the blue water. It brings
meekness and inspiration from the decency of nature, charity
toward tackle makers, patience toward fish, a mockery of profits
and egos, a quieting of hate, a rejoicing that you do not have to
decide a darned thing until next week. And it is discipline in the
equality of men—for all men are equal before fish."[1125]

During the last week of Hoover's life, in mid-October 1964,
he lay in a hospital bed especially set up in 31-A, bleeding to
death from his esophagus. The doctors worked frenetically to
stop the bleeding, but despite some two hundred transfusions, all
of their efforts failed. Calvin Albury, Hoover's fishing guide of
fourteen years, knew what ailed Hoover and had said so when
Hoover left Florida and gave up fishing in April 1962: "The old
man was beat out. I tell you the old man was just beat out."
Hoover quietly died near noon on October 20, sedated and comfortable in the Waldorf apartment that had become synonymous
with his name. On the wall in his writing room was a copy of the
"Fisherman's Prayer":

> God grant that I may fish
> Until my dying day!
> And when it comes to my last cast
> I humbly pray,
> When in God's landing net
> I'm perfectly asleep
> That in His mercy I be judged
> As good enough to keep.[1126]

It was his deeply held belief that he would join Lou, the love
of his life, a woman he had missed daily since her death twenty
some years before. With the announcement of his passing, thousands of condolences flooded in from around the world. His
body lay in state in the Capitol rotunda in Washington, D.C.,
where thousands of mourners came to pay tribute to the man
who had been at the center of American life for so many years.
Then the coffin was loaded on a train bedecked with black crepe

for the journey back to West Branch, Iowa. On a beautiful late Indian summer afternoon, Herbert Hoover, thirty-first president of the United States, was laid to rest in the rich prairie earth that so shaped his character.

Very few men have ever experienced the towering heights of success and depths of defeat that Hoover had. As Bill Nichols put it, "Hoover was a man who had lived twice."[1127] His eulogist, Dr. Trueblood, said that his story, however, "is essentially . . . triumphant."[1128] One of the essentials in understanding his persistence, his triumph, was his love of fishing and the outdoors. Fishing sustained him and was a constant source of renewal. Hoover may have been raised a simple Quaker, but for him the glories of nature were a cathedral, a celebration of life. In the trout stream or on the reefs and shoals of the Florida Keys, Hoover was closer to God than he had been in his youth, when he spent long hours in a cold, mostly silent Quaker meetinghouse.

When Hoover was lowered into the ground on that fine fall Iowa afternoon, America lost not only one of its most uncommon men, but also one of its most accomplished fishermen, a man for whom the rod and reel and the open road were all tightly woven into his love for America and its seemingly limitless possibilities. At the age of ninety, Herbert Hoover was finally fished out. In the gathering darkness, as a last tribute, a bugler on a hillside above the gravesite played taps, but a fisherman's send-off seems more appropriate.

Tight lines, Mr. Hoover—*semper pesco!*

Notes

Chapter 1: A Boyhood in Iowa

1. Herbert Hoover, *The Memoirs of Herbert Hoover: Years of Adventure, 1874–1920*, vol. 1 (New York: Macmillan, 1951), 3.
2. Herbert Hoover, *Fishing for Fun and to Wash Your Soul* (New York: Random House, 1963), 32.
3. Herbert Hoover, *A Boyhood in Iowa* (New York: Aventine Press, 1931), 19.
4. Agnes Minthorn Miles to Harriette Miles Odell, January 21, 1920, Miles, A–K, 1907–1940, Genealogy File, Herbert Hoover Library (HHL).
5. Kendrick A. Clements, *Hoover, Conservation, and Consumerism: Engineering the Good Life* (Lawrence: University Press of Kansas, 2000), 10.
6. Clements, *Hoover, Conservation, and Consumerism*, 10, and Levi D. Johnson to Herbert Hoover, April 6, 1926, Commerce Period, Personal File, Box 268, Herbert Hoover Papers (HHP), HHL.
7. Theodore J. Hoover, *Memoranda* (Stanford University, 1939), 15, unpublished manuscript in HHL; and David Burner, *Herbert Hoover: A Public Life* (New York: Knopf, 1979), 6.
8. Levi Johnson to Herbert Hoover, April 6, 1926, HHP, HHL.
9. Clements, *Hoover, Conservation, and Consumerism*, 10.
10. Theodore Hoover, *Memoranda*, 24.
11. George H. Nash, *The Life of Herbert Hoover*, vol. 1 (New York: W. W. Norton, 1983), 8.
12. Hulda Hoover to Agnes Miles, October 24, 1883, Genealogy File, HHL.
13. Theodore Hoover, *Memoranda*, 8–10.

14. Hoover, *Memoirs*, 1:4–5.
15. Hoover, *A Boyhood in Iowa*, 14.
16. Theodore Hoover, *Memoranda*, 18.
17. Hoover, *Fishing for Fun and to Wash Your Soul*, 36.
18. Theodore Hoover, *Memoranda*, 34.
19. Ibid., 22.
20. Harriette Miles Odell to Lori, October 18, 1939, Genealogy File, HHL; West Branch *Local Record*, March 29, 1883, West Branch, Iowa, HHL; and *Memoirs*, 1: 7.
21. Hoover, *Memoirs*, 1: 4–5.
22. Louise Morse Whitman, "Herbert Hoover and the Osages," *Chronicles of Oklahoma* 25 (Spring 1947): 2–4.
23. Theodore Hoover, *Memoranda*, 21–22.
24. Hoover, *Memoirs*, 1: 1.
25. Theodore Hoover, *Memoranda*, 19.
26. Hoover, *Memoirs*, 1: 1–2.
27. Burner, *Herbert Hoover*, 6.
28. Theodore Hoover, *Memoranda*, 18.
29. Hoover, *Memoirs*, 1: 2.
30. Ibid.
31. Curtis Harnack, *Gentlemen on the Prairie* (Ames: Iowa State University Press, 1985), 90–91; and Theodore Hoover, *Memoranda*, 36–37.
32. Ibid., 187–88.
33. Theodore Hoover, *Memoranda*, 27.
34. Hoover, *Memoirs*, 1: 5.
35. Theodore Hoover, *Memoranda*, 30.
36. Ibid., 31.
37. Hoover, *Memoirs*, 1: 5.
38. Theodore Hoover, *Memoranda*, 35.
39. Ibid., 18.
40. Nash, *Life of Herbert Hoover*, 1: 11; and Hoover, *Memoirs*, 1: 5–6.
41. Burner, *Herbert Hoover*, 12.
42. Nash, *Life of Herbert Hoover*, 1: 7–8.
43. Clements, *Hoover, Conservation and Consumerism*, 12.
44. Rose Wilder Lane, *The Making of Herbert Hoover* (New York: Century Co., 1920), 58.
45. Ibid., 61–62.
46. Theodore Hoover, *Memoranda*, 31–32.
47. Agnes Minthorn Miles to Harriette Miles Odell, January 21, 1920, Genealogy File, HHL.
48. Nash, *Life of Herbert Hoover*, 1: 12.
49. Lane, *Making of Herbert Hoover*, 58.
50. Ibid., 68.

Chapter 2: A New World in the Great American West

51. *Gleanings from the Life of Burt Brown Barker* (unpublished autobiography), 41–42, HHL.
52. Hoover, *Memoirs*, 1: 10.
53. George Bailey, *Germans: A Biography of an Obsession* (New York: World Publishing, 1972), 2.
54. Ed Kidd, "Hoover: A Rags and Riches Saga," in *A Century to Remember: Newberg, 1889–1989* (Newberg, OR: Newberg *Graphic*), 64.

55. Hoover, *Memoirs*, 1: 11.
56. Agnes Minthorn Miles to Harriette Miles Odell, January 21, 1920, "Odell, Harriette Miles," Genealogy File, HHL.
57. Hoover, *Memoirs*, 1: 12.
58. Kidd, "Hoover: Rags and Riches Saga," 64.
59. Nash, *Life of Herbert Hoover,* 1:14.
60. Theodore Hoover, *Memoranda,* 57.
61. Henry John Minthorn to Rose Wilder Lane, "Lane, Rose Wilder," Genealogy File, HHL.
62. Ibid.
63. Hoover, *Memoirs*, 1: 2.
64. Ibid., 1:11.
65. Harriette Miles Odell to Theodore Hoover, n.d., "Lane, Rose Wilder," Genealogy File, HHL.
66. Minthorn to Lane, February 28, 1920.
67. "Hoover through the Eyes of His Puget Sound Cousin," Seattle *Daily Times,* February 12, 1928.
68. Clements, *Hoover, Conservation, and Consumerism,* 17.
69. Kidd, "Hoover: Rags to Riches Saga," 64.
70. Hoover, *Memoirs*, 1: 13.
71. Minthorn to Lane, February 28, 1920.
72. Theodore Hoover, *Memoranda,* 71; and James Prosek, *Trout: An Illustrated History* (New York: Knopf, 1977), 45–49.
73. "Hoover Popular Lad at Newberg," Portland *Sunday Oregonian,* March 3, 1929.
74. Alva W. Cook to Burt Brow∴ Barker, October 22, 1928, attached to Oral History Interview (OHI), Burt Brown Barker, October 17, 1967, HHL.
75. Hoover, *Memoirs*, 1: 11.
76. Minthorn to Lane, February 28, 1920.
77. Theodore Hoover, *Memoranda,* 57.
78. Ibid.
79. Minthorn to Lane, February 28, 1920; and Theodore Hoover, *Memoranda,* 56, 67, 68.
80. Burner, *Herbert Hoover,* 13.
81. Theodore Hoover, *Memoranda,* 67.
82. Hoover, *Memoirs*, 1: 2.
83. Clements, *Hoover, Conservation, and Consumerism,* 15.
84. Theodore Hoover, *Memoranda,* 71.
85. Hoover, *Memoirs*, 1: 13.
86. Theodore Hoover, *Memoranda,* 68.
87. Minthorn to Lane, February 28, 1920.
88. Burt Brown Barker, OHI.
89. Ibid.
90. Herbert Hoover, "Thank You, Miss Grey!" *Reader's Digest* (July 1959): 119.
91. Ibid.
92. Burt Brown Barker, OHI.
93. Ibid.
94. "Portland Uncle of Hoover Recalls Lesson in Fishing," Portland *Morning Oregonian,* no date, 1928.
95. Theodore Hoover, *Memoranda,* 72.
96. Ibid., 71.
97. Minthorn to Lane, February 28, 1920.

98. Hoover, "Let's Go Fishin'" *Colliers Weekly,* April 22, 1944; and Hoover, *Memoirs,* 1: 13–14.

99. Hoover, *Memoirs,* 1: 13–14.

100. Ibid.

101. Richard Dillon, *Siskiyou Trail: The Hudson's Bat Company Route to California* (New York: McGraw Hill, 1975), 16; and T. T. Greer, *Fifty Years in Oregon* (New York: Neale Publishing Co., 1911).

102. Madelynne Diness Sheehan and Dan Casali, *Fishing in Oregon,* 8th ed. (Portland, OR: Flying Pencil Publications, 1995), 123.

103. A. David Rodriguez, "The McKenzie Drift Boat," *Lane County [Oregon] Historian* vol. 29, no. 1 (Spring 1984), 25–26.

104. "The Boat the McKenzie River Spawned," Eugene [Oregon] *Register-Guard,* Section C, December 14, 1975; "Drifting through Time," Eugene [Oregon] *Register-Guard,* June 17, 1990; and the Springfield [Oregon] *News,* April 22, 1987.

105. Theodore Hoover, *Memoranda,* 72.

106. Hoover, *Memoirs,* 1: 14–15.

107. Professor Joseph Swain to Vernon Kellogg, 1920 in "Lane, Rose Wilder," Genealogy File, HHL.

108. Hoover, *Memoirs,* 1: 13.

Chapter 3: From Stanford to the Stars

109. Lane, *Making of Herbert Hoover,* 101.

110. Ibid., 105.

111. Nash, *Life of Herbert Hoover,* 1: 27.

112. Hoover, *Memoirs,* 1: 18.

113. Ibid.

114. Ibid., 19.

115. H. C. Hoover to Nell May Hill, July 19, 1894, *Call Number* 27, no. 2 (Spring 1966), 4, 6.

116. Hoover, *Memoirs,* 1: 19.

117. *America's National Parks* (Lincolnwood, IL: Publications International, 1990), 170–77.

118. John Muir, *My First Summer in the Sierra* (Boston: Houghton Mifflin, 1998).

119. Hoover, *Memoirs,* 1: 19.

120. H. C. Hoover to Nell May Hill, July 19, 1894, 4, 6.

121. Herbert Hoover to John C. Branner, September 2, 1894, Branner Papers, Box 25, HHL.

122. Ibid.

123. H. C. Hoover to Nell May Hill, November 9, 1894, 6, 8.

124. Hoover, *Memoirs,* 1: 23.

125. Lane, *Making of Herbert Hoover,* 155–56.

126. Burner, *Herbert Hoover,* 21.

127. Anne Beiser Allen, *An Independent Woman: The Life of Lou Henry Hoover* (Westport, CT: Greenwood Press, 2000), 7.

128. Ibid., 8.

129. Nancy A. Colbert, *Lou Henry Hoover: The Duty to Serve* (Greensboro, NC: Morgan Reynolds, 1998), 12.

130. Lou Henry Hoover Diary (LHHD), February 2, 1890, Subject File (SF), Lou Henry Hoover Papers (LHHP), HHL.

131. Ibid.

132. Ibid.

133. "Articles, Addresses and Statements, circa 1886–1898," SF, LHHP, HHL.
134. Allen, *Independent Woman*, 15.
135. Lane, *Making of Herbert Hoover*, 159.
136. H. C. Hoover to Nell May Hill, July 9, 1895, 9, 10.
137. Lane, *Making of Herbert Hoover*, 159.
138. Nash, *Life of Herbert Hoover*, 1: 39; and Smith, *Uncommon Man*, 70.
139. H. C. Hoover to Nell May Hill, July 9, 1895, 9, 10.
140. Ibid.
141. Ibid.
142. Herbert Hoover to May Hoover, August 4, 1895, Hoover, May 1895, Box 7, Pre-Commerce Correspondence, HHP, HHL.
143. Mark Twain, *Roughing It* (New York: Penguin Books, 1985), 188.
144. Herbert Hoover to May Hoover, August 4, 1895.
145. Ibid.
146. Hoover to Nell May Hill, July 9, 1895, 9, 10.
147. Edward B. Scott, *The Saga of Lake Tahoe* (Crystal Bay, Lake Tahoe, NV: Sierra Tahoe Publishing Co., 1957), 151.
148. Ibid.
149. Twain, *Roughing It*, 193.
150. Scott, *Saga of Lake Tahoe*, 156.
151. Hoover to Hill, September 7, 1895.
152. Twain, *Roughing It*, 273–74.
153. Hoover to Hill, September 7, 1895.
154. Ibid.
155. Ibid.
156. Ibid.
157. Burner, *Herbert Hoover*, 23.
158. Hoover, *Memoirs*, 1: 25.
159. Ibid.
160. Ibid.
161. Ibid., 1: 26.
162. Hoover comment (circa 1911) reported by Donald H. McLaughlin to George H. Nash, 1979, in Nash, *Life of Herbert Hoover*, 1: 46, 601.
163. Theodore Hoover, *Memoranda*, 95.
164. Hoover, *Memoirs*, 1: 27.
165. Smith, *Uncommon Man*, 73.
166. Burner, *Herbert Hoover*, 25–26.
167. Nash, *Life of Herbert Hoover*, 1: 50–51.

Chapter 4: A Relentless Pursuit of Money

168. Herbert Hoover to Burt Brown Barker, October 5, 1897, HHP, HHL.
169. Evelyn W. Allan, *The Key*, February 1944, quoted in Allen, *Independent Woman*, 20–21.
170. Nash, *Life of Herbert Hoover*, 1: 86–96 and Allen, *Independent Woman*, 21.
171. Burner, *Herbert Hoover*, 43.
172. "Chinese Character Studies," unpublished manuscript, LHHP, HHL.
173. Allen, *Independent Woman*, 29.
174. Nash, *Life of Herbert Hoover*, 1: 62.
175. LHHD, October 27, 1900, SF, LHHP, HHL.
176. Diana Preston, *The Boxer Rebellion* (New York: Berkley Books, 2000), 47–48.
177. Frederick Palmer, *Ladies Home Journal* (March 1929), Reprint File (RF), HHP, HHL.

178. Lou Henry Hoover to Evelyn Wight Allan, ca. August 1, 1900, Evelyn Wight Allan Papers, HHL.
179. Burner, *Herbert Hoover,* 38.
180. Hoover, *Memoirs,* 73.
181. Allen, *Independent Woman,* 43.
182. Nash, *Life of Herbert Hoover,* 1: 241.
183. Hoover to Theodore Hoover, July 21, 1904, McLean Papers, HHL.
184. Nash, *Life of Herbert Hoover,* 1: 348.
185. Ibid.
186. Map, Yosemite National Park California, U.S. Department of Interior, 2000.
187. Theodore Hoover, *Memoranda,* 131.
188. Ibid., 132.
189. Ibid.
190. Ibid.
191. Ibid., 132–33.
192. Ibid., 133.
193. Nash, *Life of Herbert Hoover,* 1: 348–49.
194. Allen, *Independent Woman,* 44–45.
195. Nash, *Life of Herbert Hoover,* 1: 497.
196. Hulda Hoover McLean, OHI, August 14, 1985, HHL; and Hulda Hoover McLean, *Uncle Bert: A Biographical Portrait of Herbert Hoover,* (no publisher, copyright by Hulda Hoover McLean, reprinted 1998), 8.
197. Nash, *Life of Herbert Hoover,* 1: 489.
198. Smith, *Uncommon Man,* 76.
199. Hoover, *Memoirs,* 1: 123.
200. Ibid., 124.
201. Smith, *Uncommon Man,* 76.
202. Will Irwin, *Herbert Hoover: A Reminiscent Biography* (New York: Century Co., 1928), 115–16.
203. Allen, *Independent Woman,* 47.
204. Eugene Lyons, OHI, October 4, 1968, HHL.
205. Lane, *Making of Herbert Hoover,* 310; and Victoria French Allen, OHI, no date, HHL.
206. Hoover, *Memoirs,* 1: 119

Chapter 5: The Great Humanitarian
207. Hoover, *Memoirs,* 1: 99.
208. Nash, *Life of Herbert Hoover,* 1: 569.
209. Smith, *Uncommon Man,* 80.
210. Hoover, *Memoirs,* 1: 124.
211. Nash, *Life of Herbert Hoover,* 1: 573.
212. Hoover, *Memoirs,* 1: 141.
213. Allen, *Independent Woman,* 62.
214. Smith, *Uncommon Man,* 80–81.
215. George H. Nash, *The Life of Herbert Hoover: The Humanitarian, 1914–1917,* vol. 2 (New York: W. W. Norton, 1988), 6.
216. Smith, *Uncommon Man,* 80.
217. Allen, *Independent Woman,* 62.
218. Nash, *Life of Herbert Hoover,* 2: 12.
219. Allen, *Independent Woman,* 67.
220. www.FirstWorldWar.com
221. Smith, *Uncommon Man,* 81.

222. Irwin, *Herbert Hoover*, 135.
223. Smith, *Uncommon Man*, 87.
224. Nash, *Life of Herbert Hoover*, 2: 362.
225. Benjamin M. Weissman, *Herbert Hoover and Famine Relief to Soviet Russia, 1921–23* (Stanford, CA: Hoover Institution Press, 1974), 24.
226. Smith, *Uncommon Man*, 87.
227. Nash, *Life of Herbert Hoover*, 2: 341.
228. Ibid., 351.
229. Horace Marden Albright, OHI, September 22, 1967, HHL.
230. Hoover, *Memoirs*, 1: 148.
231. Hugh Gibson to His Mother, November 11, 1917, Diaries and Notes, 1 Nov. 1917–Dec. 1917, Box 1, Hugh Gibson Papers, HHL.
232. Hugh Gibson to His Mother, April 25, 1920, Diaries and Notes, Jan. 1920–May 1920, Box 3, Hugh Gibson Papers, HHL.
233. Dale C. Mayer, *Dining with the Hoover Family* (West Branch, IA: Herbert Hoover Presidential Library, 1991), 50–51.
234. Allen, *Independent Woman*, 75.
235. Robert Cubbage, OHI, March 22, 1971, HHL.
236. Nina Emlen Judd and H. Lee Judd, OHI, November 1, 1970, HHL.
237. Hoover, *Memoirs*, 1: 482.
238. Gary Dean Best, *The Politics of American Individualism: Herbert Hoover in Transition, 1918–1921* (Westport, CT: Greenwood Press, 1975), 24.
239. John Maynard Keynes, *The Economic Consequences of the Peace* (New York: Harcourt, Brace and Howe, 1920), 247.

Chapter 6: The Restorative Blessings of Nature
240. Theodore Hoover, *Memoranda*, 218–19.
241. George H. Nash, *The Life of Herbert Hoover: Master of Emergencies, 1917–1918*, vol. 3 (New York: W. W. Norton, 1996), 438–39.
242. Hoover, *Memoirs*, 2: 3–4.
243. Lynette Iezzoni, *Influenza 1918: The Worst Epidemic in American History* (New York: T. V. Books, 1999), 17.
244. Marguerite Rickard Hoyt, OHI, May 30, 1967, HHL.
245. Herbert Hoover, *The Ordeal of Woodrow Wilson* (New York: McGraw-Hill, 1958), 271–78.
246. Robert Weibe, *The Search for Order, 1877–1920* (New York: Hill and Wang, 1967), quoted in Clements, *Hoover, Conservation, and Consumerism*, 1–2.
247. Hoover, *Memoirs*, 2: 3–4.
248. Ibid., 24–25.
249. Lucia Shepardson, "Camping with the Hoovers," June 23, 1929, New York *Herald Tribune Magazine*, 24–25.
250. "Don't Forget Joy!: Lou Henry Hoover and the Girl Scouts," in *Lou Henry Hoover: Essays on a Busy Life*, edited by Dale C. Mayer (Worland, WY: High Plains Publishing Co., 1994), 35–47.
251. "Hoover Here to Find Out If Fish Will Bite as of Yore," August 23, 1926, Portland *Oregonian*, Aug. 27–31, 1926, Box 13, CF, HHP, HHL.
252. John Roberts, *Illustrated Dictionary of Trout Flies* (Edison, NJ: Castle Books, 1998).
253. Herbert Hoover to Lou Henry Hoover, telegram, May 14, 1917, HHP, HHL.
254. Allen, *Independent Woman*, 89.
255. Ibid., 80.
256. Herbert Hoover to Lou Henry Hoover, telegram, April 14, 1917, HHP, HHL

257. Smith, *Uncommon Man*, 94.
258. Allen, *Independent Woman*, 80.
259. Bernice "Bunny" Miller, OHI, December 7, 1966, HHL.
260. Hulda Hoover McLean, *Uncle Bert*, 15; and Theodore Hoover, *Memoranda*, 225–34.
261. Mr. and Mrs. Van Ness Hoover Leavitt, OHI, September 23, 1967, HHL.
262. Burner, *Herbert Hoover*, 153; and Best, *Politics of American Individualism*, 65.
263. Best, *Politics of American Individualism*, 84.
264. Unidentified correspondent to Hugh Gibson, March 6, 1920, Ray Lyman Wilbur Papers, "Political—1920," Herbert Hoover Collection (HHC), Hoover Institution on War, Revolution and Peace (HI), in Craig Lloyd, *Aggressive Introvert* (Columbus: Ohio State University Press), 82.
265. Leslie Taylor, "Reflections in the Lake," 1, July 17, 1954, Bohemian Club and Grove, General, 1937–64, Box 36, Post-Presidential Subject (PPS), HHP, HHL.
266. G. William Domhoff, *The Bohemian Grove and Other Retreats* (New York: Harper and Row, 1974), 4.
267. Taylor, "Reflections in the Lake," 3.
268. Ibid.
269. Domhoff, *Bohemian Grove and Other Retreats*, 33.
270. Ibid., 46.
271. Ibid., 20–21.
272. "Bohemian Club Midsummer Encampment Notice 1927," HH Personal Clubs, HHP, HHL.
273. Alexander Bode, "Roughing It—with Comfort," October 15, 1954, Palo Alto [California] *Times*, Bohemian Club and Grove, General 1937–64, Box 36, PPS, HHP, HHL.
274. Will Rodgers, "Three Weeks; or, What Happens in Bohemia," August 18, 1928, Greensboro [North Carolina] *Daily Record*, CF, HHP, HHL.
275. Domhoff, *Bohemian Grove and Other Retreats*, 11.
276. Robert H. Fletcher, *The Annals of the Bohemian Club* (San Francisco: Hicks-Judd Company, 1900), vol. 1, 1872–80, 236–37.
277. Frank Brandegee to Warren Harding, December 28, 1920, Harding Papers, Box 368, Folder 2601–1, Item 174897, quoted in Robert K. Murray, "Herbert Hoover and the Harding Cabinet," in *Herbert Hoover as Secretary of Commerce: Studies in New Era Thought and Practice*, edited by Ellis W. Hawley (Iowa City: University of Iowa Press, 1981), 19.
278. Smith, *Uncommon Man*, 97.
279. Hoover, *Memoirs*, 2: 186.
280. Sydney Sullivan Parker, OHI.
281. Marguerite Rickard Hoyt, OHI.
282. Sydney Sullivan Parker, OHI.
283. Allen, *Independent Woman*, 84.
284. Sydney Sullivan Parker, OHI.
285. Mr. and Mrs. Kosta Boris, OHI, October 2, 1966, HHL.
286. Sydney Sullivan Parker, OHI.
287. Ibid., 11–12.
288. Marguerite Rickard Hoyt, OHI.
289. Herbert Hoover, *The Memoirs of Herbert Hoover: The Cabinet and the Presidency*, vol.2 (New York: Macmillan, 1952), 42.
290. "Herbert Hoover Goes Fishin'," no date, ca. October 1921, Fishing Folder, Box 331, HHC, HI.
291. Hoover, *Memoirs*, 2: 63–64.

292. "Herbert Hoover Goes Fishin'," HHC, HI
293. Grover Cleveland, *Fishing and Shooting Sketches* (New York: Outing Publishing Co., 1906), 92–94.
294. Lou Henry Hoover to Captain Dryden, July 17, 1922, SF Trips, Kilkenny: Trips on 1922–23, Box 112, LHHP, HHL and Allan Hoover to Captain Dryden, June 20, 1922, SF Trips, Kilkenny: Trips on 1922–23, Box 112, LHHP, HHL.
295. Burner, *Herbert Hoover*, 46.
296. Herbert Hoover, *American Individualism* (Garden City, NY: Doubleday, Page, & Co., 1922).
297. Smith, *Uncommon Man*, 95.
298. Hoover, *American Individualism*, 17–18.
299. Ibid., 10.
300. Ibid., 50–51.
301. Clements, *Hoover, Conservation and Consumerism*, 39.
302. Herbert Hoover, *A Remedy for Disappearing Game Fishes* (New York: Huntington Press, 1930), 5.
303. Hoover, *Memoirs*, 2: 142–45.
304. Clements, *Hoover, Conservation and Consumerism*, 70–71.
305. Ibid., 70.
306. Ibid., 71.
307. Mark Sullivan, *Our Times: America at the Birth of the Twentieth Century*, edited and with new material by Dan Rather (New York: Scribner, 2000), 550.
308. Clements, *Hoover, Conservation and Consumerism*, 71.
309. Martha Nudel, "Williamson H. Dilg: 1867–1927," *Outdoor America: The Official Publication of the Izaak Walton League of America* (Summer 1997), 7.
310. Ibid.
311. William Voigt, Jr., *Born with Fists Doubled: Defending Outdoor America* (Gaithersburg, MD: Izaak Walton League Endowment of America, 1992), 21–22.
312. Hoover, "Izaak Walton League of America, 1922–23," July 1922 Box 346, Commerce Papers, HHP, HHL.
313. Herbert Hoover, "In Praise of Izaak Walton," *Atlantic* (June 1927), 819.
314. Clements, *Hoover, Conservation, and Consumerism*, 51.
315. Nudel, "Williamson H. Dilg," 7.
316. Robert K. Murray, *The Harding Era: Warren G. Harding and His Administration* (Minneapolis: University of Minnesota Press, 1969), 439.
317. Ibid., 442.
318. Hoover, *Memoirs*, 2: 48.
319. Murray, *Harding Era*, 440.
320. Ibid., 442.
321. Robert H. Ferrell, *The Strange Deaths of President Harding* (Columbia: University of Missouri Press, 1996), 1.
322. Hoover, *Memoirs*, 2: 49.
323. Murray, *Harding Era*, 434–37.
324. Hoover, *Memoirs*, 2: 49.
325. Harold Phelps Stokes, "A Correspondent's Diary of Harding's Alaskan Trip," July 31, 1923, Part 2, New York *Evening Post*, RF, HHP, HHL.
326. Ibid.
327. William C. Mullendore Diary, July 8, 1923, 1, Mullendore Papers, HHL.
328. Ferrell, *Strange Deaths of President Harding*, 12.
329. Mullendore Diary, July 18, 1923, 7, HHL.
330. Henry C. Wallace to Family, July 23, 1923, Special Collections, Henry C. Wallace Papers, University of Iowa Libraries, Iowa City, Iowa.
331. Mullendore Diary, July 18, 1923, 7, HHP.

332. "Hoover Lands 50 Pound Fish in Hour Fight," Everett [Washington] *News*, July 26, 1923, CF, HHP, HHL; and "President Stops Campbell River, British Columbia," Seward [Alaska] *Gateway*, July 26, 1923, CF, HHP, HHL.
333. Stephen J. May, *Maverick Heart: The Further Adventures of Zane Grey* (Athens, OH: University Press, 2000), 153.
334. Mullendore Diary, July 25, 1923, 9, HHL.
335. Stokes, "A Correspondent's Diary of Harding's Alaskan Trip," Part 2, CF, HHP, HHL.
336. May, *Maverick Heart*, 153.
337. Mullendore Diary, July 25, 1923, 9, HHL.
338. Hoover, *Memoirs*, 2: 50.
339. Ibid.
340. Quoted in Ferrell, *Strange Deaths of President Harding*, 13.
341. Murray, *Harding Era*, 448–49.
342. Ibid., 449.
343. Ferrell, *Strange Deaths of President Harding*, 19–20.
344. Ibid., 24.
345. Hoover, *Memoirs*, 2: 52.
346. Ibid., 53.
347. Robert K. Murray, "Herbert Hoover and the Harding Cabinet," in Ellis W. Hawley, *Herbert Hoover, 1921–1928* (Iowa City: University of Iowa Press, 1981), 20–21.
348. Robert H. Ferrell, *The Presidency of Calvin Coolidge* (Lawrence: University Press of Kansas, 1998), 66.
349. Murray, "Herbert Hoover and the Harding Cabinet," 37.
350. Hoover, *Memoirs*, 2: 115.
351. Frederic Walcott to Herbert Hoover, March 19, 1921, Walcott, Frederic C., 1921–28, Box 682, Commerce Papers, HHL.
352. Jerry Wilkinson, "History of Long Key," www.keyshistory.org/longkey.html, 1–5.
353. Ibid., 2.
354. Ibid., 3.
355. Theodore Brooke, Review of *Tales of Fishes, Harper's* (August 1919), 831 quoted in Carlton Jackson, *Zane Grey* (Boston: Twayne Publishers, 1973), 128.
356. May, *Maverick Heart*, 189.
357. Wilkinson, "History of Long Key," 3.
358. Smith, *Uncommon Man*, 233.
359. John van der Zee, *The Greatest Men's Party on Earth: Inside the Bohemian Grove* (New York: Harcourt, Brace, Jovanovich, 1974), 92.
360. Ibid.
361. Smith, *Uncommon Man*, 233.
362. van der Zee, *Greatest Men's Party on Earth*, 173.
363. Leo C. Monahan to Captain H. Almy, September 22, 1924, "Trips on the Kilkenny," SF, Box 112, LHHP, HHL.
364. Mark Sullivan, Jr., OHI, November 30, 1968, HHL.
365. Key West *Daily News* to Herbert Hoover, June 5, 1925, telegram, "Fishing 1924–1927," Commerce Papers, HHP, HHL.
366. Ibid.
367. Miami *Herald* to Herbert Hoover, June 5, 1925, telegram, "Fishing 1924–1927," Commerce Papers, HHP, HHL.
368. Jacob Rosengrowen, President Miami Chamber of Commerce to Herbert Hoover, June 5, 1925, telegram, "Fishing 1924–1927," Commerce Papers, HHP, HHL.

369. William J. Bryan to Herbert Hoover, June 5, 1925, telegram, "Fishing 1924–1927, Commerce Papers, HHP, HHL.
370. Rosengrowen to Hoover, June 5, 1925, telegram, "Fishing 1924–1927," Commerce Papers, HHP, HHL.
371. Ancient Order of Followers of Walton to Herbert Hoover, June 5, 1925, telegram, "Fishing 1924–1927," Commerce Papers, HHP, HHL.
372. William A. Thomas, Officer in Charge to Herbert Hoover, June 5, 1925, telegram, "Fishing 1924–1927," Commerce Papers, HHP, HHL.
373. Los Angeles Chamber of Commerce to Herbert Hoover, June 5, 1925, telegram. "Fishing 1924–1927," Commerce Papers, HHP, HHL.
374. "200 Hundred Place Names in Siskiyou County," *Siskiyou Pioneer and Yearbook* 5, no. 5 (1982): 83.
375. Patricia L. Pilling, "Herbert Hoover in the Siskiyou Mountains," *Siskiyou Pioneer and Yearbook* 4, no. 7 (1974), in Patricia L. Pilling Collection, General Accession 197/3, HHL.
376. Ibid.
377. Ibid.
378. Hoover, *Memoirs,* 2: 112–24.
379. Ibid., 2: 112–13.
380. Hoover's Daily Calendar, August 14–21, 1926, HHP, HHL.
381. "Train Stops in Jerkwater Village while Hoover Welcomes Boyhood Chum," August 21, 1926, Spokane [Washington] *Chronicle,* CF, HHP, HHL.
382. David A. Hazen, "Hoover Here to Rest, Dig Worms, Fishin' Will Be Chief Concern," August 23, 1926, Portland *Oregonian,* CF, HHP, HHL.
383. Harold M. Sims, "Hoover Revisits Boyhood Scenes," August 29, 1926, Portland *Oregonian,* CF, HHP, HHL.
384. George O'Neal, "Hoover Lured by Old Fishing Hole of Boyhood Days," August 23, 1926, Portland [Oregon] *Journal,* CF, HHP, HHL.
385. Hazen, "Hoover Here to Rest."
386. Ibid.
387. O'Neal, "Hoover Lured by Old Fishing Hole."
388. Hazen, "Hoover Here to Rest."
389. Ibid.
390. Ibid.
391. Ibid.
392. Sims, "Hoover Revisits Boyhood Scenes."
393. "Wharton Moved to Grants Pass Early in 1903," October 12, 1934, Grants Pass [Oregon] *Bulletin,* Josephine County Historical Society.
394. "Hoover Fails to Land Fish from Rogue," July 31, 1928, Medford [Oregon] *Daily News,* Southern Oregon Historical Society; and Florence Arman with Glen Wooldridge, *The Rogue: A River to Run* (Grants Pass, OR: Bulletin Publishing Co., 1982), 98–99.
395. "'Toggery Bill' Isaacs Sells Rogue River Home," April 27, 1958, Medford [Oregon] *Mail Tribune,* Scrapbook, Box 4, Larry Richey Papers, HHL.
396. H. H. Pringle, "The Time of Toggery Bill," an obituary, ca. 1961, Box 1588, William Thorndike Sr. Papers, Southern Oregon Historical Society, Medford, Oregon.
397. "Hoover Casts in Rogue," August 31, 1926, Portland *Oregonian,* CF, HHP, HHL.
398. Pringle, "The Time of Toggery Bill."
399. Lou Henry Hoover to Philippi Harding, July 7, 1921, Correspondence File, LHHP, HHL.

400. Hoover, *Memoirs*, 2: 125.
401. John M. Barry, *Rising Tide: The Great Mississippi Flood of 1927 and How It Changed America* (New York: Simon and Schuster, 1997), 176–78.
402. Ibid., 200.
403. Ibid., 194–95, 200–1.
404. Ibid., 262.
405. Ibid., 273.
406. Nash, *Life of Herbert Hoover*, 3: iii; and Burner, *Herbert Hoover*, 193.
407. Quoted in Burner, *Herbert Hoover*, 193.
408. Barry, *Rising Tide*, 280.
409. Hoover, *Memoirs*, 2: 126.
410. Ibid., 194.
411. "It Seems Incredible," August 18, 1927, New York *World*, CF, HHP, HHL.
412. Burner, *Herbert Hoover*, 193.
413. Ibid.
414. Albright, OHI, 12.
415. Ibid., 20
416. Ibid., 21.
417. Ibid., 24.
418. Roger Tanner, "Special Guests, Herbert Hoover, Secretary of Commerce," no date (July 15 or 16, 1927), Patricia L. Pilling Collection, General Accession 197/3.
419. Ibid.
420. Albright, OHI.
421. Hoover, *Memoirs*, 2: 190.
422. "Hoover's Fish Snub Him," August 18, 1927, New York *World*, CF, HHP, HHL.
423. Ferrell, *Presidency of Calvin Coolidge*, 66.
424. Ibid., 190–91.
425. "Hoover Will Fish while Aids Fight," February 14, 1928, New York *World*, CF, HHP, HHL; and "Hoover Speaks Here on Feb. 21; Goes Fishing," February 14, 1928, New York *Herald Tribune*, CF, HHP, HHL.
426. Ibid., 191.
427. Hoover, *Memoirs*, 2: 191.
428. "Hoover Lands 5 Dolphin on First Day of Fishing," August 16, 1928, New York *Herald Tribune*, CF, HHP, HHL.
429. Quoted in Burner, *Herbert Hoover*, 198.
430. "Miami Plans Events for Secretary Hoover and Wife on Visit," February 16, 1928, New York *Evening Post*, CF, HHP, HHL.
431. Burner, *Herbert Hoover*, 198–99.
432. "Mellon on Hoover," May 14, 1928, New York *Evening Post*, CF, HHP, HHL.
433. Judd and Judd, OHI.
434. John M. McCullough, "Hoover Hooks Fish after Lonely Vigil in Lycoming Hills," May 15, 1928, Philadelphia *Inquirer*, CF, HHP.
435. "Hip-Booted Hoover Shows His Trout," May 16, 1928, New York *Evening Post*, CF, HHP, HHL.
436. Ibid.
437. Ibid.
438. Judd and Judd, OHI.
439. Burner, *Herbert Hoover*, 199–200.
440. Donald R. McCoy, "To the White House: Herbert Hoover, August 1927–March 1929," in *The Hoover Presidency: A Reappraisal*, edited by Martin L. Fausold and George T. Mazuzan (Albany: State University of New York Press, 1974), 39.

441. Dorothy E. Weyandt, *I Was a Guide for Three U.S. Presidents* (no publisher, 1976), 11.
442. Helen Hullitt Lowry, "Anglers' Eden Hides the President," newspaper clipping, July 1928, in Rebekah Knight Cochran, President Coolidge Brule River Scrapbook (Brule River Scrapbook), 1928, microfilm, 1052, P91 3546, Madison, Wisconsin State Historical Society.
443. Weyandt, *I Was a Guide for Three U.S. Presidents,* 10–12.
444. Ibid., 12.
445. Lowry, "Anglers' Eden Hides the President," Brule River Scrapbook.
446. Ibid., 12–13.
447. "Clay Pierce Plans Brule Visit in Fall," newspaper clipping, Brule River Scrapbook.
448. Smith, *Uncommon Man,* 45.
449. Allan Reid to Hebert Hoover, January 17, 1928, Fisheries Bureau to FUC, Fishing 1928, Box 205, Commerce Papers, HHP, HHL.
450. Lowry, "Anglers' Eden Hides the President," Brule River Scrapbook.
451. "Guide Injured President Tries Trap Shooting," July 1928, Duluth *Herald,* Brule River Scrapbook.
452. Ibid.
453. Weyandt, *I Was a Guide for Three U.S. Presidents,* 74–78.
454. Ferrell, *Presidency of Calvin Coolidge,* 197.
455. "Hoover Goes through City," August 28, 1920, Superior [Wisconsin] *Telegram;* and "Herbert Hoover Superior Visitor," August 29, 1920, [Superior] Wisconsin *Sunday Times,* Douglas County [Wisconsin] Historical Society.
456. Weyandt, *I Was a Guide for Three U.S. Presidents,* 185.
457. Ibid.
458. Ibid., 188.
459. Ibid., 190–91.
460. Ibid., 195.
461. Ibid., 203.
462. Ibid., 207.
463. Ibid., 215.
464. Ibid., 218–19.
465. Ibid., 221.
466. Allen, *Independent Woman,* 117.
467. "Hoover Says He Goes Fishing to Escape Frenzies of Jazz," August 1, 1928, New York *World,* CF, HHP, HHL.
468. Ibid.
469. Ibid.
470. Herbert Hoover, "In Praise of Izaak Walton," *Atlantic Monthly* (June 1927), 813–19, RF, HHP, HHL.
471. Izaak Walton and Charles Cotton, *The Compleat Angler* (New York: Oxford University Press, 1991).
472. Ibid., xxi.
473. Ibid., xxiii.
474. Ibid.
475. Edgar A. Guest, "Fishing," in *All in a Lifetime* (Miami, FL: Granger Books, 1976, reprint), 157.
476. Andrew Genzoli, "Redwood Country," January 17, 1975, Humboldt [California] *Times-Standard,* Patricia L. Pilling Collection, Eureka, California, General Accession 197/3, HHL.
477. "Hoover Fails to Land Fish from Rogue," July 31, 1928, Medford [Oregon] *Daily News,* Southern Oregon Historical Society.

478. Ibid.
479. Ibid.
480. "Hoover Will Speak in Border States," August 1, 1928, *New York Times*, CF, HHP, HHL.
481. Philip Kinsley, "Hoover's Trout Luck Turns at His Old Resort," August 1, 1928, Chicago *Daily Tribune*, CF, HHP, HHL.
482. Ibid.
483. "Hoover, Deep in Woods, Shows Skill with Rod," August 1, 1928, Springfield [Massachusetts] *Daily Republican*, CF, HHP, HHL.
484. Philip Kingsley, "Hoover's Brief Vacation Ends; Due Home Today," August 1, 1928, Chicago *Daily Tribune*, CF, HHP, HHL.
485. "Hoover Gets Nice String of Rainbows," August 1, 1928, Medford [Oregon] *Daily News*, Southern Oregon Historical Society.
486. William K. Hutchinson, "45 with Hoover Party Share 35 Trout," August 1, 1928, Washington *Times*, CF, HHP, HHL.
487. "Hoover Enjoys His Fishing, Catches 13," August 1, 1928, Birmingham [Alabama] *News*, CF, HHP, HHL.
488. "Hoover Starts Back to Work," August 1, 1928, Louisville [Kentucky] *Courier-Journal*, CF, HHP, HHL.
489. "Hoover Hooks but Loses One, Decides Burning Issues 'More Bites Better Trout,'" August 2, 1928, New York *World*, CF, HHP, HHL.
490. Edwin S. McIntosh, "Hoover to Put Final Touches on His Speech," August 2, 1928, New York *Herald Tribune*, CF, HHP, HHL.
491. "Hoover Says Issue Now Is More Trout," August 2, 1928, New York *Evening Post*, CF, HHP, HHL.
492. Ray Lyman Wilbur, *Memoirs, 1875–1960* (Palo Alto, CA: Stanford University Press, 1960), 398.
493. Ibid., 397.
494. Herbert Hoover, *The New Day: Campaign Speeches of Herbert Hoover, 1928* (Stanford, CA: Stanford University Press, 1928).
495. Smith, *Uncommon Man*, 105.
496. McCoy, "To the White House," 42.
497. Eugene Lyons, *Herbert Hoover: A Biography* (New York: Doubleday, 1964), 179.
498. James Quinten Cahill, "Herbert Hoover's Early Schooling in Iowa and Its Place in Presidential Politics, Community Memory, and Personal Identity," *Annals of Iowa* 61, no. 2 (Spring 2002): 151–91.
499. Ibid., 161.
500. Hoover, *Memoirs*, 2: 207–8.
501. Smith, *Uncommon Man*, 104.
502. *To the Best of My Ability: The American Presidents*, edited by James M. McPherson (London: Dorling Kindersley, 2000), 412.
503. Edgar Allen McDowell, OHI, September 14, 1982, HHL.
504. Ibid.
505. Dorothy Bowen to Marjorie Bowen, November 7, 1928, courtesy of Marjorie Bowen Gal, quoted in Allen, *Independent Woman*, 117–18.
506. "Chief Yeoman," *Time*, December 3, 1928, 7.
507. Ibid.
508. Allen, *Independent Woman*, 118.
509. Eugene P. Thackrey, "Gay Throngs Greet Hoovers in Miami," January 23, 1929, New York *World*, CF, HHP, HHL.
510. Ibid.
511. Mark Sullivan, "Hoover Vacation Being Passed on Man-Made Isle," January 25, 1929, New York *Herald Tribune*, CF, HHP, HHL.

512. Eugene P. Thackrey, "Hoover Closely Guarded on Rail Trip to Florida," January 22, 1929, New York *World*, CF, HHP, HHL.
513. Sullivan, "Hoover Vacation."
514. "Hoover Returns from Angling Trip," January 27, 1929, *New York Times*, CF, HHP, HHL.
515. J. Russell Young, "Hoover Is Anxious to Land Sailfish," January 25, 1929, Washington *Star*, CF, HHP, HHL.
516. Eugene P. Thackrey, "Hoover Wrestles with His Speech," January 31, 1929, New York *World*, CF, HHP, HHL.
517. "Landed Him! Hoover Gets First Sailfish," February 1, 1929, Miami *Herald*, "Fishing Folder," Box 331, Subject File, HHC, HI.
518. Ibid.
519. "Hoover Sailing around Florida to Greet Edison," February 10, 1929, New York *Herald Tribune*, CF, HHP, HHL.
520. Ibid.
521. Carter Field, "Hoover Returns to Miami Beach without Tarpon," February 13, 1929, New York *Herald Tribune*, CF, HHP, HHL.
522. "Lindbergh Goes Fishing before Dining with Hoover," February 15, 1929, New York *World*, CF, HHP, HHL.
523. Thomas F. Healey, "Hoover Returning Early Next Week," February 13, 1929, New York *Evening Post*, CF, HHP, HHL.
524. Willis J. Abbott, "Watching the World Go By," November 27, 1932, *Christian Science Monitor*, RF, HHP, HHL.

Chapter 7: The Fisherman President

525. Joan Hoff Wilson, *Herbert Hoover: Forgotten Progressive* (Prospect Heights, IL: Waveland Press, 1975), 134–36.
526. Ibid.
527. "Hoover Turns to Outdoors Early for His Exercise," April 13, 1929, Washington *Times*, CF, HHP, HHL.
528. John Chamberlain, "New Glory for the Medicine Ball," April 7, 1929, *New York Times;* and "Exercise with Hoover," April 13, 1929, *New York Times*, CF, HHP, HHL.
529. Edmund W. Starling, *Starling of the White House* (New York: Simon and Schuster, 1946), 283–84.
530. Albright, OHI.
531. Ibid.
532. Thomas Lomay Hunter, *The President's Camp on the Rapidan* (Roanoke: Virginia State Commission on Conservation, 1930), 6.
533. Albright, OHI.
534. Darwin Lambert, "Herbert Hoover's Hideaway," *Shenandoah Natural History Association Bulletin*, no. 4, (1971): 9–10.
535. Allen, *Independent Woman*, 124–125.
536. "Hoover Bars Press Men and Photographers on Trip Today to Virginia Fishing Preserve," March 30, 1929, *New York Times*, CF, HHP, HHL.
537. Herbert Hoover, "Address to the Gridiron Club," April 13, 1929, *Herbert Hoover, Public Papers of the Presidents of the United States, 1929* (Washington, DC: United States Government Printing Office, 1974), 69
538. "Rain Puts an End to Hoover Fishing Trip," March 30, 1929, Washington *Times*, CF, HHP, HHL.
539. "President and Mrs. Hoover Enjoy Outing, Seeking Site in Virginia for Fishing Camp," April 7, 1929, *New York Times;* and "President Selects Camp Site On

Visit to Shenandoah Park," April 7, 1929, New York *Herald Tribune,* CF, HHP, HHL.

540. Hoover, *Memoirs,* 2: 322.
541. "Mayflower Ends Long Career," March 31, 1929, *New York Times,* CF, HHP, HHL.
542. Lambert, *Herbert Hoover's Hideaway,* 41.
543. Darwin Lambert, "The Rapidan Facet of Herbert Hoover," *Herbert Hoover Reassessed* (Washington, DC: United States Government Printing Office, 1981), 21.
544. Ibid.
545. "President's Vacation Land," March 20, 1929, Frederick *Daily News,* CF, HHP, HHL; and "President Goes Fishing on Maryland Preserve," May 12, 1929, New York *Herald Tribune,* CF, HHP, HHL.
546. Ibid.
547. "Hoover Catches Eight Trout on a Fishing Trip in Maryland," May 12, 1929, *New York Times,* CF, HHP, HHL.
548. "Third Fishing Ground Selected for Hoover," April 13, 1929, New York *World,* CF, HHP, HHL.
549. "President Has Muddy Outing," June 11, 1929, Washington *Times,* CF, HHP, HHL.
550. "Hoover Party Lands Fish for Two Meals," June 10, 1929, *New York Times,* CF, HHP, HHL.
551. Ibid.
552. Starling, *Starling of the White House,* 284.
553. Joel T. Boone Collection, Autobiography—Hoover Administration, Table of Contents to page 700A, Box 1, HHL.
554. Ibid.
555. Ibid.
556. Albright, OHI.
557. Lambert, *Herbert Hoover's Hideaway,* 59.
558. Ibid., 62.
559. "Marine Band Plays," August 18, 1929, Washington *Herald,* CF, HHP, HHL.
560. Ibid.
561. Lambert, *Herbert Hoover's Hideaway,* 63.
562. "Address of President Hoover at Madison Courthouse, Virginia, August 17, 1929," Rapidan Camp, Madison County Meeting, Box 191, PPS, HPP, HHL.
563. Burner, *Herbert Hoover,* 289–93.
564. Ibid., 290.
565. Ibid., 291.
566. Lambert, *Herbert Hoover's Hideaway,* 66–67.
567. Ibid., 77.
568. Burner, *Herbert Hoover,* 290–91.
569. Harris Gaylord Warren, *Herbert Hoover and the Great Depression* (New York: W. W. Norton, 1967), 103–4.
570. Smith, *Uncommon Man,* 114.
571. Warren, *Herbert Hoover and the Great Depression,* 104–5.
572. Parker, OHI.
573. David M. Kennedy, *Freedom from Fear: The American People in Depression and War, 1929–1945* (New York: Oxford University Press, 1999), 39–40.
574. "Hoover Clears Deck for Florida Trip," February 8, 1930, Boston *Evening Transcript* and "Hoover Will Leave Capital Today for Florida; Fishing Party Includes Wife and Three Friends," February 8, 1929, *New York Times,* CF, HHP, HHL.

575. Thomas F. Healey, "President Casts Line for Game Florida Fish," February 10, 1930, New York *Post*, CF, HHP, HHL.

576. "Hoover Hooks a 45-Pound Fish," February 10, 1930, New York *Sun*, CF, HHP, HHL.

577. "Hoover in First Try Lands 45-Pounder," February 11, 1929, *New York Times*, CF, HHP, HHL.

578. "Hoover Seeking Edible Fish, Gets a Mackerel, as Well as Four Bonitas and Three Barracudas," February 12, 1930, *New York Times*, CF, HHP, HHL.

579. Ibid.

580. "Hoover's Sail Fish Beaten by Guest's," February 13, 1930, *New York Times*, CF, HHP, HHL.

581. "Luckless, Mr. Hoover Sees Mrs. Stone Get Prize Fish," February 15, 1930, New York *Graphic*, CF, HHP, HHL.

582. "Hoover Halts Own Angling to Watch Mrs. Stone Wage Fight to Land Big Sailfish," February 13, 1930, New York *World*, CF, HHP, HHL.

583. "Fish Elude Hoover; Vacation Nears End," February 15, 1930, *New York Times*, CF, HHP, HHL.

584. Ibid.

585. "Hoover Begins Work in Car Bound North," February 17, 1930, *New York Times*, CF, HHP, HHL.

586. Kennedy, *Freedom from Fear*, 56.

587. Ibid., 59.

588. "President Fishing in Pennsylvania," May 31, 1930, New York *Evening Post*, CF, HHP, HHL.

589. Ibid.; and "President Leaves to Make Address," May 30, 1930, Washington *Star*, CF, HHP, HHL.

590. John T. Whitaker, "President Gets 8 Brook Trout at Cooke Camp," June 1, 1930, New York *Herald Tribune*, CF, HHP, HHL.

591. Ibid.

592. Ibid.

593. Judd and Judd, OHI.

594. Jay N. Darling, *As Ding Saw Hoover* (Ames: Iowa State College Press, 1954), 17–18.

595. J. N. Darling to George Matthew Adams, July 29, 1944, Special Collections, Jay "Ding" Darling Papers, University of Iowa Libraries, Iowa City, Iowa.

596. Burner, *Herbert Hoover*, 254.

597. Ibid., 263

598. Ibid., 262

599. Kennedy, *Freedom from Fear*, 65–66.

600. Ibid., 72–73.

601. January 13, 1932, Theodore Joslin Diary, HHL.

602. Lewis L. Gould, "A Neglected First Lady," Mayer, *Essays on a Busy Life*, 71.

603. Smith, *Uncommon Man*, 121.

604. William Allen White to M. F. Amrine, Lansing, Kansas, February 4, 1931, *Selected Letters of William Allen White, 1899–1943*, edited by Walter Johnson (New York: Henry Holt, 1947), 311.

605. Boone Diary, 22, 1207.

606. "Hoover Arrives at Dawn to Fish in Chesapeake," August 16, 1932, Washington *Herald*, CF, HHP, HHL.

607. Boone Diary, 22, 1207.

608. Ibid., 22, 208.

609. Quoted in "Hoover Catches Fifteen Trout in Chesapeake; Veteran Fisherman Guide Concedes His Skill," August 17, 1932, *New York Times*, CF, HHP, HHL.

610. Quoted in Smith, *Uncommon Man,* 143–44.
611. Geoffrey C. Ward, *A First-Class Temperament: The Emergence of Franklin Roosevelt* (New York: Harper and Row, 1989), xv.
612. Burner, *Herbert Hoover,* 317.
613. Allen, *Independent Woman,* 140.
614. Coleman B. Jones, "Hoover Passes Christmas Eve at Island Party," December 25, 1932, New York *Herald Tribune,* CF, HHP, HHL.
615. "Hoover Is Luckless as Georgia Angler," December 25, 1932, *New York Times,* CF, HHP, HHL.
616. Ibid.
617. Allen G. Breed, "What Is Natural? Pristine Island's Matriarch Fights for Beloved Feral Pigs," June 24, 2001, Savannah *Morning News;* and "General Information about Ossabaw Island," Georgia Department of Natural Resources, Wildlife Resources Division, georgiawildlife.dnr.ga.us.
618. "President Fishes but Luck Is Poor," December 25, 1932, Washington *Post,* CF, HHP, HHL.
619. Judi Griggs and Kara Norman, "Sea Island and the Cloister: A Historical Perspective," (Sea Island, GA: Sea Island Company, 2003).
620. Richard J. Lenz, *Longstreet Highroad Guide to the Georgia Coast and Okefenokee* (Decatur, GA: Longstreet Press, 1999), 4–5.
621. "Hoover and Guests Reach Savannah for Vacation Cruising," December 24, 1932, Washington *News,* CF, HHP, HHL.
622. "Hoover Fishes in Small Boat as Fleet Coals," December 24, 1932, New York *Herald Tribune,* CF, HHP, HHL.
623. Boone Diary, 22, 1382.
624. "Hoover Hits Luck, Gets 7-Foot Fish," December 31, 1932, *New York Times,* CF, HHP, HHL.
625. Boone Diary, 22, 1380.
626. Hoover, *Fishing for Fun and to Wash Your Soul,* 61.
627. "Hoover Hits Luck, Gets 7-Foot Fish," December 31, 1932, *New York Times.*
628. Boone Diary, 22, 1378.
629. Ibid.
630. "Hoover Wins 46-Minute Battle with Sailfish as Luck Keeps Up," January 1, 1933, New York *Herald Tribune,* CF, HHP, HHL.
631. Boone Diary, 22, 1379.
632. "Hoover Conquers Two More Sailfish," January 1, 1933, *New York Times,* CF, HHP, HHL.
633. Ibid.
634. Boone Diary, 22, 1378.
635. "Hoover Returning Works on Train," January 3, 1933, *New York Times,* CF, HHP, HHL.
636. Kennedy, *Freedom from Fear,* 132–33.
637. Smith, *Uncommon Man,* 164.

Chapter 8: Fishing for Fun and to Wash Your Soul

638. Bob Greene, *Duty* (New York: Harper Collins, 1998), 3.
639. Albright, OHI, 59–60.
640. Smith, *Uncommon Man,* 171.
641. "Herbert Hoover, Ogden Mills, Pay Visit to Nevada," April 2, 1933, [Reno] Nevada *State Journal;* and "Herbert Hoover and Party Enjoy Forty Hour Visit Here," April 3, 1933, Reno [Nevada] *Evening Gazette,* Nevada Historical Society.
642. Smith, *Uncommon Man,* 174–75.

643. Mr. and Mrs. William I. Nichols, OHI, October 5, 1968, HHL.
644. Ibid.
645. Ibid.
646. Ibid.
647. Ibid.
648. Ibid.
649. "Hoover Fishing at Pyramid Lake Today," July 1, 1933, Nevada *State Journal,* Nevada Historical Society, Reno.
650. David W. Toll, "A Brief History and Description of Pyramid Lake, Nevada," in *The Complete Nevada Traveler* (Virginia City, NV: Gold Hill Publishing, 1999), 71–72.
651. Ibid.
652. Ray Lyman Wilbur, Jr., OHI, November 24, 1971, HHL.
653. "Hoover Catches Smallest Trout at Desert Lake," July 8, 1933, Reno [Nevada] *Evening Gazette,* Nevada Historical Society.
654. Gary Dean Best, *Herbert Hoover: The Postpresidential Years, 1933–1964,* vol. 1 (Stanford, CA: Hoover Institution Press, 1983), 13–14.
655. Smith, *Uncommon Man,* 234.
656. Ibid.
657. Ray Lyman Wilbur to Wooley Camp Associates, December 27, 1937, PPI-Wilbur, Ray Lyman, HHP, HHL.
658. Darling, *As Ding Saw Hoover,* 22–23.
659. Ibid., 23–24.
660. Ibid.
661. Ibid., 24.
662. Ibid.
663. Coonie Briggs to Hoover, July 10, 1936, PPI-Travis, W.E., HHP, HHL.
664. Art Ryon, "Ham on Ryon: Mr. Hoover, the Fish Are Biting," August 14, 1961, Los Angeles *Times,* CF, HHP, HHL.
665. W. E. Travis to Hoover, July 18, 1936, PPI, HHP, HHL.
666. "In Fond Memory of Honolulu School Days," May 5, 1997, Siskiyou *Daily News,* Yerka, California.
667. Nicholas Roosevelt, *A Front Row Seat* (Norman: University of Oklahoma Press, 1953), 237.
668. Ibid., 238.
669. Andrew Genzoli, "Redwood Country: Recorded in History," January 27, 1975, Humboldt *Times-Standard,* Eureka, CA, Patricia L. Pilling Collection, General Accession 197/3, HHP, HHL.
670. Roosevelt, *A Front Row Seat,* 238.
671. Darling, *As Ding Saw Hoover,* 22–25.
672. Hoover to Darling, October 21, 1933, PPI-Darling, HHP, HHL.
673. Hoover to Darling, November 14, 1933, PPI-Darling, HHP, HHL.
674. Gilbert W. Davies and Florice M. Frank, *Stories of the Klamath National Forest: The First Fifty Years, 1905–1955,* 210.
675. Herbert Hoover to Theodore Joslin, Correspondence Mar.-Sept. 1933, PPI, HHP, HHL.
676. W. L. Hollingsforth, "Diary of a Deep-Sea Fishing Cruise on the Yacht *Samona II,*" Fishing—Correspondence 1933–42, PPS, HHP, HHL.
677. Ibid.
678. Ken Schultz, *North American Fishing: The Premier Guide to Angling in Freshwater and Saltwater* (Blue Ridge Summit, PA: Carlton Books, 2001), 245.
679. Ibid.

680. Hoover, *Fishing for Fun and to Wash Your Soul*, 31.
681. Hollingsforth, "Diary of a Deep-Sea Fishing Cruise."
682. Ibid.
683. Ibid.
684. Ibid.
685. Ibid.
686. Ibid.
687. Ibid.
688. Ibid.
689. Ibid.
690. Hoover to Darling, November 14, 1933, PPI-Darling, HHP, HHL.
691. Smith, *Uncommon Man*, 192.
692. Richard W. Hanna to Hoover, April 10, 1934, PPI-Hanna, Richard W., HHP, HHL.
693. Hanna to Hoover, April 6, 1934, PPI-Hanna.
694. Hoover to Elizabeth Hanna, July 28, 1934, PPI-Hanna.
695. Hoover, *Fishing for Fun and to Wash Your Soul*, 82–83.
696. Best, *Herbert Hoover*, 1: 27.
697. Herbert Hoover to William Allen White, August 23, 1934, HHP, HHL.
698. "Twelve Years, 1932–44," chapter 1, unpublished draft of memoirs, HHP, HHL.
699. Ibid., 203.
700. Best, *Herbert Hoover*, 1: 41.
701. George P. West, "Hoover Emerging from Old Privacy," June 3, 1935, *New York Times*, CF, HHP, HHL.
702. "Hoover Gets Prize Trout on Fishing Trip in Vermont," June 7, 1935, Rutland [Vermont] *Herald*, CF, HHP, HHL.
703. Donald B. Willard, "Hoover Pulls in Vermont Trout," June 7, 1935, Boston *Globe*, CF, HHP, HHL.
704. "Hoover Gets Prize Trout on Fishing Trip to Vermont," June 7, 1935, Rutland [Vermont] *Herald*.
705. "Hoover in Hip Boots Seeks Brook Trout," June 9, 1935, *New York Times*, CF, HHP, HHL.
706. Donald B. Willard, "Hoover Talks with Bridges and Spaulding," June 8, 1937, Boston *Globe*, CF, HHP, HHL.
707. Ibid.
708. "Hoover Pays N.H. First Visit, Tries Out Fishing Today," June 8, 1935, Manchester [New Hampshire] *Union*, CF, HHP, HHL.
709. Willard, "Hoover Pulls in Vermont Trout," June 7, 1935, Boston *Globe*, CF, HHP, HHL.
710. Donald R. McCoy, *Landon of Kansas* (Lincoln: University of Nebraska Press, 1966), 257–58.
711. West, "Hoover Emerging from Old Privacy."
712. "Hoover Angles, Raps Spending," July 5, 1936, newspaper unknown, CF, HHP, HHL.
713. Ibid.
714. "Herbert Hoover Loses 'Biggest' Catch of Outing," July 6, 1936, newspaper unknown, CF, HHP, HHL.
715. Ibid.
716. Steve Raymond, *Steelhead Country* (Seattle: Sasquatch Books, 1994), 183.
717. "Herbert Hoover Loses 'Biggest' Catch of Outing," July 6, 1936, newspaper unknown.

718. "Four Noted Montana Anglers Are Hosts to Herbert Hoover," August 1938, Jefferson Valley [Montana] *News*, Fishing Folder, HC, HI.
719. Jeff Findley and John Holt, *The Madison* (Portland, OR: Amato Publications, 1992), 1–2.
720. Ibid., 5–6.
721. "Hoover to Figure in Landon's Drive," August 21, 1936, newspaper unknown, CF, HHP, HHL.
722. "Hoover Finds Fish Choosey, Rivals Happy," August 24, 1936, Bend [Oregon] *Bulletin*.
723. Ibid.
724. Ibid.
725. Ibid.
726. Helen S. Carlson, *Nevada Place Names: A Geographical Dictionary* (Reno: University of Nevada Press, 1974), 147.
727. Stanley W. Paher, *Nevada Ghost Towns and Mining Camps* (San Diego, CA: Howell-North Books, 1984), 148.
728. "Hoover Catches Bluefish on Montauk Point Trip," September 14, 1936, New York *Herald Tribune*, CF, HHP, HHL.
729. John Hersey, *Blues* (New York: Vintage Books, 1987), 13.
730. Schultz, *North American Fishing*, 25–26.
731. "Hoover Tries Luck on Fishing Cruise," September 15, 1936, New York *Herald Tribune*, CF, HHP, HHL.
732. Ibid.
733. Hersey, *Blues*, 5.
734. Smith, *Uncommon Man*, 238.
735. Quoted in Best, *Herbert Hoover*, 1: 74.
736. "Hoover at Palm Beach Has Little Luck Fishing," December 13, 1936, New York *Herald Tribune*, CF, HHP, HHL.
737. "Hoover on Fishing Cruise in Gulf," December 16, 1936, *New York Times*, CF, HHP, HHL.
738. Gilbert and Sullivan, *H.M.S. Pinafore*.
739. "Son of Hoover Leaves Miami on Nassau Trip," March 1937, New York *Daily News*; and "Hoover Back from Fishing Trip," April 13, 1937, New York *Herald Tribune*, CF, HHP, HHL.
740. Smith, *Uncommon Man*, 244.
741. www.flyfishingconnection.com/pequest.html.
742. "Hoover Hooks Prize Trout, Gets Limit," May 2, 1937, *New York Times*, CF, HHP, HHL.
743. Hoover to W. D. Thornton, June 29, 1937, PPI-Thornton, W.D., HHP, HHL.
744. "Hoover Goes Fishing Misses Birthday Fete," August 9, 1937, *New York Times*, CF, HHP, HHL.
745. Hoover to Will Thornton, telegram, August 2, 1937, PPI-Thornton, W.D., HHP, HHL.
746. www.flyfishingconnection.com/madison.html.
747. "Hoover, Saying Nothing, Goes to Yellowstone," August 9, 1937, *Christian Science Monitor*, CF, HHP, HHL.
748. "Hoover Has 'Heard of' Rally for Republican Leaders but Prefers to Talk of Fishing," August 11, newspaper unknown, CF, HHP, HHL.
749. "Hoover Comments Briefly on Roosevelt's Court Bill," August 18, 1937, newspaper unknown, CF, HHP, HHL.
750. "Hoover Too Busy Fishing to Talk about Party Rally," August 11, 1937, New York *Herald Tribune*, CF, HHP, HHL.

751. "Hoover After Fish, Bars Political Talk," August 12, 1937, newspaper unknown, CF, HHP, HHL.
752. Ibid.
753. David Hinshaw, *Herbert Hoover: American Quaker* (New York: Farrar, Straus and Co., 1950).
754. Ibid.
755. Ibid.
756. "Former President, at Four Horsemen's Camp, Comes Out for 'Inalienable Right of Men, Boys to Fish and Catch Fish,'" August 15, 1937, newspaper unknown, CF, HHP, HHL.
757. Ibid.
758. Ibid.
759. Ibid.
760. Ibid.
761. Ibid.
762. "Hoover Comments Briefly on Roosevelt's Court Bill," August 18, 1937, Yakima [Washington] *Herald-Republic.*
763. Smith, *Uncommon Man,* 247.
764. Best, *Herbert Hoover: The Postpresidential Years,* 1: 102.
765. Smith, *Uncommon Man,* 251.
766. Lewis L. Straus, *Men and Decisions* (Garden City, NY: Doubleday, 1962), 65; and Herbert Hoover, *An American Epic,* 4 vols. (Chicago: Henry Regnery, 1964), 4: 280.
767. Best, *Herbert Hoover: The Postpresidential Years,* 1: 116–42.
768. "Hoover on Fishing Trip in Wisconsin," May 16, 1938, Chicago *Herald,* CF, HHP, HHL.
769. "Herbert Hoover Fishes in County," May 20, 1938, Marinette [Wisconsin] *Times-Union,* CF, HHP, HHL.
770. "Herbert Hoover in State 21 Years Ago as He Relaxed at Trout Fishing Lodge," October 20, 1959, newspaper unknown, Menasha, Wisconsin, HHP, HHL.
771. "Herbert Hoover Fishes In County," May 20, 1938, Marinette [Wisconsin] *Times-Union.*
772. Ibid.
773. Ibid.
774. Ibid.
775. "It's Time Voters Started to Experiment! Says Hoover," June 29, 1938, newspaper unknown, CF, HHP, HHL.
776. "Fishing and Politics," July 2, 1938, *New York Times,* CF, HHP, HHL.
777. Ibid.
778. Ibid.
779. "Reception to Fete Hoover Here," June 27, 1938, Seattle *Post Intelligencer,* CF, HHP, HHL.
780. "Hoover and Dr. Wilbur Go Fishing," June 28, 1938, San Francisco *Chronicle,* CF, HHP, HHL; and *Memoirs of Ray Lyman Wilbur,* 599.
781. A. L. Hager to Hoover, June 11, 1938, PPI-Hager, A. L., HHP, HHL.
782. "Hoover and Dr. Wilbur Go Fishing," June 28, 1938.
783. "Hoover to Be Invited to Hunt Grizzly Bear," June 27, 1938, New York *Herald Tribune,* CF, HHP, HHL.
784. Hager to Wilbur, August 1, 1938, PPI-Wilbur, Ray Lyman, HHP, HHL.
785. Hager to Editor, *Life,* August 27, 1938, Fishing Folder, Hoover Papers, Hoover Collection, HI.

786. "Indians Dub Hoover 'Chief Bread Giver,'" July 7, 1938, newspaper unknown, CF, HHP, HHL.

787. "Hoover 'Adopted' by Tribal Folks," July 6, 1938, Palo Alto [California] *Times,* CF, HHP, HHL.

788. Ray Lyman Wilbur, Jr., OHI, November 24, 1971, HHL.

789. Hoover to Thornton, July 18, 1938, PPI-Thornton, W.D., HHP, HHL.

790. John W. Schofield to Thornton, December 31, 1938, PPI-Thornton, W.D., HHP, HHL.

791. "Four Noted Montana Anglers Are Hosts to Herbert Hoover," August 1938, newspaper unknown, CF, HHP, HHL.

792. W. Cameron Forbes to Lawrence Richey, September 28, 1938, PPI-Forbes, W. Cameron, HHP, HHL; and "Hoover Visits Naushon Island: Finds Rest Fishing for Bass," October 15, 1938, Cape Cod [Massachusetts]*Standard Times,* CF, HHP.

793. Smith, *Uncommon Man,* 264.

794. Ibid., 265.

795. "Hoover Here as Cruise Guest, Lands Sailfish, Large Shark," Stuart [Florida] *News,* March 9, 1939, CF, HHP, HHL.

796. Ibid.

797. Ibid.

798. Ibid.

799. Mrs. Jeremiah Milbank, OHI, November 6, 1967, HHL.

800. Ibid.

801. Elizabeth Hanna to Lou Henry Hoover, n.d., Personal Correspondence, 1938–1942, LHHP, HHL.

802. "Hoover Ends Fishing Trip," April 17, 1939, New York *Herald Tribune,* CF, HHP, HHL.

803. "Hoover Leaving M'Kenzie Camp," April 17, 1940, Portland *Oregonian,* CF, HHP, HHL.

804. "Mr. Hoover on Our McKenzie," April 16, 1939, Eugene [Oregon] *Register-Guard,* CF, HHP, HHL.

805. "Hoover Thinks War Will Be Small, If at All," April 18, 1939, newspaper unknown, CF, HHP, HHL.

806. Herbert Hoover to W. E. Travis, April 21, 1939, PPI-Travis, W.E., Correspondence 1936–1939, HHP, HHL.

807. "Hoover Gets His Limit of Maine Trout; Guide Welch Says He's Swell," May 30, 1939, newspaper unknown, CF, HHP, HHL.

808. Ibid.

809. "Hoover Fishes in Maine," May 30, 1939, newspaper unknown, CF, HHP, HHL.

810. "Hoover Gets His Limit of Maine Trout."

811. Frank A. Hoisington, "Hoover Fears for Democracy but Is Silent on Politics as He Stops in City Enroute to Fishing Streams," August 3, 1939, Grand Junction [Colorado] *Sentinel,* CF, HHP, HHL.

812. "Herbert Hoover Enjoys Fishing Gunnison," August 4, 1939, Montrose [Colorado] *Daily News,* CF, HHP, HHL.

813. Frank L. Fetzer, "Narrative of Vacation Trip in Colorado," August 2–8, 1939, PPI-Fetzer, Frank L., HHP, HHL.

814. Ibid.

815. Ibid.

816. Ibid.

817. Ibid.
818. "Gilmore's Photo of Hoover in Today's Press," August 5, 1939, Montrose [Colorado] *Daily Press,* CF, HHP, HHL.
819. "Hoover Takes Time Off for Luncheon Meet," August 4, 1939, Gunnison [Colroado] *Courier,* CF, HHP, HHL.
820. Frank L. Fetzer, "Narrative of Vacation Trip to Colorado," August 2–8, 1939, PPI-Fetzer, Frank L., HHP, HHL.
821. Ibid.
822. "The Pendulum," August 1939, Calhan [Colorado] *News,* CF, HHP, HHL.
823. W. D. Thornton to Hoover, telegram, August 15, 1939, PPI-Thornton, W.D., HHP, HHL.
824. Public Statement File (PSF), September 1, 1939, HHP, HHL.
825. George H. Quinion, OHI, July 10, 1970, HHL.
826. George H. Quinion to Hoover, December 15, 1939, PPI-Quinion, George H., HHP, HHL.
827. Quinion to Hoover, June 3, 1940, PPI.
828. Quinion, OHI.
829. Ibid.
830. "Hoover, Off To Fish, Rules Out Politics," June 29, 1940, *New York Times,* CF, HHP, HHL.
831. Ibid.
832. "Hoover Home, Goes Fishing," July 1, 1940, Palo Alto [California] *Times,* CF, HHP, HHL.
833. George W. O'Bannon, "The Grand Gesture: The Ahwanee Hotel, Phyllis Ackerman and Arthur Upham Pope," *Oriental Rug Review* 8/3 (February–March 1988), 1–30.
834. Ibid.
835. Best, *Herbert Hoover,* 1: 167.
836. Smith, *Uncommon Man,* 287.
837. Ibid., 288.
838. Hoover to Wilbur, January 22, 1941, PPI.
839. Wilbur to Richey, January 27, 1941; and Wilbur to Hoover, January 27, 1941, PPI.
840. Smith, *Uncommon Man,* 294.
841. George H. Nash, *Herbert Hoover and Stanford University* (Stanford, CA: Hoover Institution Press, 1988), 108–10.
842. LHH to Aunt Jessie Jones, September 1, 1941, "Trips, Camping Trip Notes," SF, LHHP, HHL.
843. Ibid.
844. Ibid.
845. Ibid.
846. Hoover to William R. Castle, December 8, 1941, Pearl Harbor, Hoover Diary of Events, PPS; and Hoover to Robert A. Taft, December 8, 1941, PPI-Taft, Robert A., HHP, HHL.
847. Herbert Hoover, *Addresses upon the American Road, World War II, 1941–1945* (New York: D. Van Nostrand Co., 1946), 3.
848. Smith, *Uncommon Man,* 309.
849. Susan Estabrook Kennedy, "Blessed Are the Peacemakers: The Hoover-Gibson Collaboration," unpublished paper, 3.
850. Ibid., 4.
851. Hoover to Walcott, May 26, 1942, PPI-Walcott, Frederick, HHP, HHL.

852. Ibid., 4.
853. Lawrence K. and Frances Bean Requa, OHI, October 4, 1966, HHL.
854. www.rural network.net/~weisercc/page3.html.
855. www.snakeriverguides.com/fishing.html.
856. Requa, OHI, October 4, 1966, HHL.
857. Hoover to M. M. Meyers, September 14, 1942, PPI-Meyers, M. M., HHP, HHL.
858. Richard E. Darilek, *A Loyal Opposition in Time of War* (Westport, CT; Green-wood Press, 1976), 53.
859. Lincoln County Historical Museum, Pioche, Nevada.
860. Allen, *Independent Woman*, 171.
861. Rickard Diary, January 7, 1944.
862. Allen, *Independent Woman*, 172–73.
863. Henning Heldt, "Hoover Here on Fishing Trip To Keys," no date, ca. 1945, Miami *Herald*, HC, HI.
864. Smith, *Uncommon Man*, 300.
865. Ibid.
866. Tate to His Mother, February 16, 1944, Tate Papers, Manuscript Division, Library of Congress, Washington, D.C.
867. Ibid.
868. Ibid.
869. Ibid.
870. Warren to Hoover, April 9, 1944, PPI-Warren, George, HHP, HHL.
871. Warren to Hoover, May 22, 1944, PPI.
872. Walcott to Hoover, May 9, 1944, PPI-Walcott, Frederick, HHP, HHL.
873. Hoover, *Fishing for Fun and to Wash Your Soul*, 57–58.
874. Walcott to Hoover, May 25, 1945, PPI.

Chapter 9: It's the Old Horse for the Long Race
875. Ted Morgan, *FDR: A Biography* (New York: Simon and Schuster, 1985), 763–64.
876. Hoover to Warren, April 24, 1945, PPI.
877. www.liglobal.com/t_I/stateparks/connetquot.shtml.
878. espn.go.com/outdoors/flyfishing/s/f_map_NY_connetquot_river.html.
879. Ibid.
880. Hoover to Macy, May 14, 1945, PPI-Macy, Kingsland W., HHP, HHL.
881. Smith, *Uncommon Man*, 344.
882. Bunny Miller to Kitty Milbank, July 27, 1945, General Accession 80, Milbank, Katherine, HHP, HHL.
883. July 7, 1945, Rickard Diary.
884. Jeremiah Milbank to Hoover, August 5, 1945, PPI-Milbank, Jeremiah, HHP, HHL.
885. Hoover to Clarence B. Kelland, October 1, 1945, PPI-Kelland, C. B., HHP, HHL.
886. Heldt, "Hoover Here on Fishing Trip to Keys," no date, Miami *Herald*, HC, HI.
887. Capt. John Spear, "Bonefish," members.aol.com/poonstruck/bonefish.htm.
888. Calvin Albury, OHI, April 14, 1967, HHL.
889. John Kluytmans, OHI, May 11, 1967, HHL.
890. Best, *Herbert Hoover*, 2: 286–87.
891. Smith, *Uncommon Man*, 353.
892. H. R. Aiken to Hoover, May 6, 1946, "Fishing Correspondence, 1943–1948," PPS, HHP, HHL.
893. Paula Marren to Bernice Miller, April 26, 1946, "Fishing Correspondence, 1943–1948," PPS, HHP, HHL.

894. Hoover to Quinion, May 15, 1950, PPI, HHP, HHL.
895. Allen Corson, "Wildlife—Conservation Fishing," January 9, 1947, Miami *Herald*, HC, HI.
896. Ibid.
897. Ibid.
898. James C. Austin, "Mr. Hoover on Fishing," *Conversation Volunteer*, Official Bulletin Minnesota Department of Conservation, March–April 1949.
899. Dr. Nicholas and Mrs. Tierney, OHI, April 12, 1967, HHL.
900. Hoover to Kelland, January 17, 1947, PPI, HHP, HHL.
901. Smith, *Uncommon Man*, 362.
902. Telegrams, Hoover to Warren, April 21, 1947, and Warren to Hoover, April 22, 1947, PPI, HHP, HHL.
903. Herbert Hoover, *Addresses upon the American Road*, 1945–1948 (New York: D. Van Nostrand, 1949), 152–55.
904. "Mr. Herbert Hoover Discusses Fishing on a CBS Program, 'Invitation to Learning,'" May 18, 1947, PSF, HHP, HHL.
905. Ibid.
906. Bill Corum, "Sports," July 7, 1947, New York *Journal American*, CF, HHP, HHL.
907. Ibid.
908. Ibid.
909. Best, *Herbert Hoover*, 2: 317.
910. Floyd L. Majors, Lower Matecumbe, "News and Views of the Upper Keys," June 1963, Key West [Florida] *Citizen*, HC, HI.
911. Jerry Wilkinson, "North Key Largo," www.keyhistory.org.
912. "Fishing: From Camp to Key," January 31, 1955, *Newsweek*, Fishing, PPS, HHP, HHL.
913. Ibid.
914. Ibid.
915. Darlene Brown, "A Tribute to a Man and His Legend," June 4, 1980, [Key Largo, Florida] *Conch Shell*, CF, HHP, HHL.
916. Ibid.
917. Albury, OHI.
918. Ibid.
919. Alexander Gifford, "Travel," January 25, 1948, Baltimore *American*, CF, HHP, HHL.
920. Hinshaw, *Herbert Hoover*, 396–97.
921. Smith, *Uncommon Man*, 378.
922. Hinshaw, *Herbert Hoover*, 335–48.
923. James C. Austin, "Hoover the Fisherman," March 19, 1949, Waterbury, [Connecticut] *American*, CF, HHP, HHL.
924. Ibid.
925. Ibid.
926. Ibid.
927. Ibid.
928. "Hoover Report on Fishing," March 16, 1949, San Antonio *Texas News*, CF, HHP, HHL.
929. Edward O. Bodkin, OHI, March 9, 1970, HHL.
930. Smith, *Uncommon Man*, 381.
931. Milbank, OHI.
932. Mr. and Mrs. Allan Hoover, OHI.
933. "Herbert Hoover Cancels Fishing—Aug. 10 Is His 75th," August 3, 1949, Buffalo [New York] *Evening News*, CF, HHP, HHL.

934. Smith, *Uncommon Man*, 383.
935. Hinshaw, *Herbert Hoover*, 363–88.
936. Albury, OHI.
937. Floyd L. Majors, "News and Views of the Upper Keys," June 1963.
938. Ibid.
939. James Blocker and Don Bowers, OHI, April 14, 1967, HHL.
940. Kluytmans, OHI.
941. Best, Herbert Hoover: The Postpresidential Years, 2: 377.
942. "Beginner's Luck," March 12, 1951, New York *World-Telegram* and [New York] *Sun,* In House Finding Aid, HHL.
943. Albury, OHI.
944. Ibid.
945. Brig. Gen. Bonner Fellers, OHI, no date, HHL.
946. Smith, *Uncommon Man*, 400.
947. "Hoover Flees Fire in His Night Clothes," August 26, 1952, New York *Mirror,* CF, HHP, HHL.
948. "Hoover Escapes Death as Sierra Lodge Burns," August 26, 1952, San Francisco *Chronicle,* CF, HHP, HHL.
949. CF, HHP, HHL.
950. "Hoover Flees in Boat as Fire Razes Lodge," August 26, 1952, *New York Times,* CF, HHP, HHL.
951. "Hoover Escapes Flames as Fishing Cabin Burns," August 26, 1952, *Newsday.*
952. Hoover to Milnor, August 28, 1952, PPI-Milnor.
953. Bernice Miller to Gertrude Kamps, October 2, 1952, Fishing Correspondence 1943–1958, PPS, HHP, HHL.
954. Dr. Nicholas and Mrs. Tierney, OHI.
955. Ibid.
956. Ibid.
957. Ibid.
958. "Hoover Fit Now, Goes after Fish," February 13, 1953, Miami *News,* CF, HHP, HHL.
959. Blocker and Bowers, OHI.
960. Albury, OHI.
961. Ibid.
962. Ibid.
963. Ibid.
964. Smith, *Uncommon Man*, 380.
965. Donald J. Sterling, "Hoover Again Seeks Trout on McKenzie," July 9, 1953, Portland *Oregon Journal,* CF, HHP, HHL.
966. Ibid.
967. Ibid.
968. Ibid.
969. Ibid.
970. Ibid.
971. Ibid.
972. William L. White, OHI, March 1, 1968, HHL.
973. Albury, OHI.
974. Ibid.
975. Richard Berlin to Hoover, June 8, 1954, PPI-Berlin, Richard E., HHP, HHL.
976. Hoover to Berlin, June 11, 1954, ibid.
977. Richey to Hoover, July 22, 1954, PPI-Richey, Lawrence, HHP, HHL.

978. Eisenhower to Hoover, August 2, 1954, Eisenhower's Papers as President, 1956–52 (EPP); Administration Series (AS), Box 19, Hoover, Herbert, H. (2), Dwight D. Eisenhower Library (DEL), Abilene, KS.
979. Hoover to Eisenhower, August 4, 1954, ibid.
980. Eisenhower to Hoover, August 6, 1954, ibid.
981. Ibid.
982. Eisenhower to Hoover, August 9, 1954, EPP, AS, Box 19, Hoover, Herbert, H. (2), DEL.
983. Michael J. Birkner, "Elder Statesman: Herbert Hoover and His Successors," in *Uncommon Americans: The Lives and Legacies of Herbert and Lou Henry Hoover,* edited by Timothy Walch (Westport, CT: Praeger, 2003), 243.
984. Smith, *Uncommon Man,* 414.
985. "Ike, Hoover Off for 3-Day Fishing Trip," August 8, 1954, unknown newspaper, CF, HHP, HHL.
986. "Jack Calhoun Is Ike's Guide at Iowa Fair," September 8, 1954, [Omaha, Nebraska] West Hotel *Reporter,* CF, HHP, HHL.
987. Hoover, *Fishing for Fun and to Wash Your Soul,* 20.
988. Neil MacNeil, OHI, February 25, 1967; and Madeline Kelly O'Donnell, OHI, July 7, 1969, HHL.
989. Andrew Tully, "Ike Misses a Whopper," no date, newspaper unknown, CF, HHP, HHL.
990. "Back after Fishing with Ike," September 4, 1954, newspaper unknown, CF, HHP, HHL.
991. "Herbert Hoover Says That Newspaper Boys' Fish Stories Aren't Fair to Ike (Walton)," September 4, 1954, Birmingham [Alabama] *News,* CF, HHP, HHL.
992. "May Be Just What This Nation Needs!" September 3, 1954, White Plains [New York] *Reporter-Dispatch,* CF, HHP, HHL.
993. "All Boys Together!" September 4, 1954, Fort Worth [Texas] *Morning Star-Telegram,* CF, HHP, HHL.
994. Earl Selby, "In Our Town," September 5, 1954, Philadelphia *Bulletin,* CF, HHP, HHL.
995. Ibid.
996. Ibid.
997. Best, *Herbert Hoover: The Postpresidential Years,* 2: 385.
998. Smith, *Uncommon Man,* 415.
999. Michael O'Neal, "In the Florida Keys, 'Bonefish Oblivion,'" May 2, 2003, *New York Times.*
1000. Albury, OHI.
1001. Ibid.
1002. Blocker and Bowers, OHI.
1003. Grey, *Tales of Fishes,* 111.
1004. "Ex-President Herbert Hoover's Elder Brother Dies at Ranch," February 5, 1955, Santa Ana [California] *Register* and "H. Hoover's Brother Dies at 84," February 5, 1955, Pasadena [California] *Independent,* CF, HHP, HHL.
1005. George Mardikian, *Song of America* (New York: McGraw-Hill, 1956), 305.
1006. Ibid.
1007. George Mardikian, "Three Meals for the Chief," no date, (fall 1955), PPI-Mardikian, George, Correspondence 1947–1957, HHP, HHL.
1008. Ibid.
1009. Ibid.
1010. Smith, *Uncommon Man,* 417.

1011. "Newberg Welcomes Herbert Hoover," August 10, 1955, Baker [Oregon] *Democrat-Herald;* Mervin Shoemaker, "State Pays Birthday Tributes," August 10, 1955, Salem [Oregon] *Capital Journal,* CF, HHP, HHL.
1012. Herbert Hoover, "Saying 'Something Good about Ourselves,'" August 19, 1955, *U.S. News and World Report,* CF, HHP, HHL.
1013. "Hoover—Intent on Relaxing—Heads for Fishing Streams," July 9, 1955, Tucson *Arizona Daily Star,* CF, HHP, HHL.
1014. Bernice Miller to George Mardikian, September 10, 1955, PPI-Mardikian, HHP, HHL.
1015. Ibid.
1016. Ibid.
1017. Ibid.
1018. Ibid.
1019. Mardikian to Miller, September 20, 1955, PPI-Mardikian, HHP, HHL.
1020. Miller to Mardikian, September 26, 1955, PPI.
1021. Mardikian to Bunny, September 26, 1955, PPI.
1022. Hoover to Wilbur D. Matson, December 20, 1955, PPI-Matson, Wilbur D., HHP, HHL.
1023. "Hoover in Florida for Vacation," December 29, 1955, newspaper unknown, CF, HHP, HHL.
1024. Blocker and Bowers, OHI.
1025. Ibid.
1026. Ibid.
1027. Majors, "News and Views of the Upper Keys," June 1963.
1028. Ibid.
1029. Ibid.
1030. Neil MacNeil, OHI, Second Session, May 7, 1967, HHL.
1031. Ibid.
1032. Smith, *Uncommon Man,* 418.
1033. MacNeil, OHI.
1034. Ibid.
1035. Ibid.
1036. Best, *Herbert Hoover: The Postpresidential Years,* 2: 400.
1037. Ibid., 402.
1038. "Herbert Hoover Hooks One," March 20, 1957, Miami *Herald,* CF, HHP, HHL.
1039. Nichols, OHI.
1040. MacNeil, OHI.
1041. Ibid.
1042. Richard Norton Smith, "On the Outside Looking In: Herbert Hoover and World War II," in *Prologue* 26, no. 3 (Fall 1994): 146.
1043. Vernon S. Hidy to Hoover, April 9, 1963, Fishing Correspondence 1959–1964, PPS, HHP, HHL.
1044. Wayne Fields, *What the River Knows: An Angler in Midstream* (Chicago: University of Chicago Press, 1990), 164.
1045. van der Zee, *Greatest Men's Party on Earth,* 86–87.
1046. "Cave Man Camp Members Attending 1957 Encampment—July 12–27, Incl." Key Largo Anglers Club, General Accession 215, HHP, HHL.
1047. "Herbert Hoover Anecdotes," Neil MacNeil Papers, HHL.
1048. Ibid.
1049. Ibid.
1050. Ibid.
1051. Albury, OHI.

1052. Ibid.
1053. Ibid.
1054. Ibid.
1055. Majors, "News and Views of the Upper Keys."
1056. Ibid.
1057. Ibid.
1058. Ibid.
1059. Ibid.
1060. Virginia Green, OHI, April 14, 1967, HHL.
1061. "Francesca's Blue Book, 'Caveman's Camp' Invites the Ladies," August 3, 1959, San Francisco *Call-Bulletin*, Katherine Milbank, General Accession 80, HHP, HHL.
1062. "Auberge la Maison Donohue," www.aubergedonohue.com/Eaccueil.htm.
1063. Philippe Dube, *Charlevoix: Two Centuries at Murray Bay* (Quebec City: McGill-Queen's University Press, 1990).
1064. "Tourisme Charlevoix Tourism," www.quebecweb.com/charlevoixtourisme/introang.html.
1065. Ibid.
1066. Nichols, OHI.
1067. Albury, OHI.
1068. Ibid.
1069. Ibid.
1070. Ibid.
1071. Ibid.
1072. Ibid.
1073. Ibid.
1074. Ibid.
1075. Ibid.
1076. Ibid.
1077. Majors, "News and Views of the Upper Keys."
1078. Ibid.
1079. Ibid.
1080. Herbert Hoover, "Meet the Press," August 9, 1959, in *Addresses upon the American Road, 1955–1960* (Caldwell, ID: Caxton Printers, 1961), 69.
1081. Telephone interview with Senator Mark O. Hatfield, April 7, 1998.
1082. Ibid.
1083. Ibid.
1084. George Mardikian, "Reminiscences on a Distinguished Son of Iowa: 'The Chief,'" August 15, 1971, Cedar Rapids [Iowa] *Gazette*, RF, HHP, HHL.
1085. Herbert Hoover, "Meet the Press," August 9, 1959, in *Addresses upon the American Road, 1955–1960* (Caldwell, ID: Caxton Printers, 1961), 75.
1086. Herbert Hoover, "Boys Club Ideals Combat Spread of Youth Crime," October 8, 1959, United Press International, in *Addresses upon the American Road,* 346–48.
1087. Ibid.
1088. Richey to Hoover, November 9, 1959, PPI-Richey, Lawrence, HHP, HHL.
1089. Albury, OHI.
1090. Ibid.
1091. Mrs. J. Clinton Campbell, OHI, April 15, 1967, HHL.
1092. Blocker and Bowers, OHI.
1093. Ibid.
1094. Majors, "News and Views of the Upper Keys."

1095. Ibid.
1096. Best, *Herbert Hoover: The Postpresidential Years*, 2: 419.
1097. "Remarks by Honorary Commodore Herbert Hoover," March 3, 1961, Key Largo Anglers Club Induction of Flag Officers, Herbert Hoover Files, Accession 215, HHP, HHL.
1098. Green, OHI; and "Key Largo Anglers Commodores' Weekend," March 12, 1961, Miami *Herald*, Fishing Folder, HC, HI.
1098. Quoted in Smith, *Uncommon Man*, 423.
1100. Herbert Hoover, *On Growing Up: His Letters from and to American Children* (New York: William Morrow, 1962), 77.
1101. Nichols, OHI.
1102. Vincent Antle, OHI, July 8, 1972, HHL.
1103. Bernice Miller to Hugo Meier, February 19, 1962, Correspondence 1934–1964, PPI-Meier, Hugo; and Miller to David Packard, January 2, 1962, Correspondence 1959–1964, PPI-Packard, David, HHP, HHL.
1104. Ibid.
1105. Antle, OHI.
1106. Ibid.
1107. Ibid.
1108. Harry A. Bruno, "Rescue by a Fisherman," October 1962, *Outdoor Life*, RF, HHP, HHL.
1109. Ibid.
1110. Ibid.
1111. Ibid.
1112. "Hoover Hero of Rescue," September 28, 1962, Washington *Post*, Fishing Folder, HC, HI.
1113. Blocker and Bowers, OHI.
1114. "Remarks by Herbert Hoover, Commodore's Party Key Largo Anglers Club," March 2, 1962, Herbert Hoover Files, Key Largo [Florida] Anglers Club, General Accession 215, HHP, HHL.
1115. Ibid.
1116. Ibid.
1117. "Commodores Enjoy a Ball," March 5, 1962, Miami *Herald*, Fishing Folder, HC, HI.
1118. Albury, OHI.
1119. Ibid.
1120. Ibid.
1121. George Mardikian, OHI, September 27, 1967, HHL.
1122. George Mardikian, "Reminiscences."
1123. Best, *Herbert Hoover: The Postpresidential Years*, 2: 423.
1124. Michael J. Petti, OHI, February 29, 1968, HHL.
1125. Hoover, *Fishing for Fun and to Wash Your Soul*, foreword.
1126. "The Fisherman's Prayer," Fishing Folder, HC, HI.
1127. Nichols, OHI.
1128. Dr. Elton Trueblood, Eulogy, October 20, 1964, RF, HHP, HHL.

Index

Page numbers in italics indicate illustrations.

A Boyhood in Iowa (Hoover), 7
Ahwanee Hotel, 274
Albright, Horace, 95, 144–46, *147*, 183
Albury, Calvin, 298–99, 302–4, *303*,
    308–9, 312–13, 318–19, 325–28, *326*,
    330–32, 334–35, *336*, 338–39,
    342–43, 345, 348
amberjack controversy, 131–33
American Committee, 89–91
American Electric Railway Association
    address, 112
American Individualism (Hoover),
    113–14, 117
American Relief Administration
    (ARA), 95
An American Epic (Hoover), 323, 328,
    334, 336, 340, 342
Atlantic Monthly, 162, 296
automobiles, 76
Avalon Tuna Club, 149

Bailey, George, on Oregon, 24–25
Baja California, fishing off coast of,
    228–33
banking system, American, 202–3
Bawdwin mine, 85
Belgium, relief efforts for, 91–93
Bewick and Moreing, 70–71
    as senior partner with, 76
bicycles, adventures with, 38–39
Block Island Sound, 245
Blue River, 46
bluefish, 245
Bohemian Grove Club, 105–9, 275, 280,
    282, 320
    establishing separate camp at,
        129–30
    inducted into Old Guard of, 309–12
    lakeside talks at, 324
    return to, 222–23
    see also Cave Man Camp

bonefish, 293
   fishing, 318–19
   rig used for, 308–9
Book of the Black Bass (Henshall), 116
Boxer Rebellion, 73–74
Boys' Clubs of America, 245, 336
British Columbia, fishing streams and
   lakes in, 257–58
Broadmoor Hotel, 275
Brown, Mollie. *See* Carran, Mollie
   Brown
Brown's Camp, 225
Brule River, 157–61
   trout in, *158*
Brussels World's Fair, 332
Bureau of Fisheries, 114
Burma, 84–85
Burrows, Lewis O., *262*, 264
Butler, Philippi, *193*

Calhan, Colorado, *News,* 268
Camp Rapidan, 185–91, *186*
   giving to government, 219
   inauguration of, 189–91
   interior of cabin at, *193*
   Roosevelts at, 219
   visit to, 338
Cape San Lucas, 174
Carran, Mollie Brown, 22, 39, 171–72
Carter, Eland, *169*
Cave Man Camp, 129–30, 224, 319–21,
   329–30, 337–38
   last visit to, 345–46
Cedar River, family outings on banks
   of, 9–11
The Challenge to Liberty (Hoover), 233,
   235
Chesapeake Bay, 113, 130, 206–8
Children's Feeding Program, 295
China
   Boxer Rebellion, 73–74
   the Hoovers in, 71–74
Churchill, Winston, 99
   defeated in general election, 291–92
Ciel sur Terre, 333
Circle S Ranch, 233–34
   last visit to, 307
Civilian Conservation Corps (CCC),
   228
Coleman Fishing Club, 254–56
Columbia Irrigation League, 135

Commission on Organization of the
   Executive Branch of the Govern-
   ment, 297
Commission for Relief in Belgium
   (CRB), 92–93
Committee on Monetary Policies,
   222–23
The Compleat Angler (Walton), 234, 296
Congress of Industrial Organizations,
   247
Connetquot River, 289–90
Coolidge, Calvin, 126
   on Brule River, *156*
   choosing not to run for president,
      148
   and Hoover fishing on Brule River,
      157–59
   summer vacation of 1928, 152–57
   transition to fly fishing, 155–57
Corbin Park estate, 238–39
Covered Wagon (Hough), 116
Craig's Camp, 246
Cresent Lake, Oregon, family outing
   to, 286

De Re Metallica (Agricola), 86–87
Democratic Party, House majority in
   1934, 235–36
Deschutes River, 243–44
Dewey, Thomas, 260, 262, 285–86
Dilg, Williamson H., 116–17, *118*
Donner Lake, 66

Eel River, 163
Eisenhower, Dwight, 304, *316*
   Hoover fishing trip, 313–17
El Rancho Silverado, 332–33
Esberg, Milton, 163, *169*
Eugene *Register-Guard,* 262

family outings
   in Appalachians, 96–97
   childhood, 7–11
   at Cresent Lake, Oregon, 286
   in Florida, 294–95
   in High Sierras and Yosemite, 102–3
   Minthorns, 32–34
   in Washington D.C., 95–96
family reunion, *11*
Famine Emergency Committee, 292–94

First Aid for Hungary, 325
Fisherman's Prayer, 348
Fishing for Fun and to Wash Your Soul
    (Hoover), xii, xiii, 286, 342
    excerpt from, 286–87
    foreword, 347–48
Fishing with a Hook (Berners), 234
Fishing in Oregon, 45
Fishing and Shooting Sketches (Cleve-
    land), 234
fishing trips
    Alaskan, 121–24
    Avalon Tuna Club, 149
    Baja California coast, 228–33
    Block Island Sound, 245
    British Columbia, 257–58
    Brule River, 157–61
    Cape San Lucas, 174
    Chesapeake Bay, 113, 130, 206–8
    Connetquot River, 289–90
    Corbin Park estate, 238–39
    Deschutes River, 243–44
    Eel River, 163
    Florida coast, 212–17
    Florida inland waterways, 276
    Florida Keys, 127–29, 131–33, 150,
        176–78, 195–98, 246, 292–93, 302–4,
        305, 308–9, 312–13, 318–19, 322–23,
        325–28, 330–32, 334–36, 338–39,
        342–43, 345
    Georgia coast, 210–12
    Grand Tetons, 268, 281
    Grebe Lake, 268
    Gunnison River, 264–67
    High Sierras and Yosemite, 102–3
    Hobe Sound, 261
    Idaho, 252–53
    Klamath River, 165–66, 225–28
    Lake Kennebago, 264
    Lake Lakota, 237–38
    Lake Mead, 269–70
    Lake Mitchell Trout Club, 238
    Larry Creek, 151–52, 200–1
    McKenzie River, 138–39, 226, 240–41,
        247, 274, 279, 309–12, 329
    Madison River, 241–43, 249, 251–52,
        268
    Mill Creek, 233–34
    New Mexico, 277–78
    Ogontz Fishing Club, 97–98
    Pequest River, 247, 256

    with press, 161–70
    Pyramid Lake, 221–22
    Rogue River, 139–40, 165, 241
    Sacramento River, 166–68
    St. Louis Creek, 315
    Schenob Brook, 271–72, 279–80, 294
    Silver Lake, 306–7
    Snyder's Camp, 296–97
    South Pike River, 254–56
    Twin Lakes, 279–80
    Wooley Creek, 224–25, 235
    Yellowstone Park, 145–48
Fishing the Virgin Sea (Grey), 234
Florida
    fishing along coast of, 212–17
    Keys, fishing in, 127–29, 131–33, 150,
        176–78, 195–98, 246, 292–93, 302–4,
        305, 308–9, 312–13, 318–19, 323–24,
        325–28, 330–32, 334–36, 338–39,
        342–43, 345
    real estate boom in, 131
flu epidemic, 101
Fly-Fishing (Grey), 234
Fort St. James, 258
Freedom Betrayed. See Magnum Opus
Friends Pacific Academy, 26–27, *28*
Friends Polytechnic College, 37

Georgia, fishing along coast of, 210–12
Gibson, Rainbow, *164*, 165
Grand Tetons, 268, 281
Gray, Jenny, 40–42
    and family, *41*
Great Depression, 198–218
    icons, xxi
    jingles, xx–xxi
Grebe Lake, 268
Grey, Zane, 116, 127–28, 174, 234, 270,
    293, 318
Gunnison River, 264–67

Hager, A. L., *258*
Harding, Florence K., *120*
Harding, Warren G., 109, *120*
    death of, 125
    funeral train, 125–26
    voyage of discovery trip, 117–25
Harris, Fred, 226, 247, 309, *310*
Hatfield, Mark O., 337, *337*
    foreword by, xi–xiv
Henry, Lou. *See* Hoover, Lou Henry

Henry Clay Pierce Estate, 154–55
Herbert Hoover Presidential Library,
 dedication of, 346
hitchhiker incident, 250
Hobe Sound, 261
Holiday Farm, 226, 275, 279
 last visit to, 328–29
Honolulu school, 227–28
Hoover, Allan Henry, 163, *236*
 birth of, 84
Hoover, Herbert, *12*
 administration, 181–218
 aiding American citizens stranded in
  London, 89–90
 ancient mining texts collection, 86
 battles a sailfish, *196*
 birth of, 4
 birthplace of, *5*
 breaking rules and rebelling, 31–32
 brings in catch on the *Orca*, *216*
 and Bunny Miller at Key Largo
  Anglers Club, *346*
 in Burma, 84–85
 business success, 43
 called "Bertie," 4
 and Calvin Albury, *303, 326, 336*
 campaign of 1923, 170–72
 in China, 71–74
 and companions encircling a giant
  redwood, *169*
 conservation efforts, 114–26
 contracting malaria, 85
 contribution, greatest, 338
 conversion to fly fishing, 44
 and Coolidge fishing on Brule River,
  157–59
 cruise to South Africa, 76–77
 daily chores, 29–30
 dealing with loss of parents & separation from siblings, 19–21
 death of, 348
 demand for privacy vs. craving for
  publicity, 133–34
 diagnosed with abdominal cancer,
  346
 displays sailfish, *199*
 during four month interregnum,
  209–18
 eating habits, 320–21
 Eisenhower fishing trip, 313–17
 and Eisenhower grilling steaks, *316*
 entry into California politics, 105

European trip, 253–54
 Famine Emergency Committee
  chairman, 293–94
 on favorite fishing, 300
 first sailfish, 177, *179*
 fishing in Bernard, Vermont, *239*
 fishing books collection, 234
 fishing with Lewis O. Burrows, *262*
 fishing Pyramid Lake, 223
 fishing in West Yellowstone, *242*
 and Frank Knox at Coleman Fishing
  Club, *255*
 and Fred Harris on McKenzie River,
  310
 geology class, *62*
 and George Warren on Pequest
  River, *248*
 gives Richey fishing tackle, 313
 good neighbor policy with Latin
  America, 174–75
 with granddaughter Lou Henry, *327*
 growing enmity toward Roosevelt
  and New Deal, 233
 growing up in Oregon with
  Minthorns, 26–47
 on Gunnison River, *269*
 on Harding's voyage of discovery
  trip, 117–25
 with Horace Albright, *147*
 on horses, 50–51
 on how to eat a peach, 338
 inauguration day, 181
 induction into Stuart Lake tribe,
  258–59
 Izaak Walton League address, xi–xii
 on Kennebago Lake, Maine, *ii, 265*
 on Klamath River, *167*
 laid to rest in West Branch, Iowa, 348
 on Lake Mead, *270*
 on Larry Creek, *153*
 last address by, 346
 with Lou at Camp Rapidan, *190*
 Lou Henry courtship and marriage,
  53–60, 71
 and Lou on McKenzie River, *140*
 on McKenzie River, *141, 311*
 mapping High Sierras and Nevada
  desert, 50, 52–53, 60–67
 with Mark O. Hatfield, *337*
 mining industry career, 68–69, 70–87
 move to Oregon to live with
  Minthorns, 22

move to Salem with Minthorns, 35–37
near death as child, 4–5
nomination at 1928 Republican Convention, 152
off Long Key, Florida, *132*
on Old Billy, Camp Rapidan, *189*
one year old, *8*
on Oregon Trail by train, 23–24
at Osage nation, 12–14
playing canasta, 301–2
the press and, 205, 317–18
the public and, 161–70, 205–6, 225–26
with Quinion and Walcott, 272
reeling in rockfish on Chesapeake Bay, *207*
refusing to hold up fish he didn't catch, *266*
releasing fish, 271
reputation, regaining, 296
at Resurrection Bay in Seward, Alaska, *123*
retiring from fly fishing, 333
and Richey with wahoo, *331*
as Secretary of Commerce, 109–10
severing relationship with Larry Richey, 276
with siblings, *36*
Silver Lake incident, 306–7
at Stanford, 48–59
at Stuart Lake, *258, 259*
as surveyor in Arkansas mountains, 49
telling off-color jokes, 251
Truman meeting, 290–91
trying out fiberglass fly rod, 297
on wading streams, 286–87
and Walcott near Schenob Creek, *273*
as war food administrator, 93–99, *94*
weeding onions, 34
at White House, Waltham on the Thames, *77*
Willkie meeting, 275
winning presidential election of 1923, 172–73
at Wooley Camp, *236*
Hoover, Herbert Charles, birth of, 76
Hoover, Hulda, 4, 6, *8, 9*
death of, 19
Hoover, Jesse, 4, *8, 9*
death of, 5–6

Hoover, Lou Henry, xix, 53–57, *55, 61*
Bailey School camping trip, *57*
at Boxer Rebellion site, *75*
at Camp Rapidan, *190, 193*
camping, *64*
death of, 282–83
father's death and, 161
fishing with father, *58*
with Kappa Kappa Gamma sorority, *63*
on McKenzie River, *140*
at White House, Waltham on the Thames, *77*
Hoover, Lou Henry (granddaughter), *327*
Hoover, Mary "May," 4, 6, 73, 104, 112, 259, 302
death of, 309
with siblings, *36*
Hoover, Rebecca Yount, 19–20
Hoover, Theodore "Tad," 4, 6, *21*, 104, 112, 259
attends William Penn College, 46
death of, 319
Mildred Brooke marriage, 78
"Orphans" poem by, 20
with siblings, *36*
Hoover Committee, 89–90
Hoover Dam, 296
Hoover Library Tower, 276
Hopkins, Timothy, *236*
Horton, Frank, ranch of, 249–50
Hughes River, 184

inaugurations
Eisenhower's, 307
Hoover's, 181
Kennedy's, 341
Roosevelt's, 218
"Invitation to Learning" CBS radio show, appearance on, 296
Iowa State Fair, 314–15
Izaak Walton League, 116
Hoover's address to, xi–xii
Izaak Walton League Monthly, 116

J. C. Penney mansion, Belle Isle, Florida, 176
jet plane incident, 305
Jumbo Gold Mine, 244

Kennedy, John F., 339, 341
Key Largo Anglers Club, 297–99, 306,
    308, 342
  Truman's visit to, 339
Kingsley, Iowa, 17–18
Klamath River, 165, 225–28
Knox, Frank, 254, *255*
Korean War, 304
Kristallnacht, events of, 260

Lake Kennebago, 264
Lake Lakota, 237–38
Lake Mead, 269–70
Lake Mitchell Trout Club, 238
Lake Tahoe, Twain fishing on, 63–65
Larry Creek, 151–52, 200–1
The Lasting Peace (Hoover), 281
Leroque, John, 155, 157
  with Coolidge on Brule River, *156*
The Light of the Western Stars (Grey), 127
Lindgren, Dr., 50, 52–53, 60
Long, Earl C., 185, *193*
Long Key Fishing Camp, 127

MacDonald, Ramsey, at Camp Rapi-
    dan, 191–92
McKenzie Bridge, 262
McKenzie River, 45–46, 138–39, 226,
    240–41, 247, 274, 279, 309–12
  last time fishing, 329
McMullin, Dare, *193*
Madison River, 241–43, 249, 251–52,
    268, 281
Magnum Opus (Hoover), 328
Mardikian, George, 319–21, 329, 330,
    332–33
  Hoover's eating habits article,
    320–22
Mayflower Mine, 68
medicine ball game, 182
"Meet the Press," guest on, 338
Memoirs (Hoover), 44, 47, 63, 148
Metlakatla, Alaska, 120–21
Metropolitan Miami Fishing Tourna-
    ment, 294
Mill Creek, 233–34
Miller, Bunny, 276, 343, *346*
Miller, Garfield, 237, *239*
Mining Magazine, 83
Minthorn, Henry John, 4–5, 22, 26–29,
    29

Minthorn, Fred and Harriet "Hattie,"
    32
  home of, *33*
Mississippi River, great flood of the,
    141–44
Mitchell, J. P., *236*
Mono Lake, Twain on, 65
Montauk Yacht Club, 244
Mullendore, William C., 119
  at Resurrection Bay in Seward,
    Alaska, *123*
Murray Bay, 333
My First Summer in the Sierra (Muir), 52

National Committee on Food for the
    Small Democracies (NCFSD), 275
National Recovery Act (NRA), 237
New Mexico, fishing trip, 277–78
New York Times, 216
  editorial, 256–57
Newberg, Oregon, 25, *25*
Nixon, Richard, 329, 339, 342
  at Cave Man Camp, *340*
North Santium River, 43–45

Ogontz Fishing Club, 97–98
Ogontz Lodge, 151–52, 200–1
"On Fishing" (Hoover), *347*
On Growing Up (Hoover), 342
One World (Willkie), 280
opossum incident, 187–88
Ordeal of Woodrow Wilson (Hoover), 328
Oregon
  fishing and camping expeditions in,
    42–43
  landscape of, 24–25
Oregon Land Company, 35–37, *38*
  Hoover as office manager of, 37
Oregon Trail, by train, 23–24
Oregonian, 140
Osage nation, Pawhusaka, Oklahoma
  Hoover at, 12–14
  wedding ceremony, *13*
Outdoor Life, 344

Palm Beach Sailfish Club, 215
Pequest River, 247, 256
permit, fishing, 330–32
Pioche, Nevada, 282
Potomac River, 187

The Problems of the Lasting Peace
   (Hoover), 279
pumpkin wars, 14
Pyramid Lake, 221–22

Quaker services, 6
Quinion, George H., 271, *272*
Quorn, Iowa, 17

Railroad Pension Act, 237
Rancho del Oso, 104–5
Rapidan River, 183–85
   the Hoovers first visit to, 184–85
rattlesnake incident, 50–51
Reader's Digest, 279
Reconstruction Finance Cooperation
   (RFC), 204–5
Republican Circles, 254
Republican National Conventions, 152,
   206, 240, 285–86
   addressing, 272–74, 324
Republican Party, after election of 1934,
   235–37
residences
   2300 S Street, Washington D.C.,
     110–12
   San Juan Hill, 103–4, 282
   Waldorf-Astoria, 219
Reward Mine, 68
Richey, Larry, *199, 331*
   death of, 338
   fishing camp of, 186–87
   receiving fishing tackle, 313
   severing relationship with, 276
Rickard, Abigail, 83, *193*
Rogue River, 45, 139–40, 165, 241
Roosevelt, Franklin D., 109, 206, 209,
   217–18, 269, 275, 279, 280
   at Camp Rapidan, 219
   death of, 288–89
   Hoover and Coolidge stories, 284–85
   inauguration, 218
Roughing It (Twain), 61

Sacramento River, 166–68
Sacramento Valley Turnpike incident,
   221
sailfish, 195
   Hoover's first, 177, *179*
St. Louis Creek, 315
Salem Street Car Company, 39
salmon incident, 344–45

San Juan Hill, 103–4
   donated to Stanford, 282
Schenob Brook, 271–72, 279–80
   last time fishing, 294
Sea Island Investments, 212
Seeing Cairo Fund, 83–84
Seminole Lodge, 178
Shasta Springs Hotel, 166
Sierras, expedition through, 78–82
Silver Lake, fire at, 306–7
Smith, Fred, *236*
Snake River, 280
Snyder's Camp, 296–97
Society of American Women in Lon-
   don, 91
Sons of Gwalia Mine, 71
South Pike River, 254–56
South Side Sportsmen's Club of Long
   Island, 289–90
Sportsman's Lodge, 265
Stanford University, 46–47
   attending, 48–59
State Insurance Company, *38*
Steelhead Country (Raymond), 241
stock market crash of 1929, 193–94
Strauss, Lewis L., 244
   incident, 341
Stuart Lake tribe, 258–59
Sullivan, Mark, 111, 130, 151–52, 174,
   194

Tales of Fishes (Grey), 127, 234
Tallac Hotel, *67*
   fishing on dock at, *66*
Tangier Island, 208
Thornton's camp, 281
Tilson, John Q., *169*
Truman, Harry S., 346
   Hoover meeting, 290–91
Twain, Mark, 61
   fishing on Lake Tahoe, 63–65
   on Mono Lake, 65
Twin Lakes, 279–80

United Mine Workers, 247
United Press release, 300

Vermejo Ranch, 277–78

Walcott, Fred C., 127, 271, *272, 273*
Waldorf-Astoria, residence at, 219

Walton, Izaak, vii, 161–62, 234, 296
War Food Administration, 98
Warren, George, 247, *248*, 295–96
Washington D.C., residence in, 110–12
Weasku Inn, 165
Weiser, Idaho, 280
West Branch, Iowa, 2
    boyhood fishing experiences in, 1–4
What the River Knows (Fields), 329
White, William Allen, 235
    on problem of Hoover's personality,
        205–6
Wilbur, Ray Lyman, 50, 83, 134, 151–52,
        163, *236, 258, 259*
wild west show incident, 90
Williams, Tom, *236*
Willkie, Wendell, 271, 272–73, 280
    Hoover meeting, 275

winter activities, 14–17
Wooley Camp, 224–25, 235
    transferring interest in to son, 286
Wooley Creek, 224–25
Wooley Creek Association, 134
Wooley Creek Ranch, 134–35
    Hoover's log cabin at, *136*
World War I, 89–93
World War II, 288
    dropping of atomic bomb in
        Hiroshima, 292

Years of Adventure (Hoover), 301
Yellowstone Park, hatchery project,
        144–48
Yosemite National Park, 274
    camping trip to, 51–52
Youth's Companion, 16